The Peak District

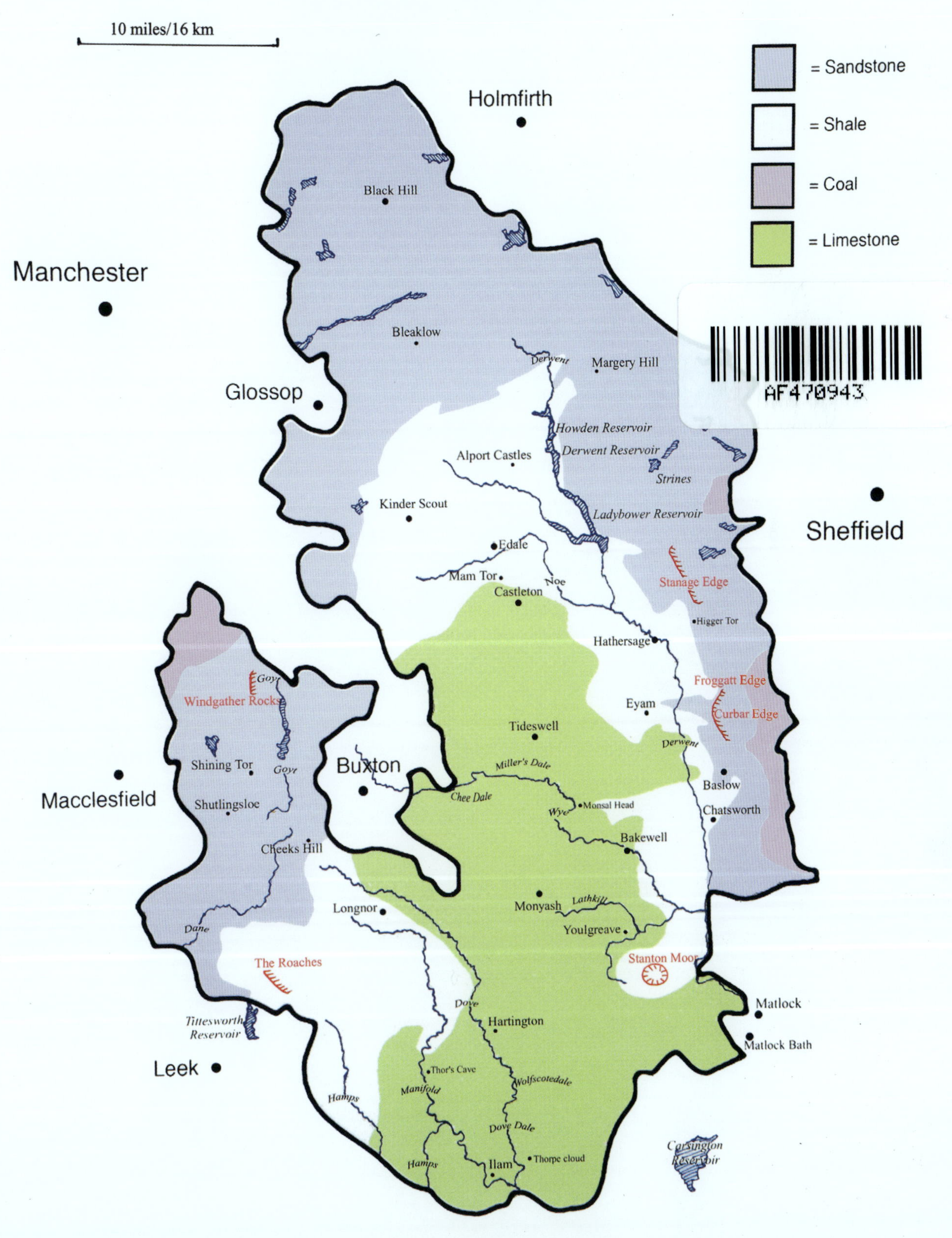

PEAK LANDSCAPE AND LIGHT

A Photographer's Guide to the Peak District

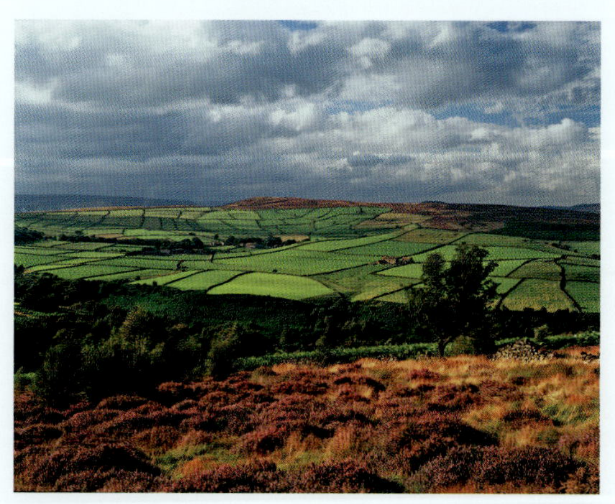

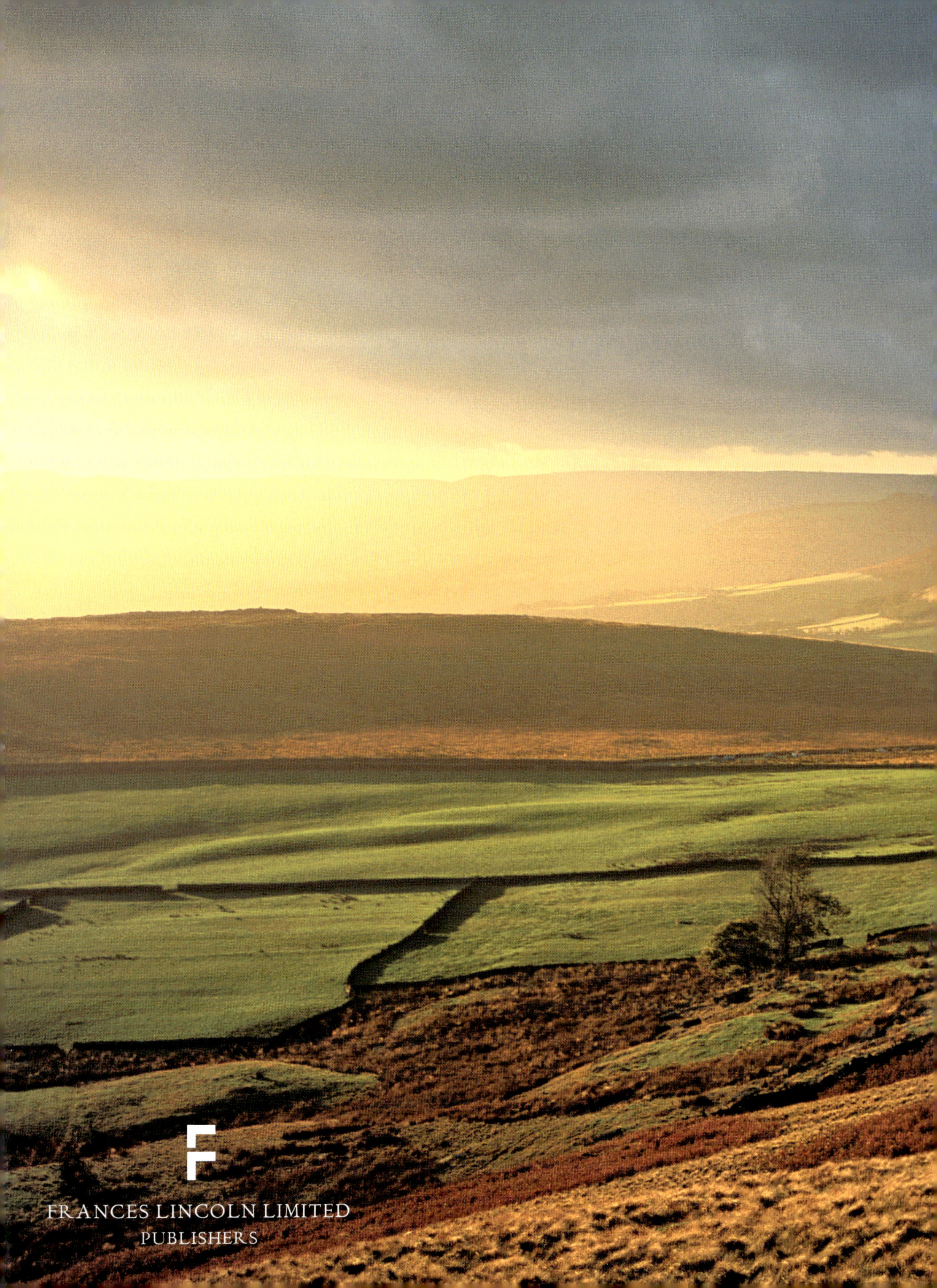
FRANCES LINCOLN LIMITED
PUBLISHERS

PEAK LANDSCAPE AND LIGHT

A Photographer's Guide to the Peak District

Karen Frenkel

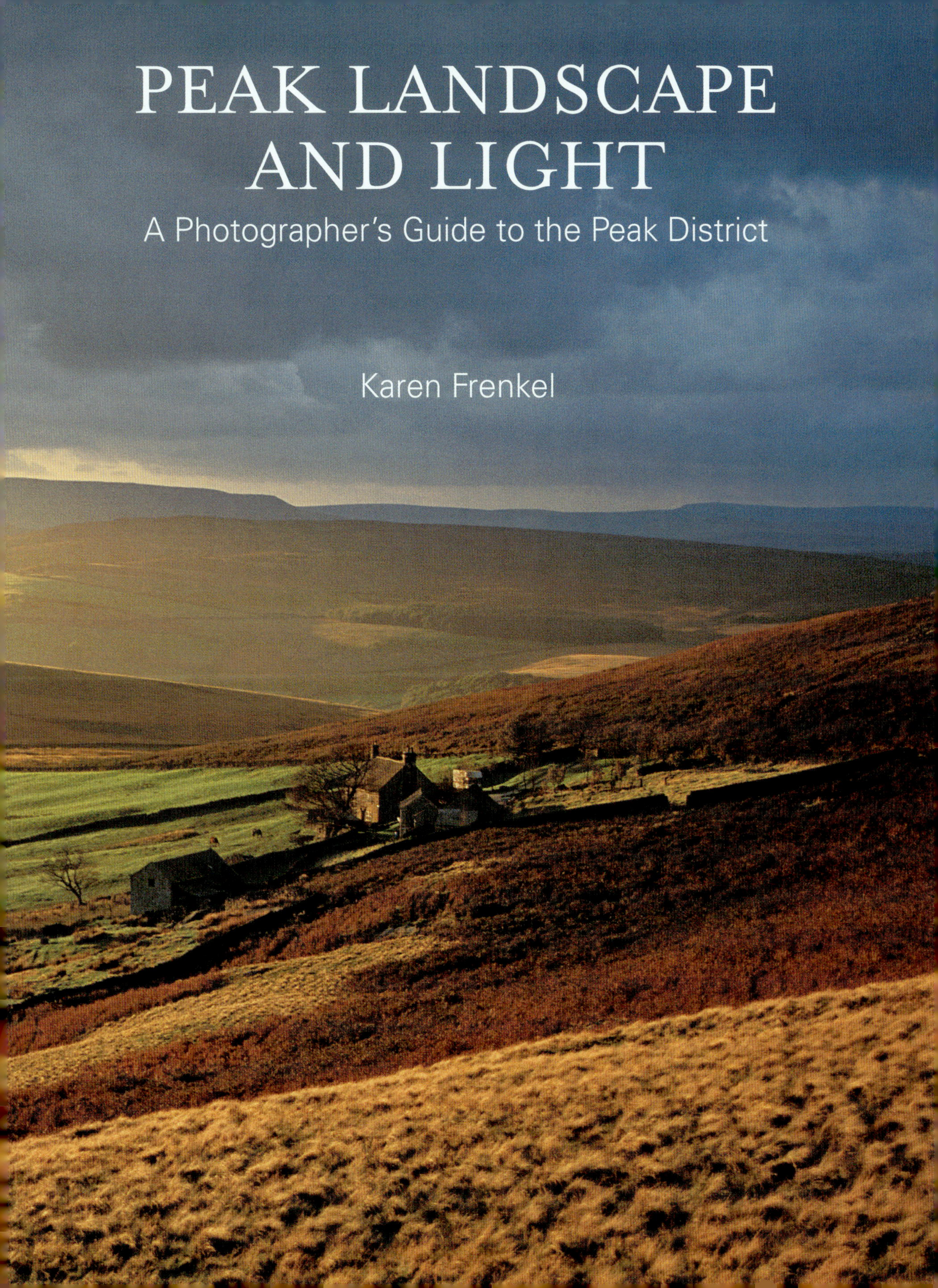

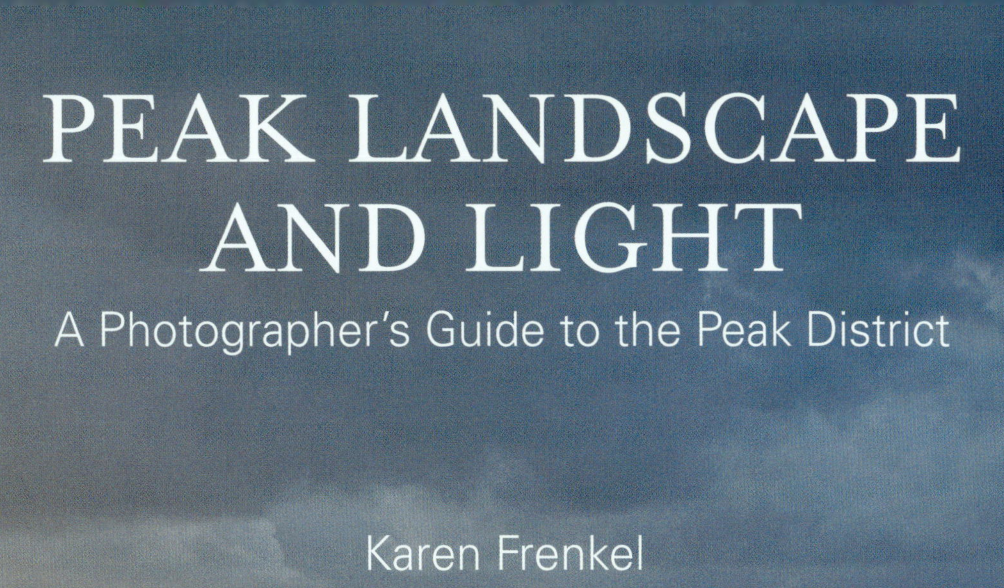

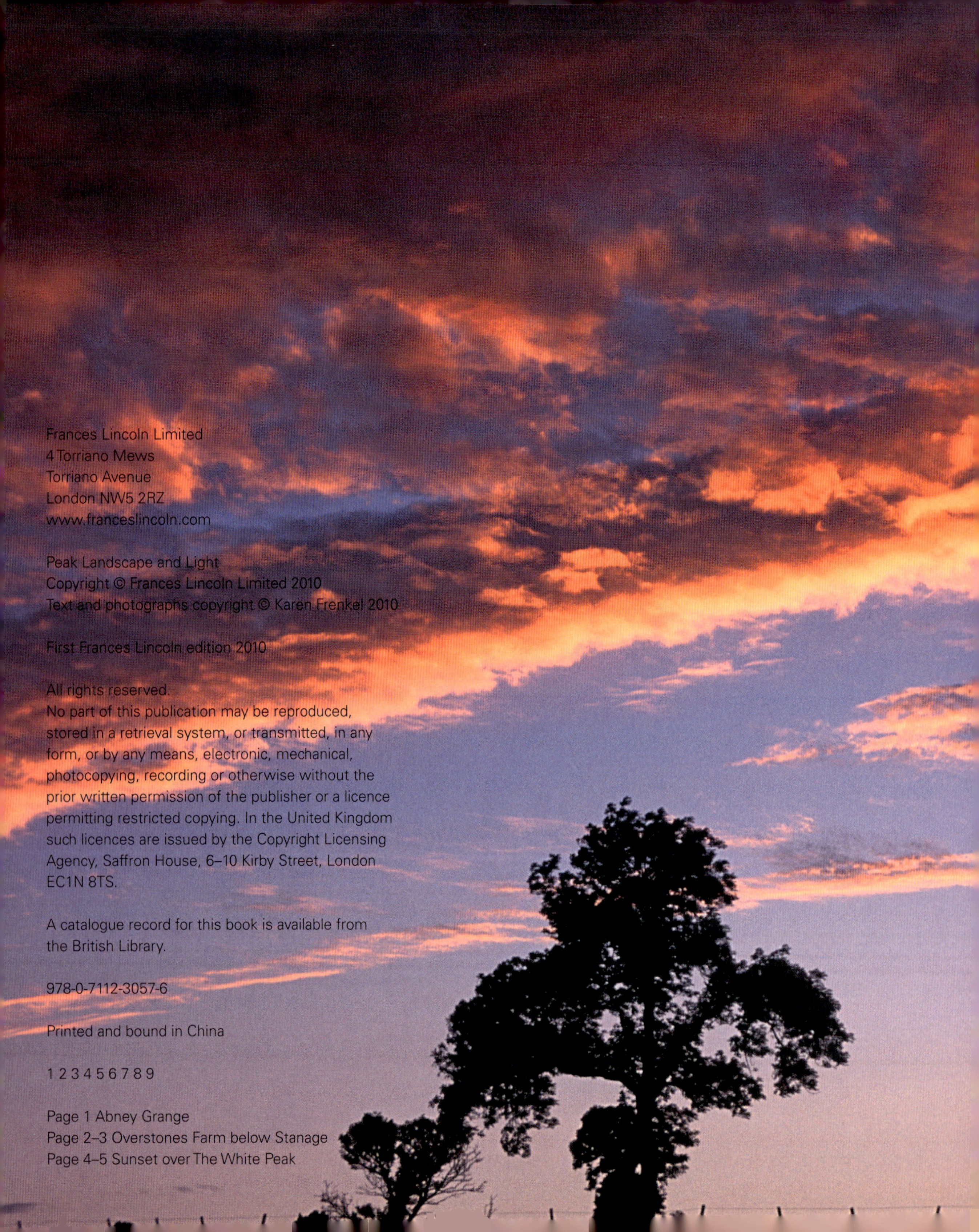

Frances Lincoln Limited
4 Torriano Mews
Torriano Avenue
London NW5 2RZ
www.franceslincoln.com

Peak Landscape and Light
Copyright © Frances Lincoln Limited 2010
Text and photographs copyright © Karen Frenkel 2010

First Frances Lincoln edition 2010

A catalogue record for this book is available from
the British Library.

978-0-7112-3057-6

Printed and bound in China

1 2 3 4 5 6 7 8 9

Page 1 Abney Grange
Page 2–3 Overstones Farm below Stanage
Page 4–5 Sunset over The White Peak

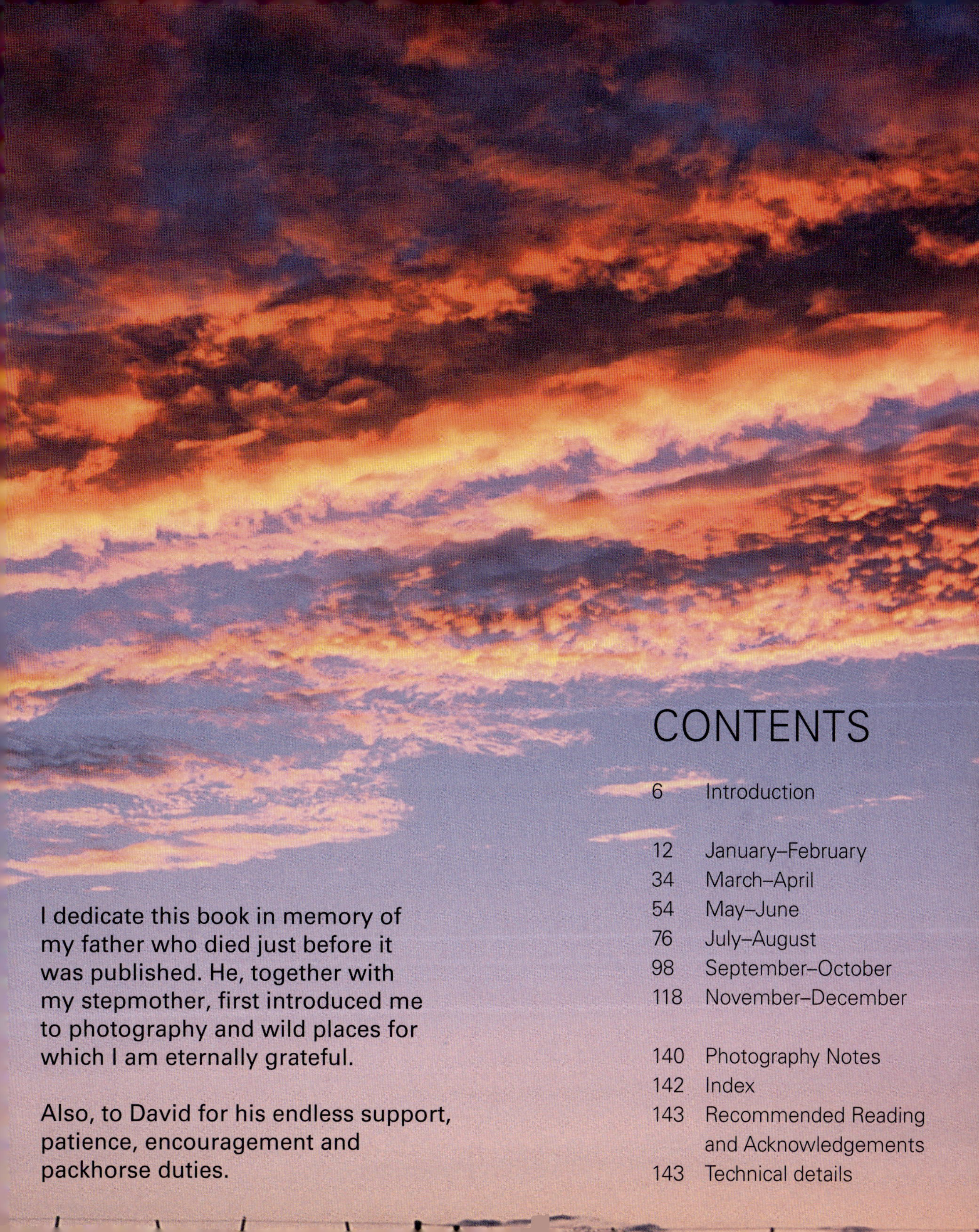

I dedicate this book in memory of
my father who died just before it
was published. He, together with
my stepmother, first introduced me
to photography and wild places for
which I am eternally grateful.

Also, to David for his endless support,
patience, encouragement and
packhorse duties.

CONTENTS

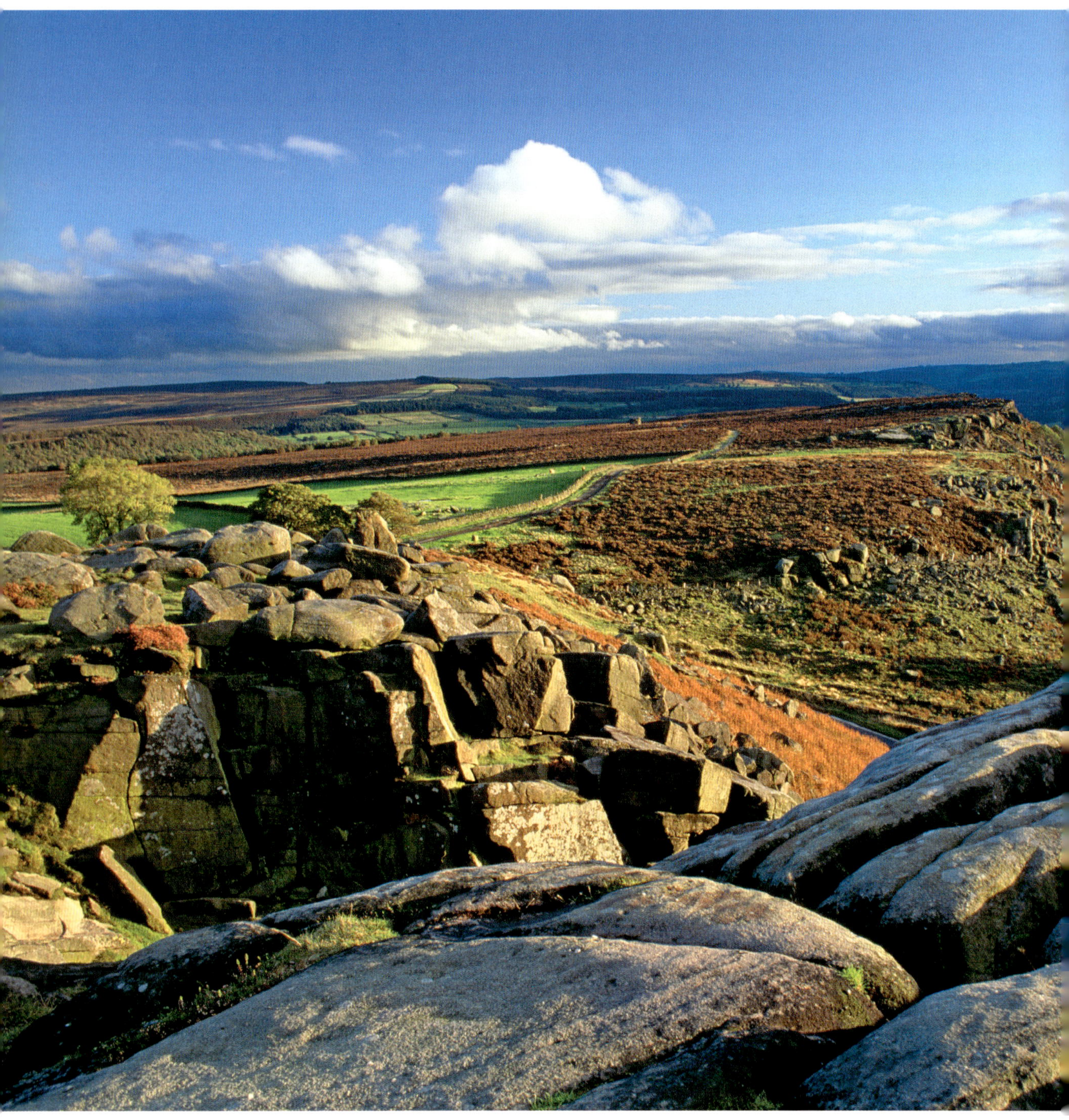

Curbar Edge

INTRODUCTION

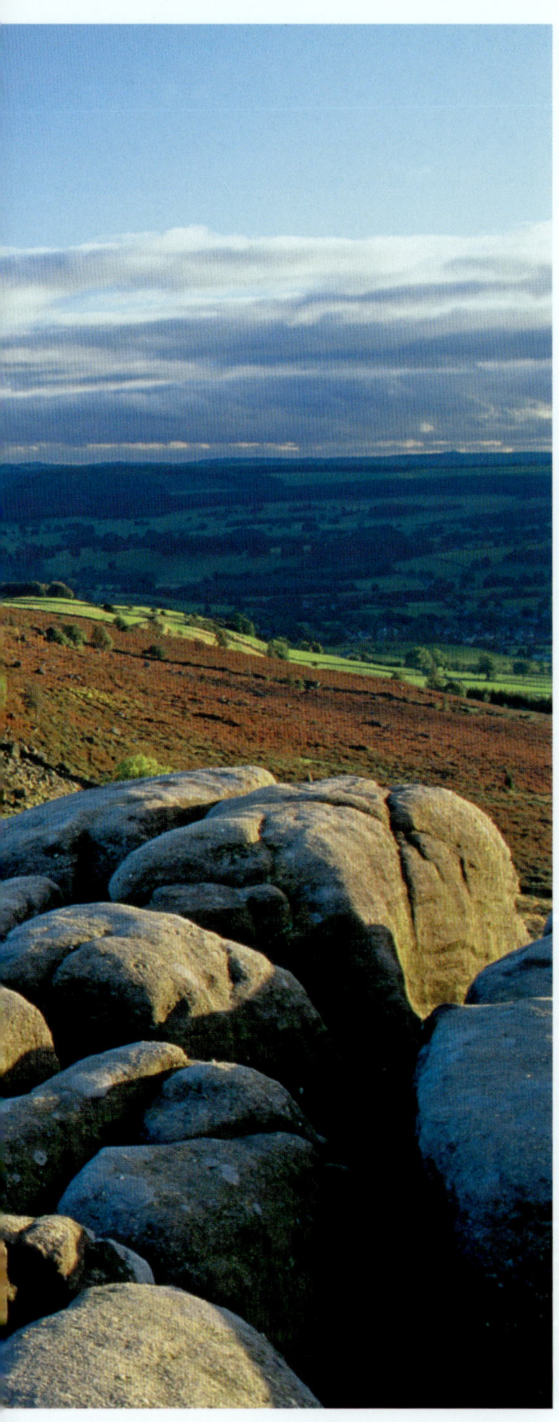

I first visited the Peak as a child on regular day trips with my parents, who were both keen amateur geologists, photographers and walkers. I was dragged to some unusual places and loved it. Those memories are deep rooted and back then, I never dreamt that one day I would be lucky enough to live and work here. In 1993, with a career in chemistry, I came to live in the Peak and in 1996 I became a full time professional landscape photographer. Those few years of being surrounded by this beautiful landscape were the catalysts which changed my life.

Over the past 17 years, I have have developed a deep love and understanding of the Peak's changing landscape, nature and moods throughout the year. I have seen how, over a relatively short period, our seasons have changed. Back in the 1990's we certainly had more snow which would not disappear as fast as it seems to in more recent times, with the noteable exception of last winter (2009-2010). This made my job much easier and less pressured if I was trying to record a snowy landscape.

On the other hand, our last two summers have been very wet and I have recorded fast flowing moorland streams in August, which in a dry year would have been just a trickle and nowhere near as spectacular. It is for this reason that I have collated some of my best images from over the years to show you how special this area is and how fragile it may be with our changing climate.

The Peak District has a wonderfully diverse landscape in a relatively small area. This is due to its varied geology which dictates the landforms, soil, flora and fauna and thus its final appearance. Like an upturned horseshoe in the north, west and eastern sides of the region, there are the

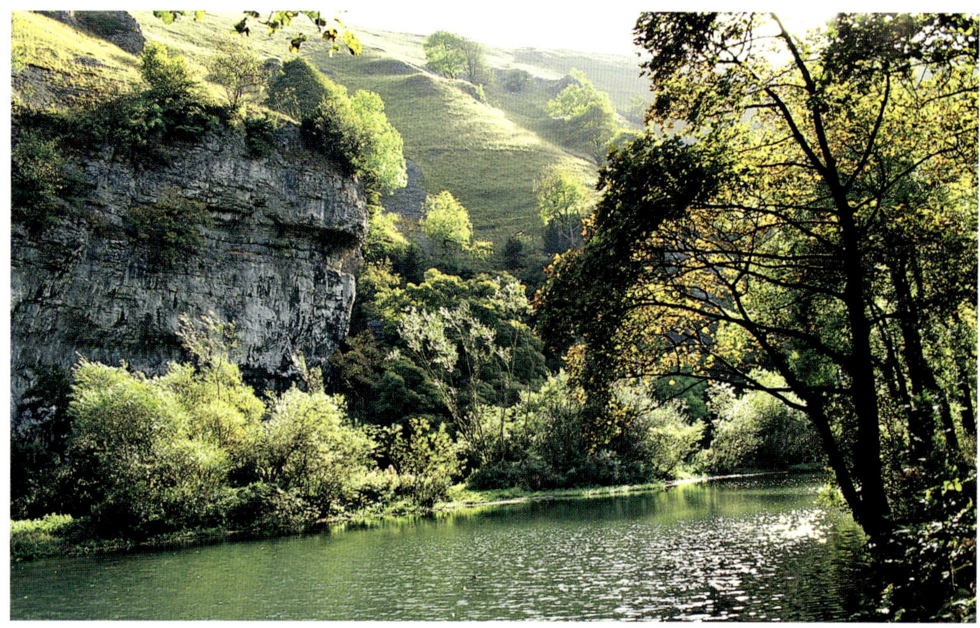

dark gritstone rocks and shales which form the dramatic landscape of the Dark Peak, with its eroded tors and wild, craggy moorland, home to heather, blanket bog and bracken. The wonderful sounds of curlew and grouse are characteristic and a fleeting glimpse of a white mountain hare in its winter coat is a special treat.

In contrast, there is the gentler, more fertile landscape of the limestone areas in the central and southern Peak, which is known as the White Peak. Often a high plateau of around 1,000feet/300metres, it is like a giant green patchwork quilt criss-crossed by a network of drystone walls. Rivers cut deep through this landscape to form steep-sided dales with crags, cliffs, caves and pinnacles. These dales are rich in birdlife and limestone-loving plants with wonderful displays of flowers throughout the spring and summer months. As these crystal clear rivers babble along, tumbling over rocky weirs, birds such as the dipper can be seen flitting between the boulders, bobbing up and down before diving in for a meal.

Not surprisingly, in recording these infinitely varied scenes, I have learnt some important lessons along the way, which I hope I will share with you in this book. For those eager to improve their landscape photography skills I have tried to incorporate an instructional element throughout the book of where-to-go and what-to-do with the light and weather, targeting suitable locations for certain conditions, explaining compositions and the thought processes that I have gone through. The aim of this book is to share the knowledge I have built up over the years and to show which locations in the Peak are at their best depending on the time of the year under certain lighting and weather conditions, together with a little information about that area and/or interesting points or stories about the pictures.

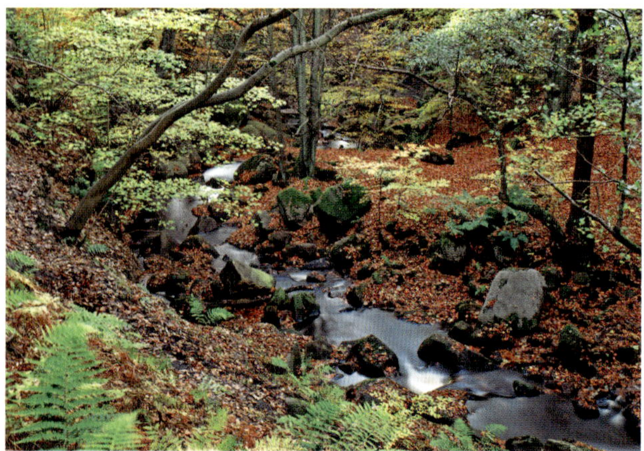

The importance of light

In order to capture that special image I realised that not only did I need to understand how our landscape changes in appearance throughout the seasons, but even more crucially, how to work with the ever-changing light which falls on it throughout the day, month and year. How the light falls on and is reflected by the landscape, and its creation of shadows and highlights, is as important as the landscape itself. This is the raw material for all our pictures.

The changing appearance of the landscape here in the Peak depends mainly on the state of the trees, plants, flowers, grasses, mosses and lichens in addition to the water levels in our rivers, streams, pools and reservoirs. Put simply, the quality of light is dependent on the angle of the sun and the weather conditions which modify it. It can be direct, dappled, diffuse, stormy or transient. There are so many variables and I am beginning at last to understand and work with whatever the light throws at me by building up a knowledge of which location would be best under those conditions and at that particular time of year.

Occasionally, you can be lucky and just be in the right place at the right time. But often hours of studying maps, reconnaissance trips, wasted trips, and waiting around are needed in order to be there and capture what is often a fleeting moment in time, when landscape and light come together to give that winning combination and an image with impact. The most beautiful composition or view in the world will look drab if lighting conditions are wrong. The photographer must feel an emotion when capturing that image in order to convey that through to the viewer. The bigger the emotion, the stronger the image will be. When it does come together, somehow all that wasted time is worth it, satisfying something deep within us. This is what makes my job so interesting, but, at times very challenging.

This collection of photographs has been taken with both film and digital cameras and in different formats. What should become clear is that it is not your equipment that really matters, but seeing that picture in the first place and reacting correctly to it by working quickly with both the light and whatever camera gear you may have to create the best possible image in that situation. Landscape photographers often pre-visualise

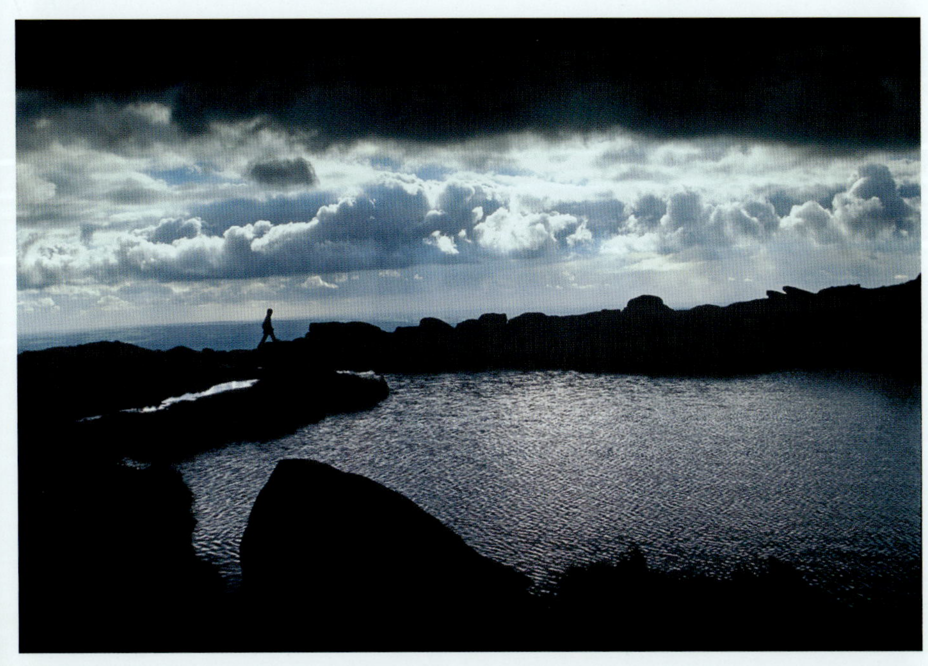

Left: Doxey Pool, The Roaches

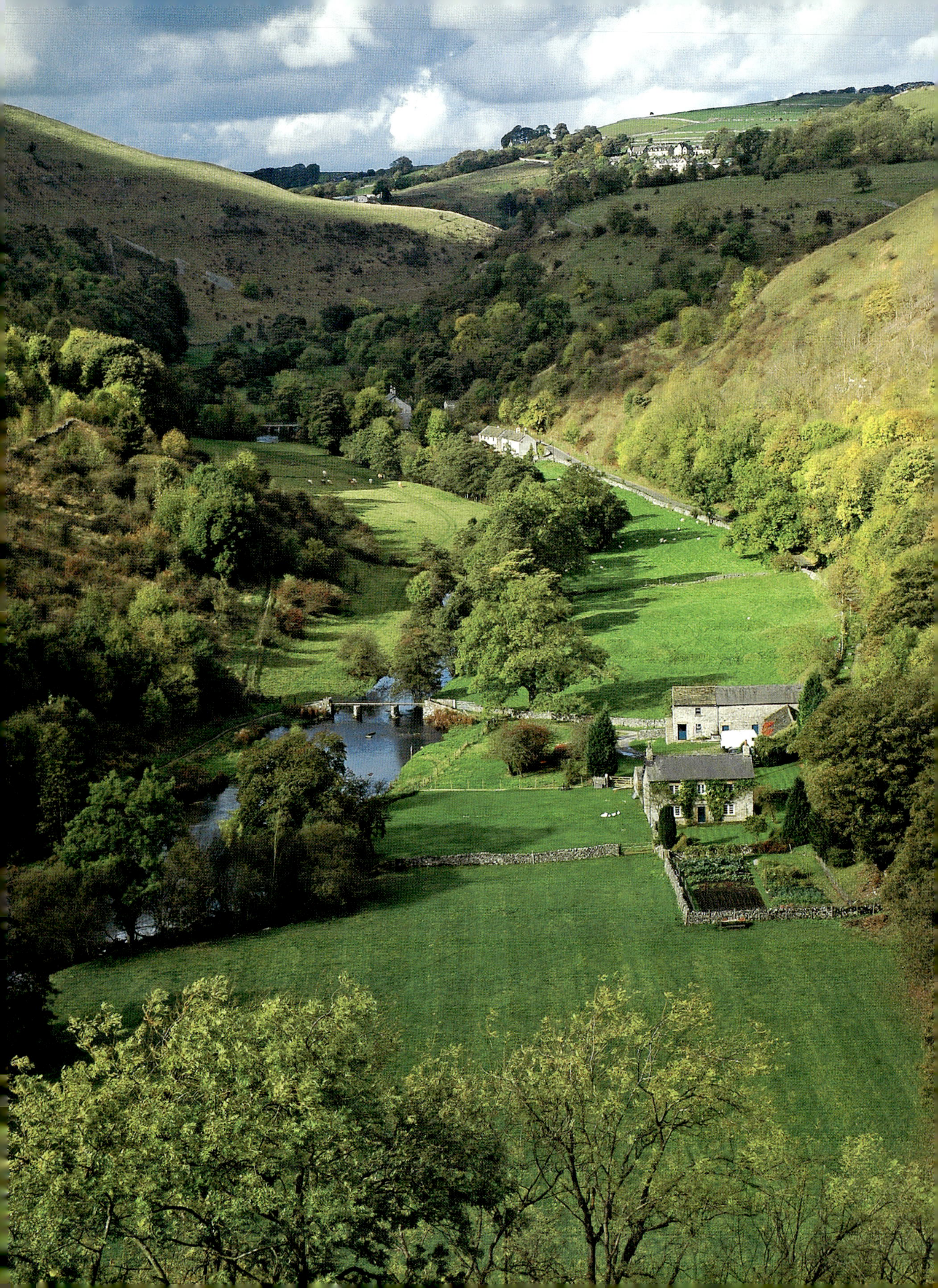

their images and strive for perfection, becoming obsessed and driven by the light, working at anti-social hours and addicted to weather forecasts. If you catch the bug, beware, as social and family lives can suffer!

Through the Peakland year

I have split the book chronologically into bi-monthly chapters where I will talk in more detail about the typical lighting, weather and features of the landscape for that particular time of the year. We must bear in mind though, that as in any year there are exceptions e.g. snow in April, drought in March, but I have been honest about when the images were taken which may often cause surprise. It makes the job of generalising monthly trends increasingly more difficult with our current freaky weather.

Technical notes and exact times are given at the back of the book for each image (if known) and cross referenced to the page numbers. There is also a brief chapter on the equipment used and more detailed notes on the photography, although this could be a book in itself. There may be some locations which I have visited at different times of year or under different lighting conditions. See the index for page numbers.

Above all, I hope this book inspires people to get out and absorb the beautiful landscape and nature which surrounds us, not just here in the Peak but everywhere, if you can tune into it. I have travelled from Pakistan to Patagonia but it's the images on my doorstep which I feel are the best. That's because they are the ones for which I feel the deepest emotion and understanding. Finally, you will notice that there are still some areas of the Peak District that I have not covered in this book. As long as I am healthy, I'll never tire of searching for new places to explore or cease to try to improve on existing locations in new light. I am still learning, this book is only the start of a lifetime's work, not the end. There is still so much to do!

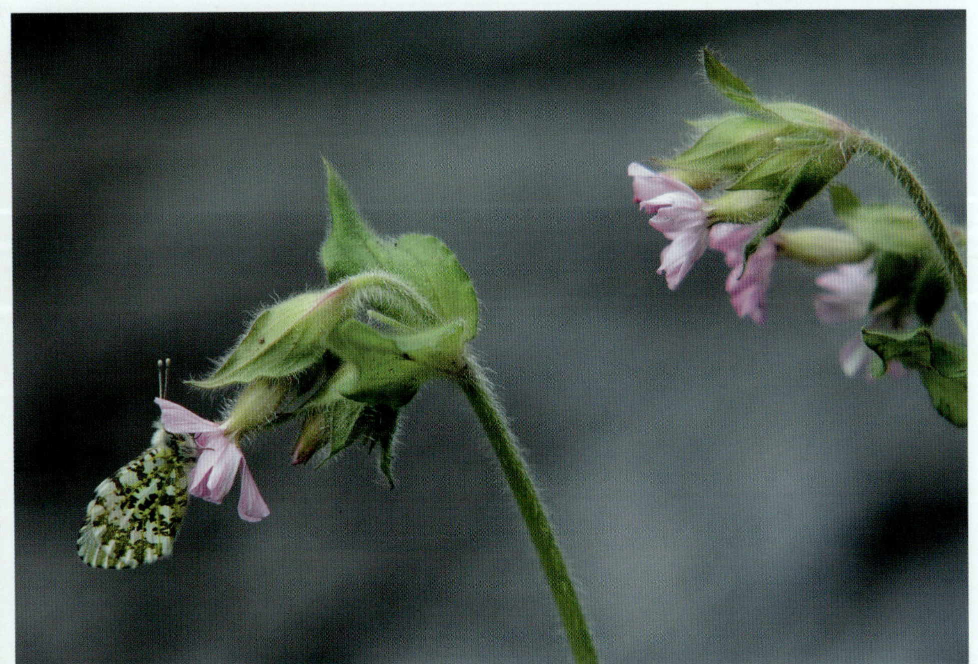

Far Left: Monsal Dale

Left: Orange tip butterfly on red campion

JANUARY–FEBRUARY

Sunrise time 08.25–06.59 **Sunset time** 16.00–17.45 **Sunrise direction** SE–ESE **Sunset direction** SW–WSW

Stark beauty, ice cool, mist and gloom

Daylight hours are brief and the sun's short arc is low in the sky throughout the day, leaving some valleys permanently in shade. In those areas which do catch the sun, it casts long shadows which sculpt out features in the landscape, giving a flattering light for your images. On the other hand, you may not see the sun at all, and there are often endless, dull, drab days to contend with. Even then we can search out details or gloomy, atmospheric scenes. If we're lucky we can get frost or snow which transforms both the White and Dark Peak into a winter wonderland. At sunrise or sunset when the sun is near to the horizon and the light more red in tone, the sky acts like a giant reflector, and snow, water or white limestone take on those pastel pink hues. Chilly nights following a mild day often sees mist form in the valley bottoms, and the hill tops and edges rise out like islands in a tranquil ocean of cotton wool. On non-snowy, frosty or misty days, the White Peak landscape can look drab, lacking in colour with no foliage, plants or flowers to liven it up apart from shapely tree skeletons which can still give strong compositions. In these conditions I favour the gritstone areas. These have more colour and interest with the golden (but by now slightly faded) bracken, moorland grasses and reflections in boggy moorland pools as well as the spectacular rock formations which can look dramatic in the winter sunlight.

It can be a season of extreme stark beauty if you're in the right place at the right time to capture it. But it can also be very chilly waiting for the right light.

Winter sunset on Higger Tor

Higger Tor stands proud at 1,423ft/434m above the Burbage Valley near Hathersage and is easily accessible by road, so is a great place to head for when searching out a winter sunset. With views all around, it is also quite exposed and on this afternoon extremely chilly as a strong northerly wind was blowing. Never have I been so cold. I waited for an hour for the sun to appear behind the clouds and only had a few moments of lovely light, but with freezing fingers managed to set up a few shots of this view towards Over Owler Tor and Millstone Edge. Feeling extremely hungry, on returning to my car, my face was so frozen I couldn't even eat my Pringles which were lying on the seat!

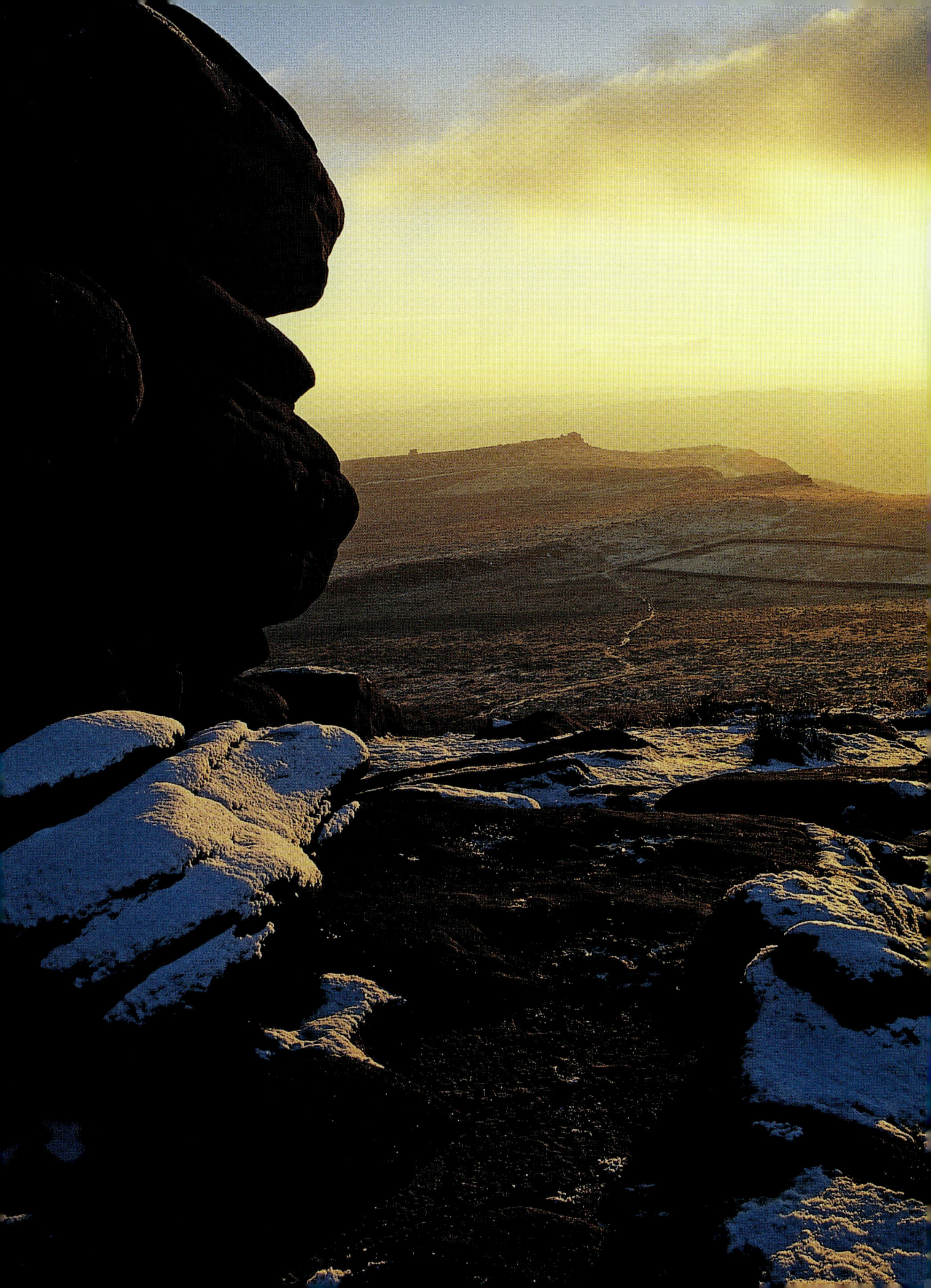

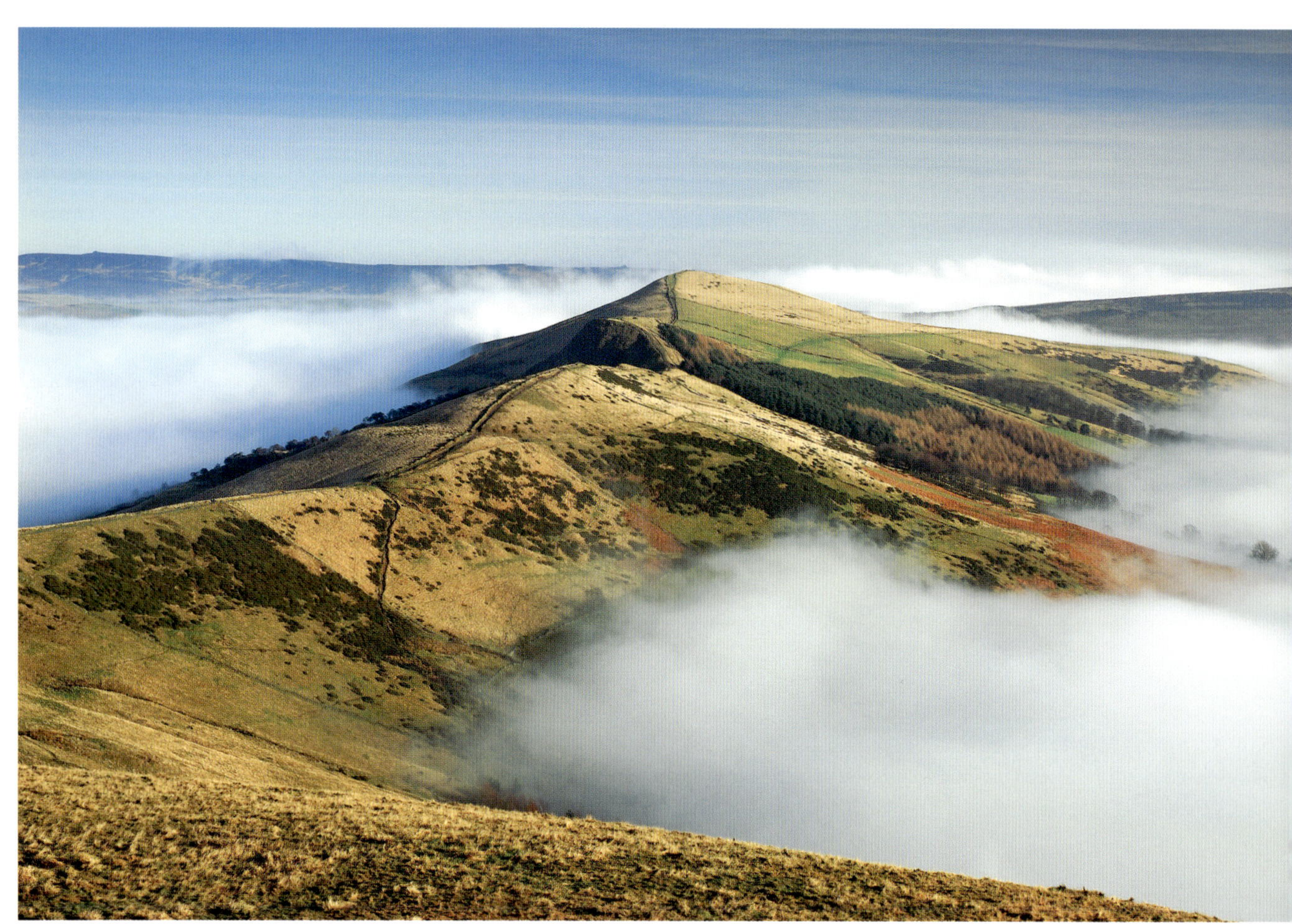

Mist below the Great Ridge

The Great Ridge stretches in a SW to NE direction
between the Hope and Edale Valleys from Mam Tor
(1,695feet/517metres), an Iron Age hillfort, to Lose Hill
(1,563feet/476metres) which we can see at the end
of the ridge.

I love mist trapped in the valley bottoms, indicating a
temperature inversion. I'm addicted to weather forecasts and
if it looks promising the night before, I pack my heavy camera
bag ready for an early morning charge up a hillside in order to
pop out of the cloud into the sunshine and look down on the
mist below. Mam Tor is ideal for this as I can park halfway up,
and then it's a short, sharp, frantic climb up the steep steps
to the top in order to get there before the sun burns it all off.
Wheezing and gasping for breath in the cold morning air,
I arrived to see The Great Ridge stretching out like a fin above
a sea of cloud as it lapped up and down the steep slopes.
On the right buried in mist is Castleton and on the left of the
ridge, the Edale Valley.

This picture was taken a few years earlier on 35mm film from the same place. Here, I was attracted by the colour contrast below the ridge between the orange bracken and green grass and also the pattern of mist which followed the line of the track. As a breeze began to strengthen, the trees in the valley bottom popped in and out of view as the mist swirled up and down, so I quickly got out my long lens and zoomed in on this composition before the transient moment passed.

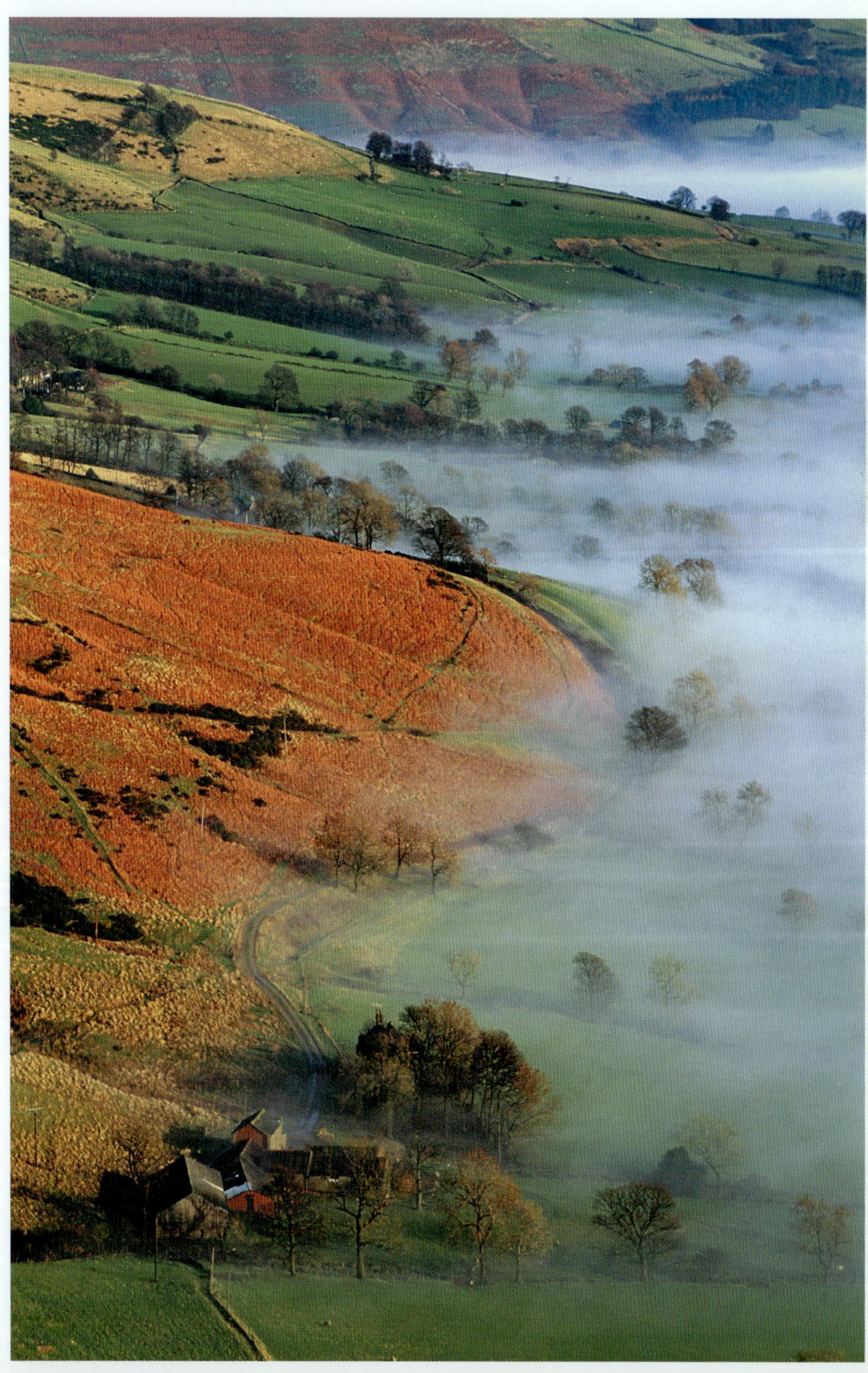

Iced grasses in Padley Brook

Padley Brook tumbles down from the gritstone moorland around Higger Tor and Carl Wark near Hathersage and runs through the Longshaw Estate, owned by the National Trust. This was a photograph where I was lucky enough to be in the right place at the right time, but with only seconds to spare. I saw this rapidly melting ice sculpture twinkling in the sunlight and had to work fast setting up my tripod and long lens before the sun moved round and cast it in shadow. Seconds after I took this, the light had gone and the magic was lost. I could never have planned this photograph if I'd tried.

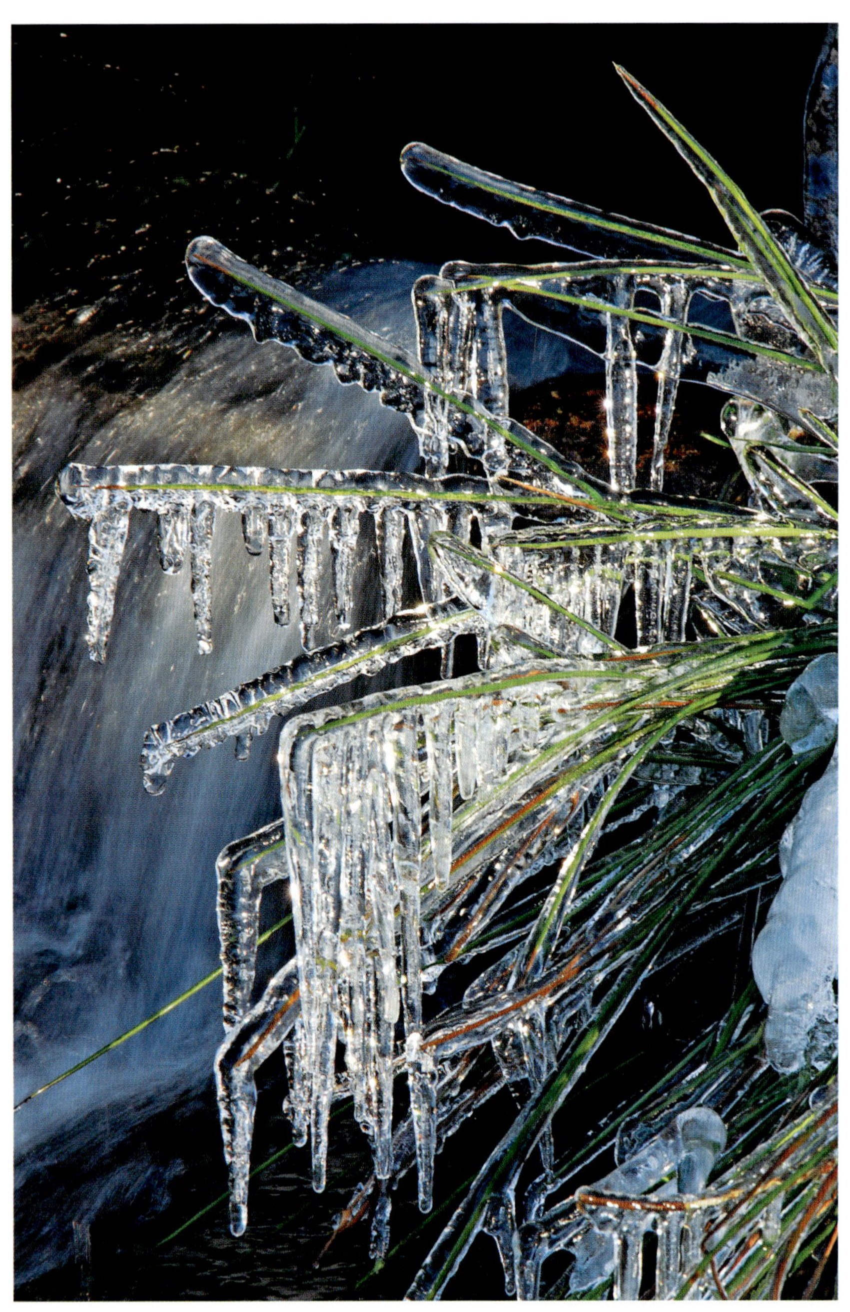

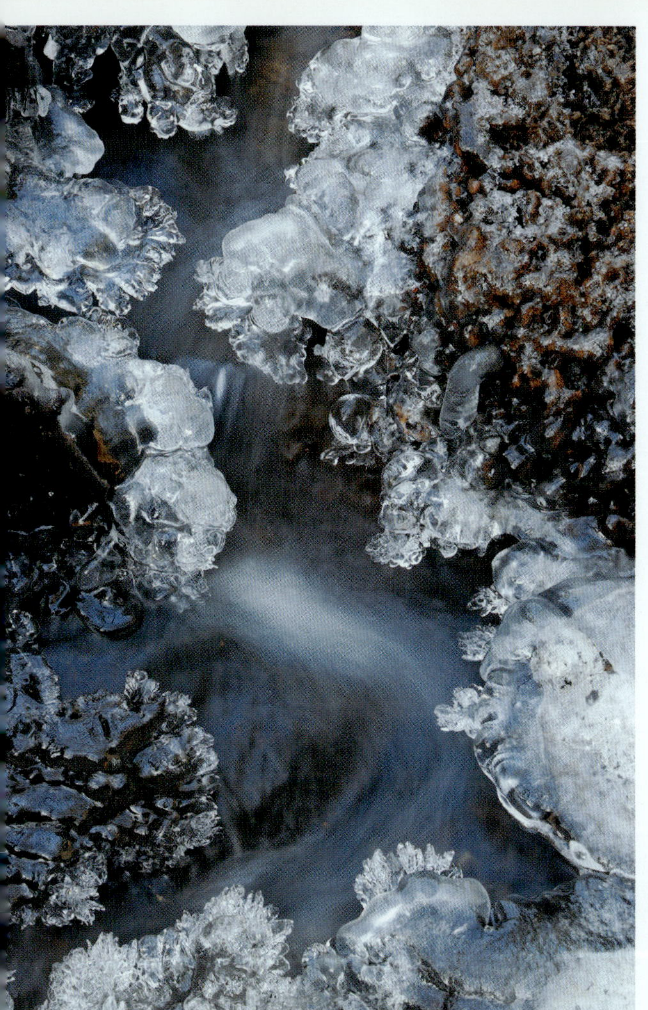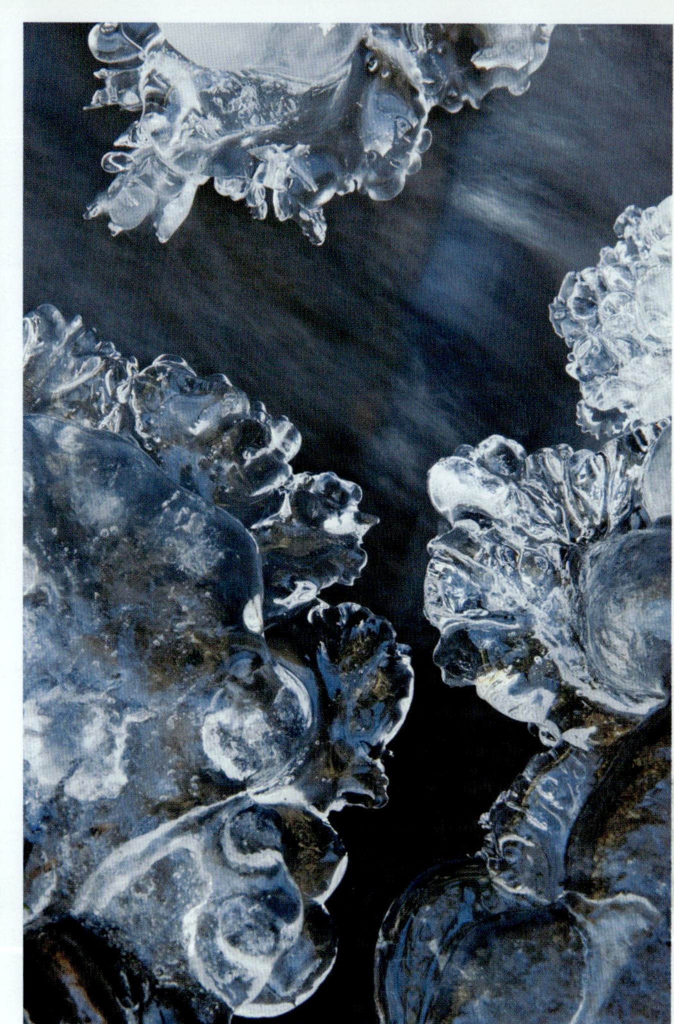

Ice formations in river

When skies are miserable and the light is flat, I tend to concentrate
on the details in the landscape, and on freezing cold days I often
head for rocky streams looking for ice formations. I spent about two
hours at this location which could be anywhere in the Peak, hardly
moving but engrossed in this minature world. I used my long lens
and zoomed in on ice structures as the water flowed beneath,
the slow shutter speed recording it as a soft streak giving an
S-shaped composition running through these shiny jewels.

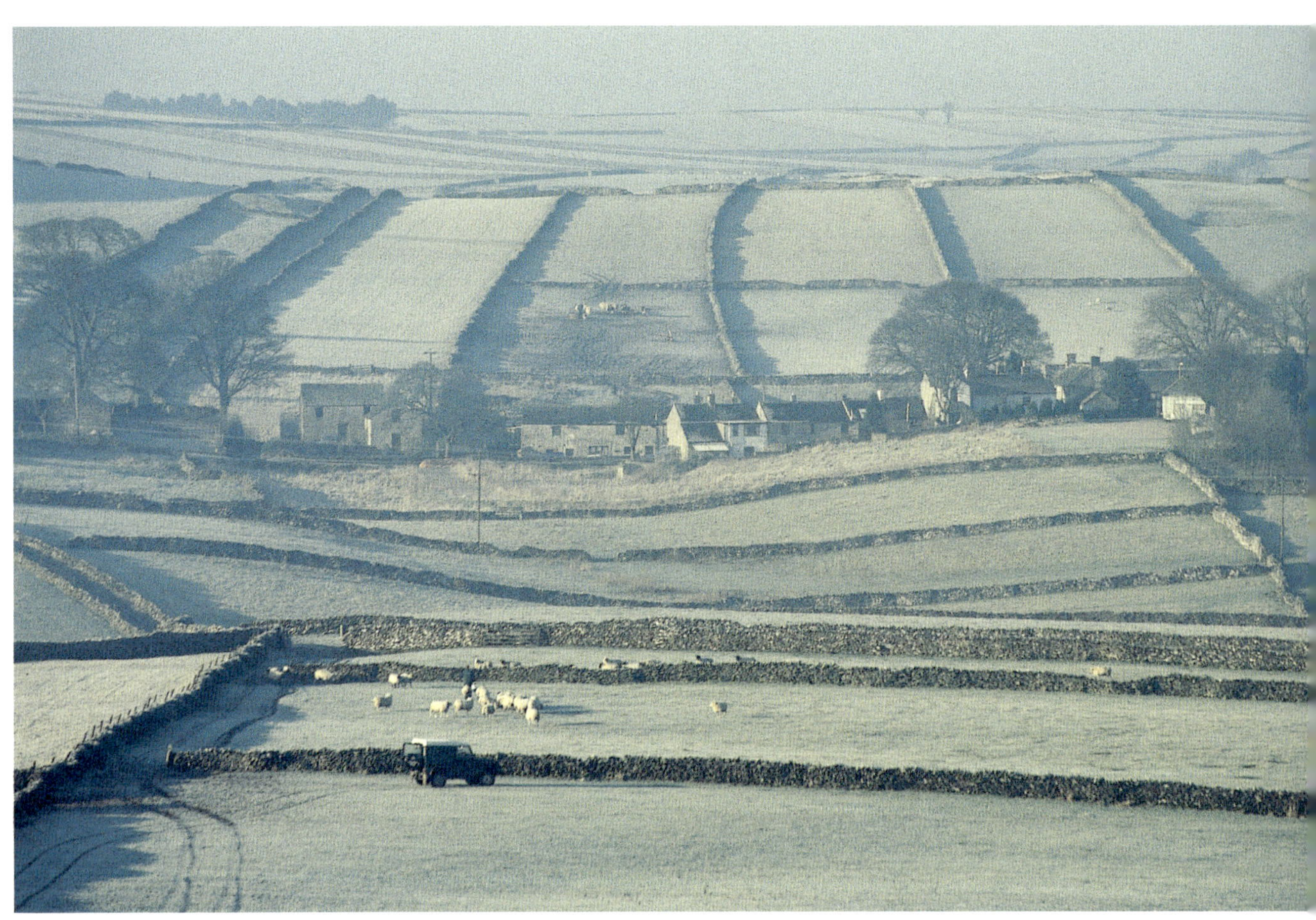

Field patterns near Wardlow

At about 820 feet/250m on the White Peak limestone
plateau, Wardlow is typical of a linear village where farms
are spaced along a single street from which lead the
medieval strip fields. I was attracted by the farmer feeding
his sheep and the wonderful, frosty field patterns etched
by the side-lighting from the low early morning sun. This
picture was actually taken on the same morning as that of
the image opposite. As lighting conditions were identical,
both images share the same grey/green effect.

Haddon Hall

Haddon Hall, the home of Lord Edward Manners, is one of the best surviving examples of a twelfth century medieval manor house in the country. Hence its popularity as a film set for classics such as *Jane Eyre* and *Pride and Prejudice*. As we look across to it from Haddon Fields, standing above the River Wye on this frosty, still winter's morning we can see it in all its glory, as it is so often obscured by trees in summer. The light was sunny but slightly misty which gave the image a monochromatic effect. With no clouds and stable light conditions, for once I had all the time in the world. I experimented and used the lovely shaped tree on the right as useful foreground for my composition.

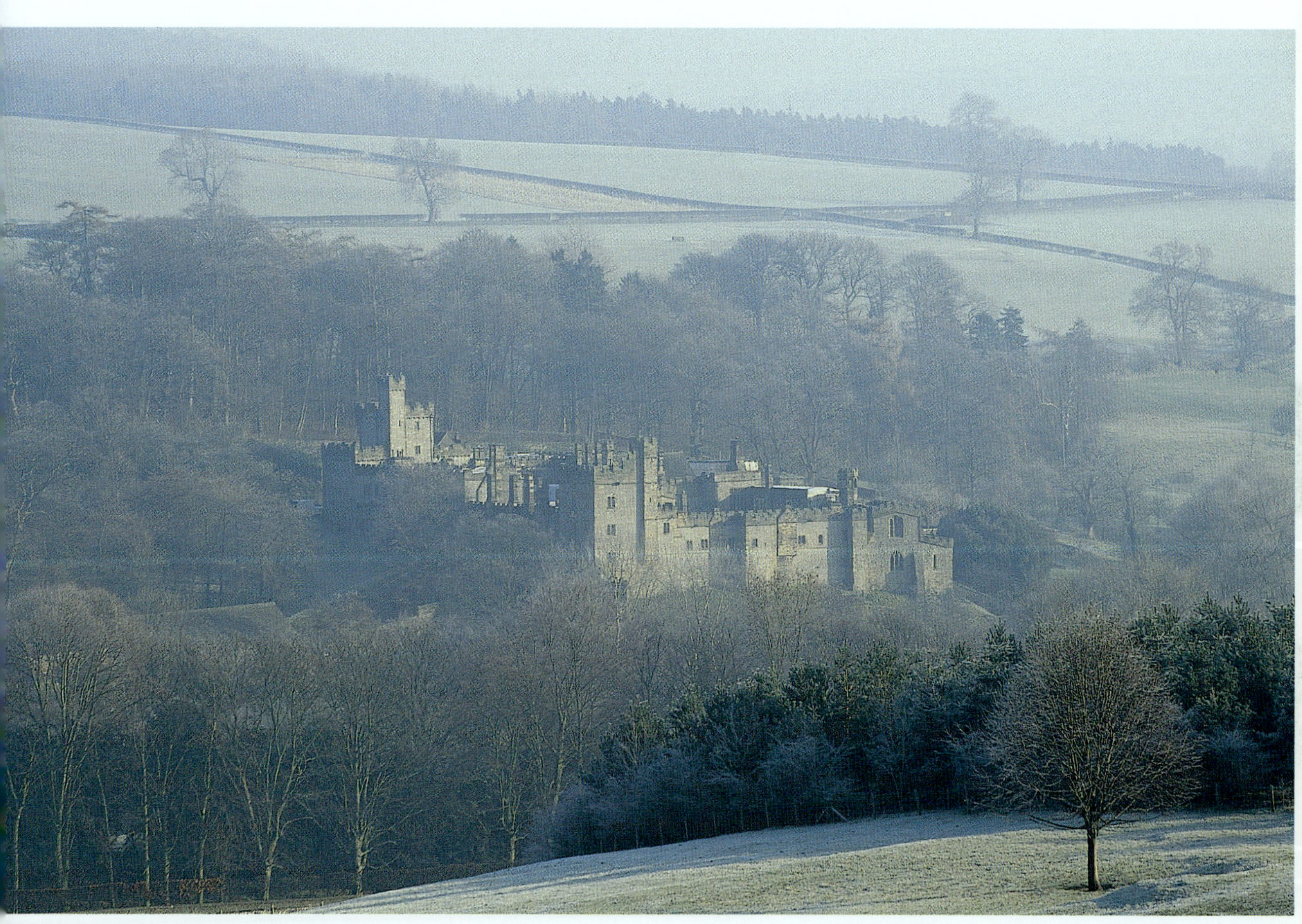

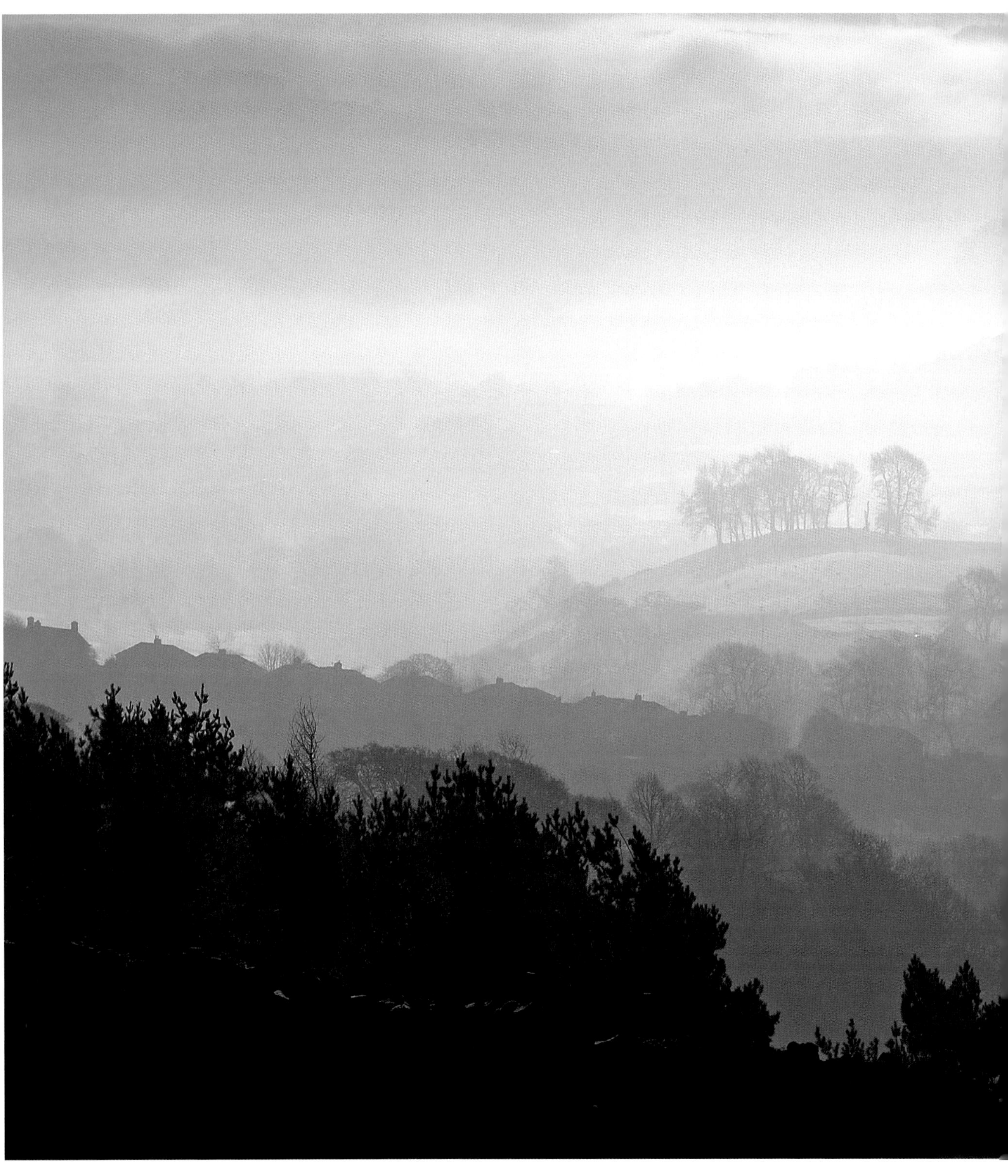

Morning mist over Eyam

The pretty village of Eyam lies below Bretton and Eyam Edge on the limestone-gritstone border. Eyam is a major tourist attraction, famous as the 'Plague village' where in 1665 a box of clothes from London arrived containing plague-carrying fleas. The disease quickly spread throughout the village but by the action of the villagers isolating themselves, the disease was contained within Eyam. Sadly, however, in just 14 months, 260 villagers died. A remarkable tale of human self-sacrifice. Back in 2001 with my film camera, I drove along Bretton Edge in the sunshine one morning and noticed a low-lying mist hanging over Eyam with the hills and trees emerging. Using a long telephoto lens I zoomed in, which gave a foreshortening effect on the hills, creating a layered, monochromatic Chinese watercolour, feel to the picture. After the success with my previous image taken on film, I revisited this spot under misty conditions with my digital camera on many occasions. Eventually in 2007 I managed to get a similar image and tried out different compositions including this landscape format version.

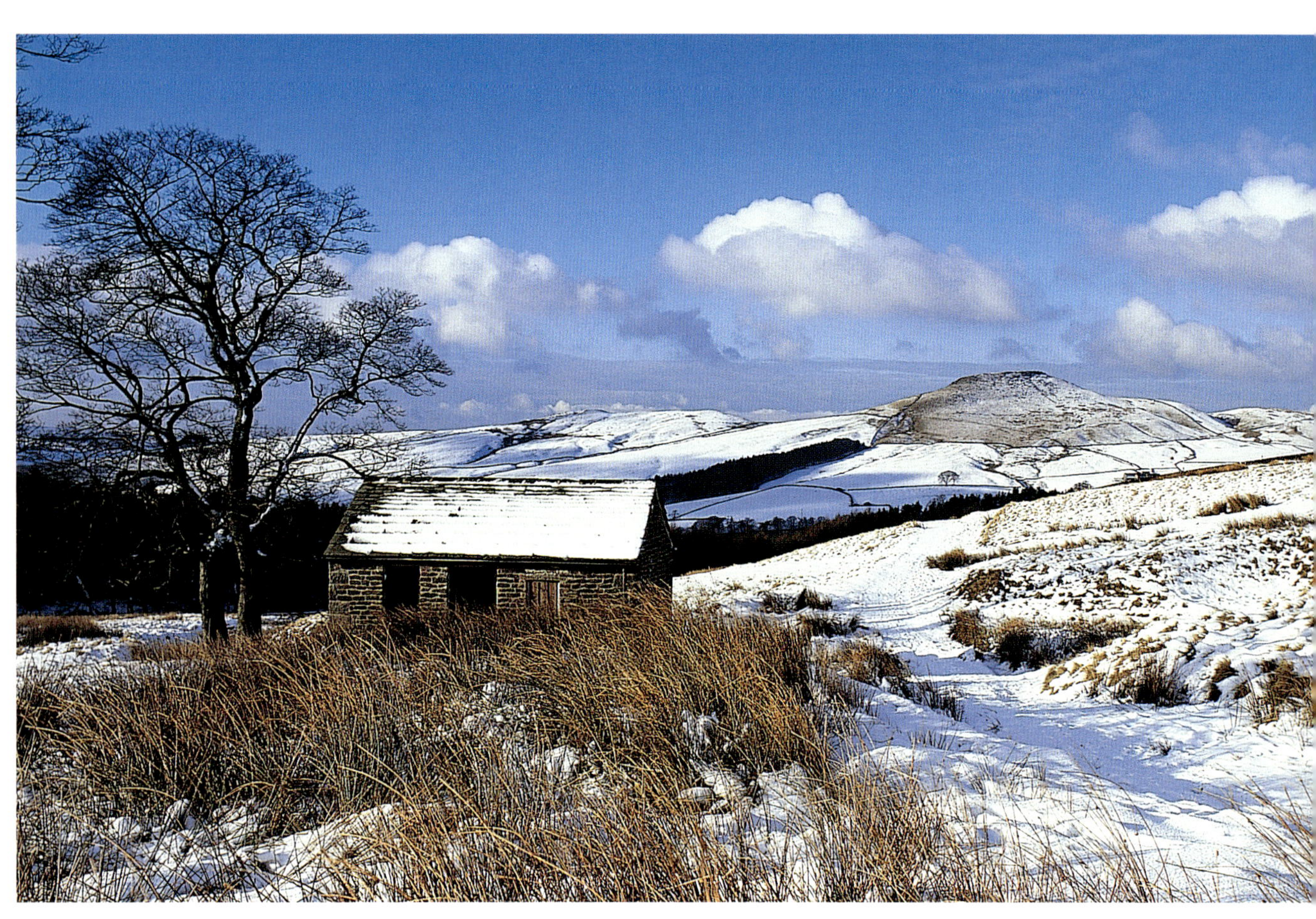

Winter near Wildboarclough

This lovely old field barn lies just off the A54, and having
driven past it many times, I had always imagined
photographing it in snow. The straw-coloured moorland
sedges create a good foreground to lead your eye through
the picture past the barn and tree to the distant summit
of Shutlingsloe(1,660ft/506m), often nick-named the
"Matterhorn of the Peak" which stands above the tiny
village of Wildboarclough. Planned side-lighting meant
I could use my polariser to full effect emphasising the
fluffy white clouds which add interest to the sky. A sunny,
still morning but cold enough not to worry about slushy
melting snow, it was perfect for winter photography.

Lone tree on Rushup Edge

I've been fascinated by this lonesome tree on Rushup Edge near Castleton for years, visiting it many times in different lighting conditions but, photographically speaking, was never satisfied. This was the result of a chance visit. Having been out of the country when we had our best snow ever, on my first sunny day back I raced up to Mam Tor and Rushup Edge to catch the last bits of lying snow before it all disappeared. There was my tree standing proud in great light. I loved the contrast of the golden grasses, patches of white snow and deep blue sky. A simple image using diagonals and contrasting colours.

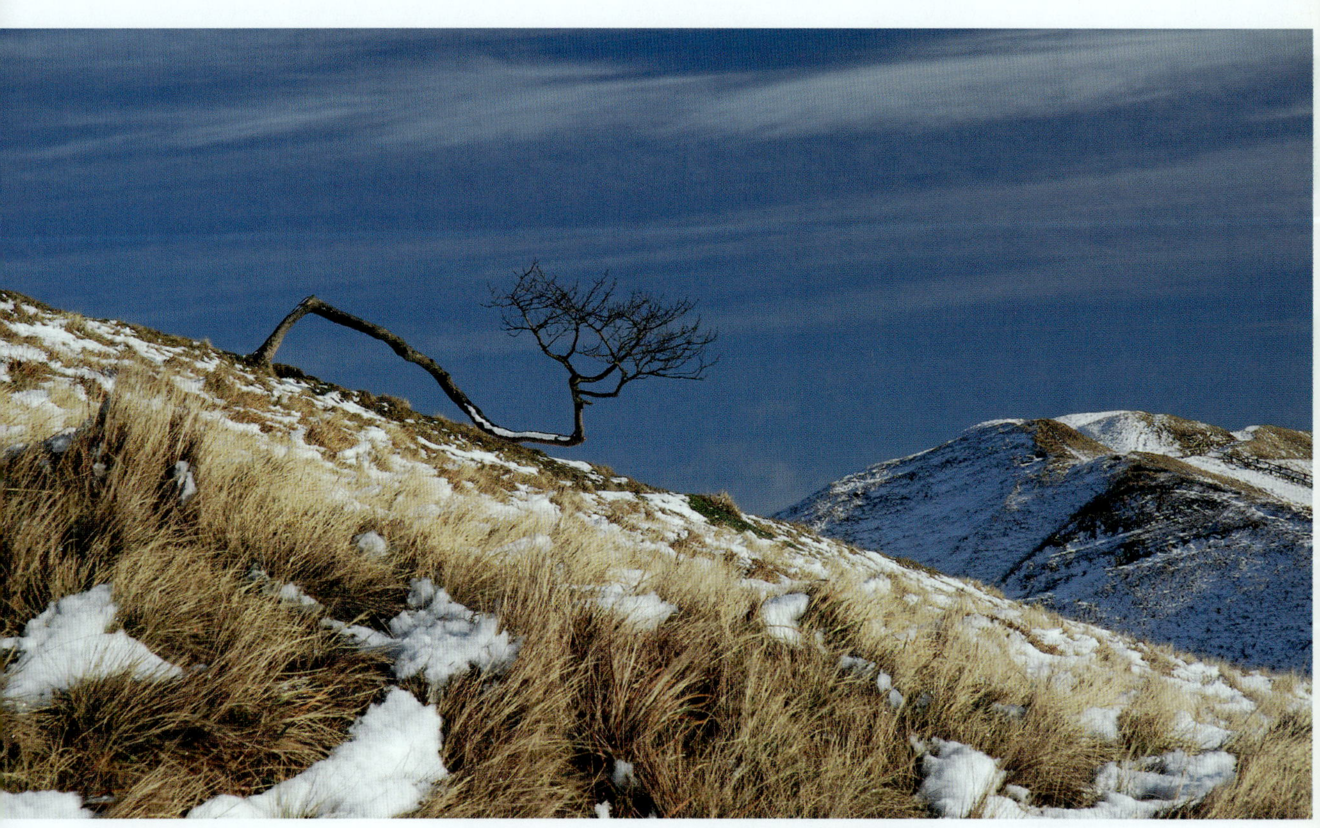

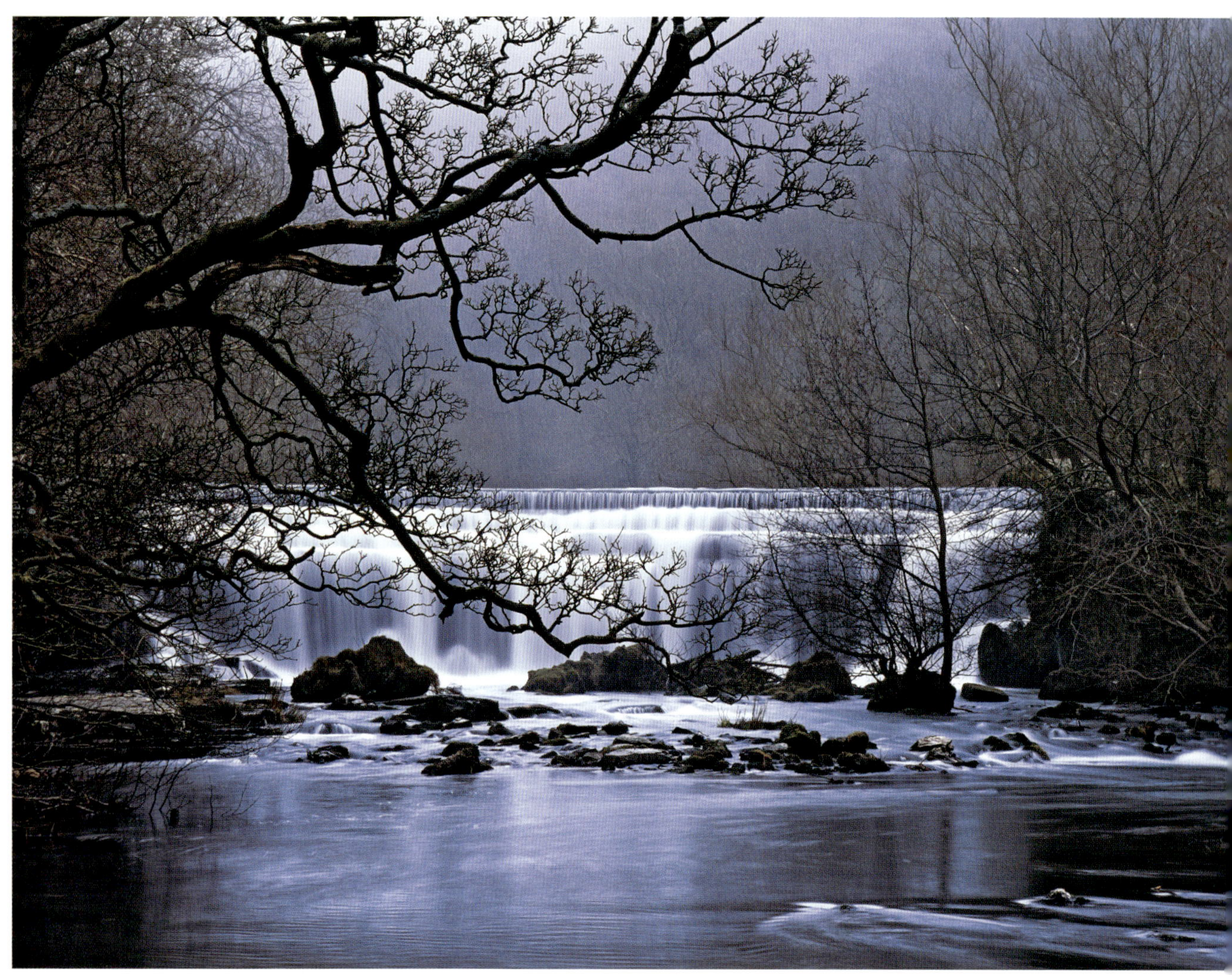

The River Wye at Monsal Weir

This beautiful river, popular for trout fishing, meanders gently
from Buxton to Bakewell through the limestone scenery of
Monsal Dale below the famous 80 foot/24 metre high Monsal
Head Viaduct, which once carried the Midland Line.

Early one cold and gloomy February morning, I set out with
my medium format camera hoping to photograph the viaduct
reflected in the misty river below. The scene was not as good as
I'd hoped, so I wandered off to Monsal Weir and was rewarded
by this wonderful softly-lit view instead, where the white water
appeared to glow. These conditions with slide film and no filters
gave this image a cool, blue cast which adds to the atmosphere.
I included the rocks in the foreground deliberately to add depth
to the picture. This is an example of a surprise shot which you
can't pre-visualise or easily replicate either.

Icy boulders in Padley Gorge

Another example of ice formations in a rocky river, but this time they coat the gritstone boulders of Padley Gorge. It was extremely treacherous as I tried to set up my tripod and medium format camera among them. The low light levels and slow film gave a very long shutter speed, recording the water as a silky blur. A bright patch in the sky briefly reflected a pinky light onto the icy boulders, which added a subtle glow and extra contrast to the image.

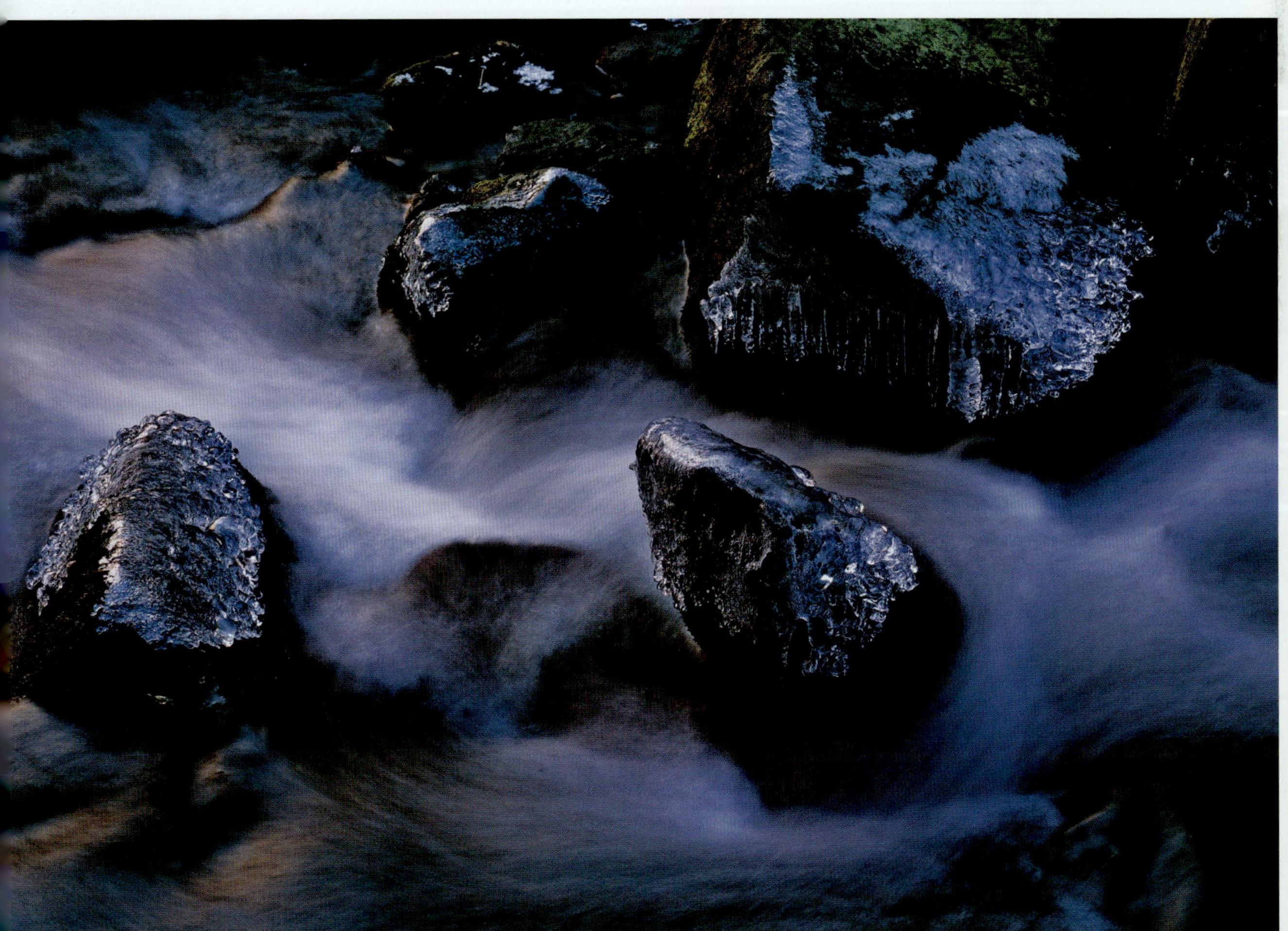

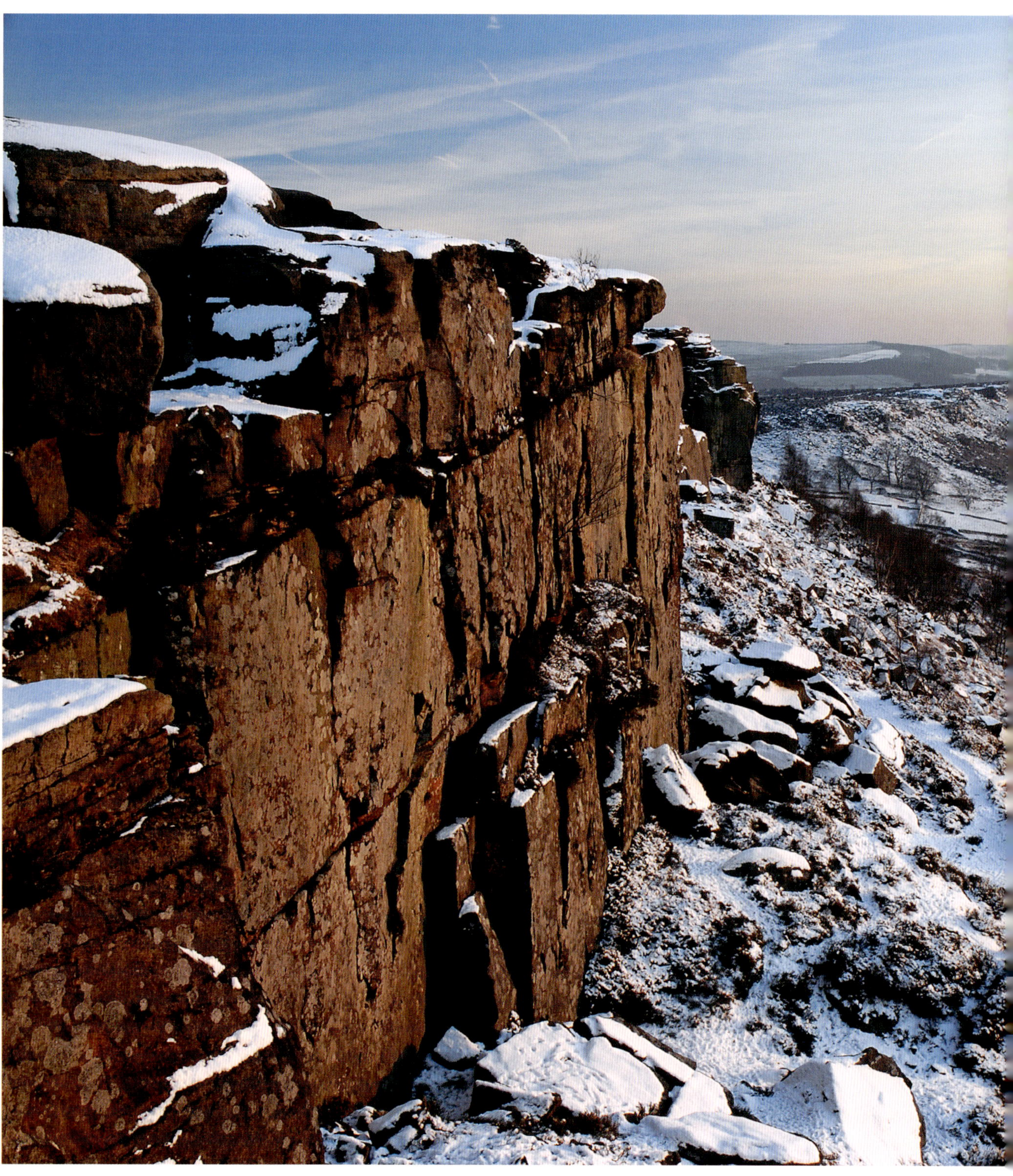

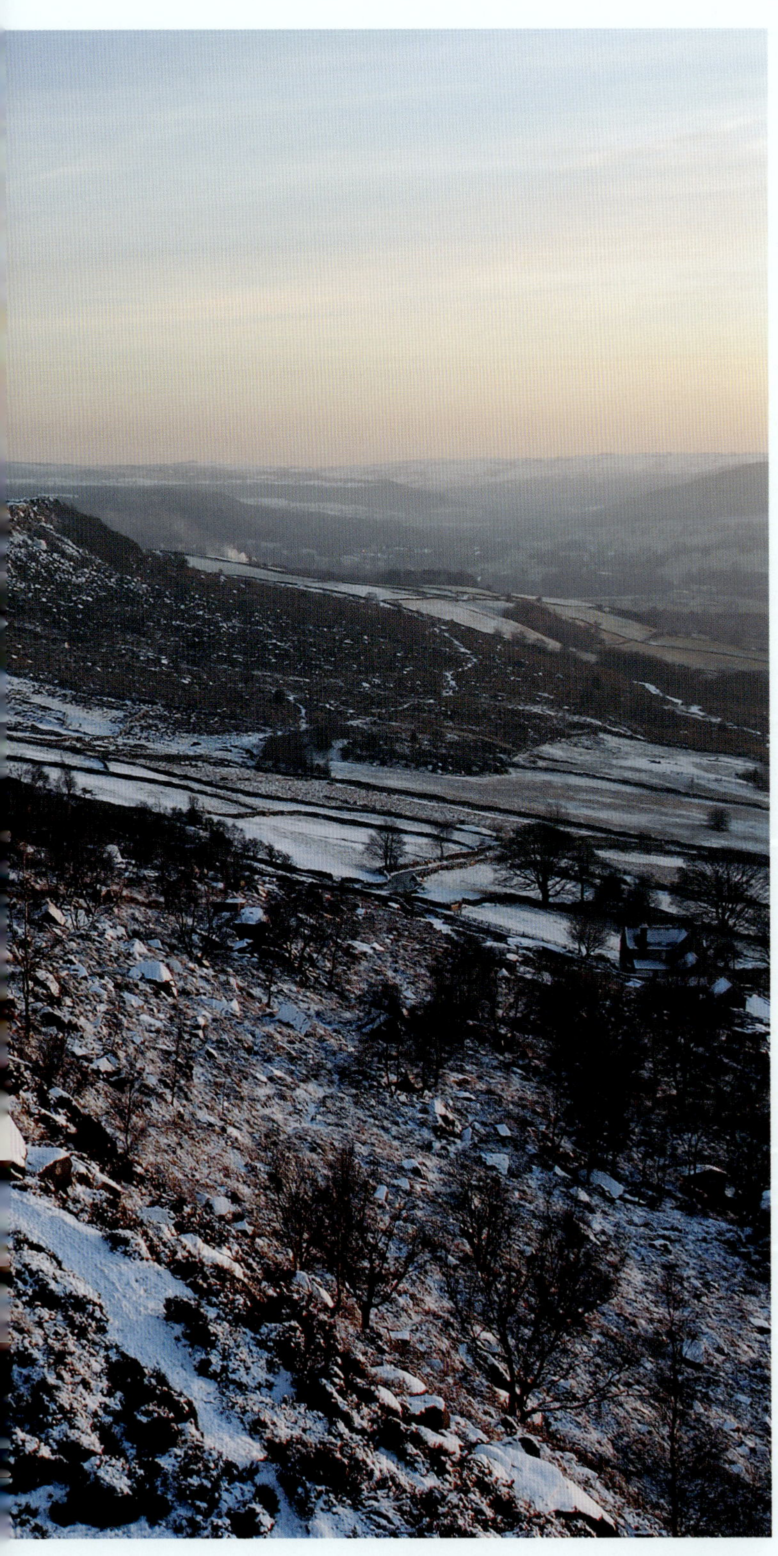

Winter sunset along Curbar Edge

As the sun dips and the sky turns to pastel shades, this westerly facing gritstone edge with its sprinkling of snow takes on a pinky hue. With the temperature plummeting and sheet ice everywhere, I had to tread very carefully setting up this shot as there were sheer drops on either side of me and an icy wind was beginning to strengthen. A covering of snow at sunset or sunrise lifts an image, reflecting back light into the landscape from what would otherwise be a dark foreground in contrast to the brighter sky.

Five Wells Chambered Cairn near Chelmorton ▼

The remains of this Neolithic tomb (built between 4500 and 2000 BC, which once contained 17 skeletons, command fantastic views northwards high above the River Wye valley at 1,410ft/430m. It is in a prime position to catch the last rays of a winter setting sun. I target high places like this in winter when the valleys are in shade. The sun had cast a pink glow onto the white limestone tomb surrounded by a pale mauve sky. The soft pastel colours of the landscape made it a magical time for photography.

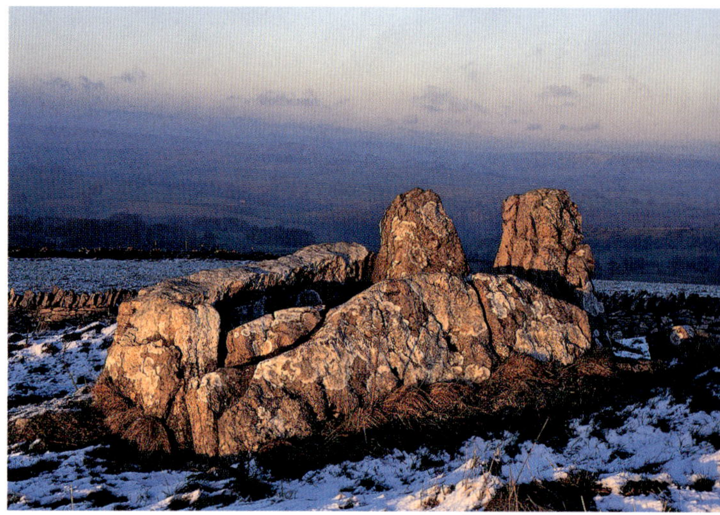

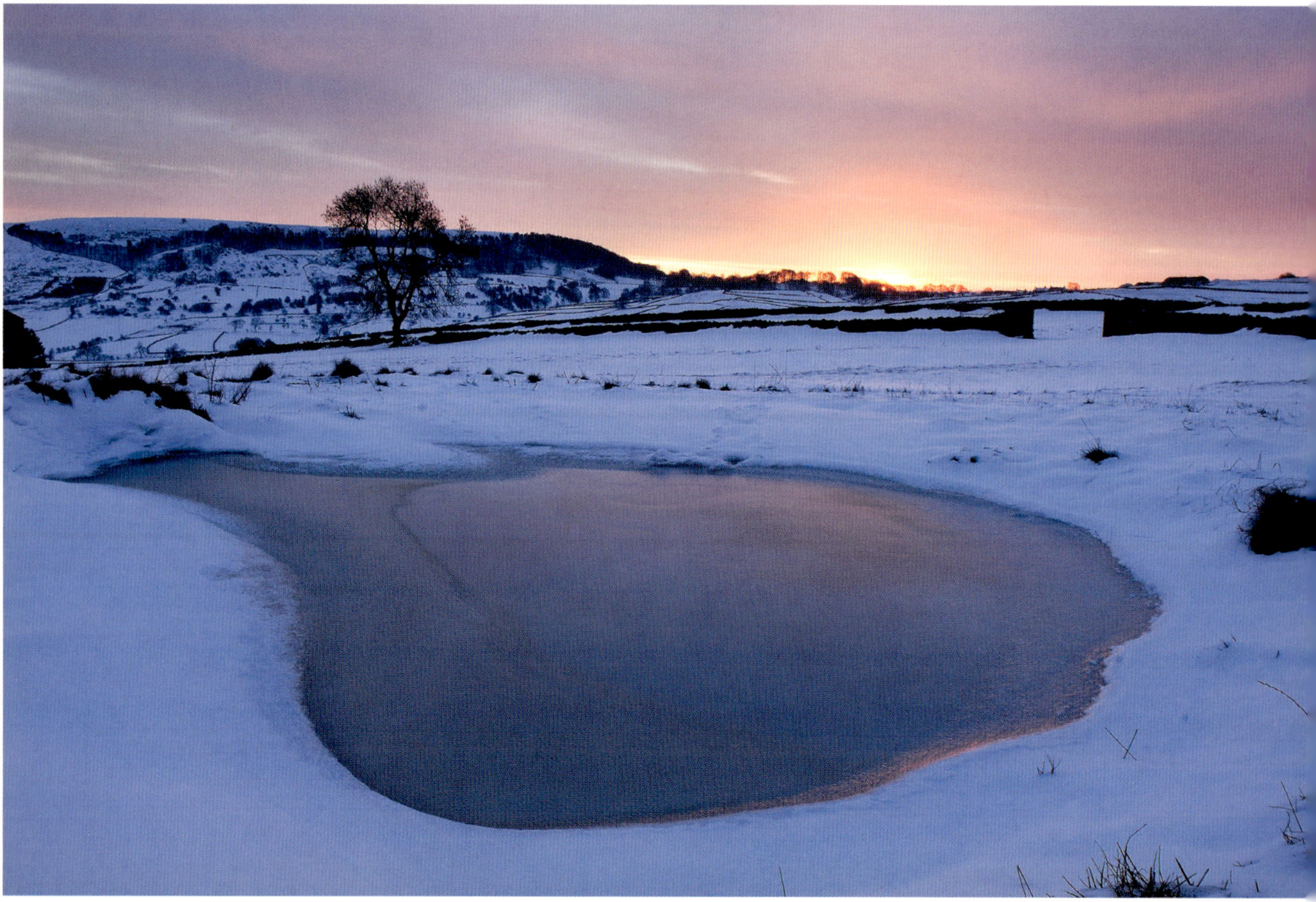

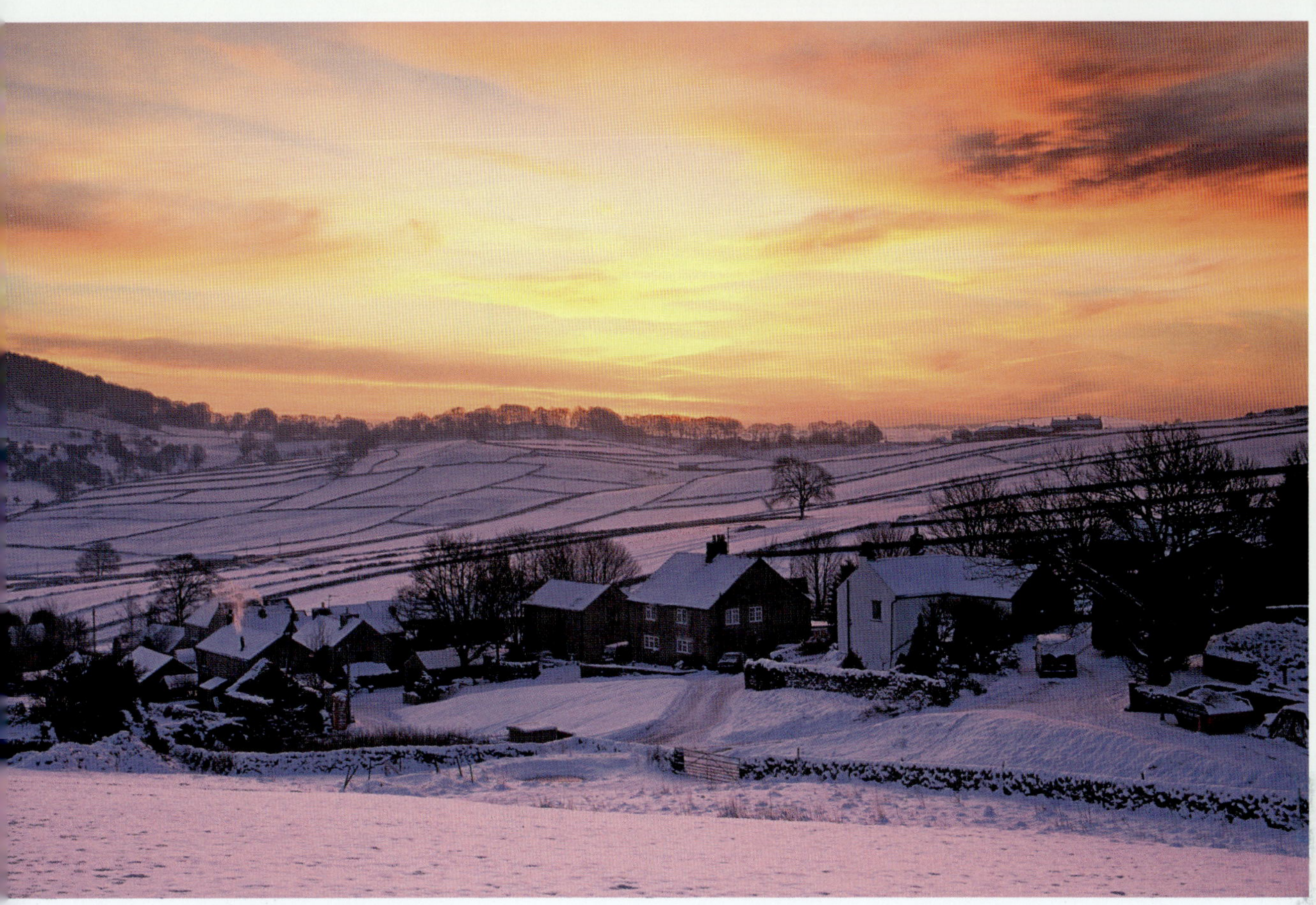

◀ Sunrise over a frosty dewpond, Little Hucklow

Dewponds can be found in fields all over the White Peak where water is quick to drain away. They are man-made circular ponds to hold rainwater ensuring livestock have enough water in dry periods. They also make very useful foreground for photographers and a nice reflective surface for pink skies at sunrise and sunset. Unlike our coastal colleagues, we are not blessed with vast expanses of water around here so have to be a bit more inventive and use any puddle we can. I loved the teardrop pattern formed by the overflow of the circular pond. Unfortunately, I arrived in a rush and had the wrong lens on my camera. By the time I had fitted my wide angle lens the sky had lost some colour. It's a shame I didn't get there earlier.

▲ Sunrise over Little Hucklow

Little Hucklow is a tiny hamlet which stands high on the White Peak plateau at around 1,000feet/300metres. It is also my home, so I am fortunate to be able to snatch photographs in all conditions. For this image I had returned (with bronchitis) the night before from a Scottish New Year trip which was somewhat lacking in snow. Through my bedroom curtains I could see a pink glow, so dragged myself outside in my dressing gown armed with camera and tripod to witness this wonderful scene. There was no time to waste as the sky was changing rapidly. Fifteeen minutes later, I returned back to bed, frozen and spluttering but satisfied that I must have captured a special moment. I couldn't wait to get my slides processed to find out. Despite what many people may think, no pink filter was used; it was just nature at its best.

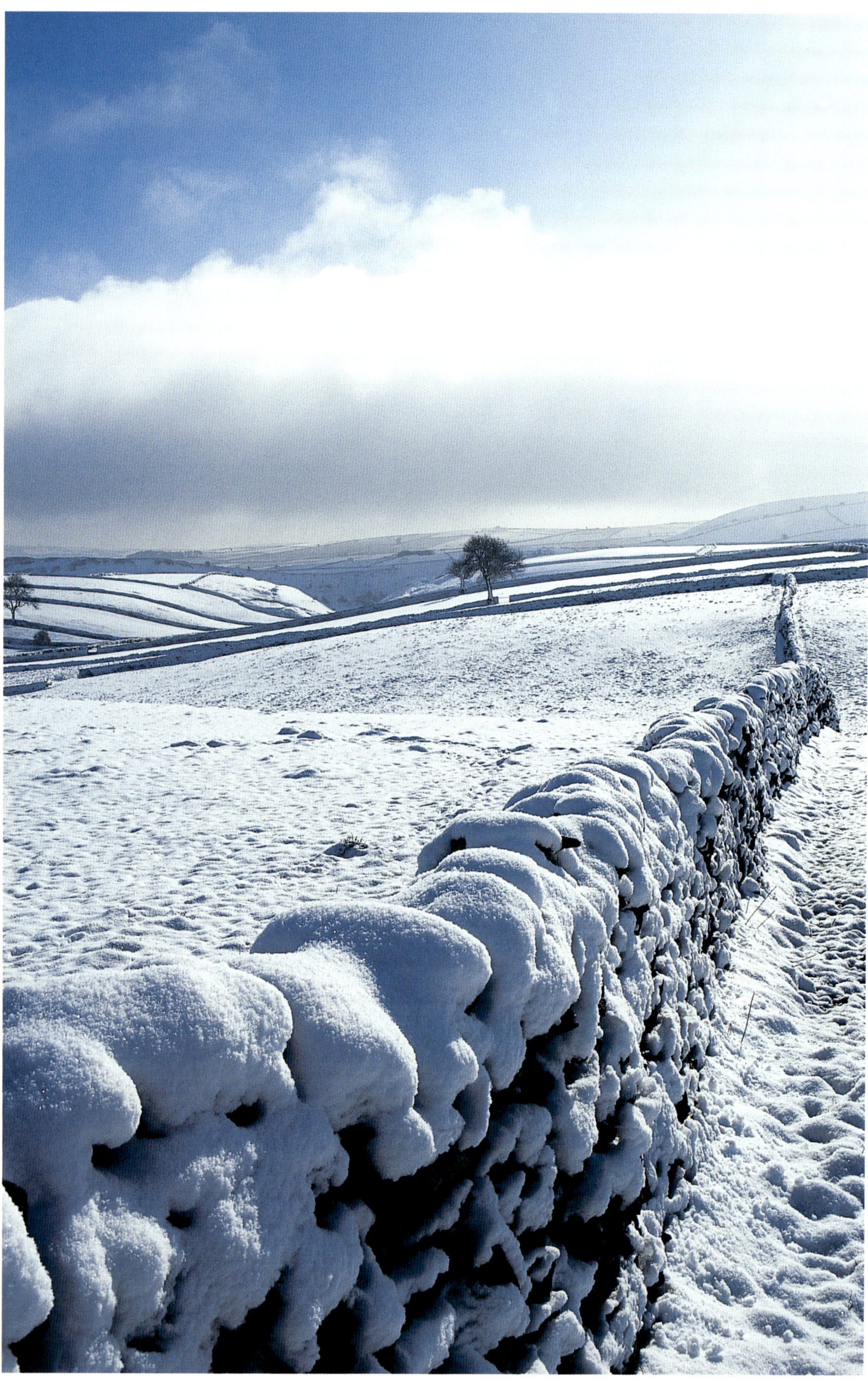

◀ Snowy walls near Litton

There are miles of limestone walls which criss-cross the landscape in this area, and on this high limestone plateau the snow tends to stay a little longer. Walls covered in snow give interesting shapes and shadows and the side-lighting along this one shows up the mounds from the cap stones as they snake diagonally into the distance. The snow was melting quickly in the sun, so I had to work fast. Luckily, the road to Litton was clear and I could access it easily, but often when snow conditions are brilliant, minor roads are blocked and walking to your location is the only option.

▼ Looking east down the Vale of Edale towards Lose Hill and Win Hill

When it snows, I often head for Edale and Kinder as there is nothing more exhilarating than a walk on Kinder's high edges, thigh deep in pristine snow. All too often now, the snow melts quickly on the lower ground to give patchy coverage so I headed off rapidly but didn't realise just how hard climbing up Grindslow Knoll would be. The path had disappeared and the gully filled with deep, drifting snow. I was wading up to my waist at times in a blustery, biting wind. Exhausted, and carrying a ridiculously heavy bag with several cameras and lenses, I had to give up. I got only to this point above the valley and took a few images looking east on both my digital and medium format cameras. I'm now more disciplined, learnt the importance of travelling light and take only one camera for long trips.

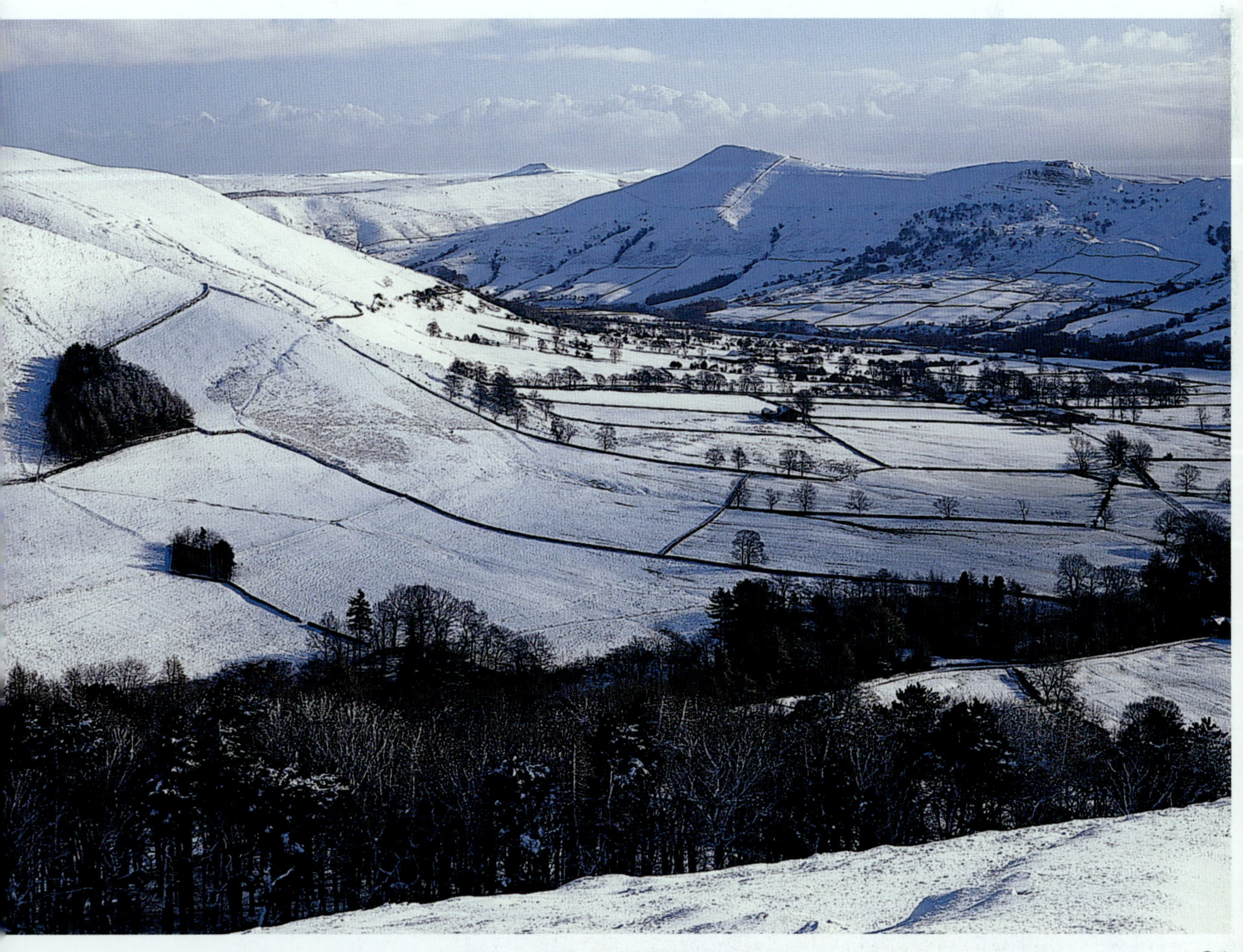

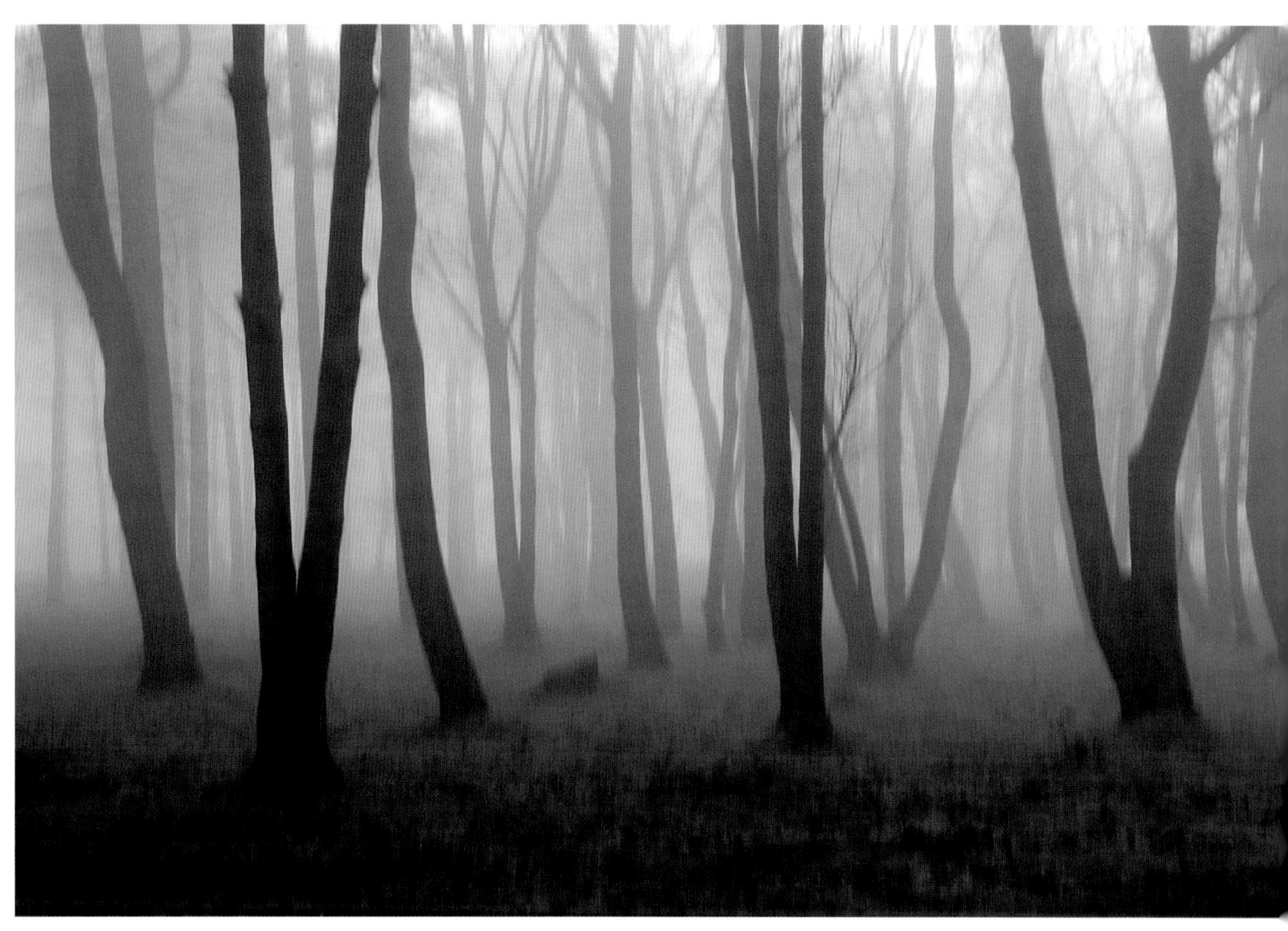

Atmospheric woods near
Sir William Hill, Bretton

One gloomy morning I headed for this woodland to carry
out an experiment with my camera. While on the tripod
and with a slow shutter speed, I let the camera pan
slowly downwards, streaking the trees to create a more
mysterious surreal image. I have not converted this to
black and white. On murky mornings like this the
landscape can look naturally monochromatic.

Hoar frost in Miller's Dale

Life is very peaceful here now, but back in the 1800s it was a hub of industrial activity with cotton mills at Cressbrook and Litton powered by the River Wye, and later the Midland Railway running through. Miller's Dale station was built in 1863, gradually bringing in new tourists to the area. The station closed in 1967 and the disused railway now forms the lovely Monsal Trail, rich in wildlife and industrial history. If there is a chance of hoar frost, then it is often in the sheltered dales where it lingers, as the moist, trapped air over the rivers freezes, coating everything it touches, as it did on this still morning.

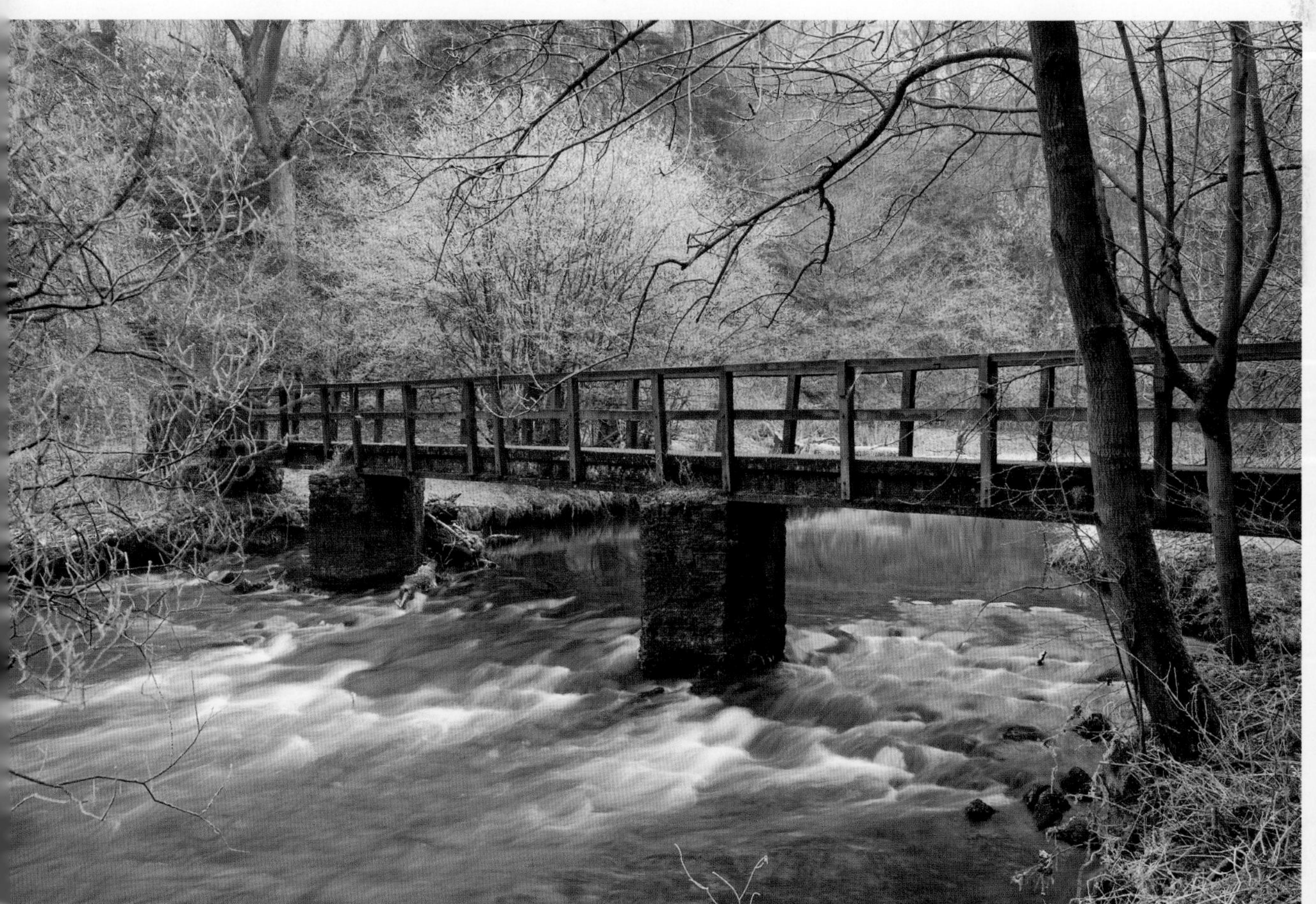

Stormy light, Bretton

This little ridge on the border between the Dark and White Peak is one of my favourite areas in the Peak District and, being close to home, I have grown to know it intimately and can get to it easily when the light is spectacular. My favourite light is strong sunlight with a stormy backdrop. In this image, the mauve grey sky contrasts well with the sunlit green fields. The raking light across the bare tree not yet in bud shows up its glossy branches in all its skeletal glory. It also picks out the distant field patterns of the ancient medieval field systems close to the hamlet of Abney.

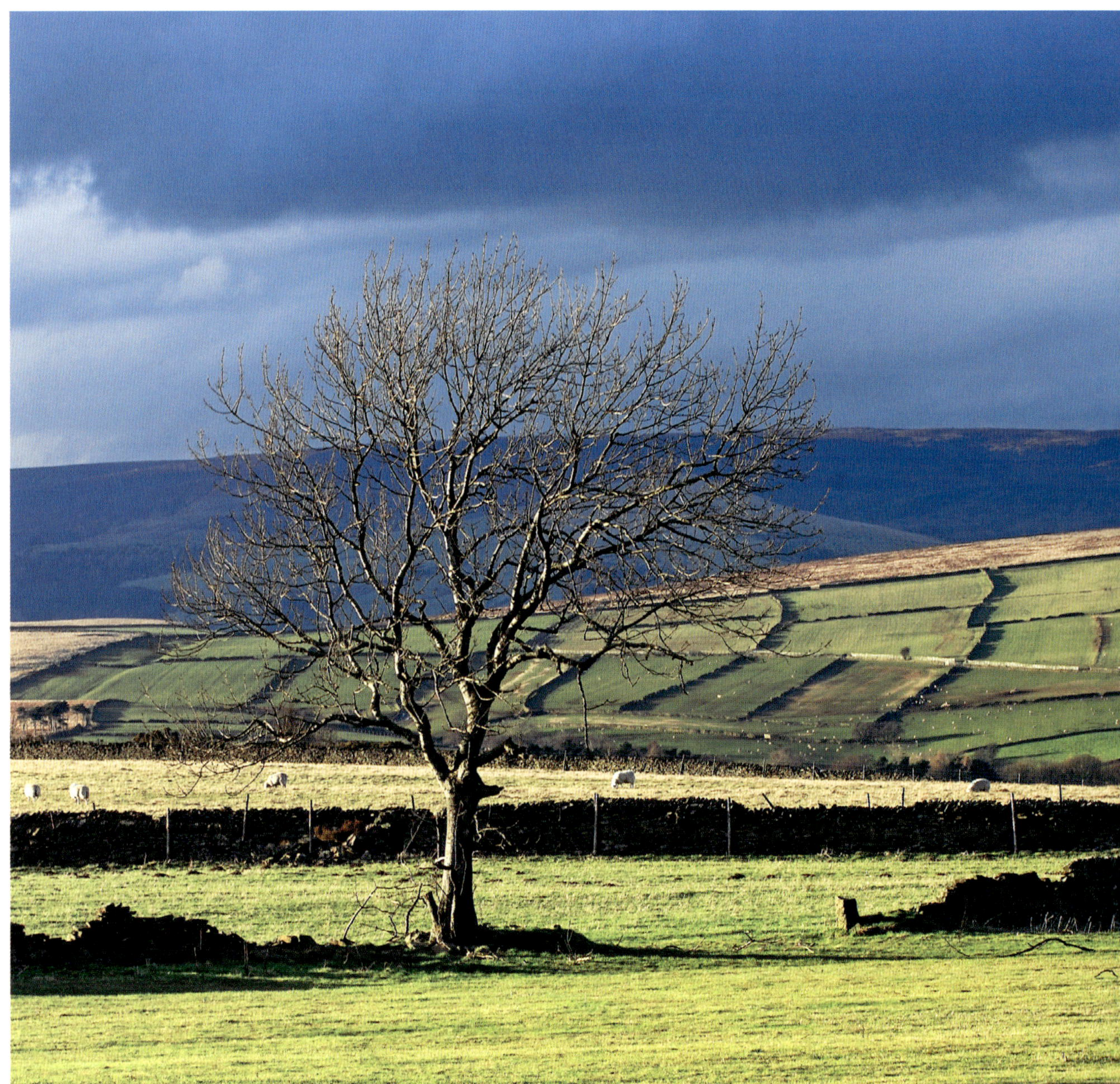

MARCH–APRIL

Sunrise time 06.12–05.36 **Sunset time** 18.22–20.37
Sunrise direction E–ENE **Sunset direction** W–WNW
Vernal Equinox March 20th **Sunrise** 06.12 **Sunset** 18.22

Raging water, chasing rainbows and new life

Days are beginning to lengthen to fill normal working hours and the landscape slowly awakens after its long winter sleep. It can still be very cold, enough even for snow and frost. But the weather is totally unpredictable and changeable. The sun is higher in the sky pumping in more heat and energy to the atmosphere which in turn gives unstable, showery conditions but with strikingly clear light from the fresh, clean air. In addition, rivers, waterfalls and reservoirs are at their best with the water table being high from the increased rainfall or snow melt of winter.

At this time, for stormy days I again favour the Dark Peak where dead bracken is still colourful, rocky brooks become torrents and skies are big and dramatic. Spring does arrive late here in the Peak and most of the limestone dales are still disappointingly bare, especially those wooded in ash whose leaves are late to emerge. However as April approaches, life re-emerges in these dales which are home to a wealth of beautiful spring plants and buds which love the damp calcareous soils, deciduous woodland and river banks. Wood anemone, butterbur, celandine and catkins are just a few that can be found in abundance. It is on the cloudy, still days with low contrast when I turn my camera to these delicate subjects although sometimes when backlit they are attractive.

With the capricious weather this is a challenging and exciting time for landscape photographers who can chase some of the most spectacular light of the year. It certainly blows the cobwebs off!

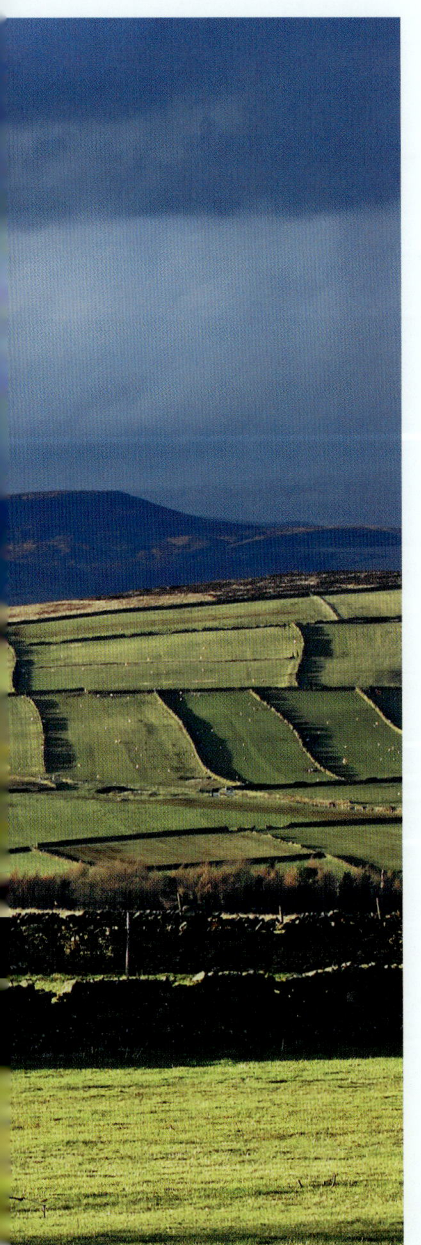

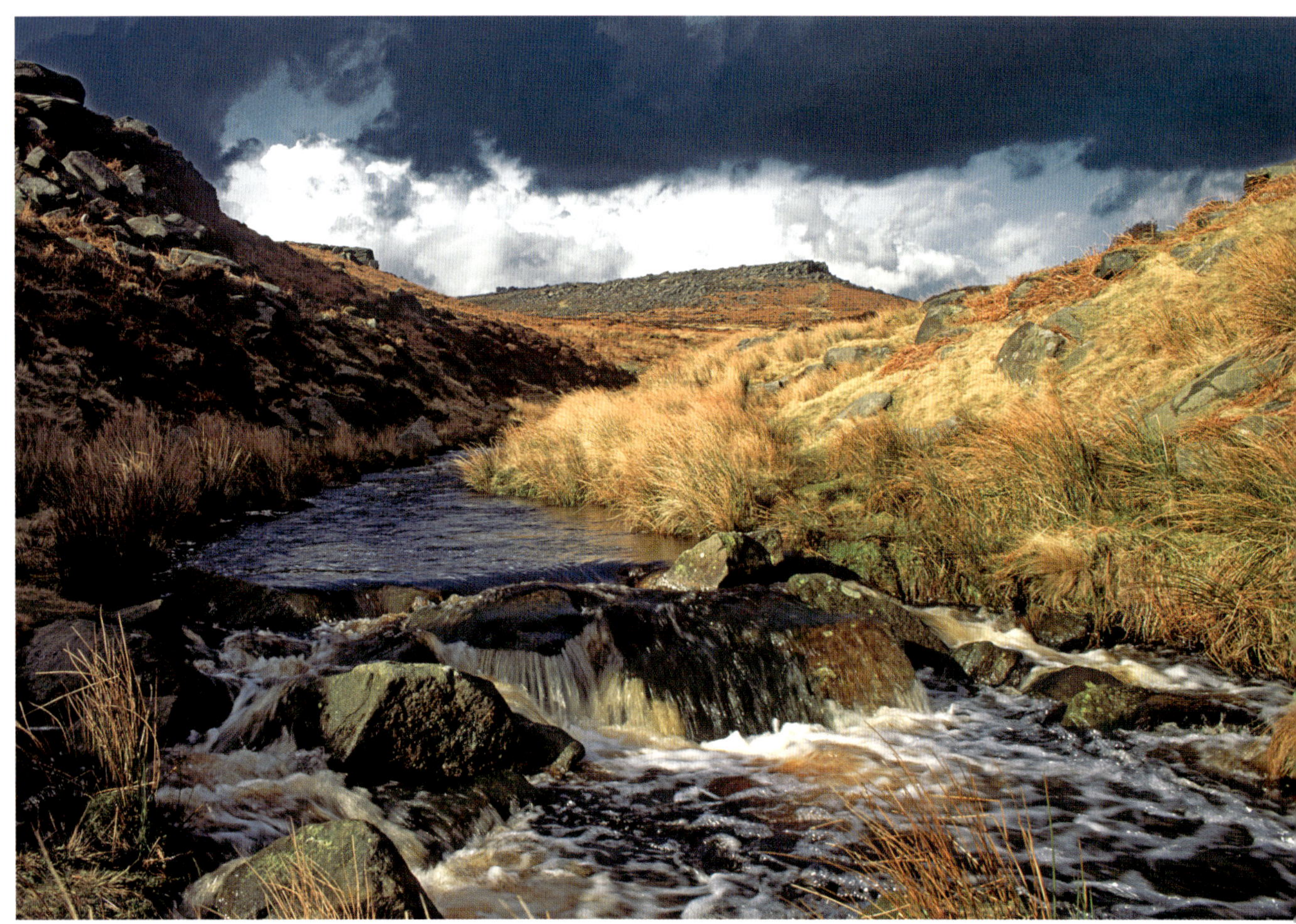

▲ Burbage Brook

Burbage Brook near Hathersage runs down through the
gritstone moorland below Higger Tor and Carl Wark, the
latter a flat- topped prehistoric hillfort which you can see
here in the distance. Latest theories suggest the fort may
be Neolithic and this whole area is littered with prehistoric
field systems and clearance cairns. This is the kind of
typical unstable, stormy spring day which I love, where the
light is clear and dark brooding clouds race across the sky.
Careful planning meant the scene was side-lit when I
arrived, giving shadows and depth to the picture. I balanced
my tripod precariously in the stream, and was frequently
battered by hail showers. With the light and sky constantly
changing, I took many images, no two the same, before
finally falling into the icy water. Squelching back to my car,
I found it had been broken into, but there was nothing to
take, and I felt my moody pictures made up for it all.

▶ Three Shires Head

From high on Axe Edge Moor, the River Dane flows under
this ancient packhorse bridge at the aptly-named Panniers
Pool, where the three counties of Staffordshire, Derbyshire
and Cheshire meet. This old trading route was used for
carrying flax, silk and buttons from the mills at Gradbach,
Macclesfield and Wildboarclough in Cheshire. It's a great
spot, very popular now with walkers instead of traders,
stopping off at the pool for lunch with their rucksacks
rather than panniers.

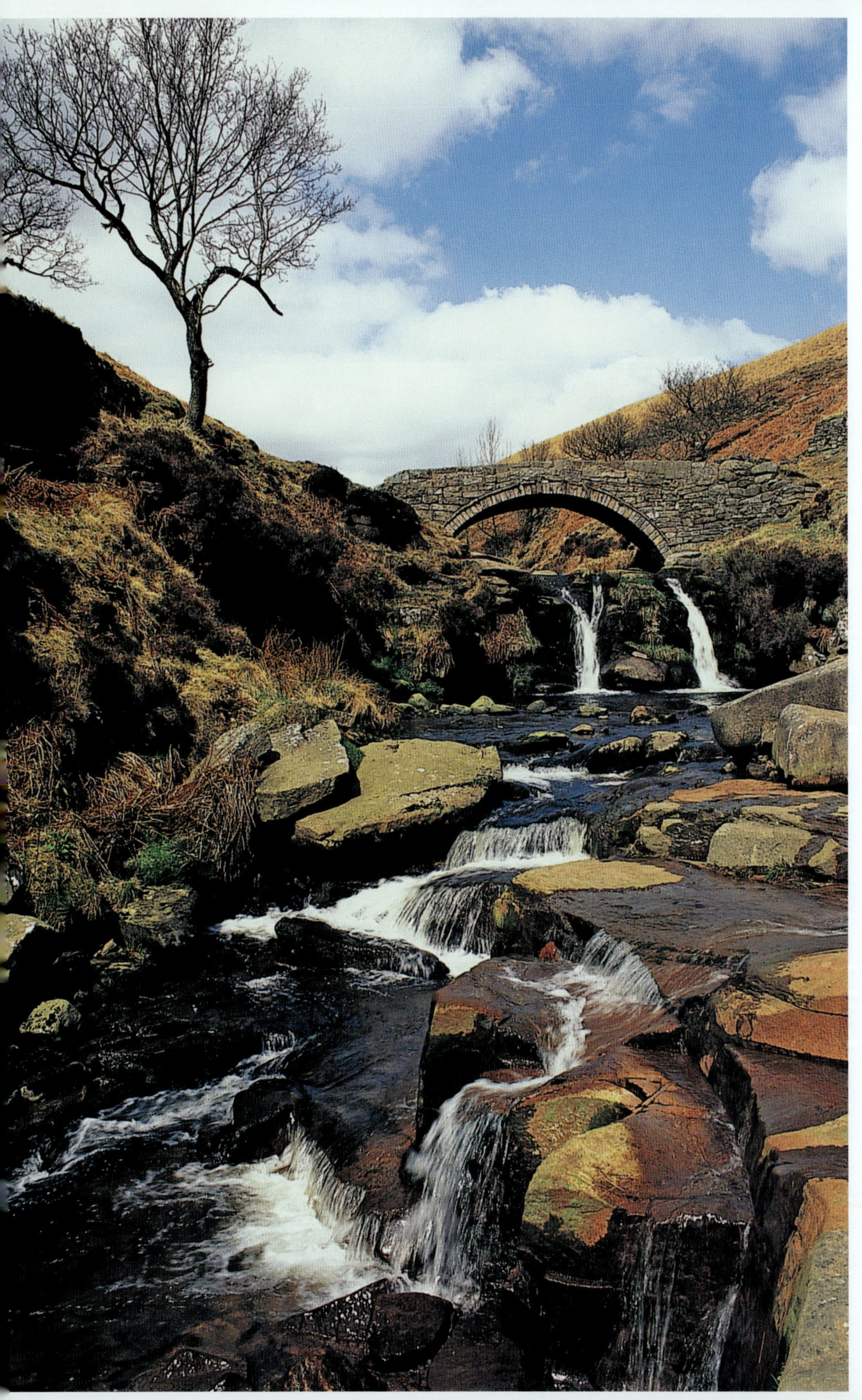

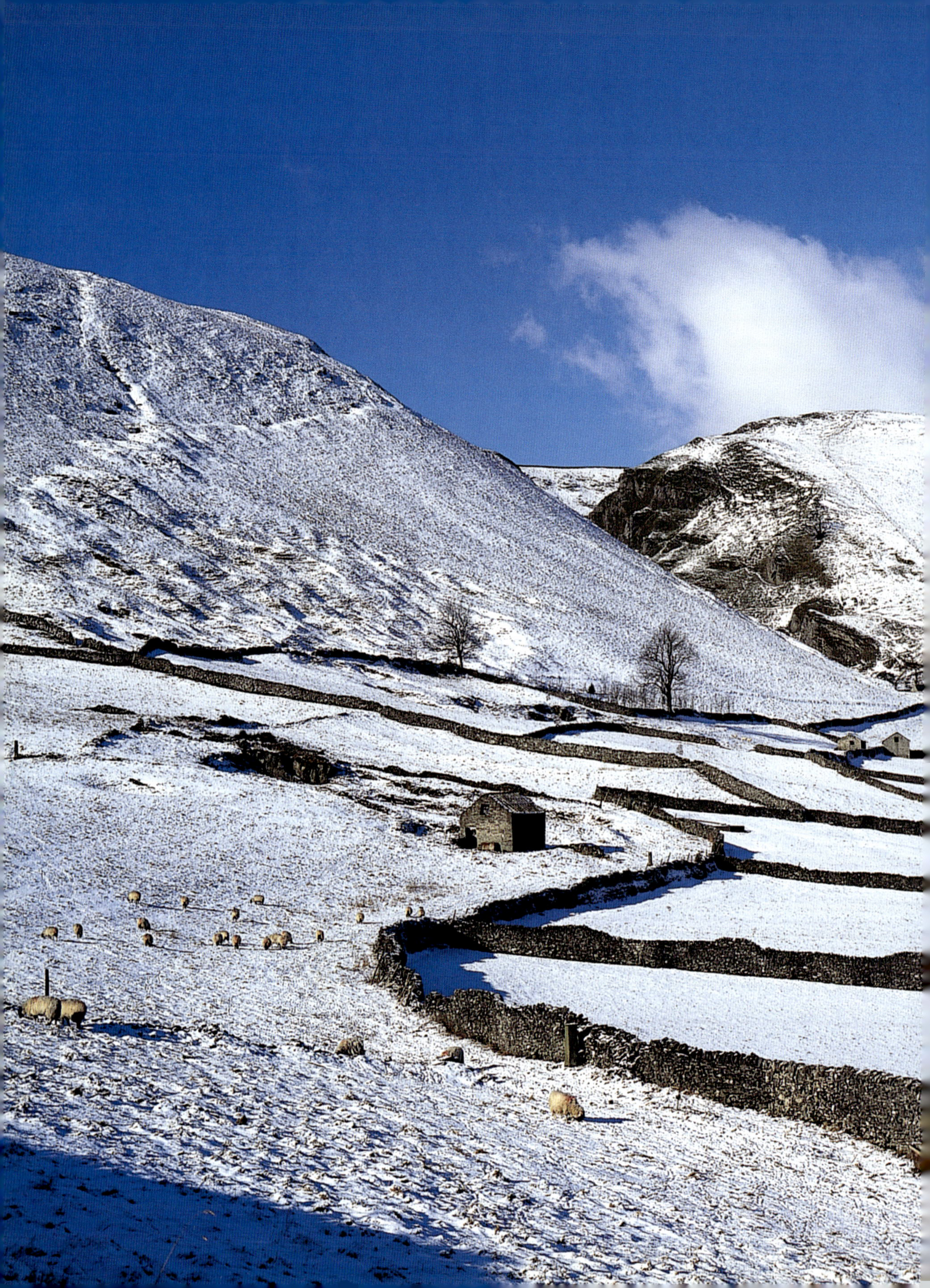

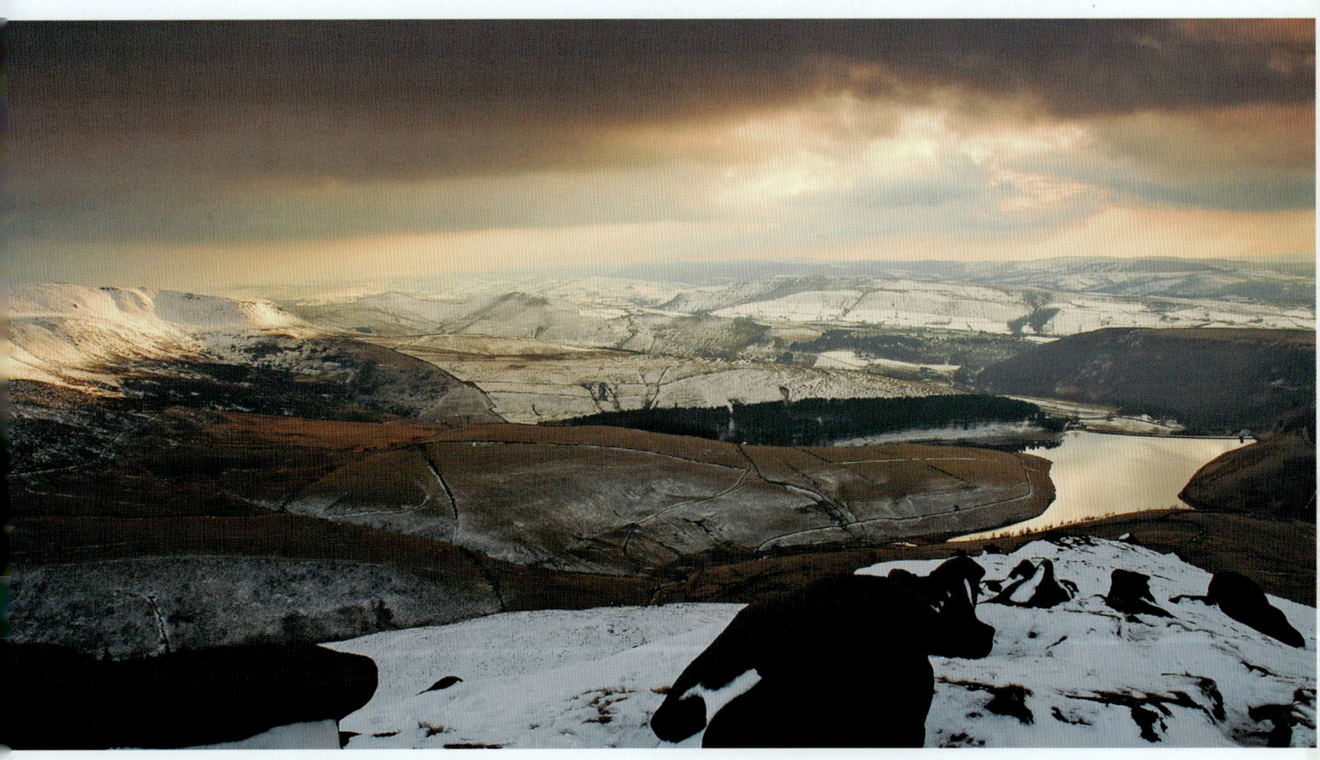

◀ Field patterns near Winnats Pass, Castleton

I have noticed over the years that often in March and April, just when we think spring is here, the weather reverts to winter and we get a dumping of snow. It usually happens overnight and with the warmer days is quick to melt. This means a frantic rush around before lunchtime to capture as many successful images as possible. This day was typical and I had to work fast. Here, looking west, the snow has picked out the wonderful field patterns between the limestone walls below Peveril Castle. The snaking wall and field barns which are dotted along into the distance lead the eye up to the entrance of Winnats Pass. In the spring sunshine, the snow was rapidly disappearing on the south facing slopes of this spectacular limestone gorge.

▲ Looking west from the Kinder Plateau

It was a late in the day decision to go up Kinder. Having missed the recent snowfall, I was desperate to capture any remaining snow on high ground, and as the skies began to clear, I made a decision to seize the moment rather than wait until the following winter. By 3.00pm I was racing like mad up slippery William Clough in order to get to the top before sunset. Unfortunately, the inevitable Kinder cloud soon drifted in and my window of light was rapidly diminishing. You can see in the foreground that Kinder Reservoir was already in shadow and the snow patchy. However, I just managed to catch the last rays of sunlight on the snow-capped southern edge of the plateau near Kinder Low. Minutes later I would have been too late. Who said landscape photography was a leisurely affair? I will have to return another winter.

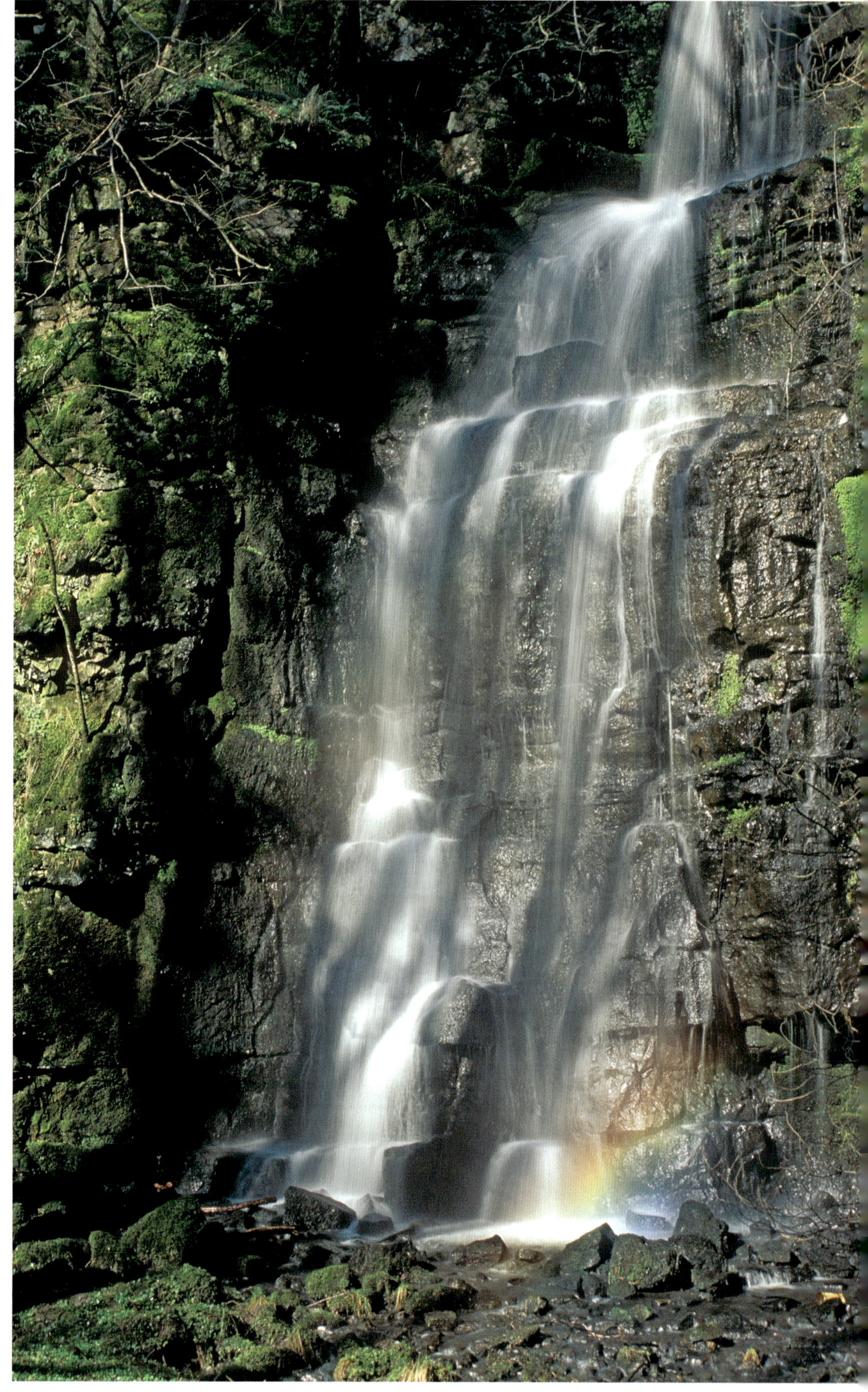

Hidden waterfall ◀

I discovered this waterfall by accident many years ago and am always fascinated by its hidden qualities. I am slightly reluctant, therefore, to broadcast its exact location for fear of spoiling the secret atmosphere. This was the first image I ever took of it. I have returned many times without ever catching the right light to reveal not only the rainbow and volume of water pouring over the 60foot/18m drop but the shadowy knight's head as well. There must be many other hidden dells like this all over the Peak that many people have discovered and want to keep secret. Selfish, I know, but we all need a few special places we like to keep to ourselves in this increasingly public world.

Rubicon Wall near Cressbrook ▼

As the River Wye flows down through Miller's Dale it passes through a lovely little amphitheatre known as Water-cum-Jolly Dale, where the river forms a tranquil pool below steep limestone crags and, being a breeding ground for water fowl, the cries of coot, moorhen and tufted duck echo around. April is the time when this dale starts to spring into life. As I look over the weir across at Rubicon Wall, a popular climbing crag, we can see the first acid greens of spring appearing from the fruits of the small-leaved elm which I used to frame the scene. A gentle breeze meant that reflections were destroyed, but one calm spring day I will return.

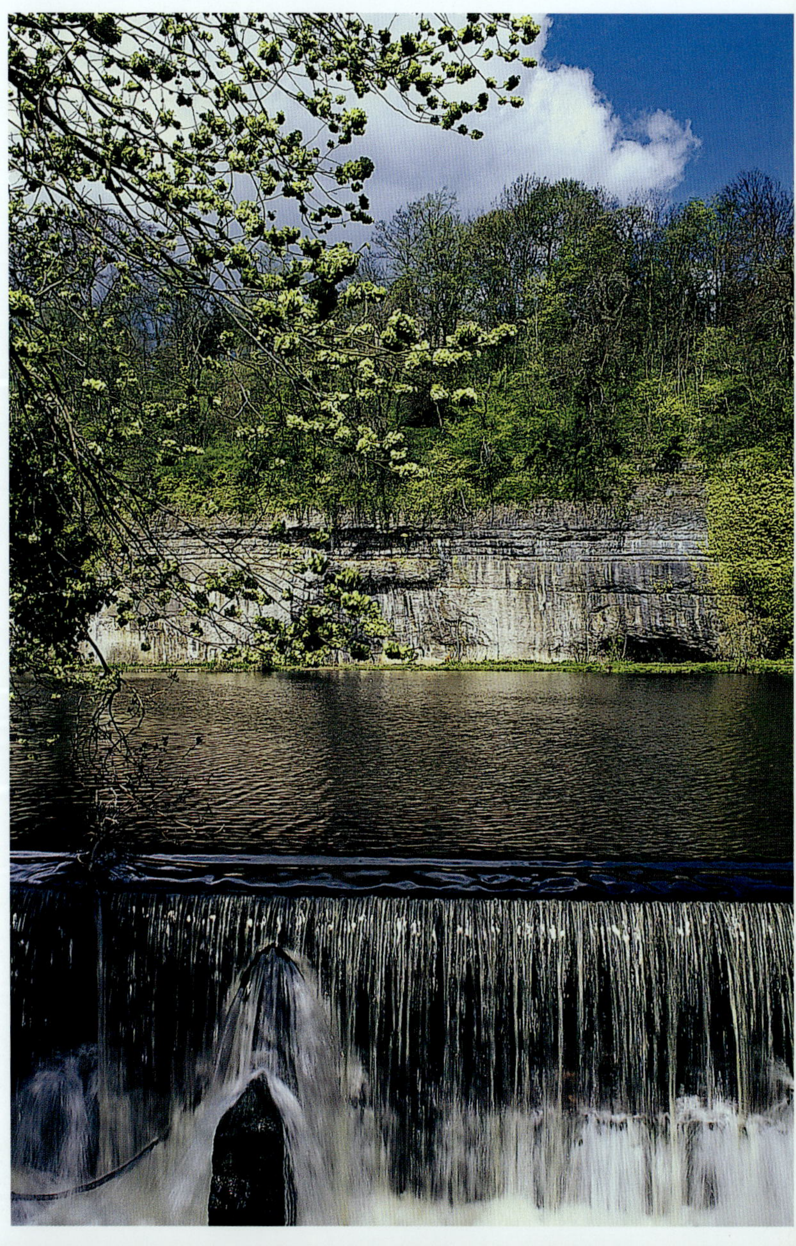

Alport Castles ▼

Lying just off the Snake Pass in the northern part of the
Peak, Alport Castles is reputed to be the biggest landslip
in England. Its instability lies in the easily eroded shales
bedded between the layers of gritstone. From this view
looking north-west, we can see more evidence of less
dramatic landslips beyond. Oblique lighting has cast dark
shadows which add to the drama. With its huge gritstone
towers, tumbled boulders and grassy mounds now well
detached from the ridge, Alport Castles is aptly named.
To give scale to this picture, on the top right is a tiny wall
where people are sheltering from the strong wind for
lunch. I was not so lucky, and blasted by its full force
was struggling to see with my streaming eyes.

Sheep grazing in "mist" along Stanage ▶

I could tell you this was taken in one of those lovely
autumnal mists which can envelop the edges. However,
that would be misleading. In reality, I was walking along
Stanage annoyed at missing the light again and thinking
I'd made another wasted trip. To top it all, someone had
decided to burn off the heather near Bamford Edge and
clouds of smoke were drifting my way. I suddenly realised
that I could try to turn this to my advantage as it looked
quite atmospheric. All I needed were a few of my favourite
models, turned a corner and there they were, grazing
peacefully in a nicely positioned group. Who says the
camera never lies?

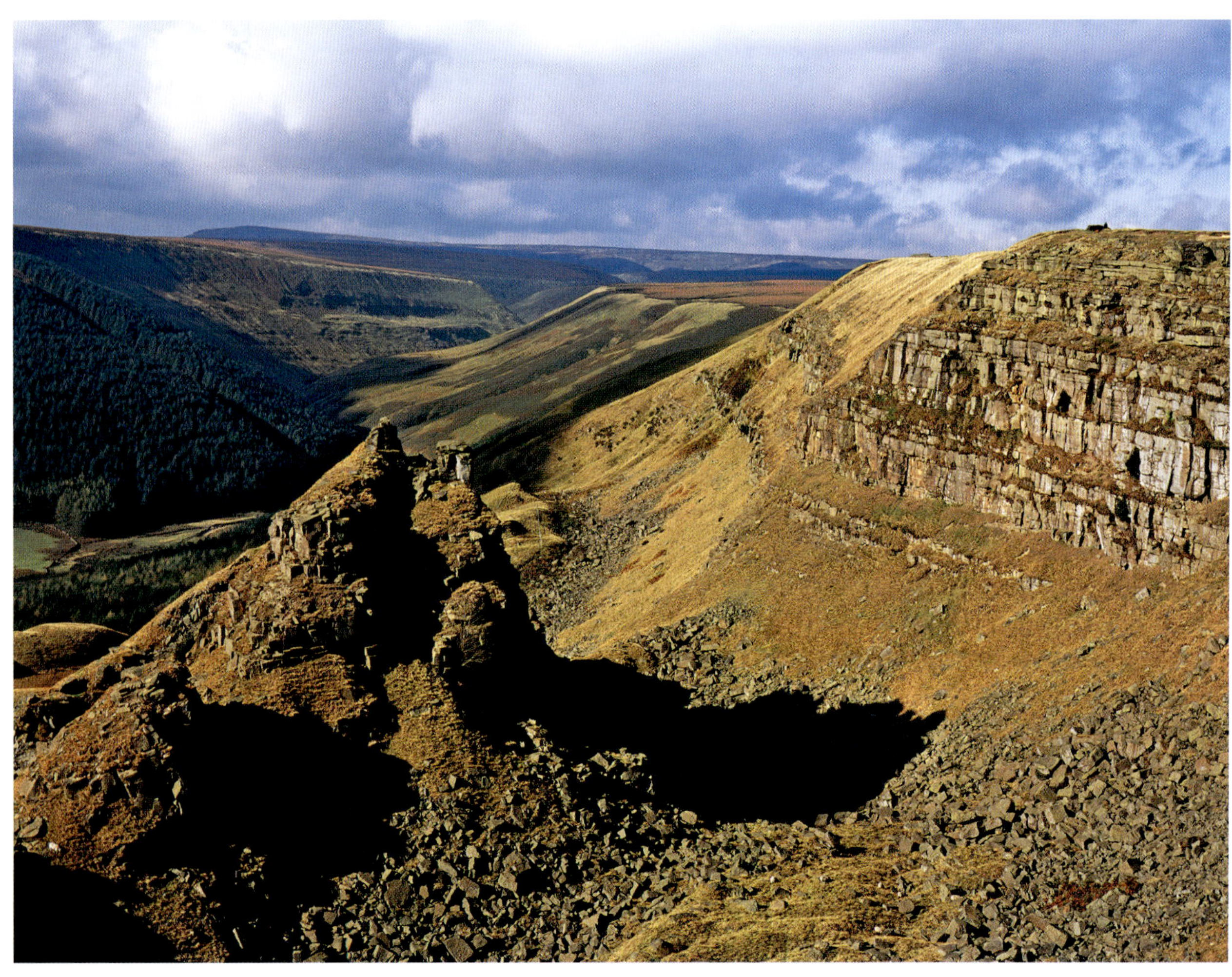

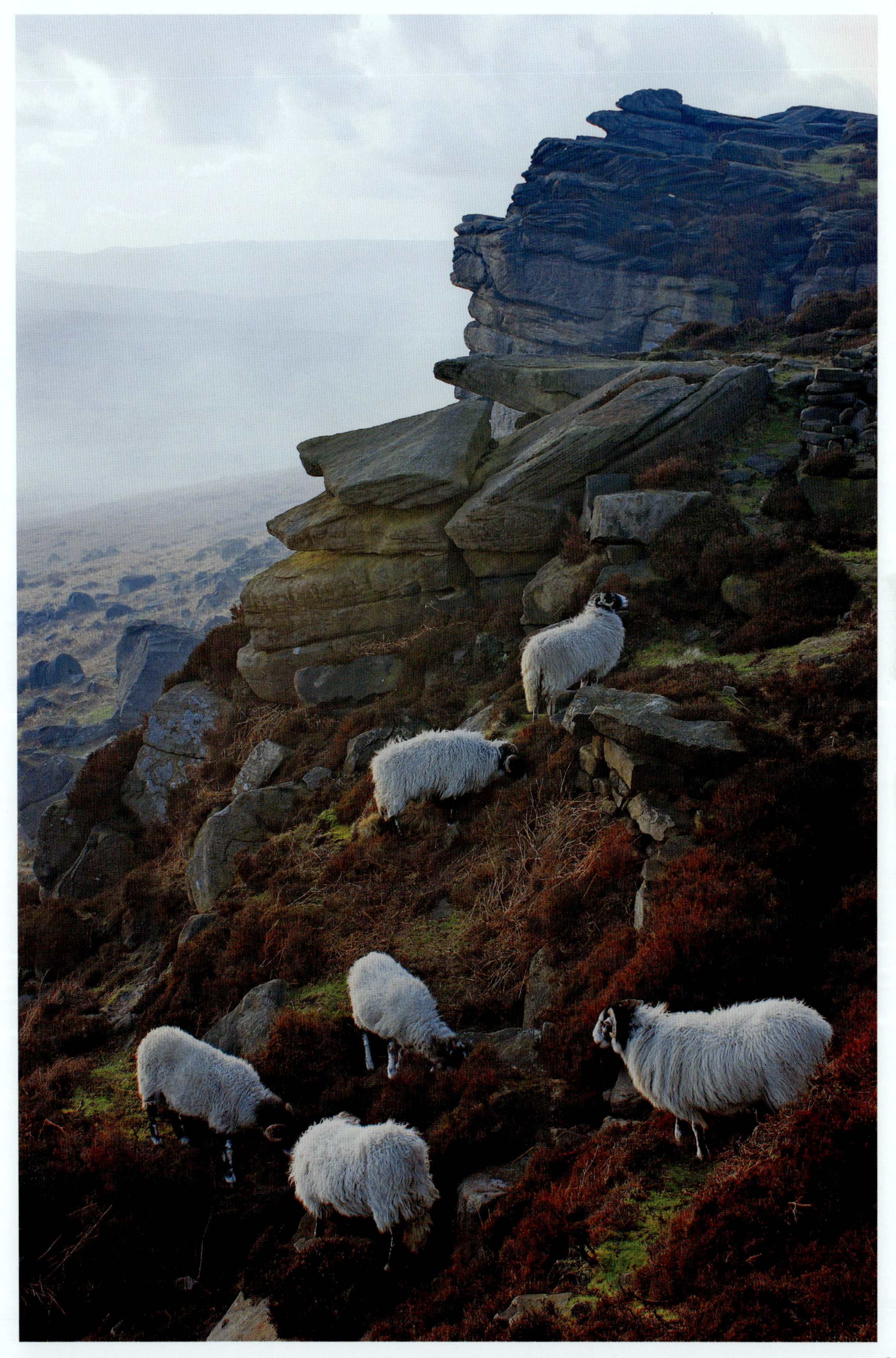

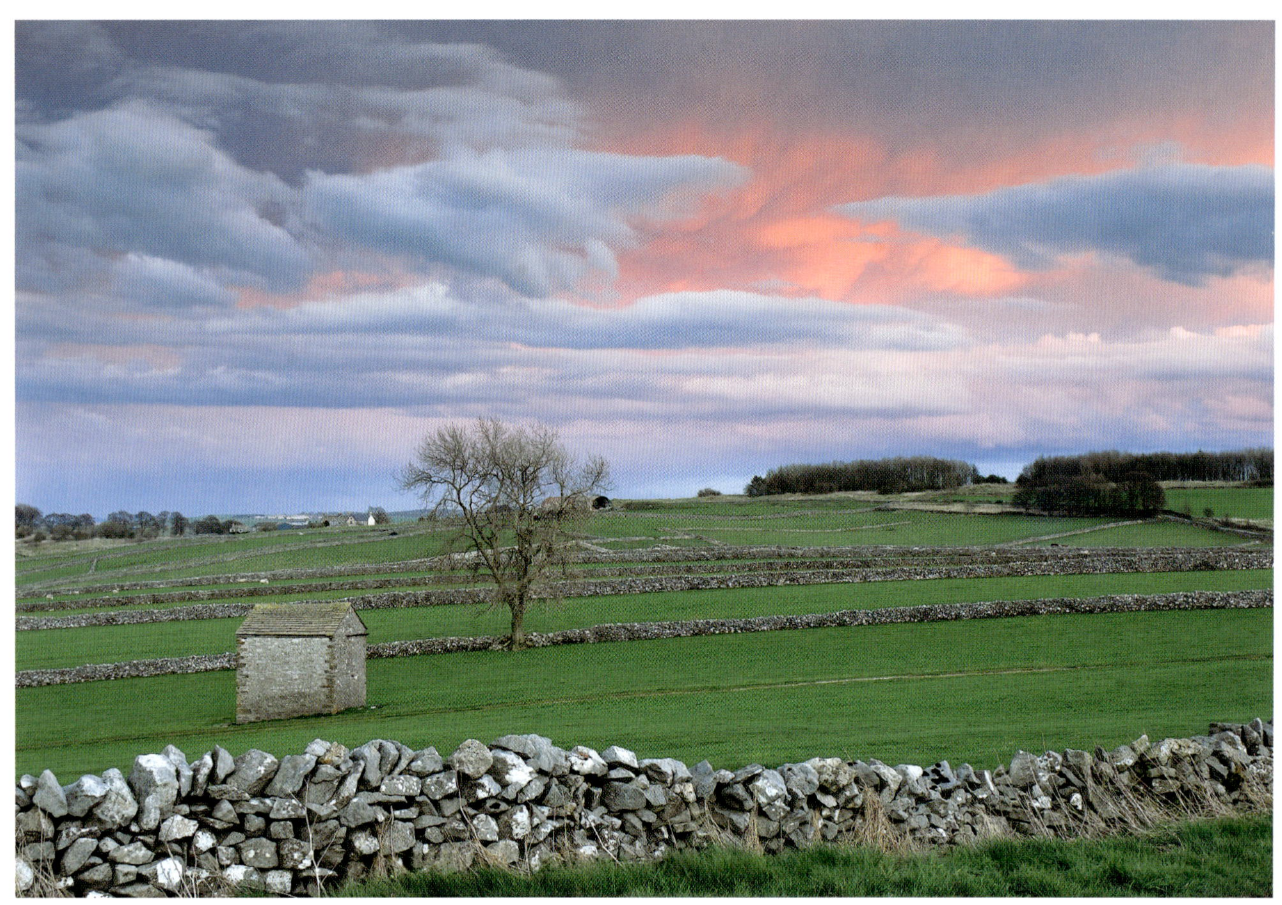

Stormy sunset over a
White Peak barn

There are only a few days a year when the evening sky
takes on a mysterious glow, usually when storm clouds are
present and the sun is about to set. The problem is being
ready with a camera and finding a suitable place for an
acceptable composition. I am fortunate to live near this
barn, so when conditions are right I can drop everything
and be there within minutes. We must all have places near
to where we live which are suitable subjects and although
they may not be the most dramatic or scenic, we stand
more chance of capturing the most dramatic light, and
consequently, an image with more impact than a
spectacular location in the wrong light.

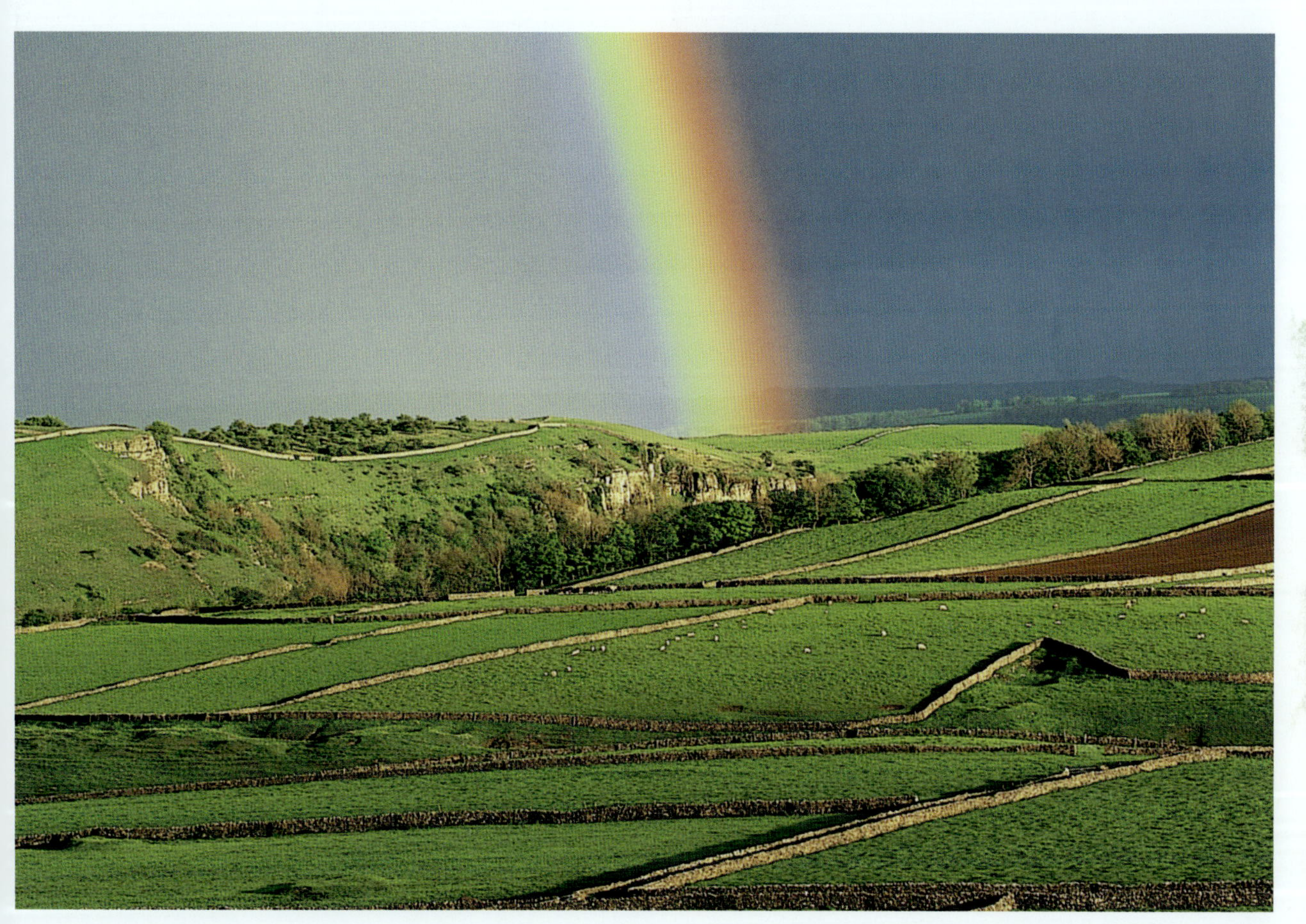

Rainbow over Ravensdale Crags

This is probably one of the strongest rainbows I've ever seen, and for once, I was in a reasonable place to photograph it. Standing on Litton Edge above the village of Litton I had to keep sheltering down behind a wall to avoid the squally showers. Popping my head up I saw this fantastic rainbow over the Ravensdale crags. It lasted ages, so I had time to put on my long lens and zoom in a little.

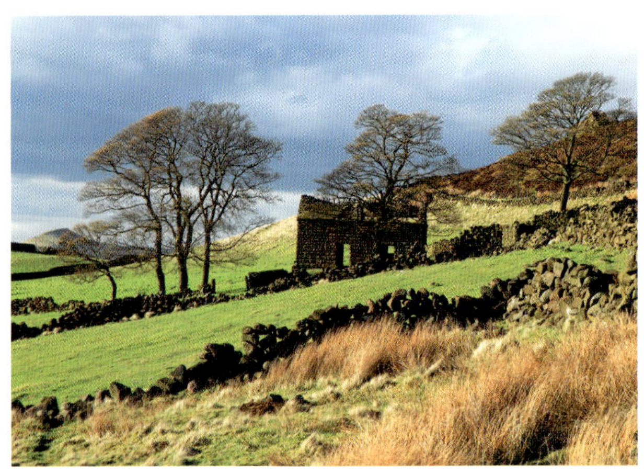

◄ Derelict barn at Roach End

There are many examples of derelict ruins scattered around the Roaches, in the Staffordshire Moorlands. I got to this one just in time before the sun moved behind to cast it in shadow. It was another stormy afternoon, fitting for my subject with its tumbledown roof. The back lit fields create vivid green curtains for the 'open plan' windows and doors contrasting well with the slate grey sky and golden sedges. Every boulder on the broken wall is also isolated. In the distance we can see Shutlingsloe just catching the fleeting sunlight.

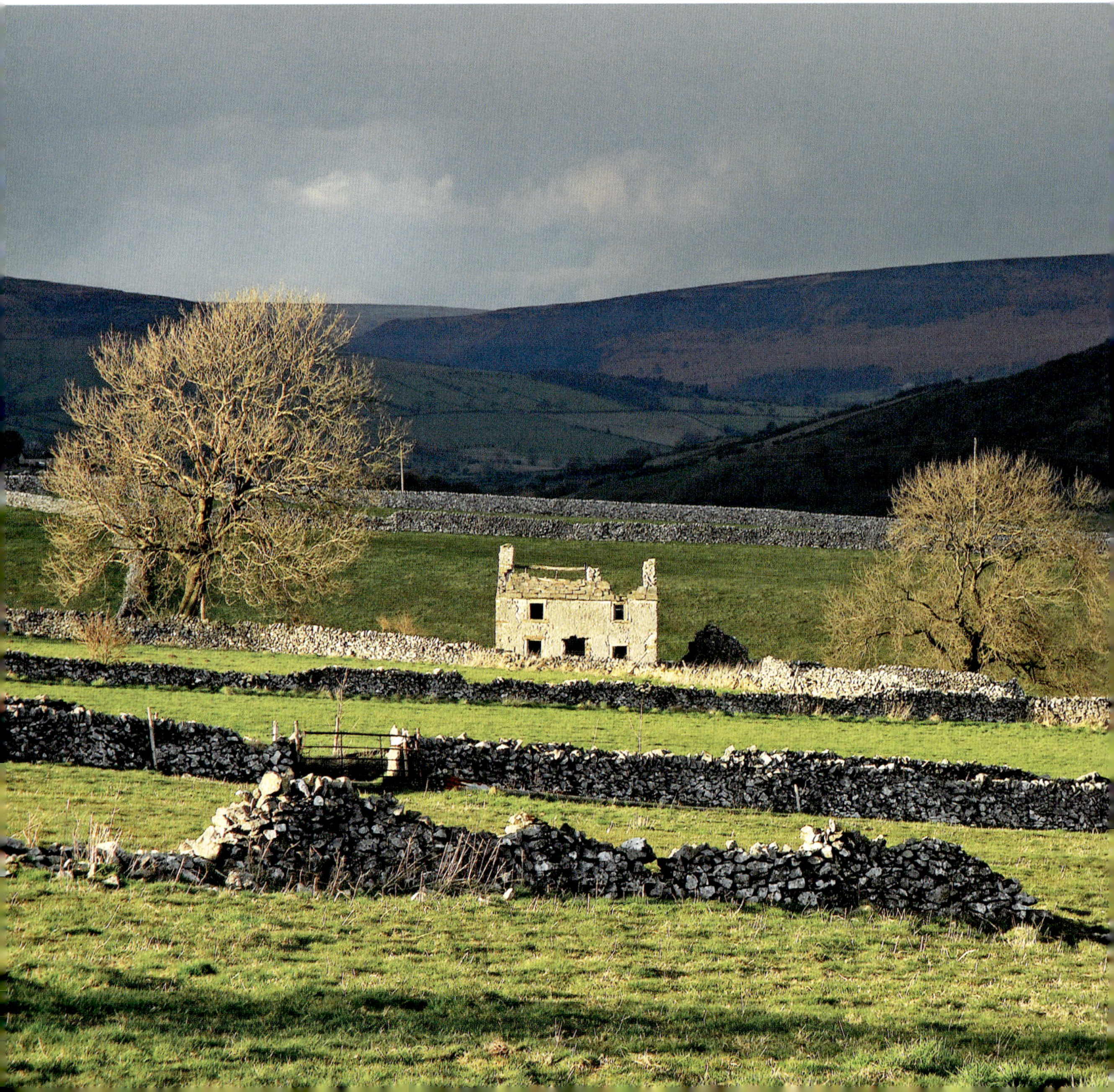

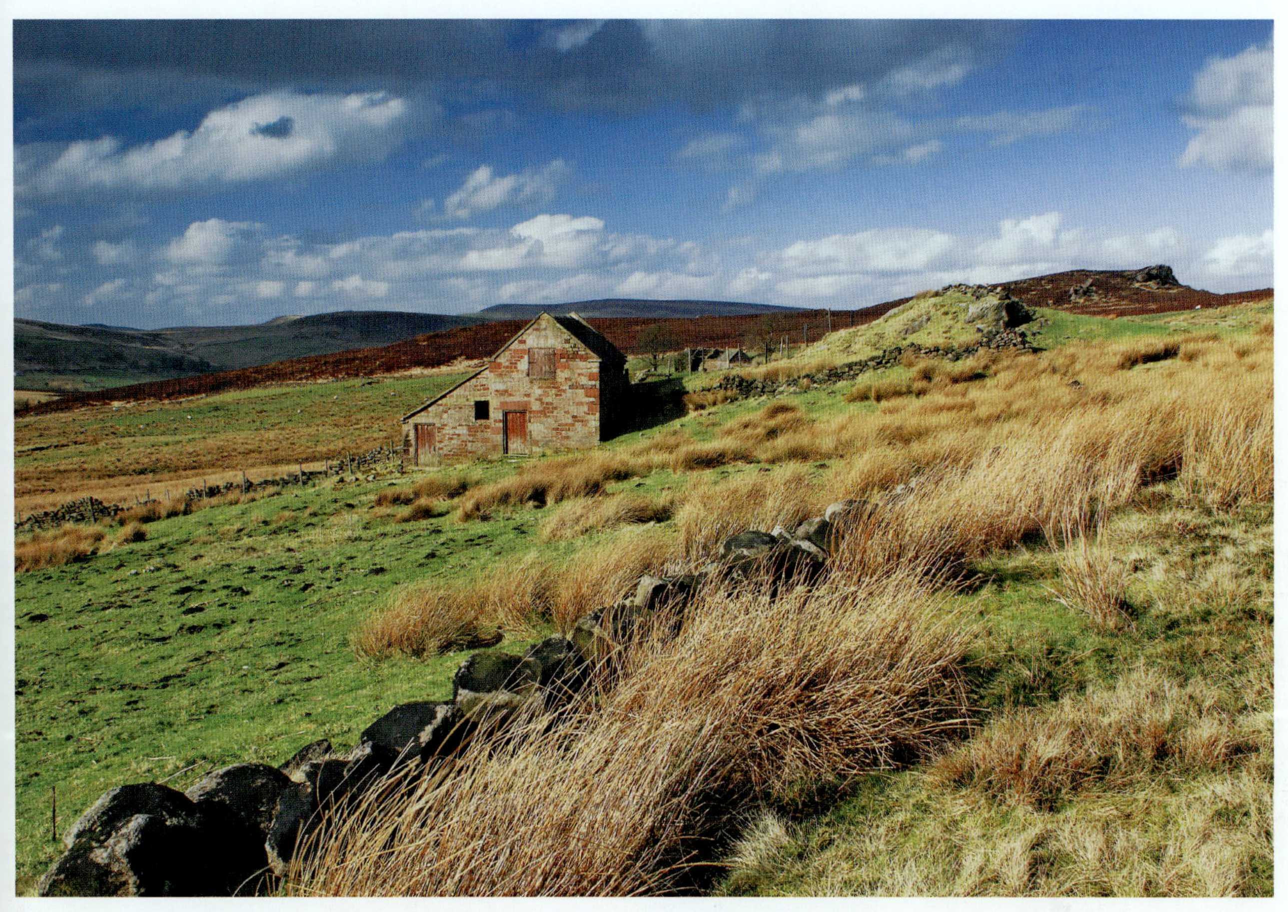

◀ Deserted homestead, Coplowdale

I'm attracted to old ruins and, sadly, there are plenty of tumbledown barns and houses left to decay and eventually disappear in the Peak District. I know planning permission for the restoration of this one to a residence has been refused many times for reasons I don't quite understand. I therefore make it my mission to photograph these before they are lost from the landscape. I prefer stormy conditions to accentuate the feeling of neglect, and this time of year is good for this type of light. The dark brooding skies and hills of the Hope Valley behind the brightly- lit limestone ruin lift it out of the landscape between the side-lit skeletal trees not yet in leaf.

▲ Barn near Gib Torr, Staffordshire Moorlands

Another barn which attracts me, although in better condition than most, is this one near Gib Torr on the gritstone moorland of the more remote part of South West Peak. I had visited this location many times in flat light, and pre-visualised a stormy day with side-lighting as my target. Here, we can barely see the remains of a gritstone wall peeping above the moorland grasses as it marches up to a rocky promontory and over the top across the grassy fields beyond. In the distance is the abrupt start of the wilder heather moorland. The barn makes this image but I positioned myself so that the wall and grasses led diagonally across the picture. Even the clouds seem to lean towards the right as they race across the blustery sky.

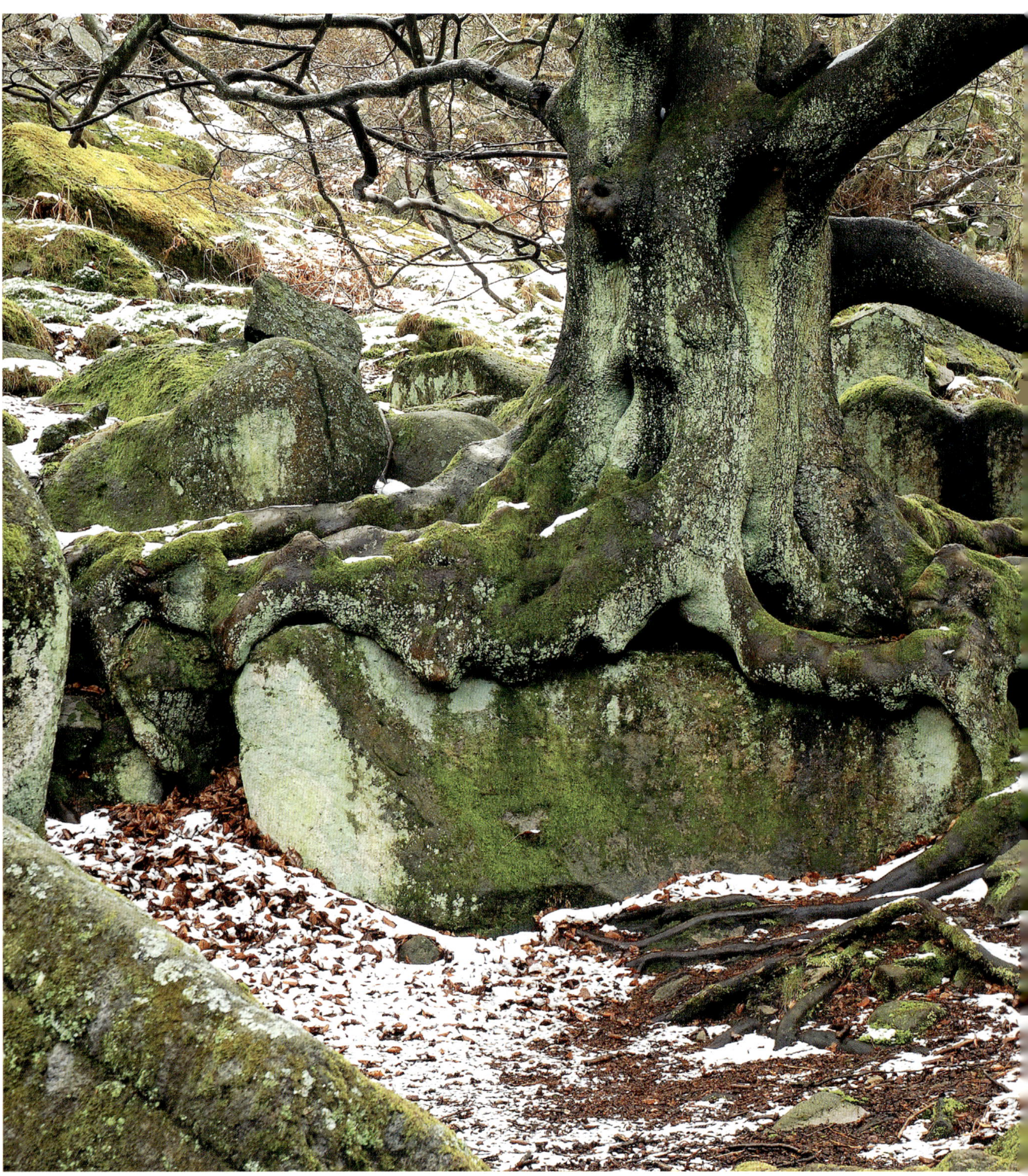

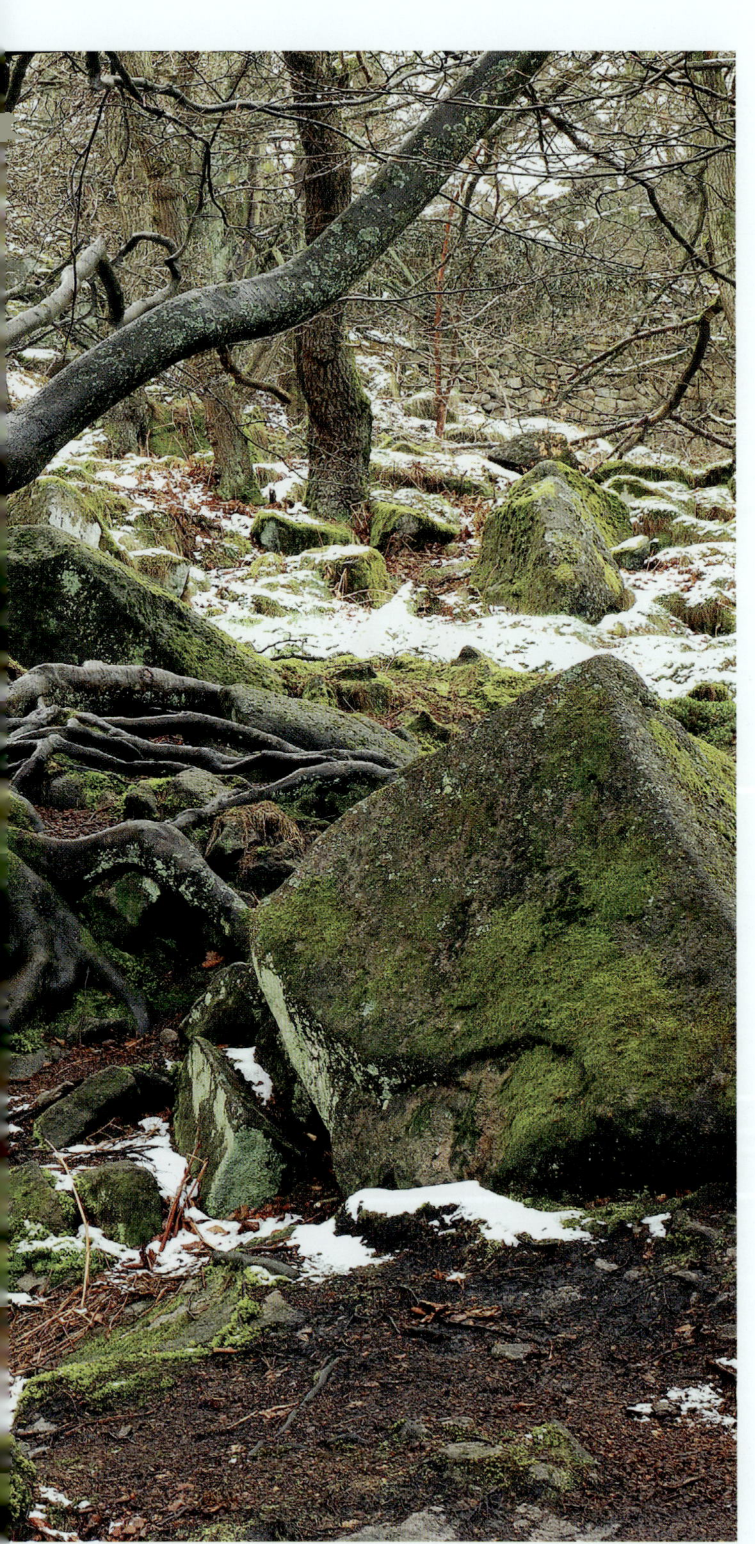

Beech tree, Padley Gorge

This lovely beech tree with its gnarled old
roots appears to be growing out of the rock.
After a long damp winter, it is covered
in green mosses and lichen adding to its
ancient Lord of the Rings earthy look.
A dusting of snow in April breaks up the
green, but it is melting rapidly as we can
see from the wet branches and roots.

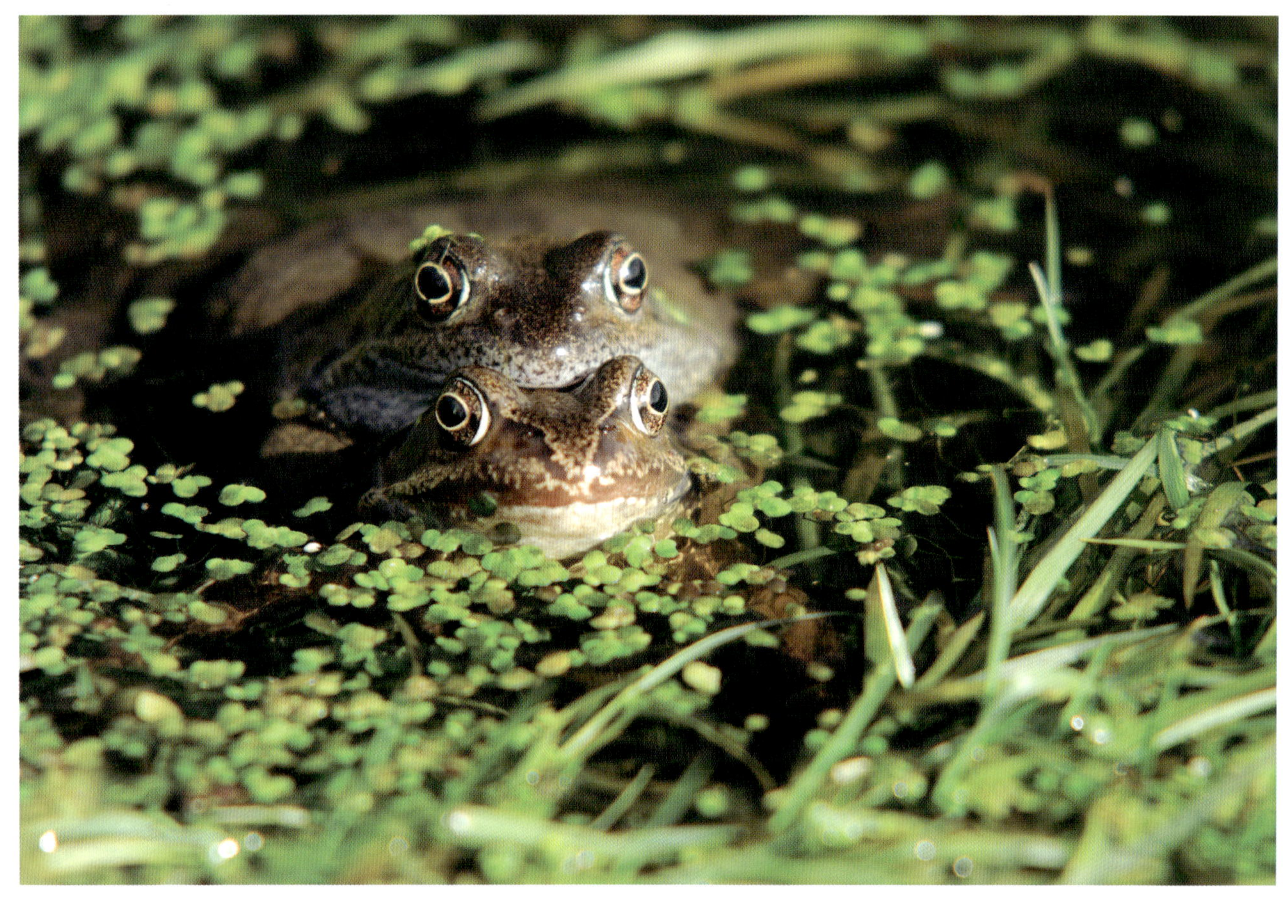

Common frogs mating in a dew pond

Driven by the need to return to the pond in which they were born and making this journey year after year to breed, the mass movement of frogs makes ponds and puddles all over the Peak District become alive with orgies of the mating amphibians for a few of days in March. I found this one close to home and, if I'm available, try and visit it every year to photograph the spectacle which may only last a couple of days. I usually cause amusement to passersby who see me grovelling on my stomach in the mud, fighting with my tripod and long telephoto lens. On my arrival, the frogs usually disappear under water, but patience pays off and one by one they pop up and carry on with their essential business.

Backlighting along the River Manifold, Ilam

About a mile/1.5km upstream from its confluence with the River Dove, the River Manifold flows through National Trust land at Ilam Park just below Ilam Hall. Built between 1821 and 1826 by Jesse Watts-Russell on the site of an older hall (built in 1546 by John Port), it is now a Youth Hostel and the old stable block a National Trust tea room. In April, the deciduous trees all around are beginning to burst into leaf and here their fresh green growth is caught in the spring sunshine alongside the glistening river. Here, the dark woodland and sparkling water add suitable contrast to the backlit tree in the centre.

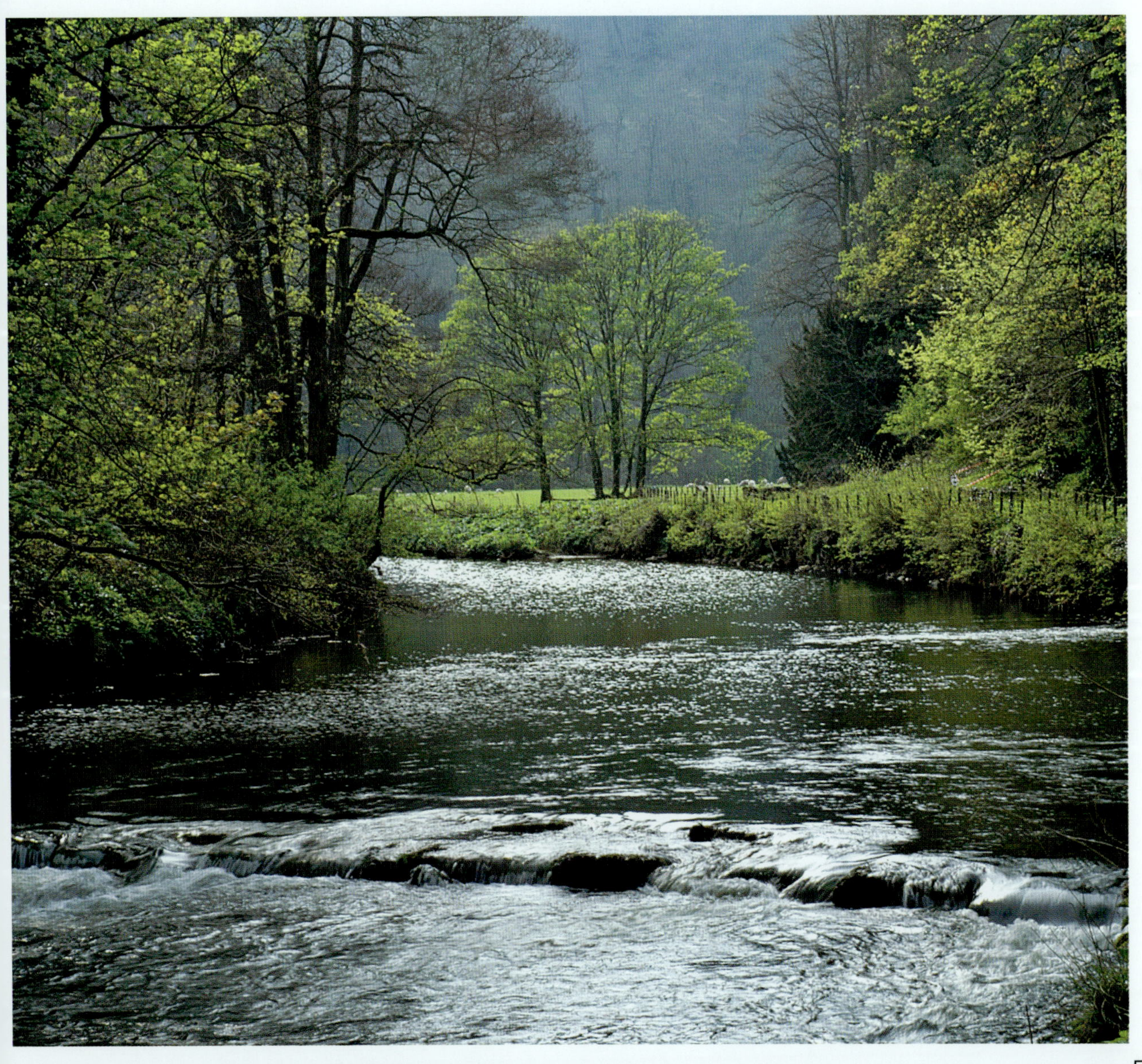

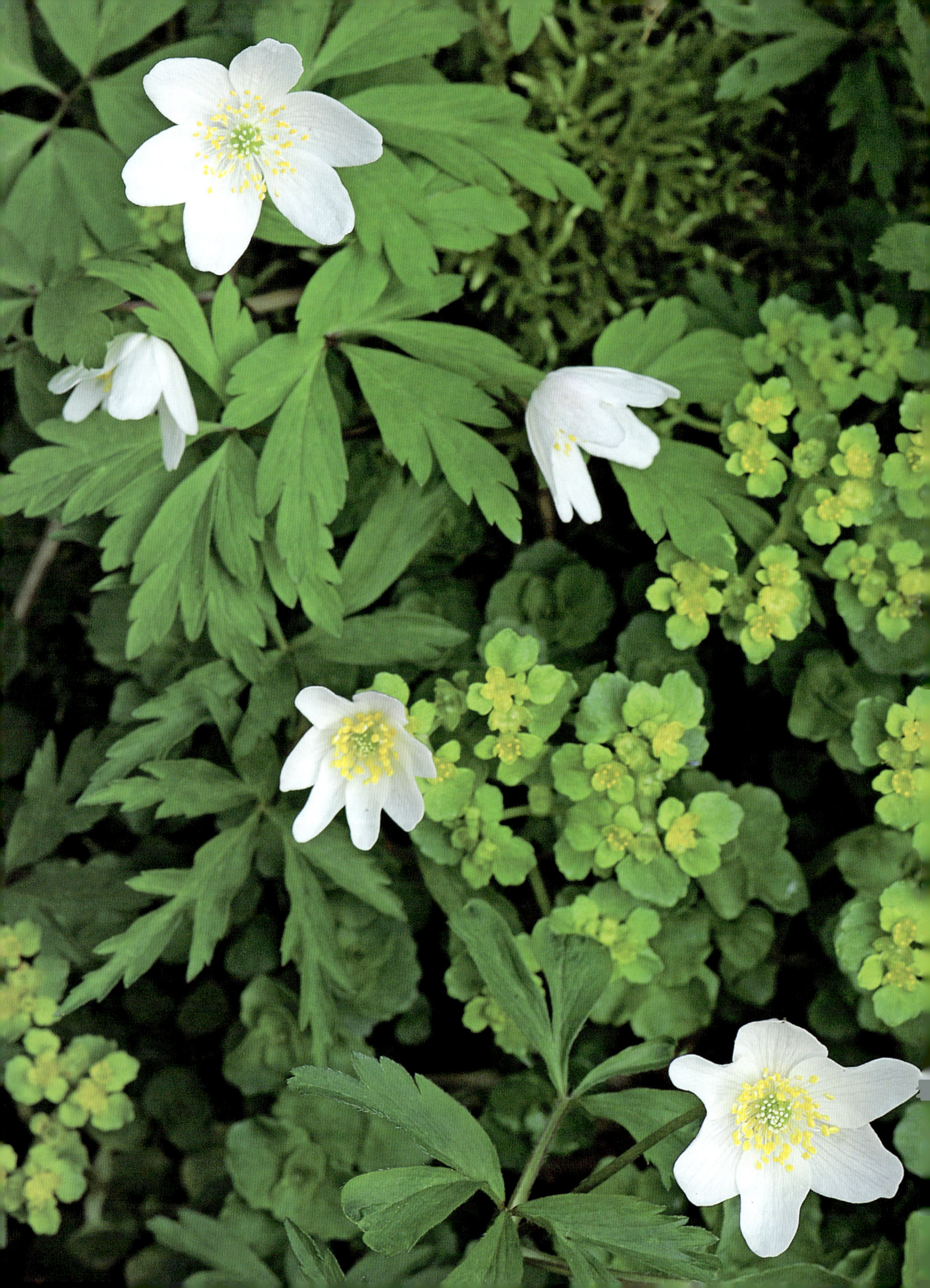

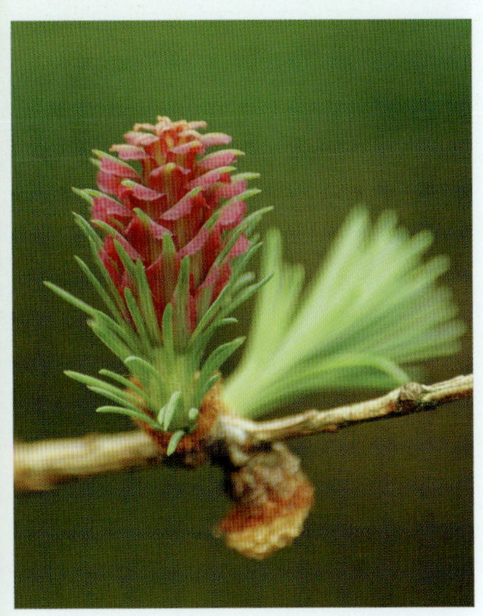

◀ Female flowers of larch in the Upper Derwent Valley

The European larch is one of my favourite trees and at this time of year it produces beautiful little female flowers in upright red and green cones. The colours are so vibrant and contrast so well together they are a delicate spectacle worth looking out for wherever larch trees grow, which tends to be the gritstone areas of the Peak.

▼ Butterbur in Miller's Dale

These plants love the damp river and stream sides of the White Peak and are often recognised later in spring by their large rhubarb-type leaves. At first glance, the flowers can look shabby but on close inspection the tall flower spikes are made up of hundreds of tiny pink star-like flowers with a white centre. I prefer to get in close with my macro lens to show the delicate beauty of these little gems. Unfortunately, this usually means grovelling up close on my knees in mud, holding a reflector to reflect the natural light back on to the plant. It's then a case of setting up the tripod in the right place, waiting for any breezes to lull and having a free hand to press the shutter release. Big landscapes are much easier.

◀ Wood anemone in Chee Dale

Wood anemones love the damp, calcareous soils of our deciduous woodland in the limestone dales and are one of the first of our spring flowers to appear. It took me ages to spot this diagonal grouping, and I felt the vivid yellowy green of the golden saxifrage and dark green of the anemone leaves formed a lovely background to the composition. By choice of aperture I made them slightly soft in focus to draw more attention to the white of the anemone flowers.

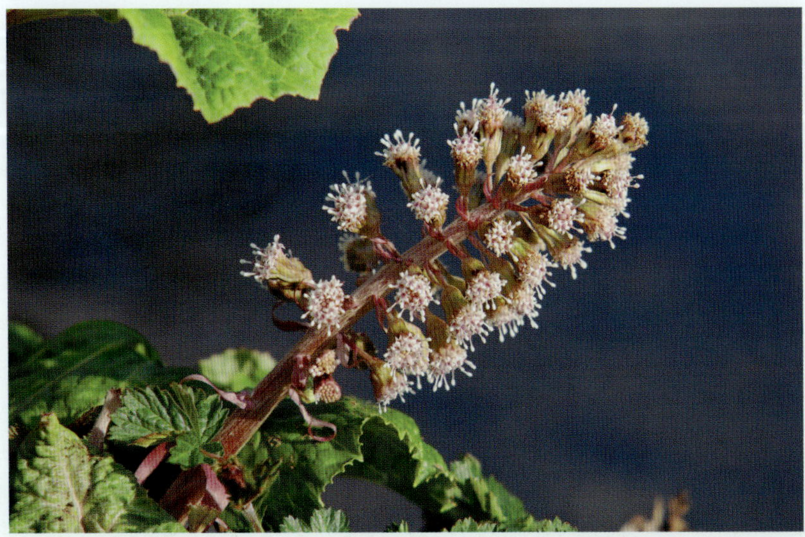

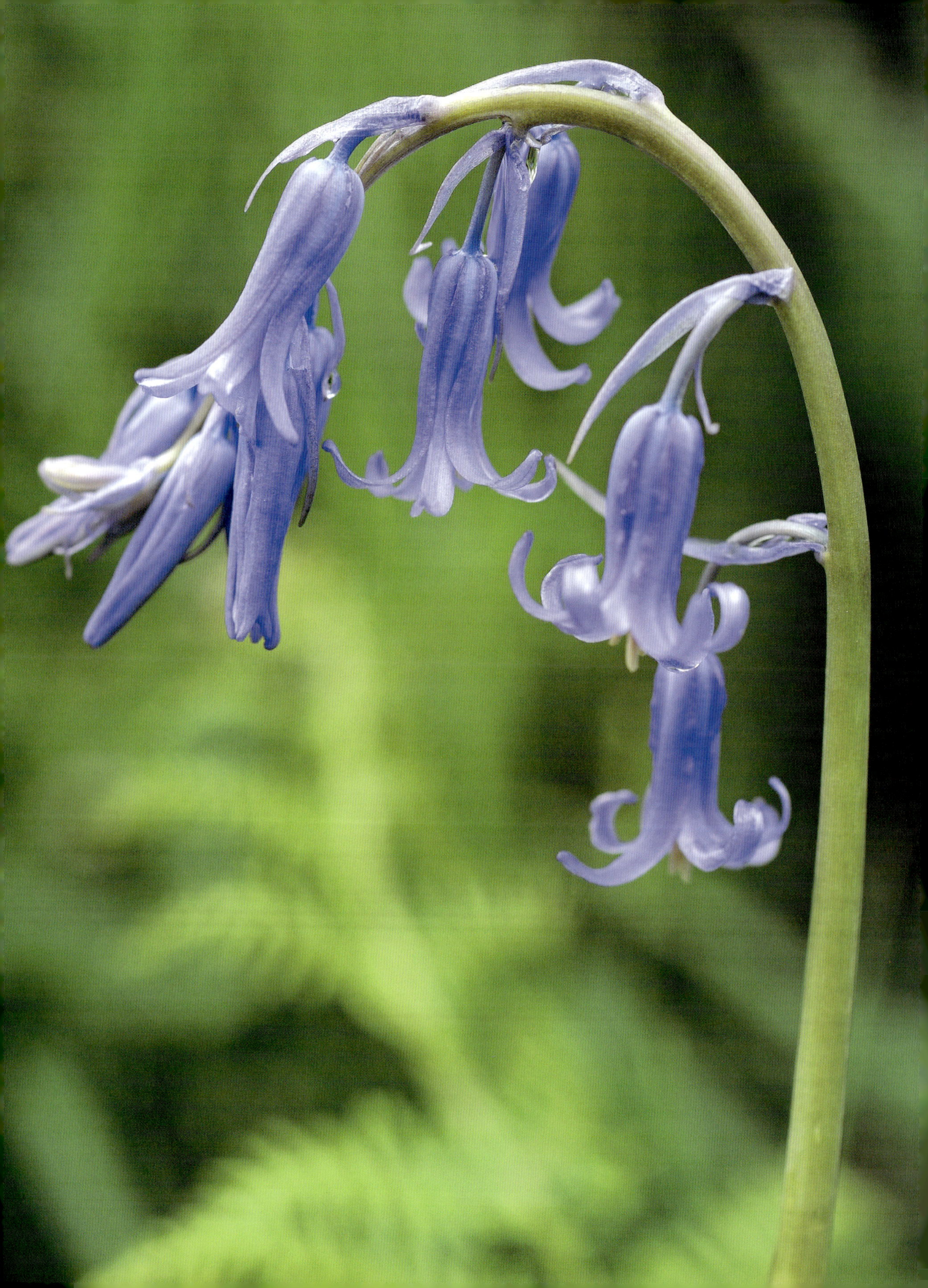

MAY–JUNE

Sunrise time 05.34–04.44 **Sunset time** 20.39–21.41 **Sunrise direction** NE **Sunset direction** NW
Summer solstice June 21st **Sunrise** 04.40 **Sunset** 21.42

Lush pastures, acid greens and spring flowers

Spring is well and truly here and with the warmer temperatures, the landscape changes extremely rapidly in the first two weeks of May, especially in our limestone dales, where the emerging buds and plants of April are now exploding into life. North facing slopes and dales now see sun for the first time.

This is an exhausting time for landscape photographers trying to keep up with these changes, having to make regular visits to places and whose working hours become stretched with dawn at around 4.30am and sunset not until 10pm. With the sun being so high in the sky for much of the day, in order to get soft more flattering lighting, these antisocial hours are necessary. I start to drift away from the wilder Dark Peak gritstone landscapes and turn my camera to our limestone dales, rivers and woodland. There is so much to do! Bluebell woods are at their best in early May, ferns are beginning to unfold and the wild garlic flowers are carpeting the damper woodland and dales creating lovely green and white compositions.

It is noticeable from the following images that it is a very 'green' time of year, but not a boring monotonous green, more vibrant acid greens, and sometimes new leaves emerge with red and yellow tinges which make some woodland look almost autumnal. Not only are the trees bursting into life but the tired-looking green fields of early spring suddenly erupt into lush pasture and swathes of sweet cicely and cow parsley flank the limestone walls and verges, the white umbellifers dancing in the wind.

Hold on tight to this whirlwind of change, there's no time to rest if we want to witness this amazing spectacle of nature to the full.

Close up of bluebells near Foolow

The delicate drooping head and pastel hues are evidence that this is our native bluebell, not the invasive Spanish variety which is a garden escape. These are brighter and brash, more upright and sturdy, and in danger of taking over some of our woodlands. Using a long lens and isolating a single bluebell shows off this beautiful plant, which must be one of Britain's favourite flowers. We are one of the few countries in the world who can boast an abundance of bluebells carpeting our ancient shady woodlands in May. As the season extends, the bluebells grow tall as they reach for the light in the thicker leaf canopy. They also lose their blue colour and turn slightly paler and more magenta with the bells curling at the ends as you can see here.

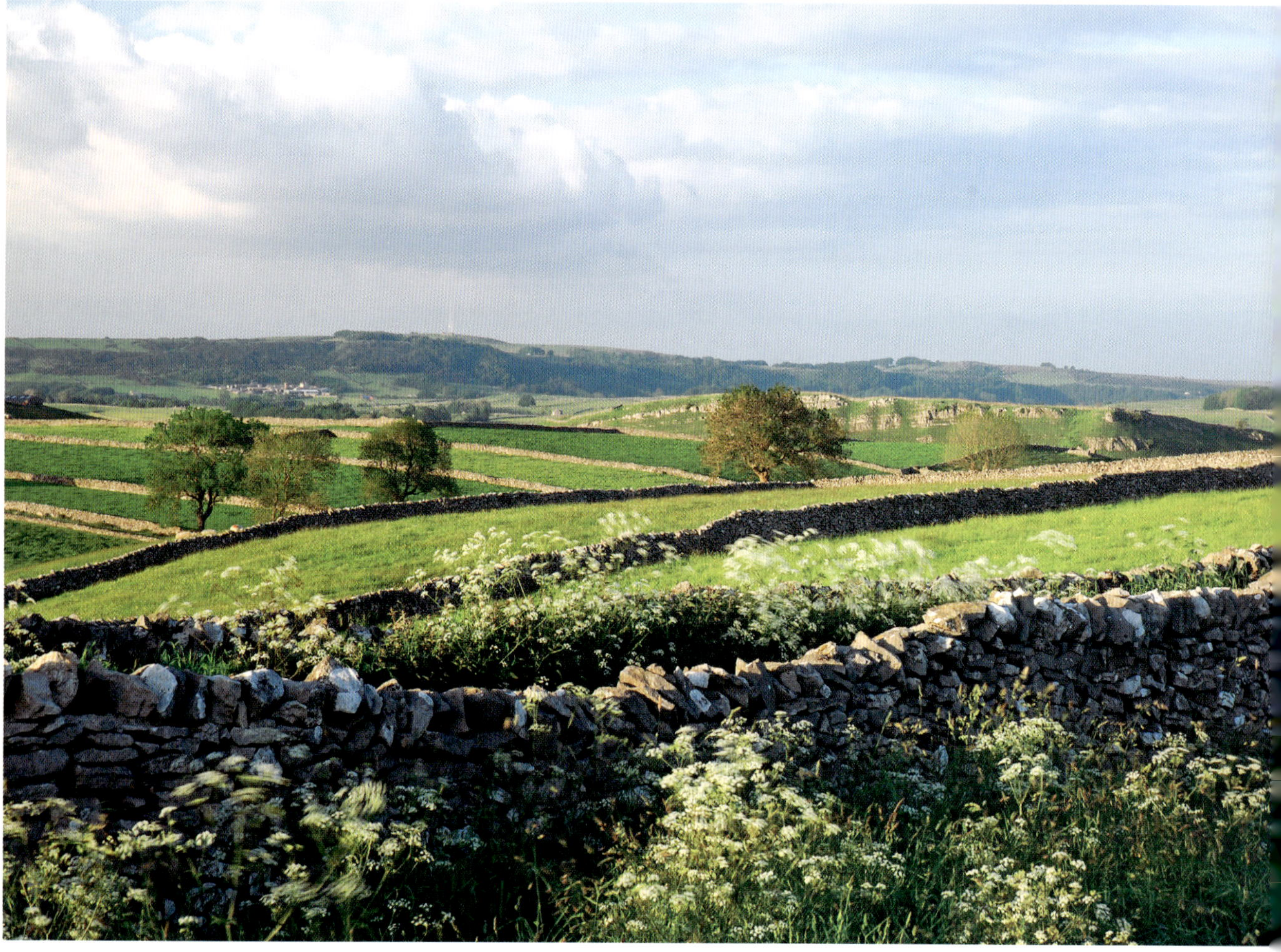

▲ Cow parsley flanked walls near Litton

Soft evening light skims the top of these limestone walls near Litton as they criss-cross the landscape, flanked by cow parsley blowing in the evening breeze. Here, we can see the medieval cultivation strips fossilised by the narrow walled fields. In some villages, farms and fields were small, as occupiers had a second income from lead mining. I was just in time for this shot as moments later the sun had dropped, leaving the foreground walls and cow parsley in total shadow.

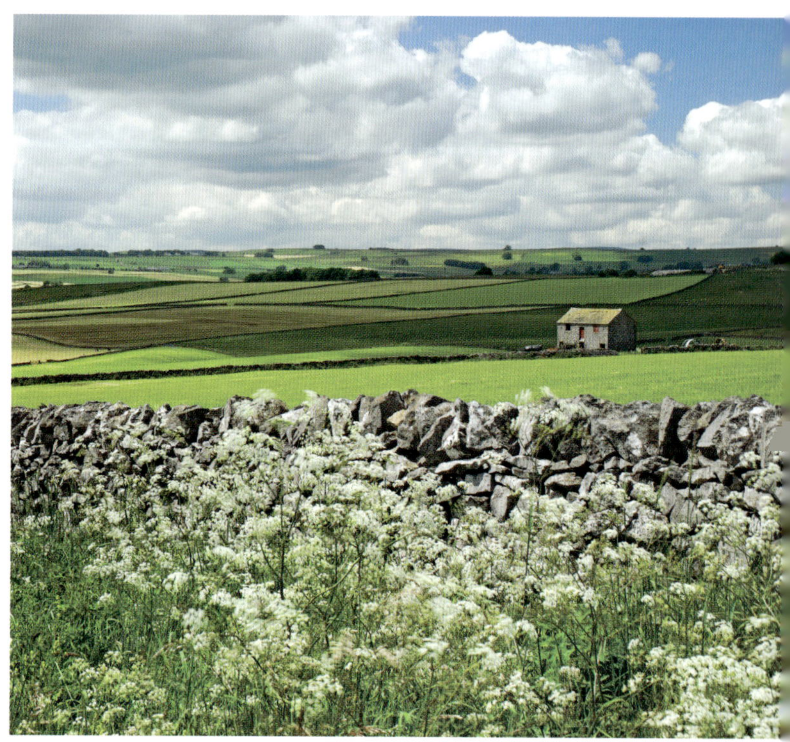

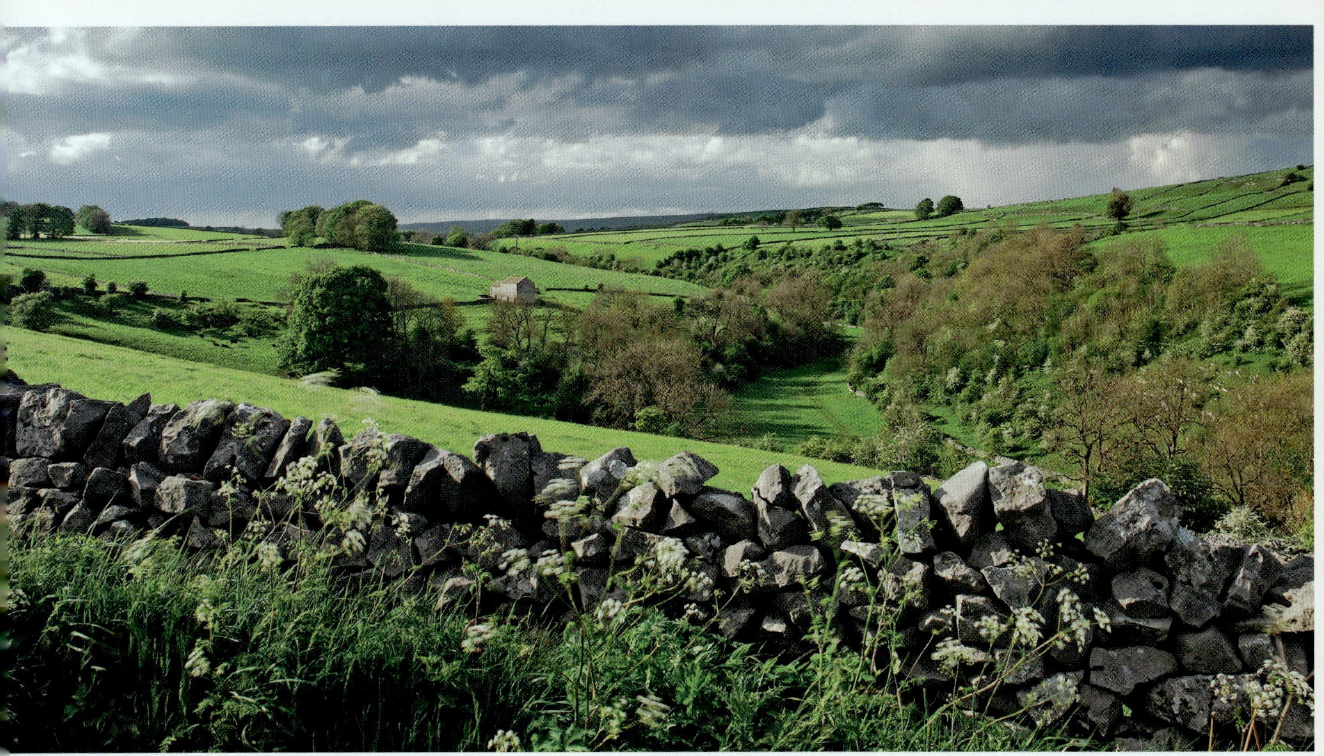

▲ Stormy skies over Peter Dale

After a wet week in Shropshire and suffering from a chest infection, I arrived home to this wonderful stormy light and couldn't resist taking my camera out to capture it. I loved the different shades of grey of the obliquely-lit limestone wall where every stone seemed to stand out, and how these colours were repeated in the distant stone barn near Wormhill with the brooding storm clouds above. These formed a great colour contrast to the back-lit grass. Although it was May, it was extremely windy and cold, typical of a post cold front day. I struggled home pleased I'd bagged a dramatic image but lost my voice completely for a week after.

◄ Cow parsley and field barn near Monyash

A sturdy field barn, still in good working order stands proudly in a patchwork quilt of brightly lit fields of lush grass. Cow parsley blows around in front of the wall on this blustery post cold front day where the air is clear and crisp. Above, we can see a cumulous cloud sheet running across the sky. Great if you're either side of it, but frustrating if your subject is underneath and refusing to be illuminated.

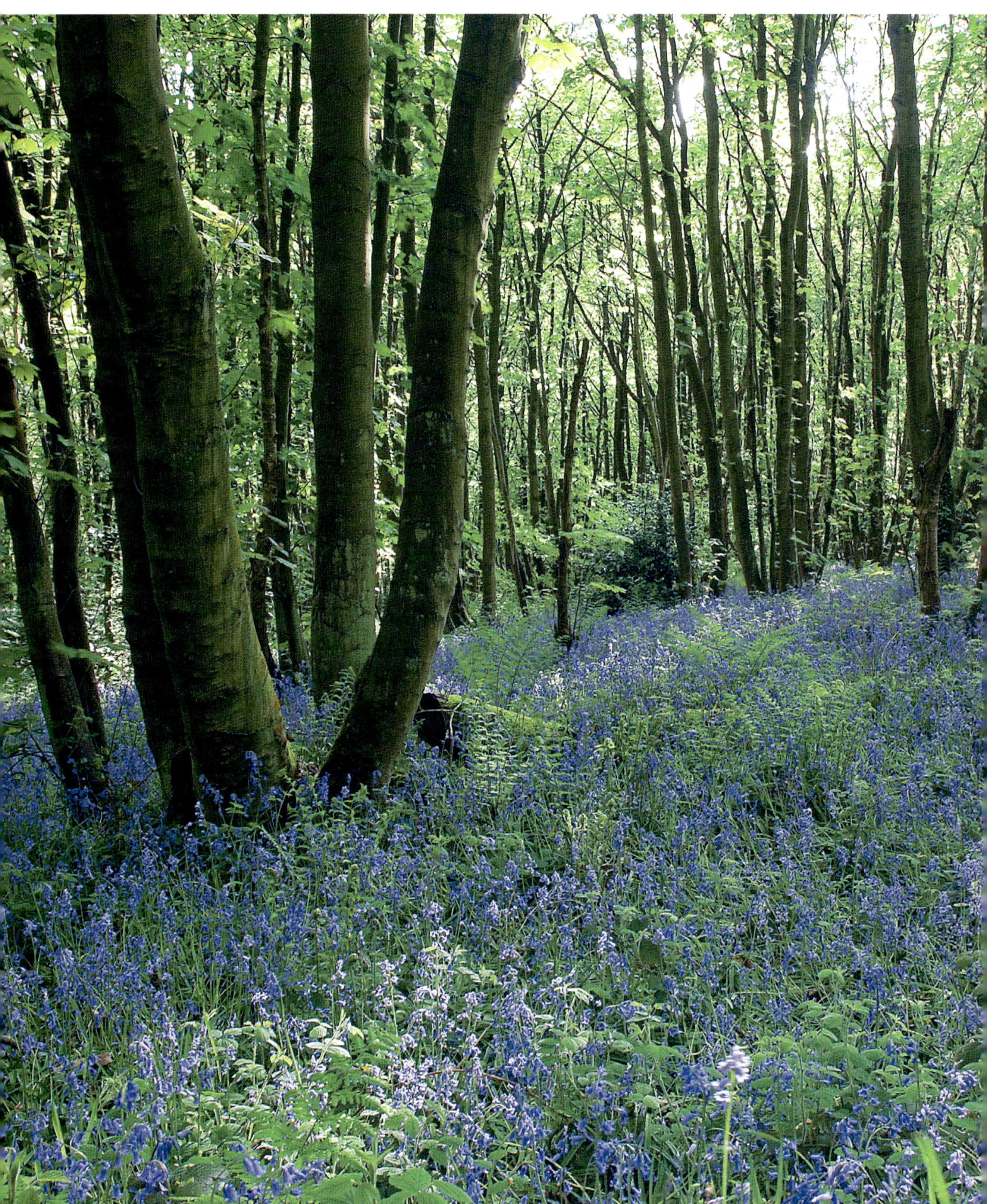

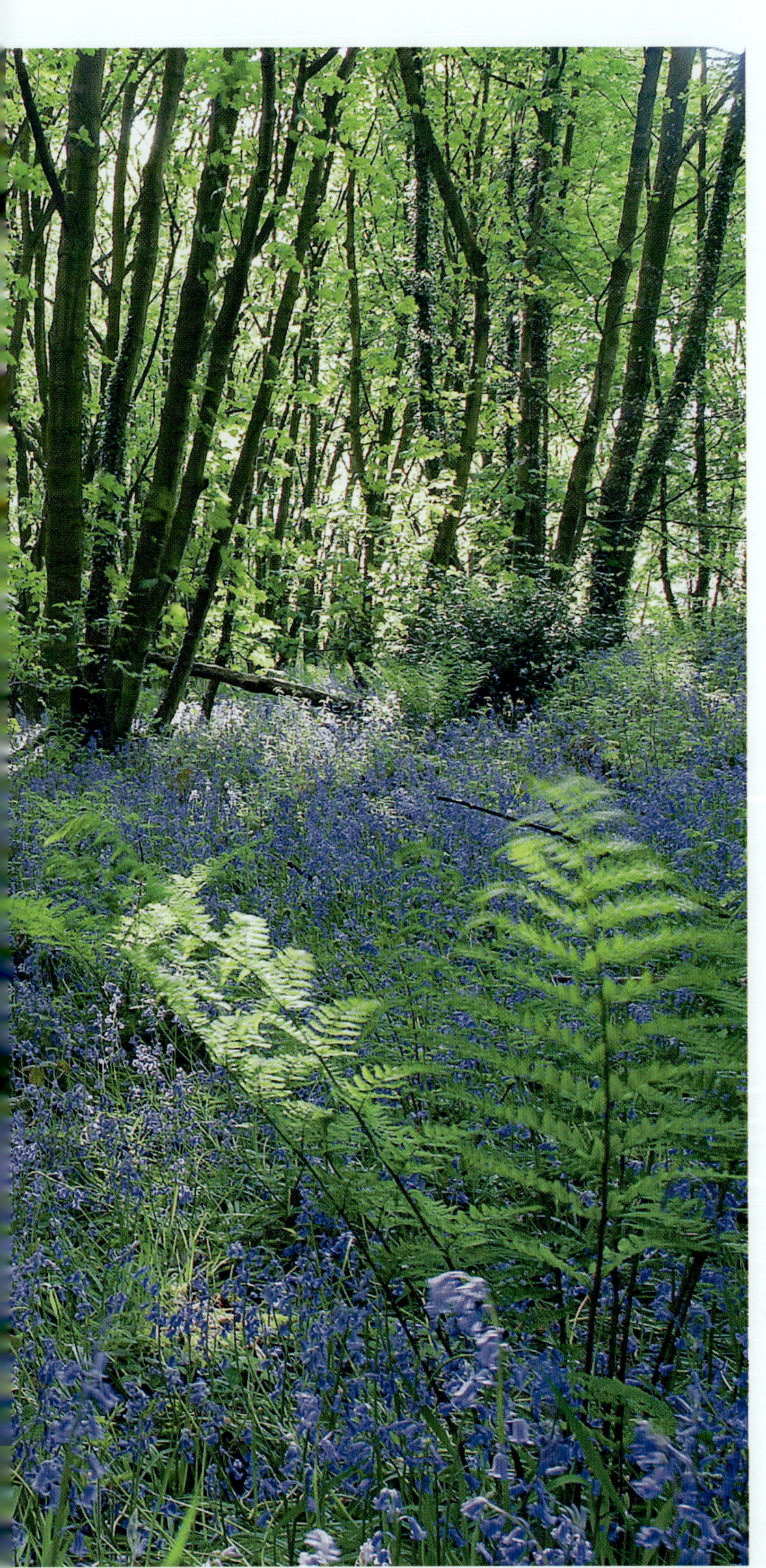

Bluebells in Tinkersley woods

I was tipped off by a friend to visit this location. It looked lovely but I find it very difficult to capture the atmosphere on camera which we experience when walking in an ancient woodland. Years ago, I was spoilt as I lived near the fantastic bluebell woods of the Chilterns. Since moving here in 1993, I have been searching for the same thickly carpeted bluebell woods to photograph and am still looking. Many, like this one near Rowsley are also covered in ferns which tend to dilute the bluebell effect. Getting down low and using a long lens sometimes helps to create a denser colour with the foreshortening effect, but composition then becomes a problem and we lose the bigger picture. The spindly saplings are difficult to compose but the evening sun shining through the single fern balance this image. Still not satisfied, next May I will carry on my quest to try and photograph the perfect Peak District bluebell wood.

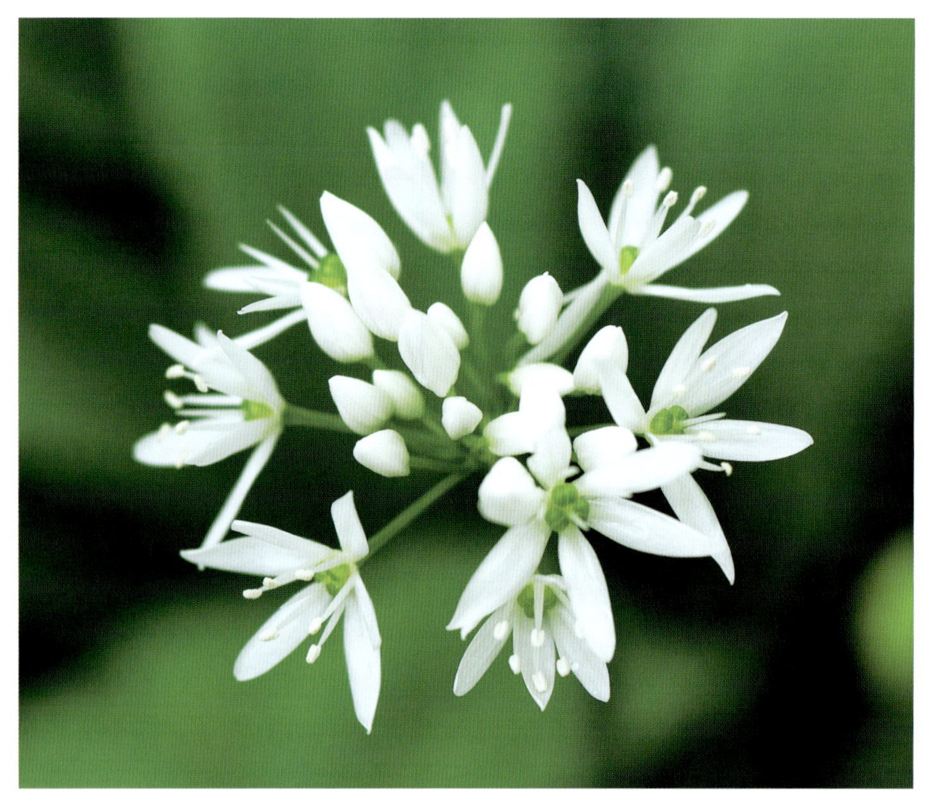

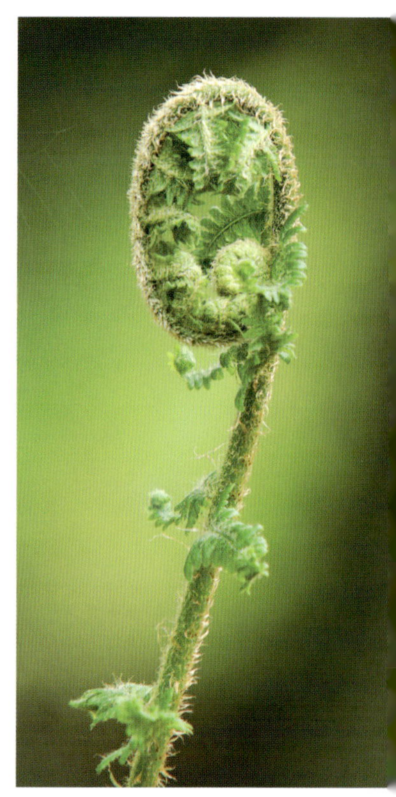

▲ Wild garlic flower, Cressbrook

Using a macro lens I got in close and drew out the detail in these tiny flowers to show the pollen covered stamens dangling down from the delicate petals which make up this attractive flower head. A whole new world of fascinating beauty opens up with macro photography and you can spend hours in one spot - perfect if you don't want to walk far.

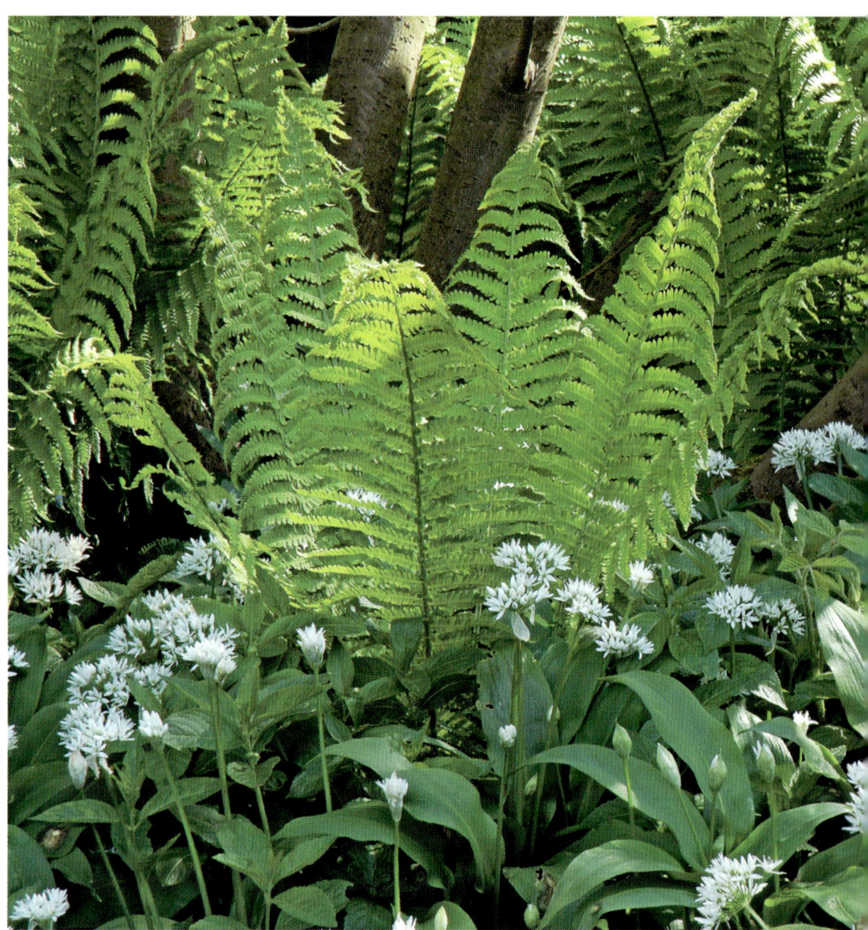

◀ Uncurling fern in Manners wood, Bakewell

There's nothing better than sitting among the earthy smell of a natural deciduous woodland surrounded by birdsong early on a May morning. But it was not so much sitting but more crawling around on my belly to create the right composition for this uncurling fern. I wanted a simple, uncluttered background of a colour which would highlight the delicacy of my subject. It was then a case of struggling with my long telephoto lens and tripod to fix my composition and wait for the breeze to calm so my subject didn't blur. Easier said than done at this long focal length with its tiny depth of field.

◀ Wild garlic and ferns

Here, wild garlic or ramsons adorn the banks of the river Manifold near Ilam. A member of the onion family, they love damp shady places and can be found (and smelt) throughout the Peak District woodlands and dales. Normally, I would photograph the flowers of these under softer, less contrasty lighting, but felt the backlighting through the ferns added a freshness to this green and white image.

▼ Backlit catkins in Tideswell Dale

The catkins of pussy willow are one of the first cheery signs of spring. Unusually, for plant photography, I like to photograph them on sunny days choosing a background of dark foliage which really sets off the freshness of their bright yellow pollen-rich stamens, resembling that of fibre optics when backlit in the spring sunshine.

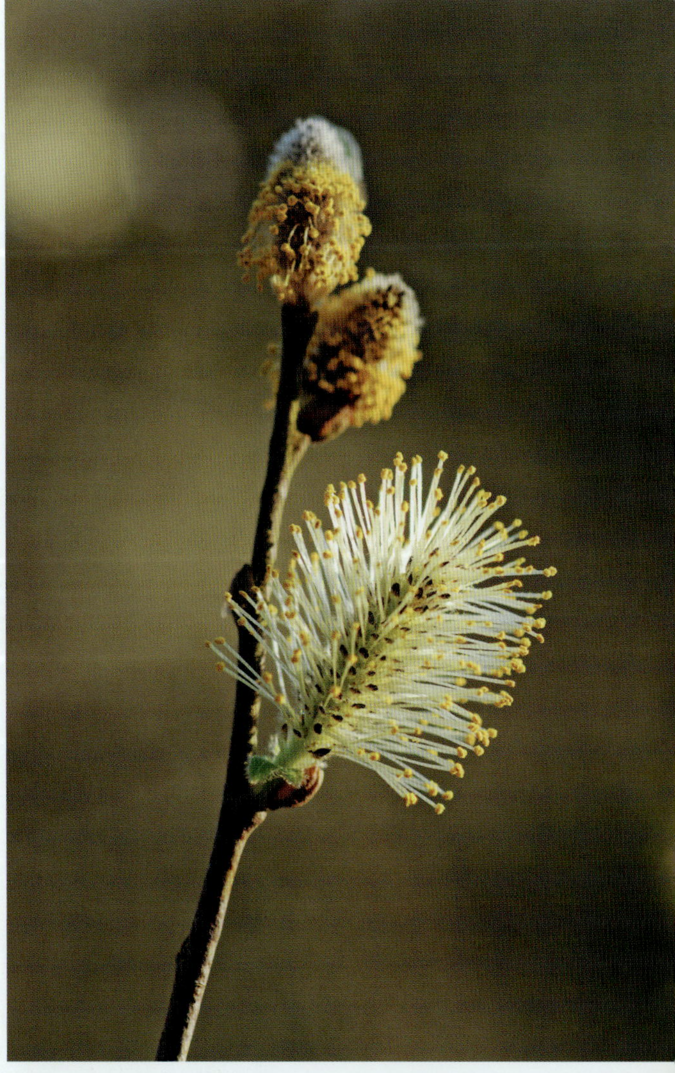

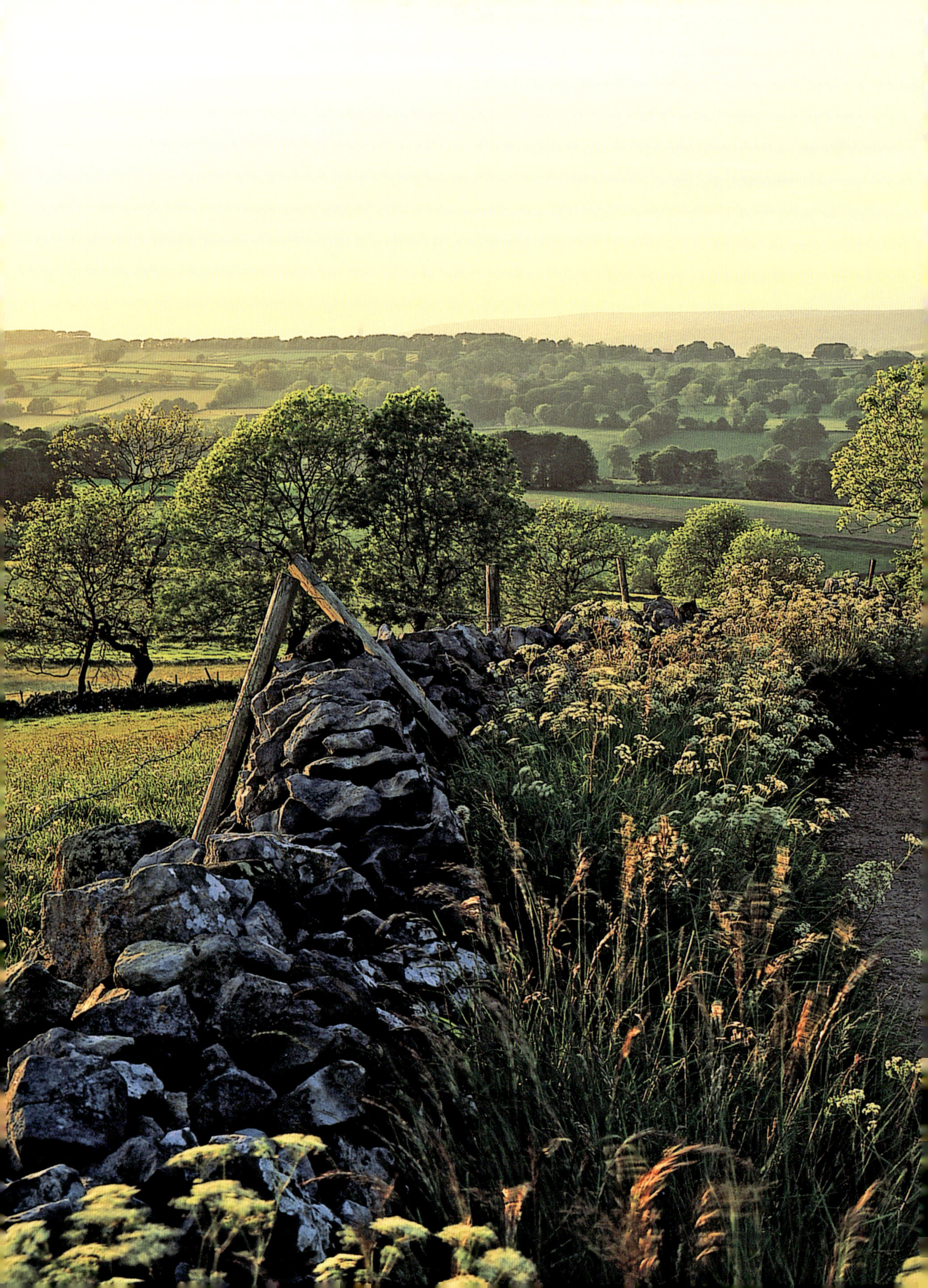

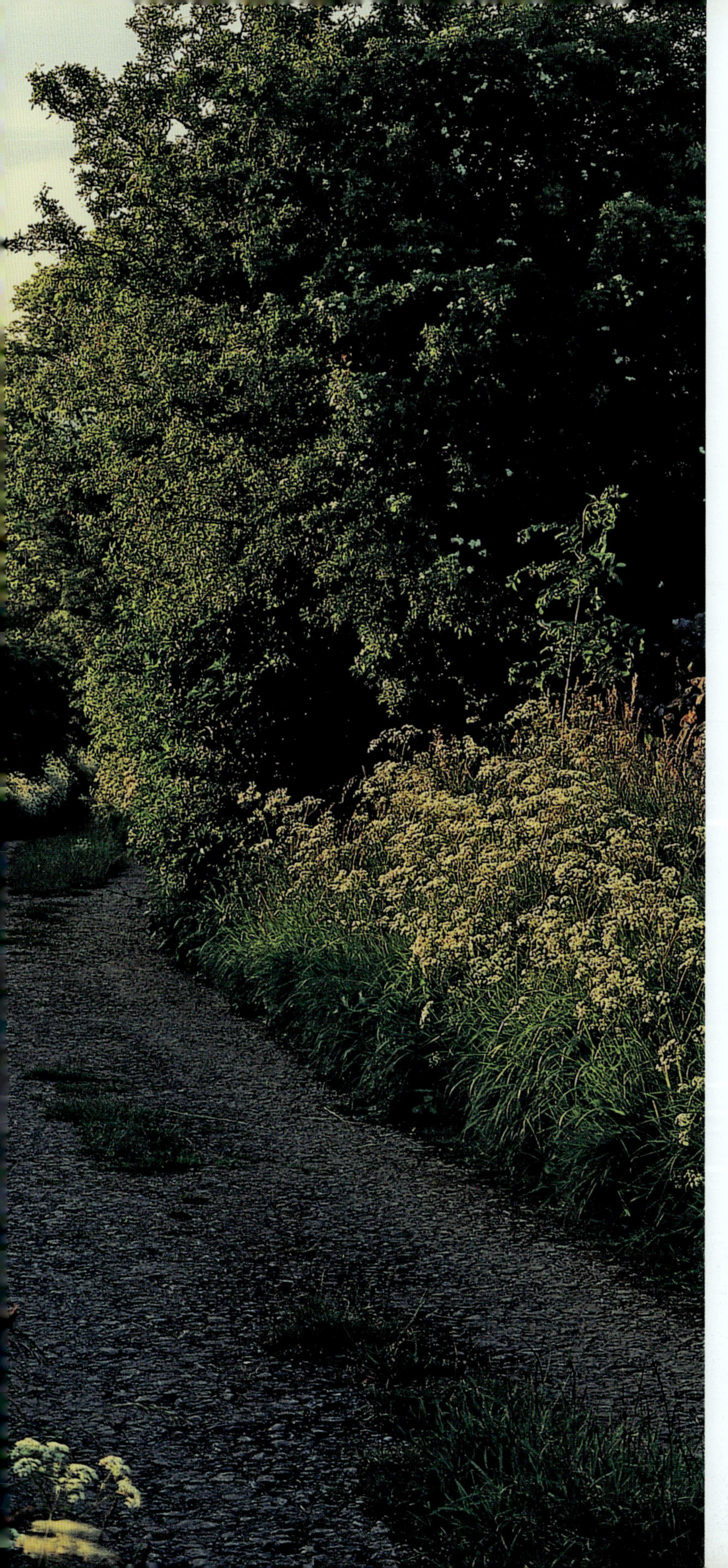

Long Lane
at Priestcliffe

I'm not sure why I like this image;
but I think it's the way the late
afternoon light plays on the cow
parsley and grasses as the old
limestone wall tumbles into the
distance. This is part of the Limestone
Way, a long distance route of about
50 miles/80km running from Rocester
near Uttoxeter in Staffordshire to
Castleton. This ancient track has
probably been used for hundreds of
years as a trading route and I can just
imagine a horse and cart plodding
around the corner.

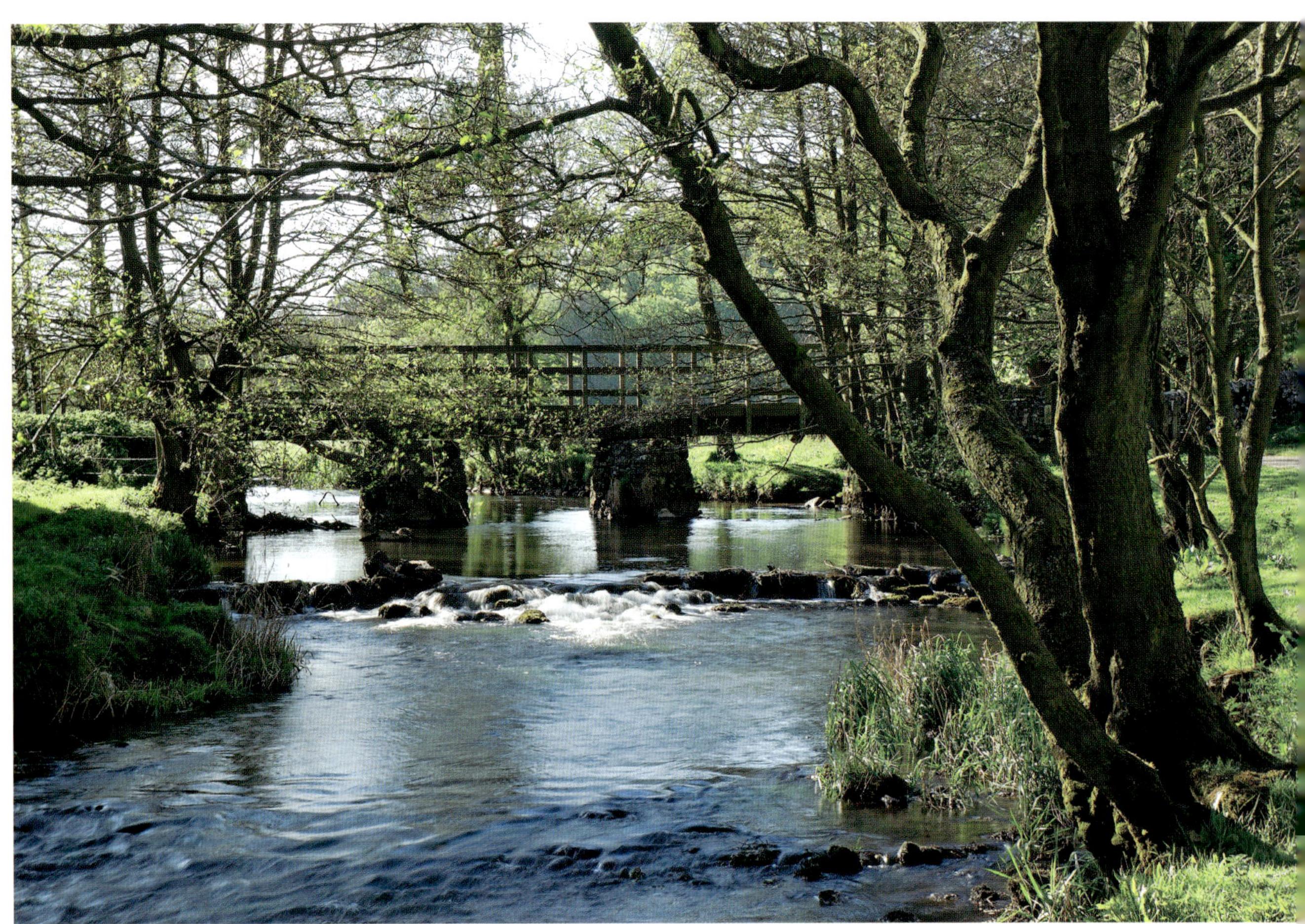

Footbridge in Wolfscote Dale

Afternoon sunlight shines through the new growth on
trees which flank the crystal clear waters of the River Dove.
This footbridge at the northern end of the dale is difficult
to photograph later in summer as it is hidden from view by
the thicker canopy of leaves. It links to a lovely route up
through Narrowdale towards Alstonefield.

Lathkill Dale Tufa Dam

Lathkill Dale, with its limestone crags, ash woodland, tumbling screes and crystal clear water, is full of wildlife and a National Nature Reserve managed by Natural England. Described by the famous fly fisherman, Charles Cotton in 1676 as the most transparent stream he had ever seen, it seems to have survived the disruption by lead mining in the eighteenth and nineteenth centuries where many remnants are scattered throughout the dale.

Here, the River Lathkill tumbles over a fresh green grassy dam, but there are times in dry periods where the river disappears completely beneath its permeable bed of limestone. Mysterious trickling noises are the only clue to its course.

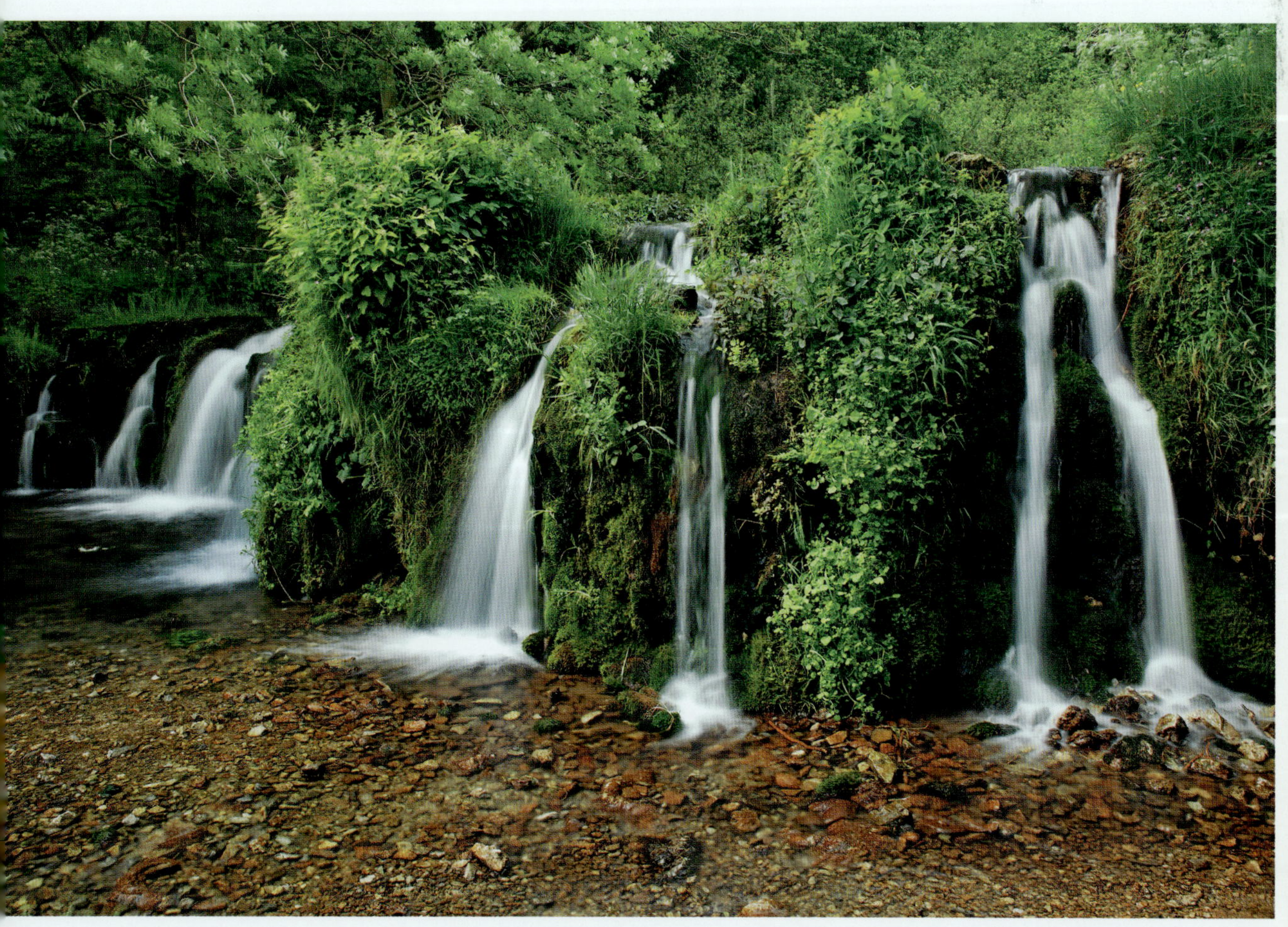

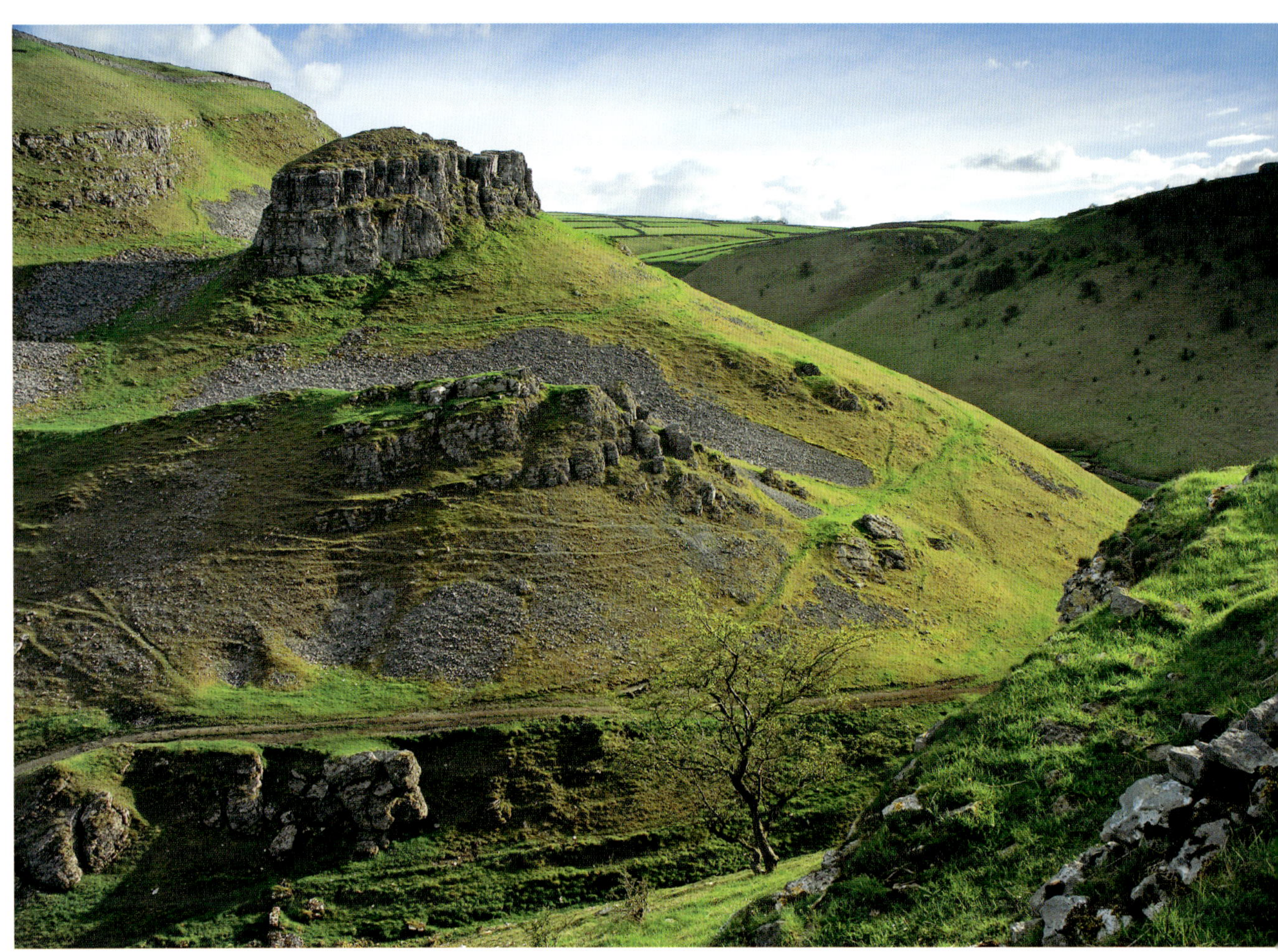

Peter's Stone in evening light

In contrast to the image opposite, this was taken in evening
light from across the valley, showing just how varied a
location can look when it is photographed under different
lighting conditions but the same time of year.

Orchids near Peter's Stone, Cressbrook Dale

Standing as a proud sentinel in the beautiful valley of Cressbrookdale is Peter's Stone, a displaced block of limestone which slipped downhill over a layer of clay. Gibbet Rock as it was once called, is reputed to be where the last gibbeting in Derbyshire took place in 1815, and bodies of executed criminals were regularly displayed there. Cressbrookdale, managed by Natural England, is famous for its wildflowers in the summer months, particularly limestone- loving plants such as rockrose and bloody cranesbill. Early purple orchids and saxifrage carpet the slopes in May and June providing a colourful foreground to the rocky pinnacle with its gruesome past, seen here in dark shadow.

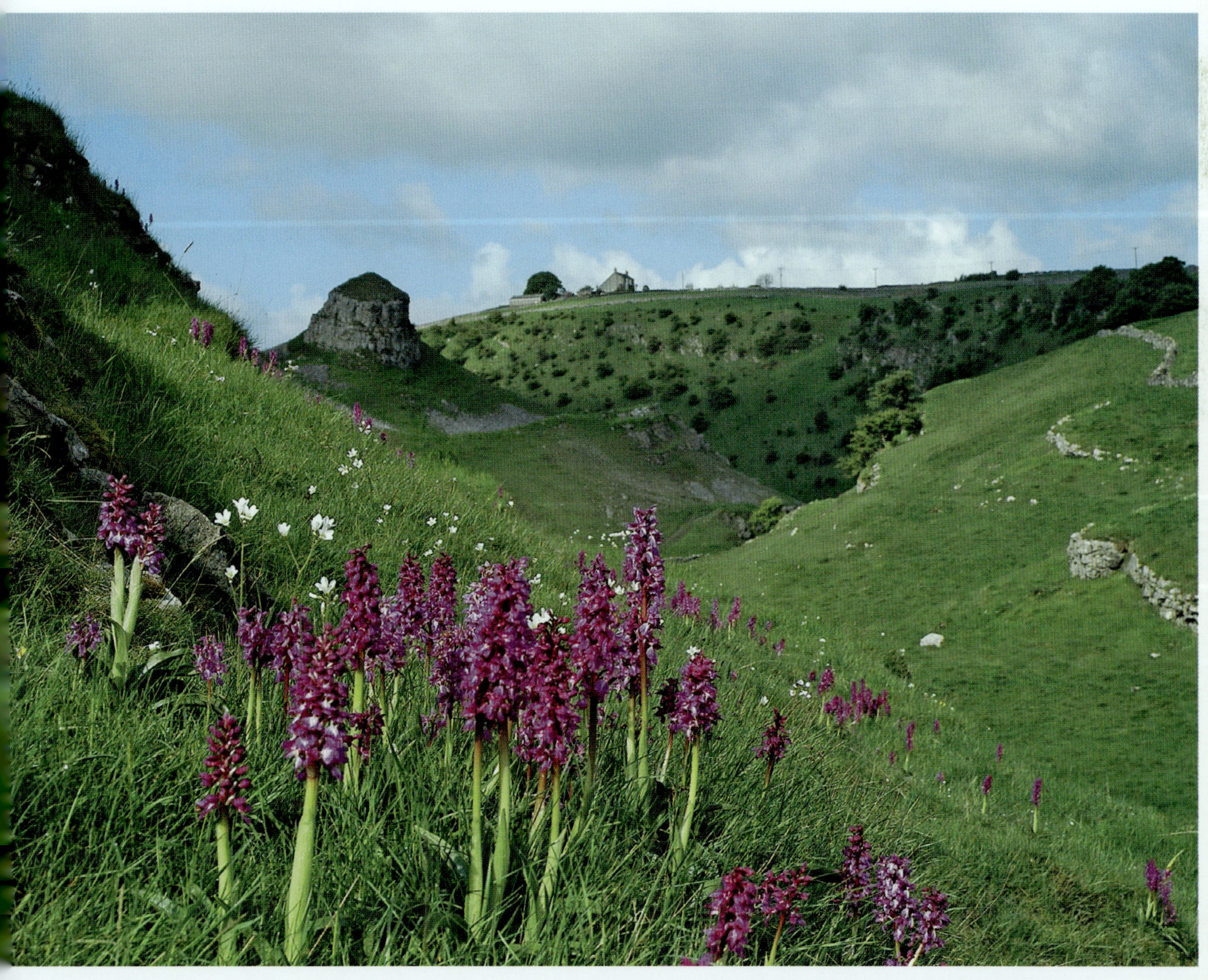

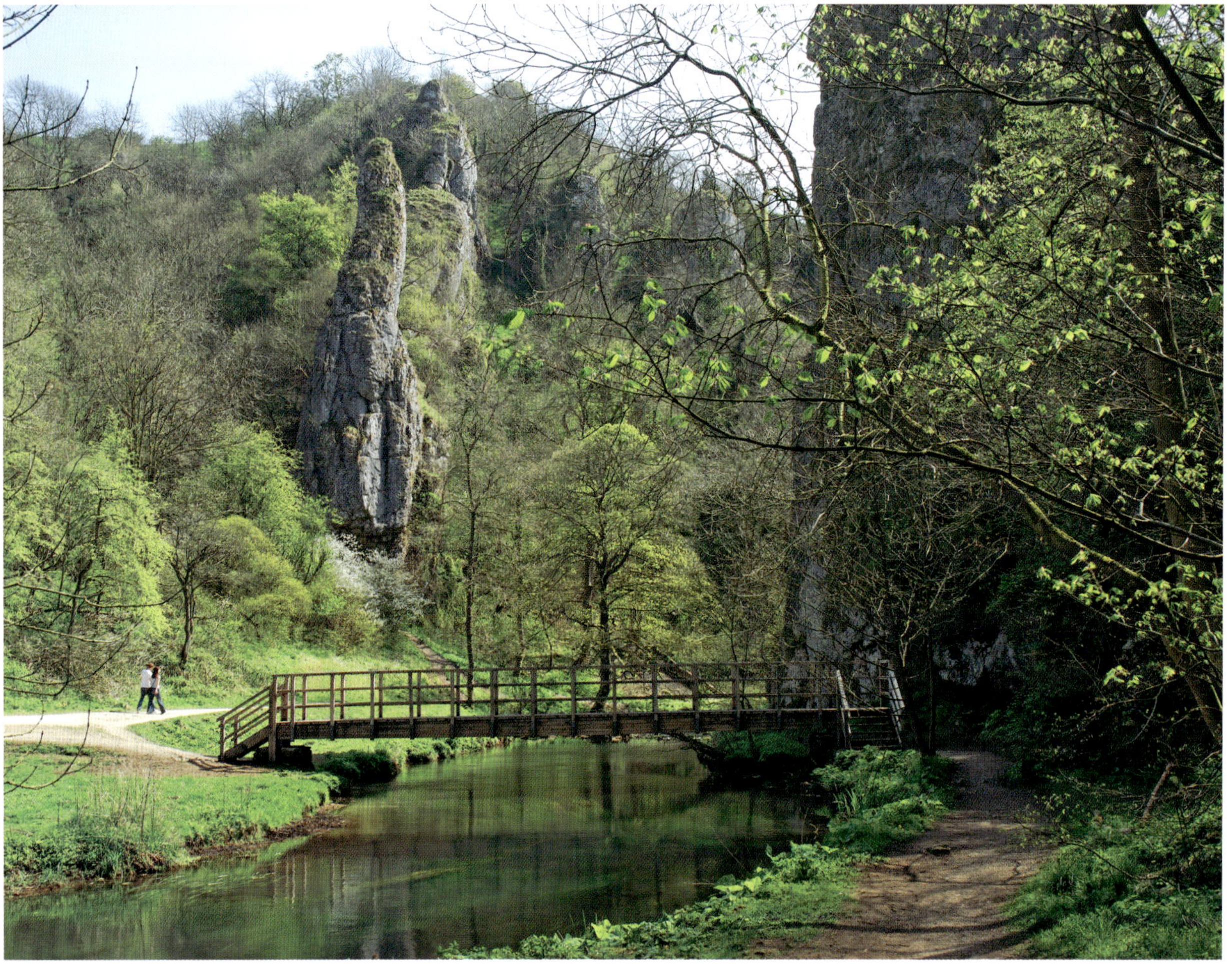

▲ Pickering Tor and Ilam Rock, Dovedale

Further upstream from the famous and busy Stepping Stones, the River Dove winds its way through an ash wooded gorge of limestone pinnacles crags and caves. Here, the valley has opened out and two giant rock stacks face each other across the river and county boundary. Pickering Tor in Derbyshire is to the left and over the newly renovated footbridge is Ilam Rock in Staffordshire. Early spring is the best time here as blackthorn blossom blooms everywhere and the emerging young leaves have a fresh vibrancy but not so dense yet that these wonderful crags are hidden behind the foliage.

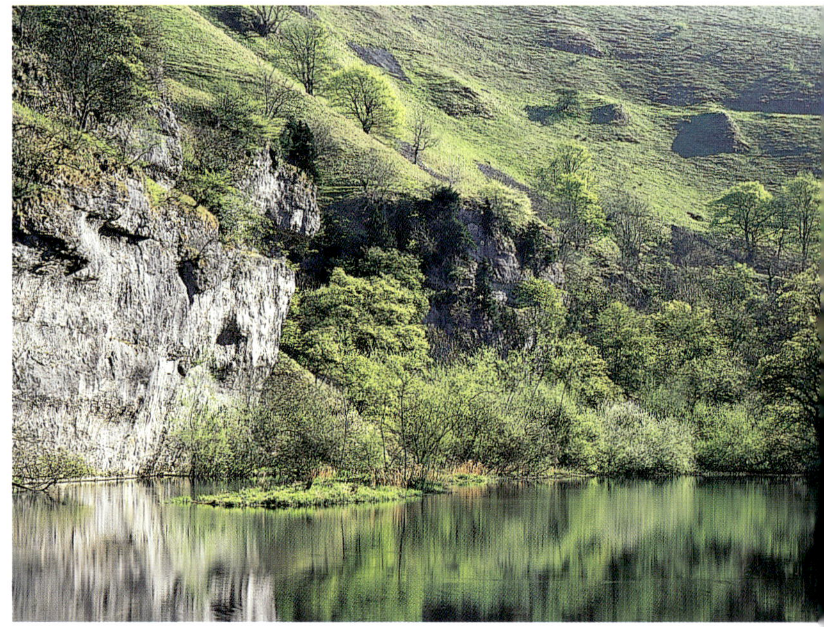

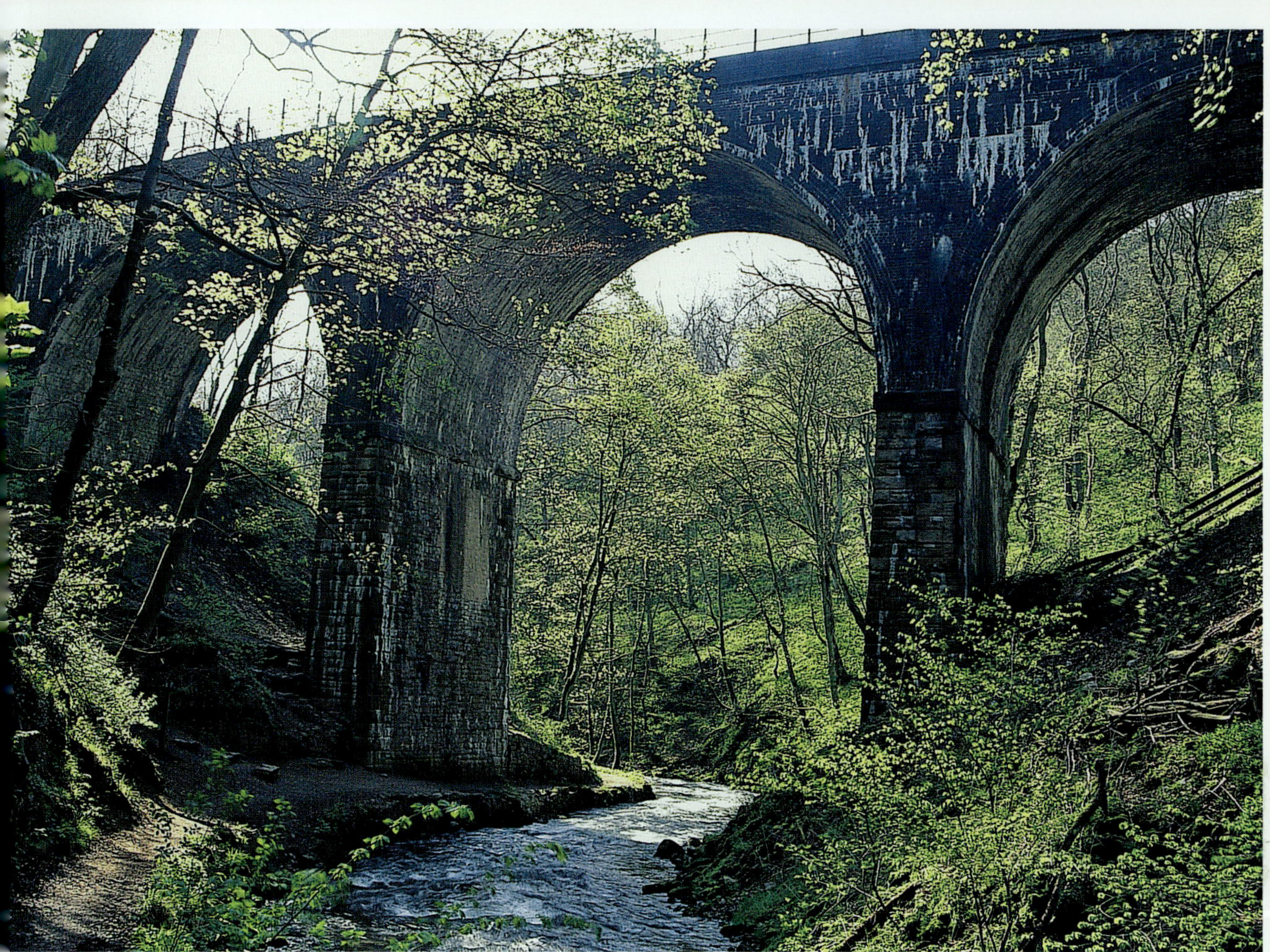

▲ Chee Dale Viaduct

Wilder than many of the limestone dales, this impressive valley is threaded by the old Midland Line, now the Monsal Trail. Here, Chee Dale viaduct towers over the River Wye. Very popular with school groups for abseiling, I can guarantee that whenever I turn up there will always be ropes dangling down with excited children on the end! Morning is best here with backlighting on the water and through the fresh spring foliage.

◀ Reflections in Water-cum-Jolly Dale

Fresh green leaves are beginning to emerge, and this is the best time to see this dale before the tree canopy of summer becomes too heavy and dark. On a still afternoon, the limestone crags and back- lit green foliage make a tranquil scene, reflected in the artificially created wide pool through which the River Wye flows gently before tumbling over the weir further downstream and speeding along the narrows past Cressbrook Mill. Now converted to apartments, this impressive Georgian building was built by William Newton in 1815 replacing Sir Richard Arkwright's mill of 1783. This was a thriving cotton mill where Newton was said to have treated his child apprentices well, unlike those from nearby Litton Mill under the employment of Ellis Needham.

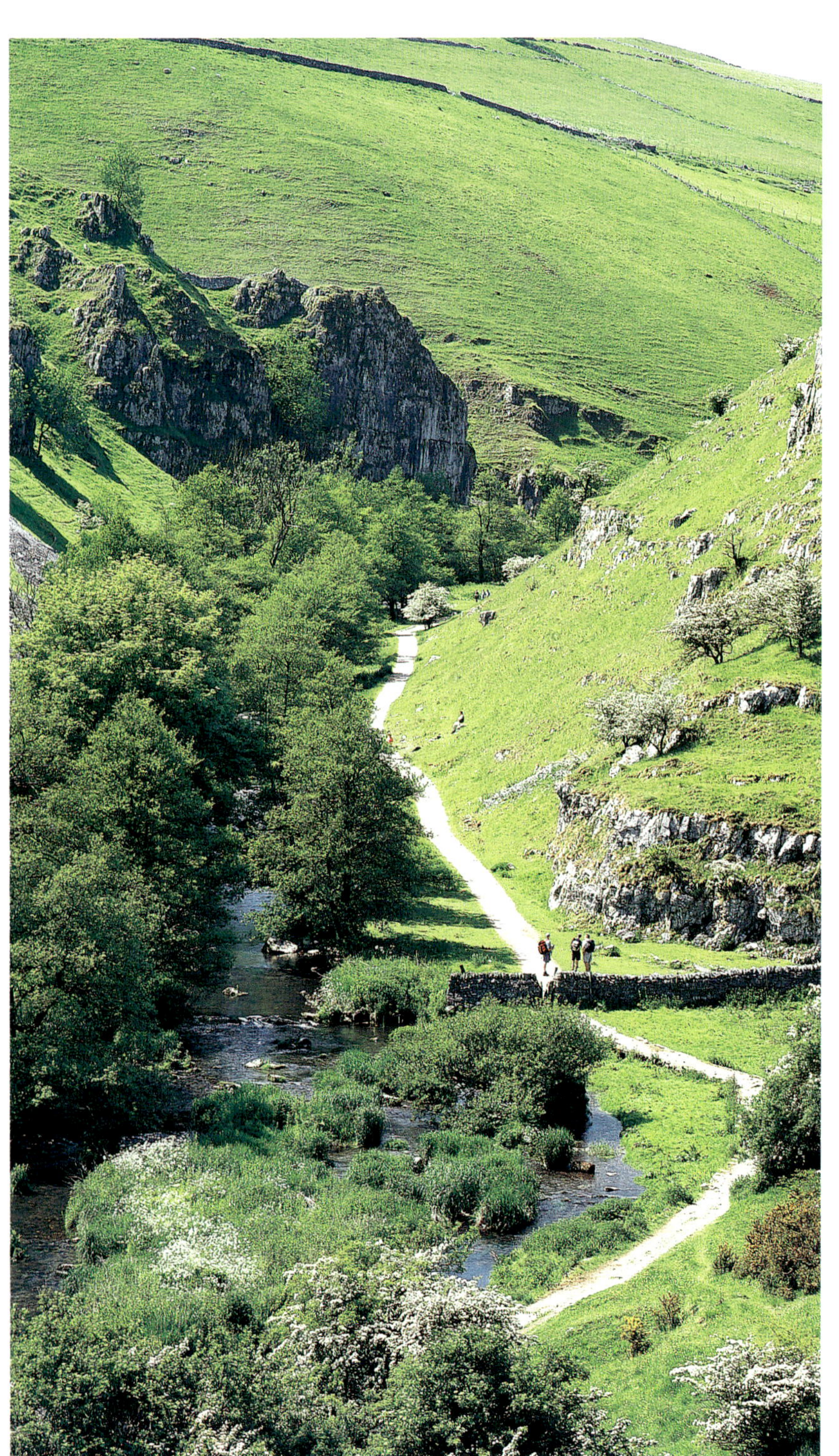

Wolfscote Dale

About a mile/2km south of Hartington, the River Dove cuts a deep twisting course through the limestone to create a lovely valley below crags, caves and tors, its slopes flanked with ash, sycamore, hawthorn and alder. It is not dissimilar to the more crowded Dovedale, but a little more open. I suspect what keeps the crowds away are the lack of nearby car parks. May is a lovely time as the hawthorn is in blossom and the grassy slopes begin to take on a lush green freshness. Dippers, herons and wagtails dip in and out of the river and limestone loving plants such as early purple orchids begin to emerge.

Here, I am standing high on the bank looking NW down the dale, using the path and side-lighting on the crags to break up the mass of green. It is a difficult dale to photograph, too early and the light is flat, too late and deep shadows appear across the dale.

Wave formations, Solomon's Temple, Buxton

Standing high above Buxton at 1,443 feet/440m on the rocky limestone hillock known as Grin Low, this folly built in 1896, commands a wonderful view northwards over the former spa town. Between the seventeenth to mid-nineteenth centuries there were hundreds of lime kilns producing large quantities of lime in this area. It is the sky which makes this image with its fantastic white wave formations marbled against the deep blue. Amongst the limestone outcrops, yellow buttercups carpet the lush grass adding a summery feel to a very simple image.

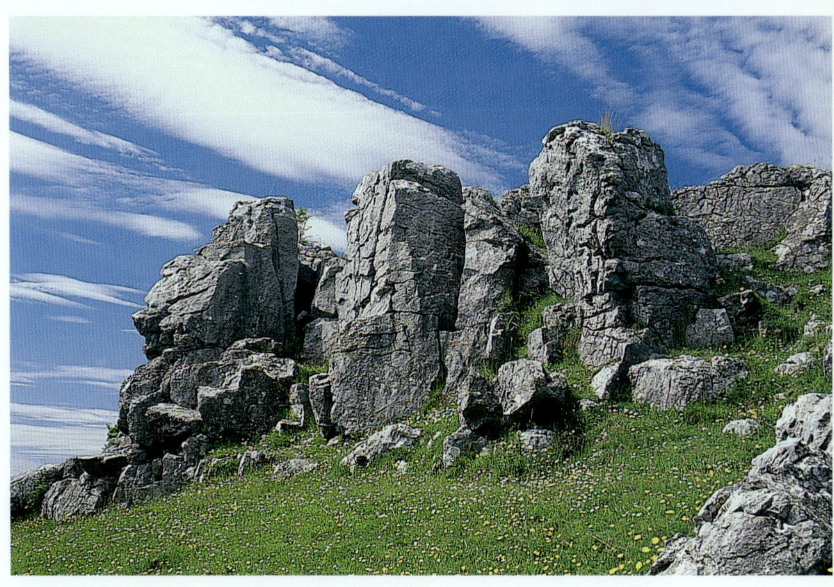

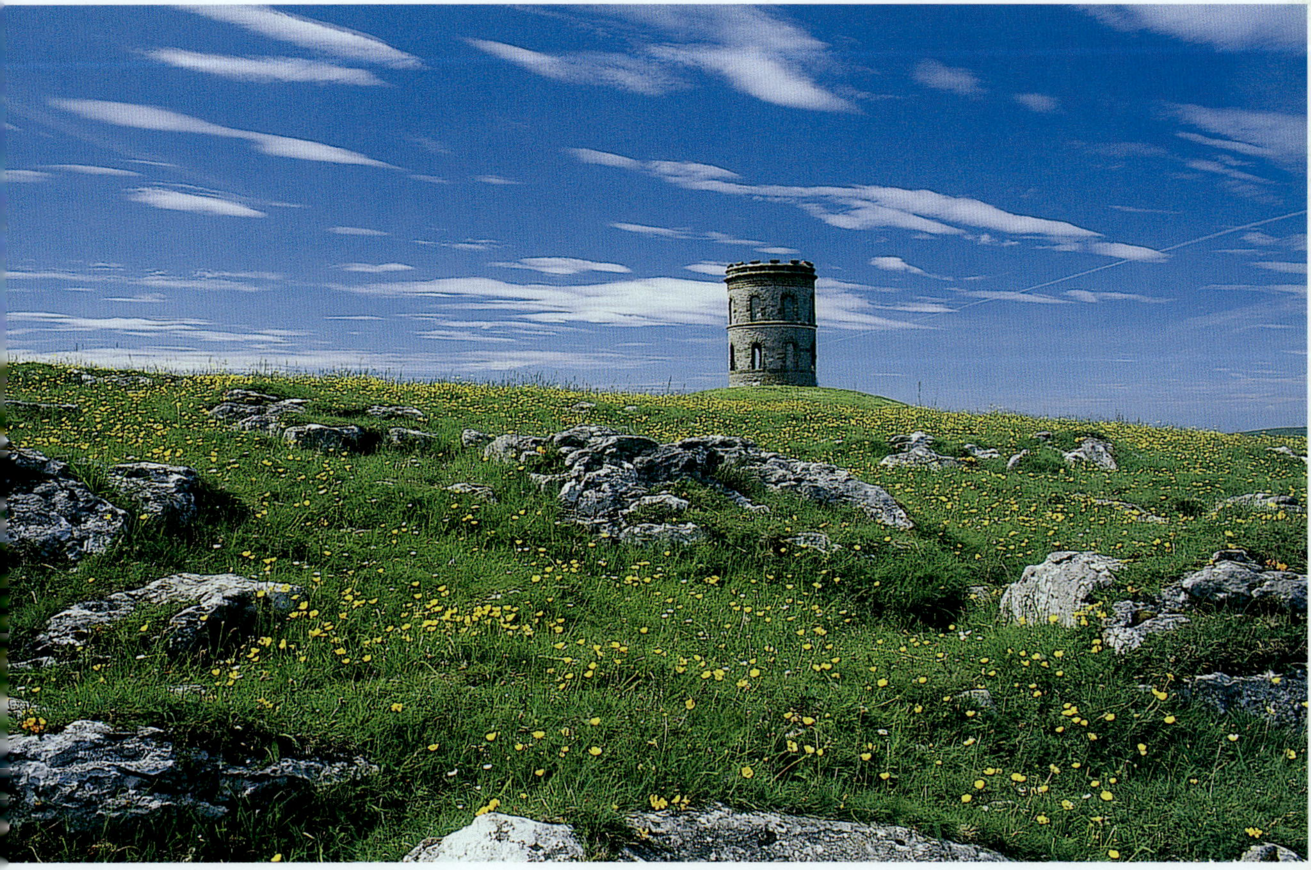

Limestone outcrops near Solomon's Temple

Just below Solomon's Temple are these wonderful limestone outcrops. As you can see from the sky, this image was taken on the same afternoon. A sky like this cannot be wasted and I whizzed off to a few locations while it lasted.

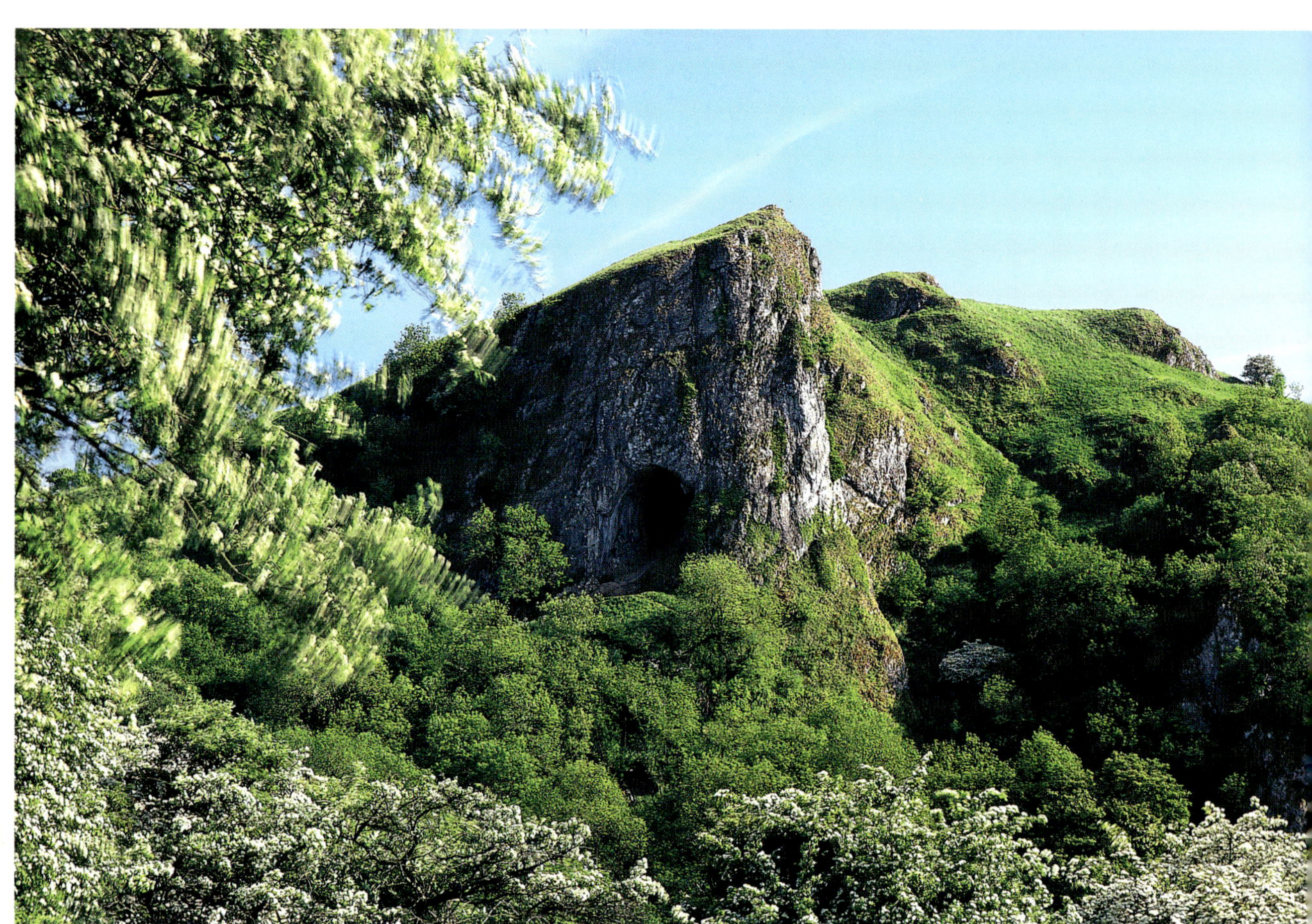

▲ Thor's Cave and May blossom

Through the spring canopy and swaying may blossom stands the gaping black mouth of Thor's Cave high above the Manifold Valley. Formed over thousands of years by erosion of the limestone and exposed by Ice Age glaciers, it must have been a useful shelter for wild animals and evidence suggests early human occupation. It's even been used as an opening sequence in Ken Russell's 1988 horror movie, *The Lair of the White Worm*. Today, however, under deep blue skies it would be difficult to imagine anything other than a rabbit or sheep popping out.

▶ Monsal Head Viaduct

May blossom adorns the slopes above Monsal Head Viaduct as we look south west down Monsal Dale towards Hob's House and Fin Cop, the site of a recently excavated Iron Age hillfort. Now part of the Monsal Trail, this wonderful viaduct built in 1867 once carried the busy Midland main line, much to the anger of the author and art critic John Ruskin back in the nineteenth century who wrote:"… you blasted its rocks away, heaped thousands of tons of shale into its lovely stream. The valley is gone and the gods with it…" Ironically, today, this view is one of the most iconic of the Peak District and the viaduct became a protected structure after the line closed in 1968.

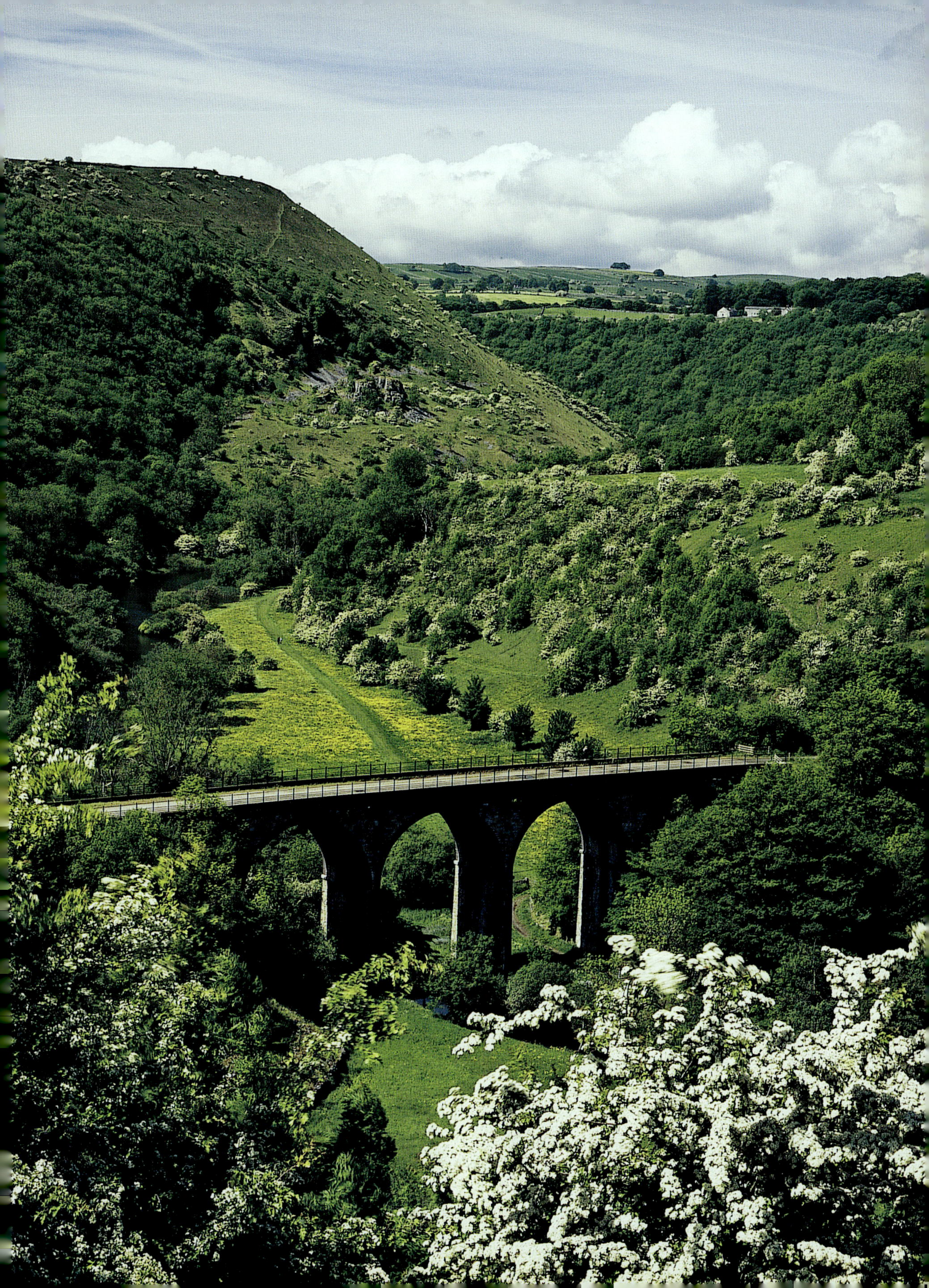

▼ Sweet cicely and phone box, Wormhill

It's the colour contrast between the intense red and green which makes this image work. The red K2 phone box (becoming more of a rarity these days) appears almost to be growing out of the clouds of fluffy, white sweet cicely which engulf it. Sweet cicely is distinguishable from cow parsley by its aniseed smell if you crush the leaves between your fingers. When the black seeds appear, they are collected and used in the local well-dressings to outline the designs of the beautiful pictures made using flower petals, seeds and other natural materials set in clay.

▶ Beech trees in Pindale

I was driving down Pindale into Castleton through this lovely avenue of beech trees, when I thought it had potential so I stopped, scouted around and then looked up. I spotted this graphic image of dark trunks like arms reaching up for the sky through a bright green canopy. It can be rewarding if you look up a bit more, as long as you don't bump into things.

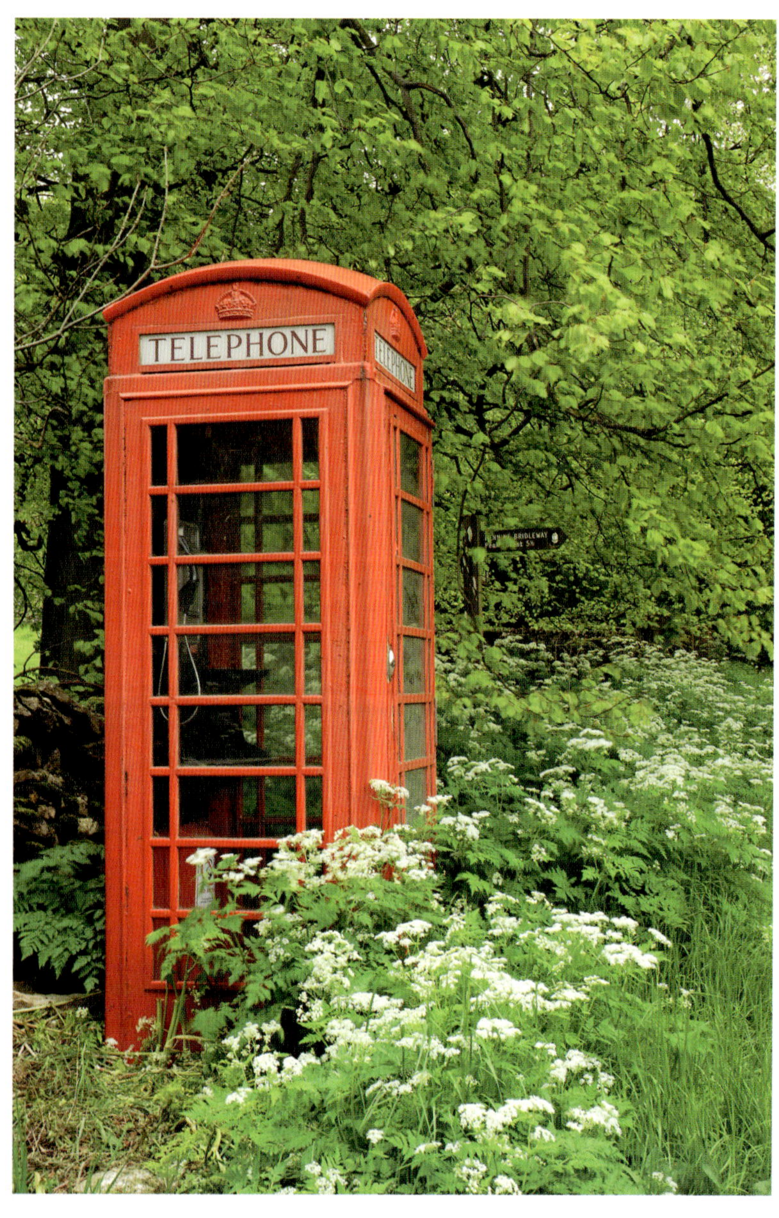

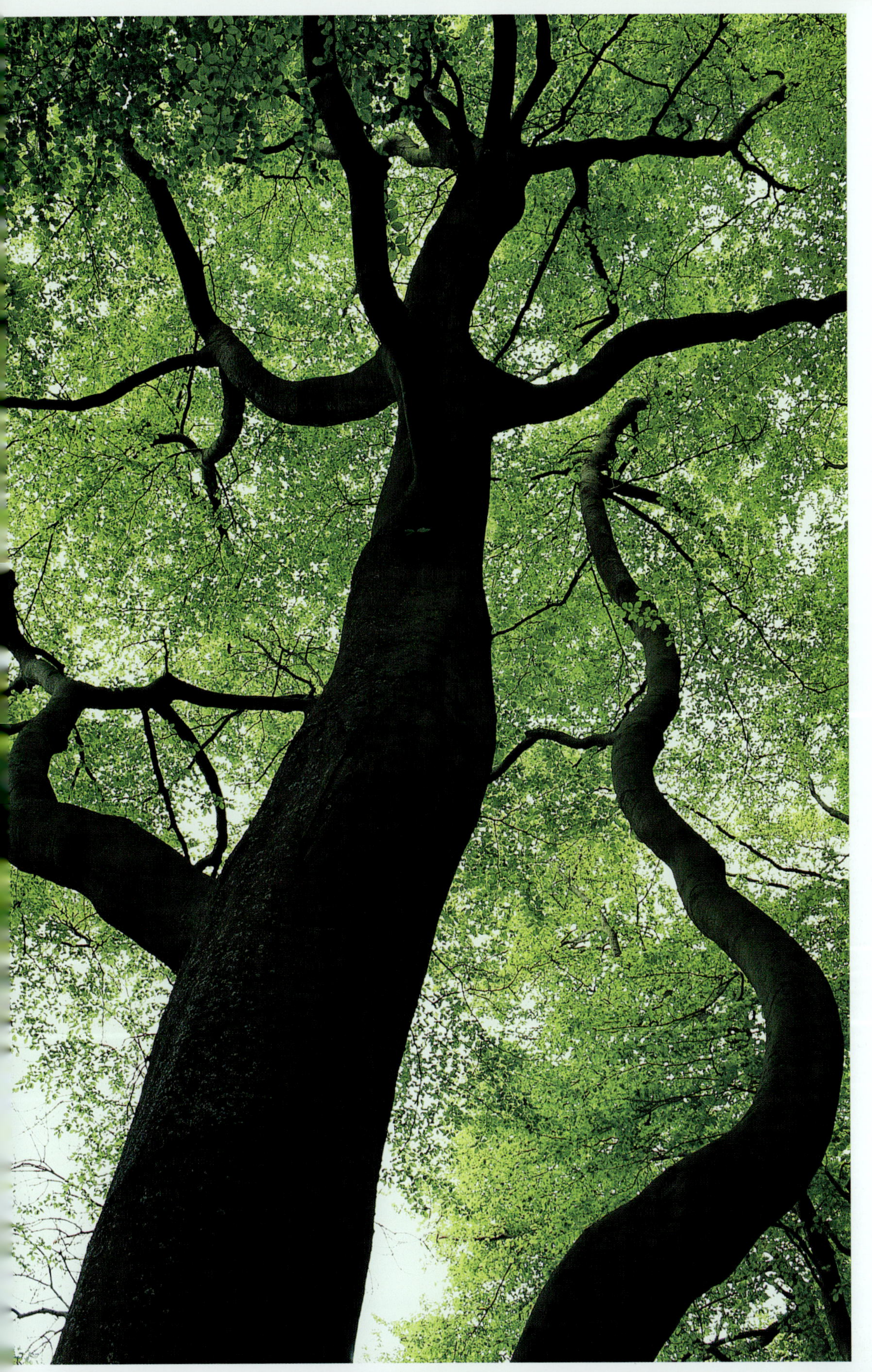

JULY – AUGUST

Sunrise time 04.44–06.16 **Sunset time** 21.41–20.01 **Sunrise direction** NE–ENE **Sunset direction** NW–WNW

Heather haven, swaying grasses and the golden hour

The spring freshness has now gone and trees are in full leaf with less variation in the green tones. The sun is still high in the sky throughout the day so, photographically, this could be a difficult time of year lacking interest. However, there are other treats which emerge from the Peakland landscape.

Apart from the soft blue scabious, harebells and purple fireweed which we see growing everywhere, grasses now move into the limelight as they grow long and soft, producing many interesting seed heads. Even the gentlest breeze creates moving waves of texture and subtle colour as they sway backwards and forwards. However, these soon become slightly over shadowed, as one of the most striking scenes here in the Peak from late July and through August is the vibrant purple haze of heather on the high gritstone areas of moorland. Although predominantly found in the northern Dark Peak, there are also wonderful displays throughout the gritstone moors of both the eastern and western boundaries of the national park and other smaller isolated pockets on grit outcrops scattered around the Peak like Stanton Moor. To do the landscape justice, it's best to work in the softer, warmer light around dawn or dusk (the 'golden hour') which means very early starts or late evenings. This also avoids the crowds as it's now the peak season for tourists.

So on warm, sunny evenings, forget the barbecues, get out on the moors and indulge your senses with the honey fragrance and sights of a vast expanse of mauve sometimes luminescent heather under a setting sun. But don't forget the midge cream!

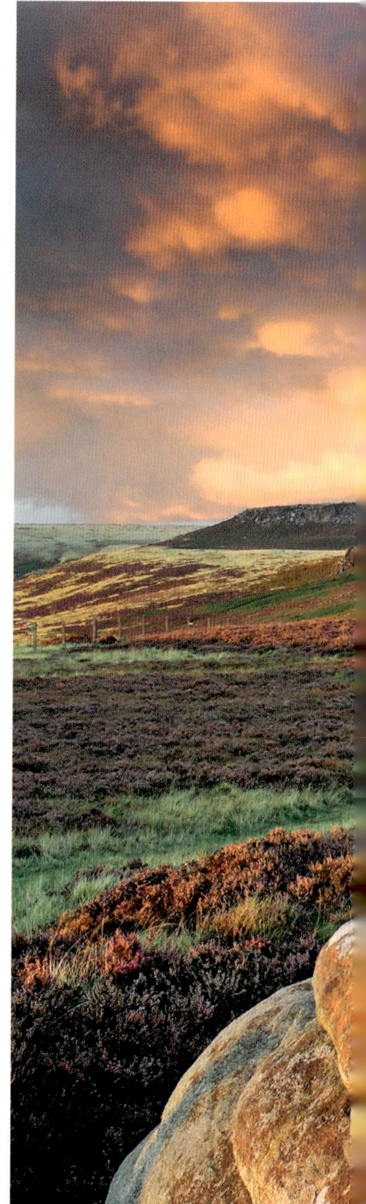

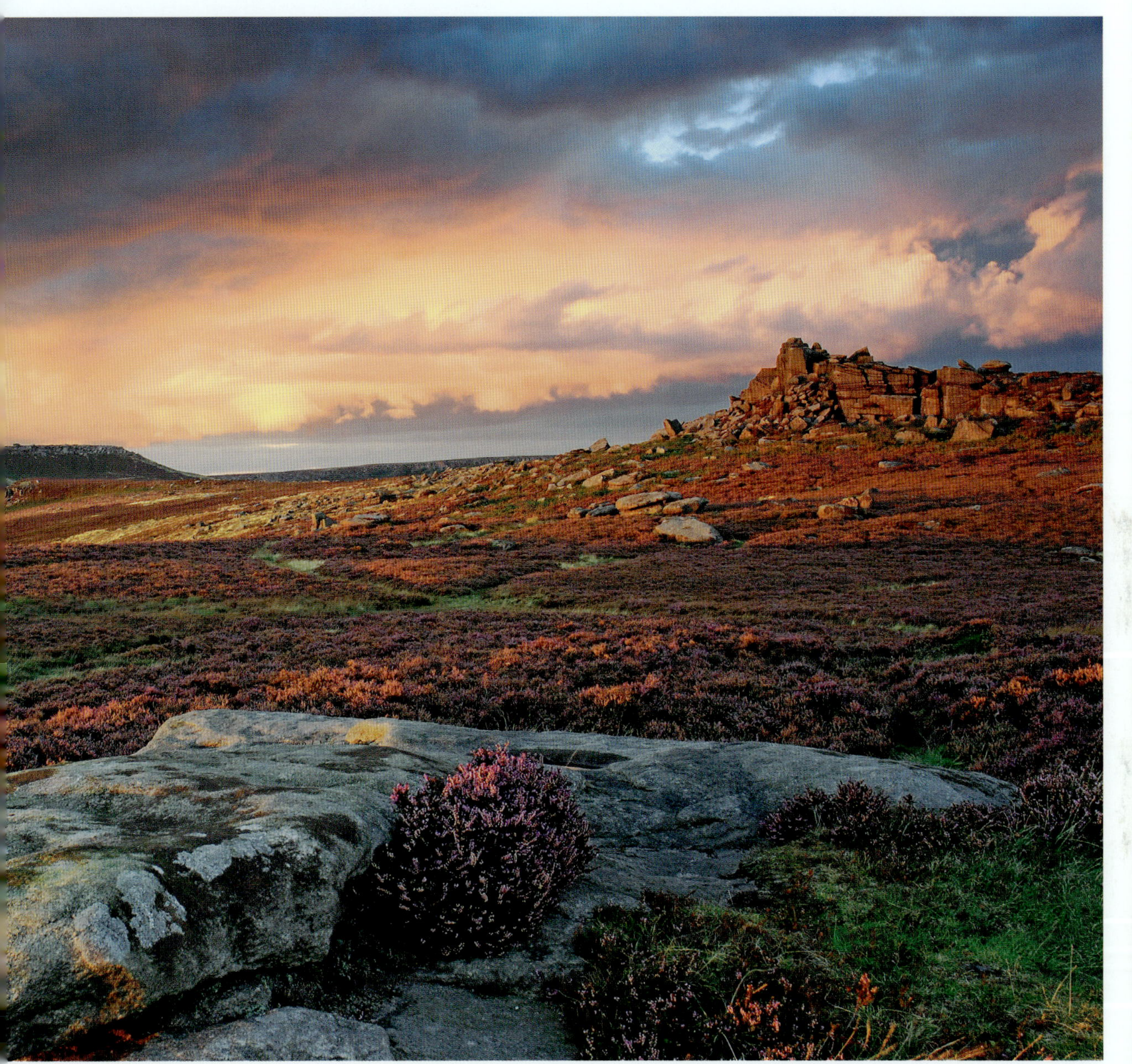

Sunset near Over Owler Tor

All year I wait for skies like this and often I have many wasted trips thinking there will be a sunset, watching and waiting to no avail. On this evening I headed to one of my favourite locations near Millstone Edge and Over Owler Tor, pacing around to find a promising composition. I met a couple of other photographers there with the same idea but, as usual, the light had faded and while chatting and putting my camera away, suddenly the sun dropped below a bank of cloud into a clear patch and the skies exploded, the soft pink glow complimenting the heather. I stopped in mid conversation and ran off to set up my gear quickly. We worked silently until dark, stumbling back to our cars knowing we had witnessed something special.

▼ Eyam Moor and Abney Grange

At last, after a few failures over the years, I managed to get the right conditions for my early morning light on the heather over Eyam Moor. I didn't bivvy, but just managed to get up in time for a change. It was a glorious morning although slightly hazy, and the heather was still in top condition despite it being the very end of August. There is always a special quality to the light at this time of day and I waited until the sun was high enough by around 6.30am for it to rake across the moor and the fields around Abney Grange. As you look northwards over Shatton Moor you can see Win Hill in the distance. There are still many areas in shadow but this adds more depth to the image.

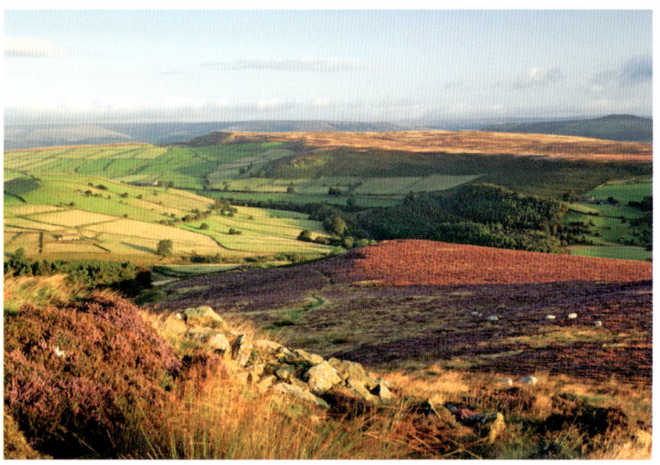

▼ Wall across Eyam Moor

This is a wonderful example of a gritstone wall marching across open heather moorland and still kept in perfect condition. Lit by evening light, I composed it to run diagonally across the image leading the eye through to Win Hill and the Hope Valley. To the right (or north east) of this wall is an ancient stone circle and field system probably dating from about 2700 years ago. A fantastic place to be with views all round – our ancient ancestors certainly knew how to pick a spot.

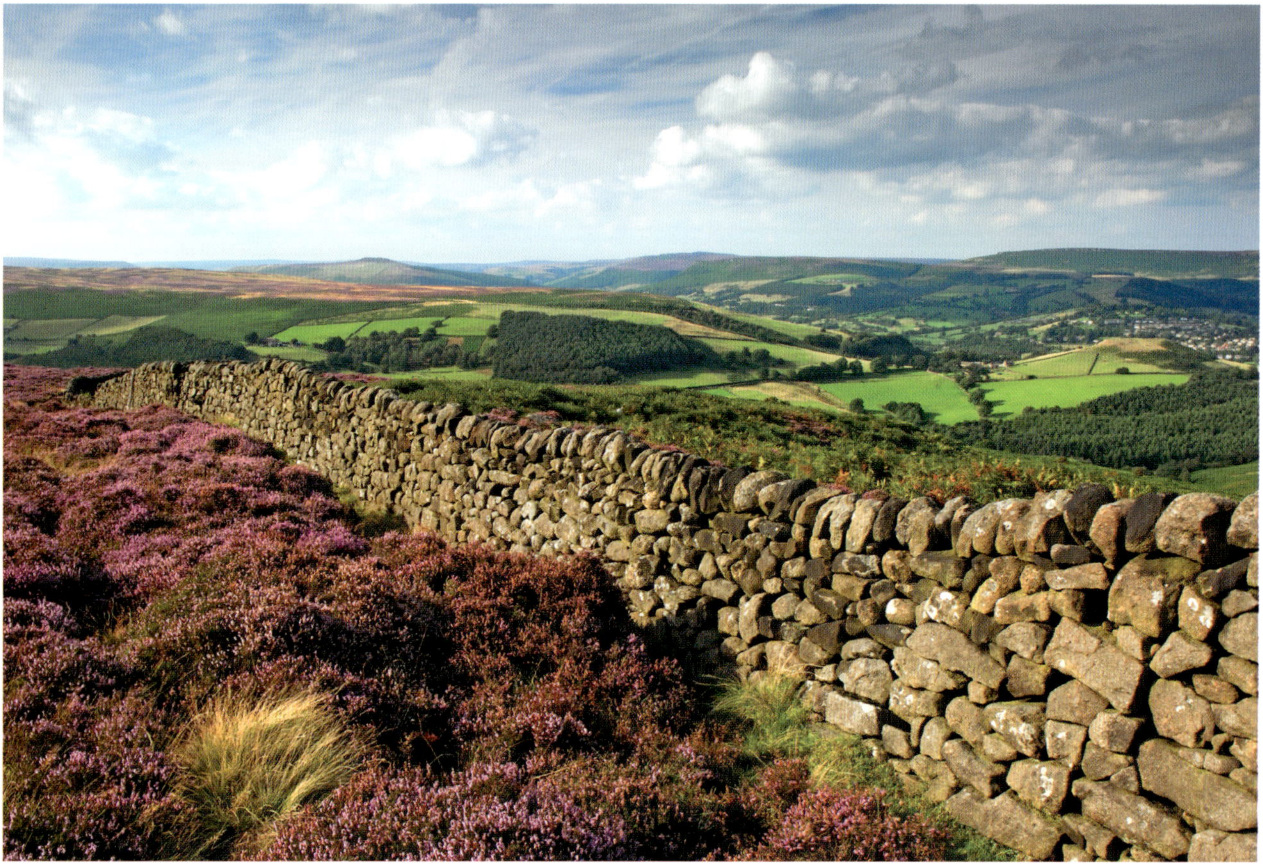

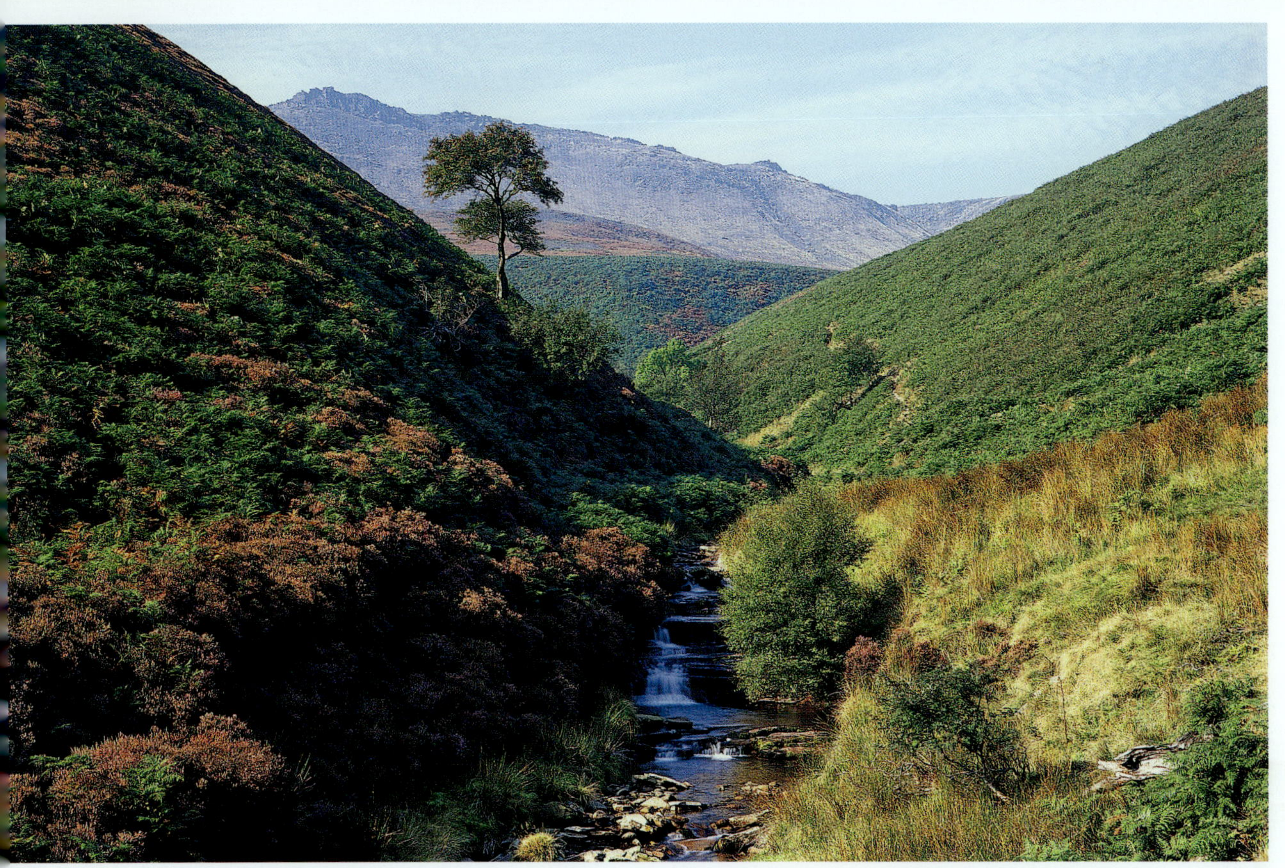

▲ Fairbrook, Kinder

This peaceful, heather- flanked valley is one of the northern routes to the top of Kinder Scout and lies just off the busy A57 Snake Pass. I've always been attracted to this little valley with its mini waterfalls but often find it difficult to get the composition I want due to the steep terrain. I'm usually balancing precariously on a ledge (as I was here) but I then tried to clamber down to the water to get a more dramatic image (see rear cover picture). Unfortunately, I slipped and clattered down to the bottom feeling somewhat battered and bruised. Working alone can be hazardous especially in areas with no mobile phone reception and no-one ever did pass me that morning, so it was a good thing I was not seriously hurt.

▶ Stormy skies over Higger Tor

On a blustery evening, the clearing skies light up the heather moorland as we look northwards across to Higger Tor. The long heather, recorded as a mauve blur with the slow shutter speed in the low light levels, provides good cover for birds and often a red grouse will be flushed out giving its wonderful 'go-back, go-back' call, all part of the atmosphere of these beautiful moors.

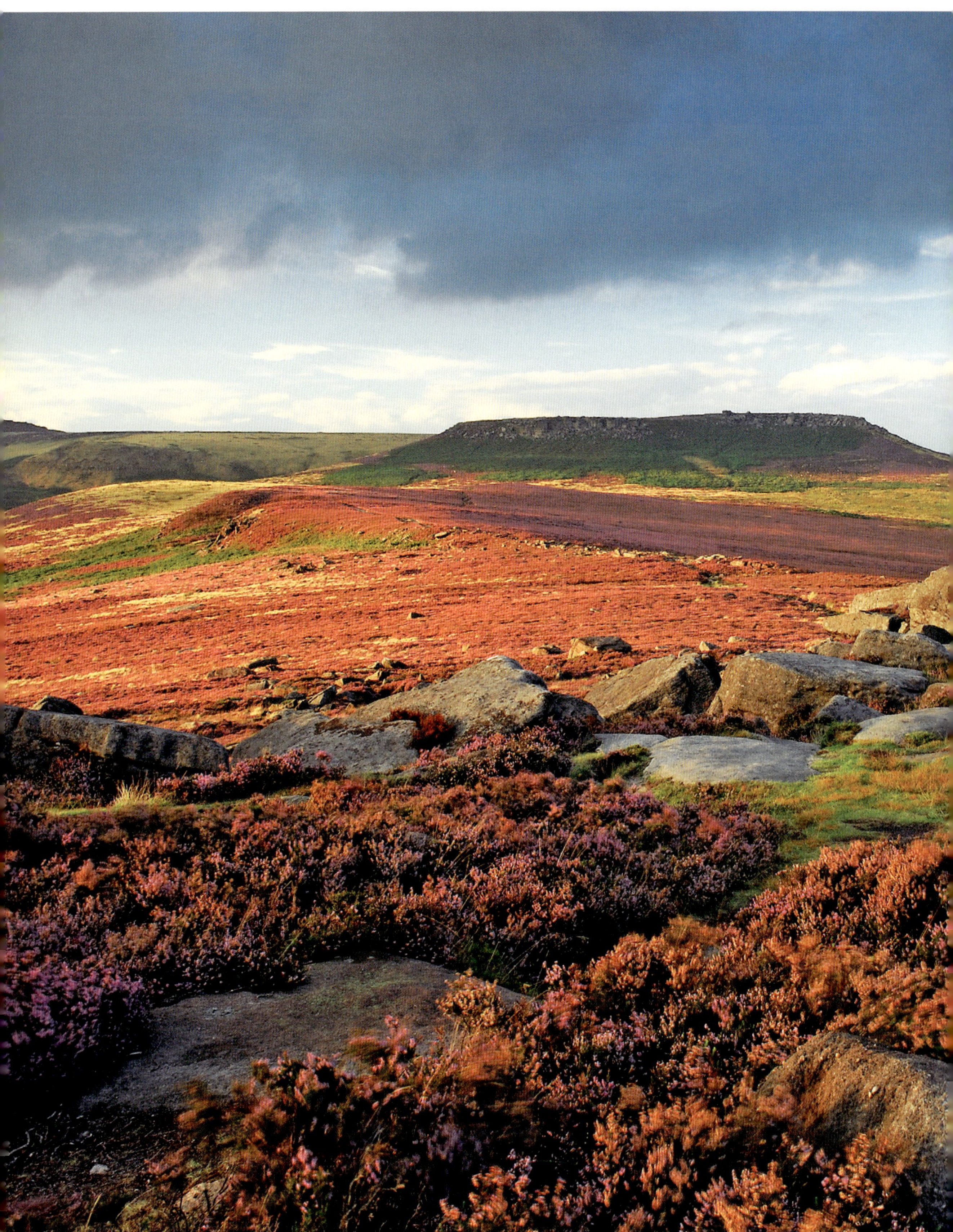

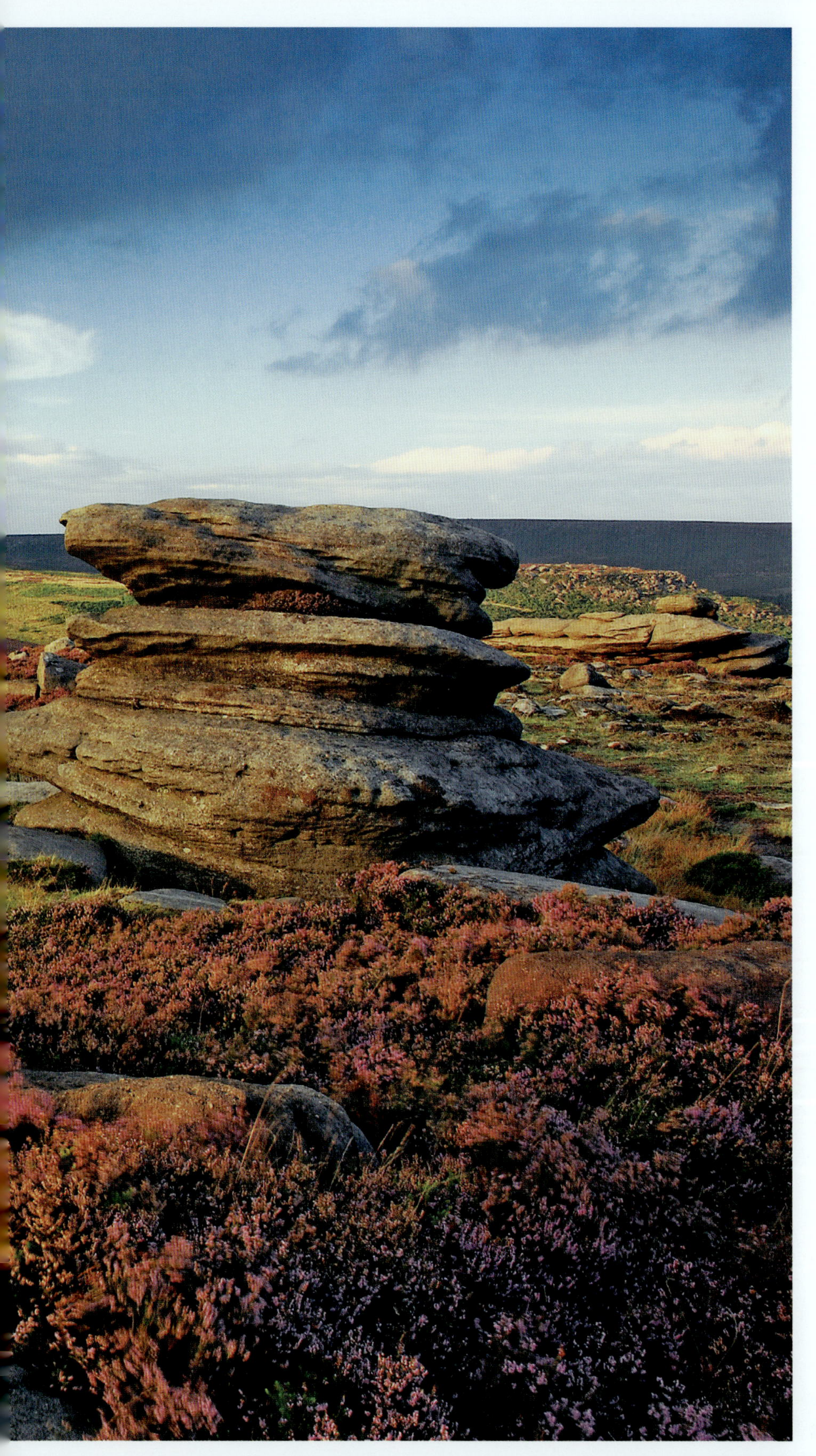

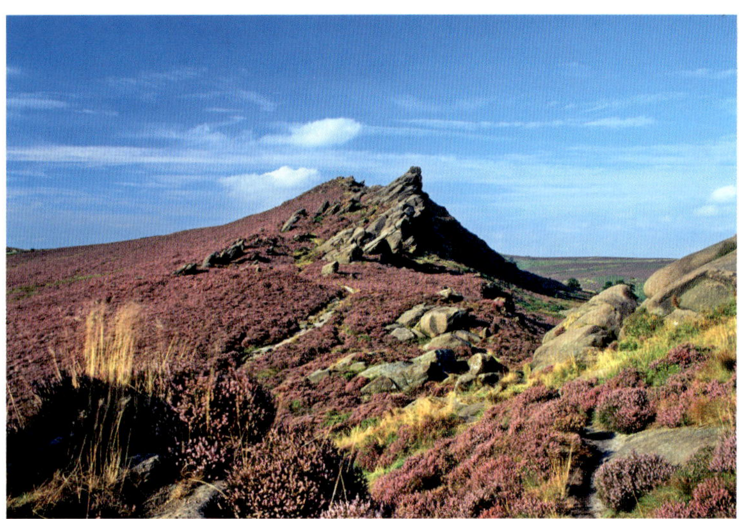

▲ Ramshaw Rocks

Just north of Leek off the A53 is this lovely little sandstone ridge with its many interestingly - shaped rocky outcrops. I often time my visits for afternoon or evening light which creates shadows and depth when looking north along the ridge. Here, I used the path and the sedges blowing in the wind to lead the eye to the top of the rocks and fluffy white clouds above. Sadly, the main thing I remember when taking this image was the invasion of big black flies with long dangling legs. One even crawled inside my camera when I was changing film.

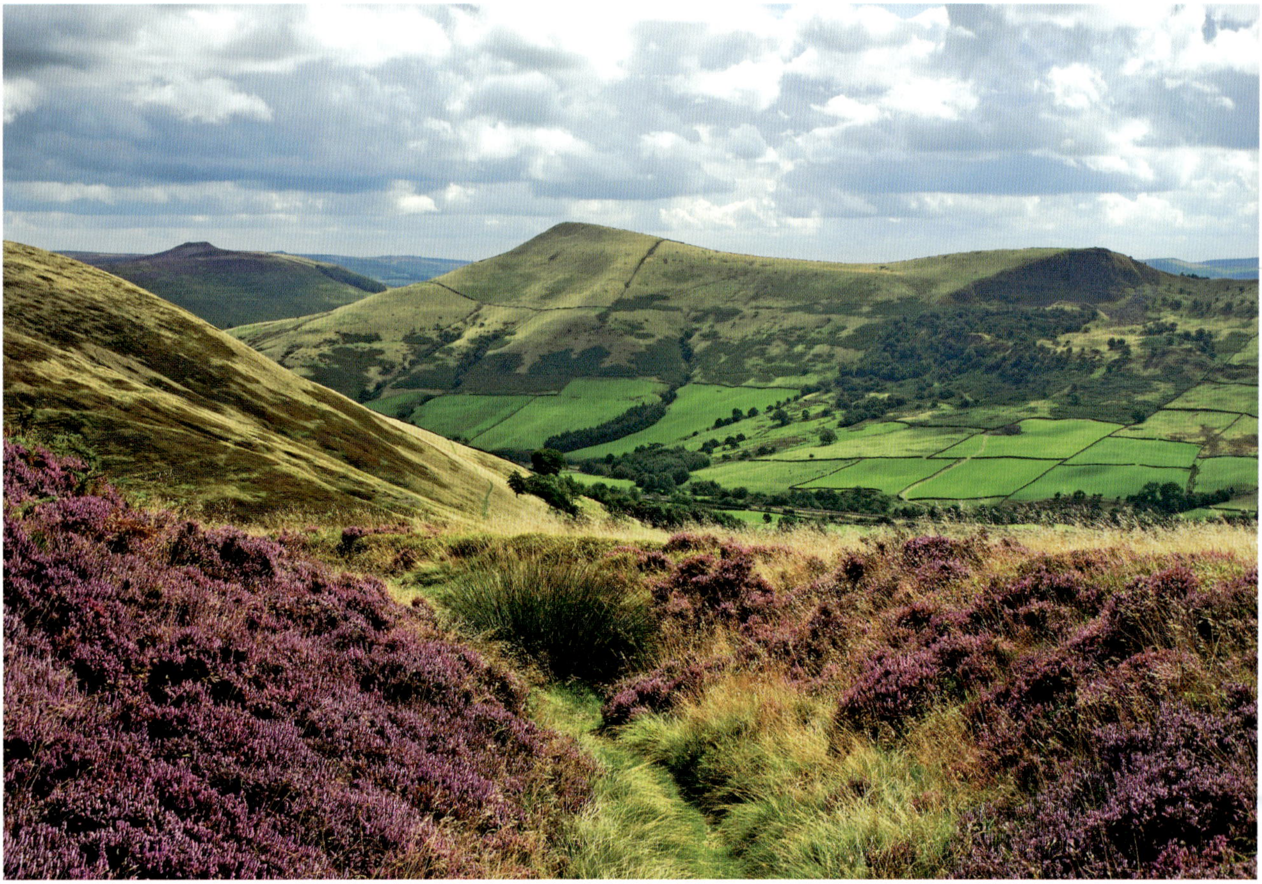

▼ Windgather Rocks

Aptly named, this little gritstone outcrop lies to the west of the Goyt Valley near Kettleshulme and is popular with rock climbers. Facing west, it gets the evening light and the rock is nicely warm to the fingers as it releases its heat of the day like a giant storage heater, with the breeze to keep midges away. At this time of year, pockets of heather cling to the crevices making interesting compositions. Here we are looking north towards Kettleshulme and Whaley Bridge. The fields we can see in the mid distance resemble a patchwork quilt.

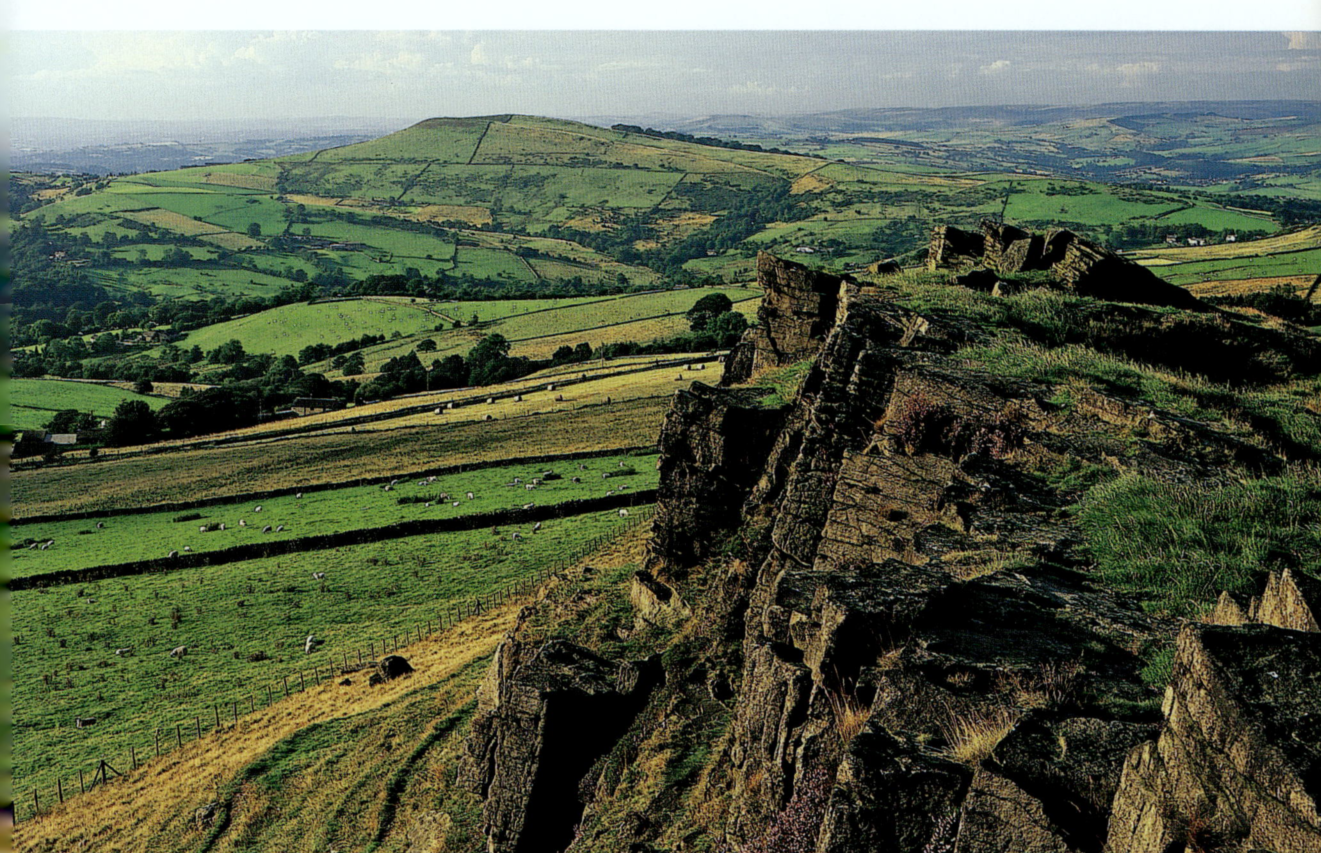

◀ Looking towards Lose and Win Hills from The Nab, Edale

I noticed this view many years ago on a circuitous route down from Kinder and loved the zig-zag formation of the hills and the path leading your eye towards Back Tor, Lose Hill and the pimple of Win Hill in the far distance. Since then, I've lost count of the number of times that I've tried to capture it in the right light and failed. It involves an energetic climb up from Edale in order to get there before cloud cover envelopes the sun and the light goes flat. With the heather in top condition and bubbly clouds forecast, today was the day. With my heart pounding, I got there just too late. However, I persevered, wandered up to Ringing Roger and back down before another chink in the clouds provided some fleeting sunlight on the heather.

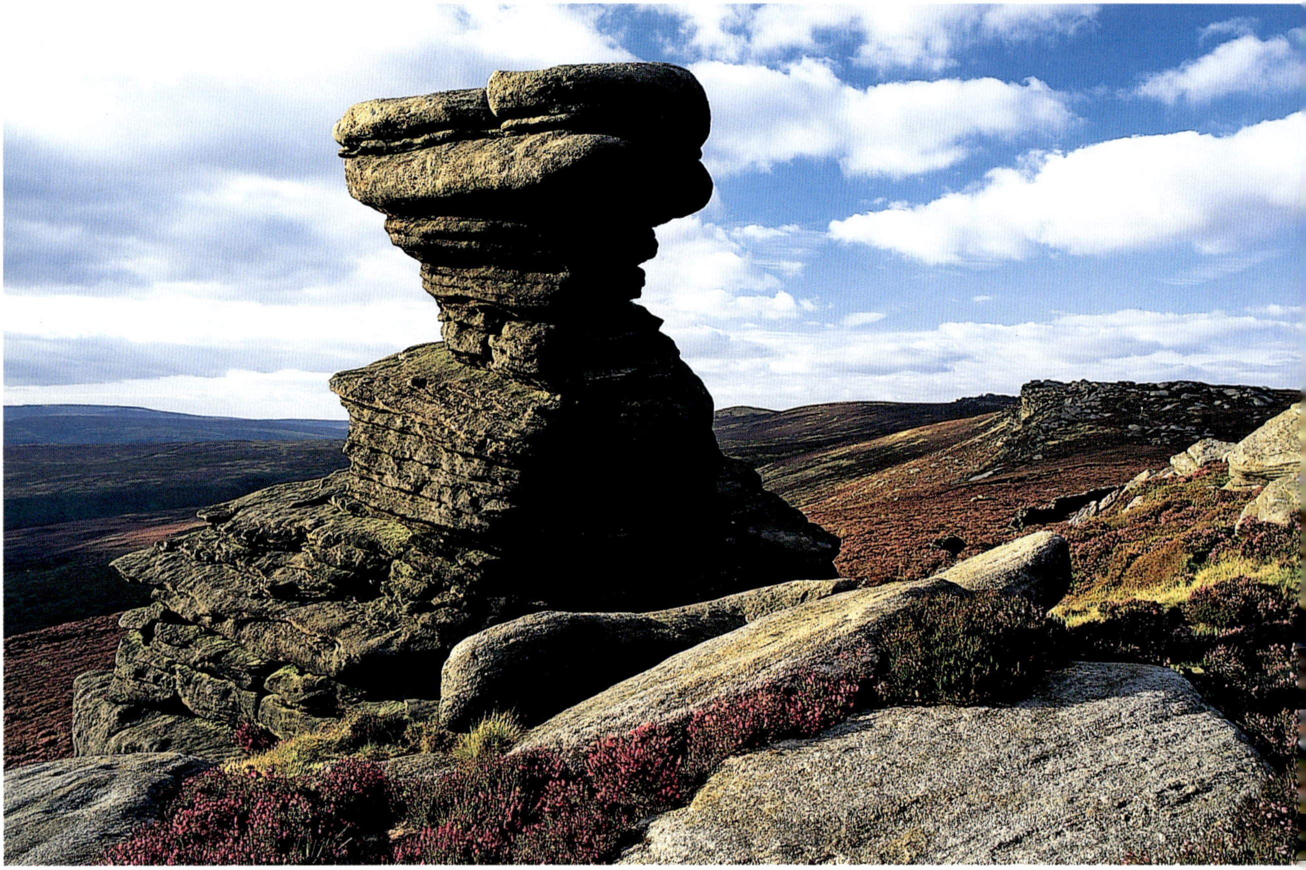

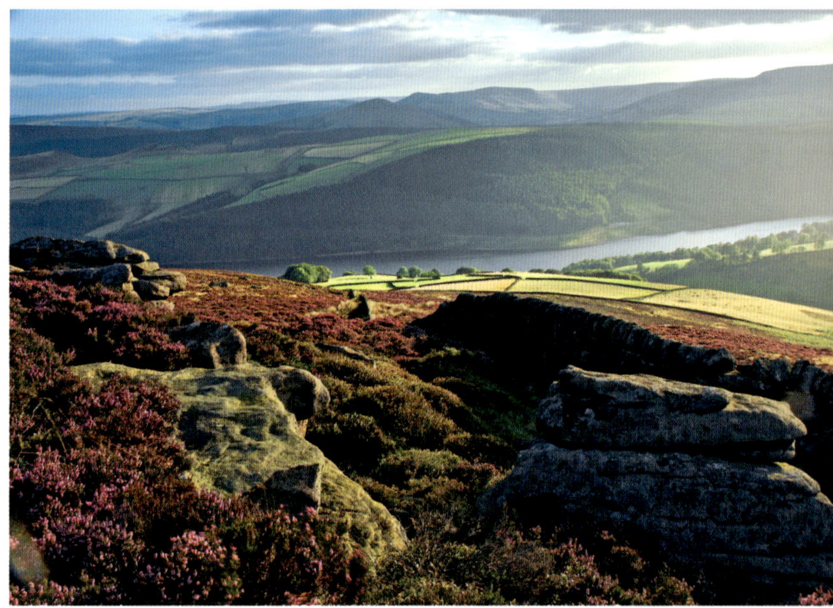

▼ View down to Ladybower from The Salt Cellar

Sometimes it's easy to get obsessed with one particular view and not look around for others, especially if it has taken years to get the right conditions. However, while at the Salt Cellar I turned my camera 180 degrees as I noticed a wonderful view down towards Ladybower, my eye being drawn through a gap between the rocks towards a distant tree standing among a patchwork of fields backlit by the evening sunlight. In the distance we can see the Edale Valley below Kinder Scout and Lose Hill. The only problem here is that when the wind drops, at sunset the midges come out for a feast.

◀ The Salt Cellar, Derwent Edge

Standing high on Derwent Edge above Ladybower Reservoir at 1,574feet/480m The Salt Cellar is a really wonderful place to be on a fine August evening, despite the considerable effort required to get there. You can guarantee to see grouse on this wild moorland, the silence broken by its distinctive call. You may also be lucky enough to see a mountain hare as it dashes for cover among the boulders. I have spent a few years of wasted photography trips to this spot in order to get the right conditions. Either the sky is too blue and featureless or a bank of cloud develops just as I struggle to the top with all my gear. Sometimes, I cut it too fine and get there just as the sun drops down below the Kinder massif. On this evening, I got there a bit earlier and caught the light sculpting the contours of this lovely weathered gritstone outcrop as the sun came in and out of the clouds. I positioned the tor on the left so that we can see Derwent Edge lit up as it snakes away into the distance towards Back Tor.

▼ Storm approaching Back Tor, Derwent Edge

Back Tor stands at 1,765feet/538m at the northern end of Derwent Edge, and is similar in shape to that of the Salt Cellar. A heavy shower is approaching from the west over Bleaklow and Kinder. There are often thunderstorms in August, but this was more of a severe April shower with the strength and chill of the wind which was blowing. The air was very clear with great visibility, typical of post cold front conditions.

▶ Spooky trees near Eyam Moor

This may look like winter but it was actually taken at about 6am on a very damp, soggy August morning after an uncomfortable overnight bivvy on Eyam Moor in order to capture a sunrise over the heather. At dawn, a vaguely promising pink mist soon turned to rain. My reward was this atmospheric photograph through the woods on my return.

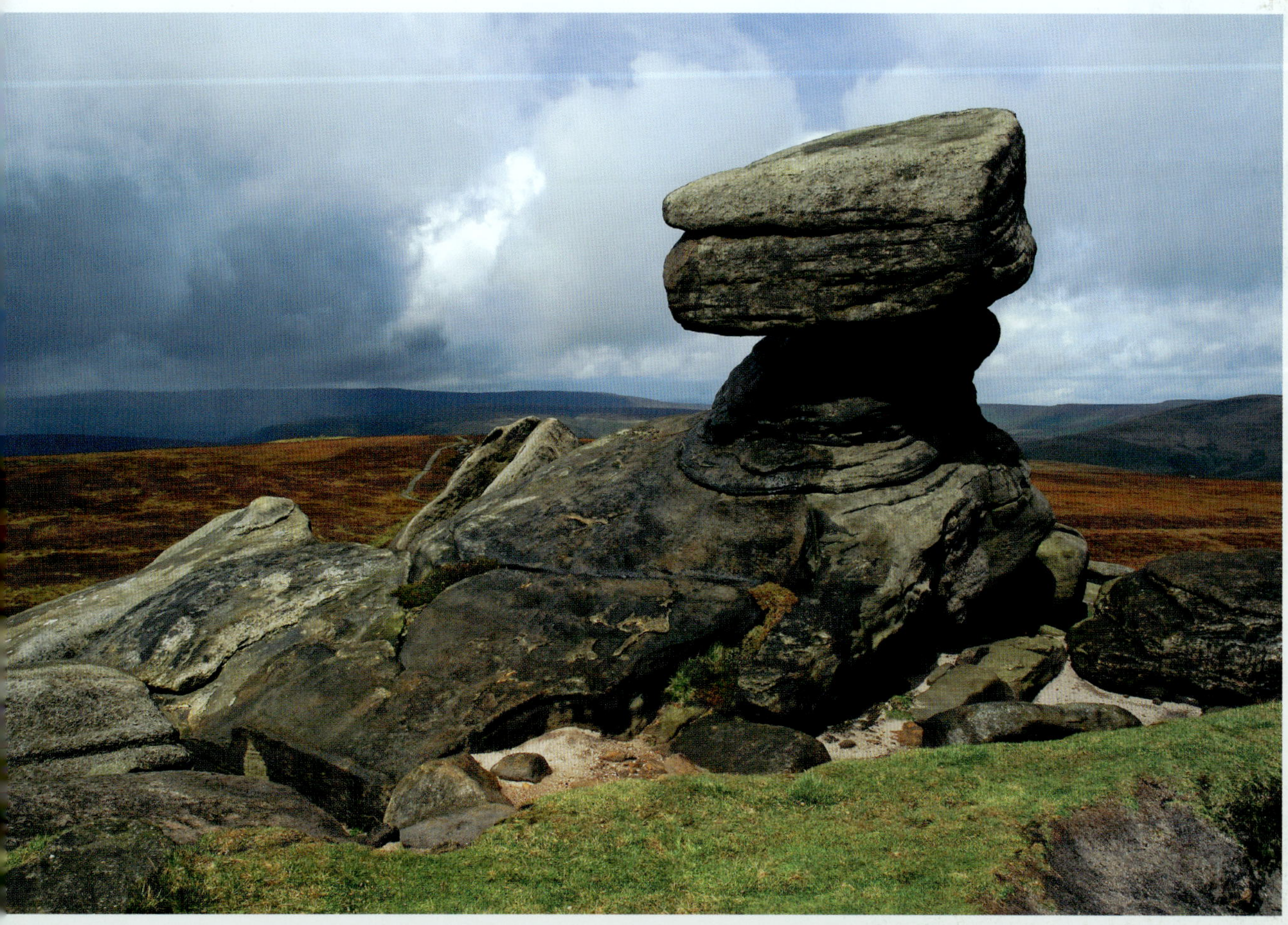

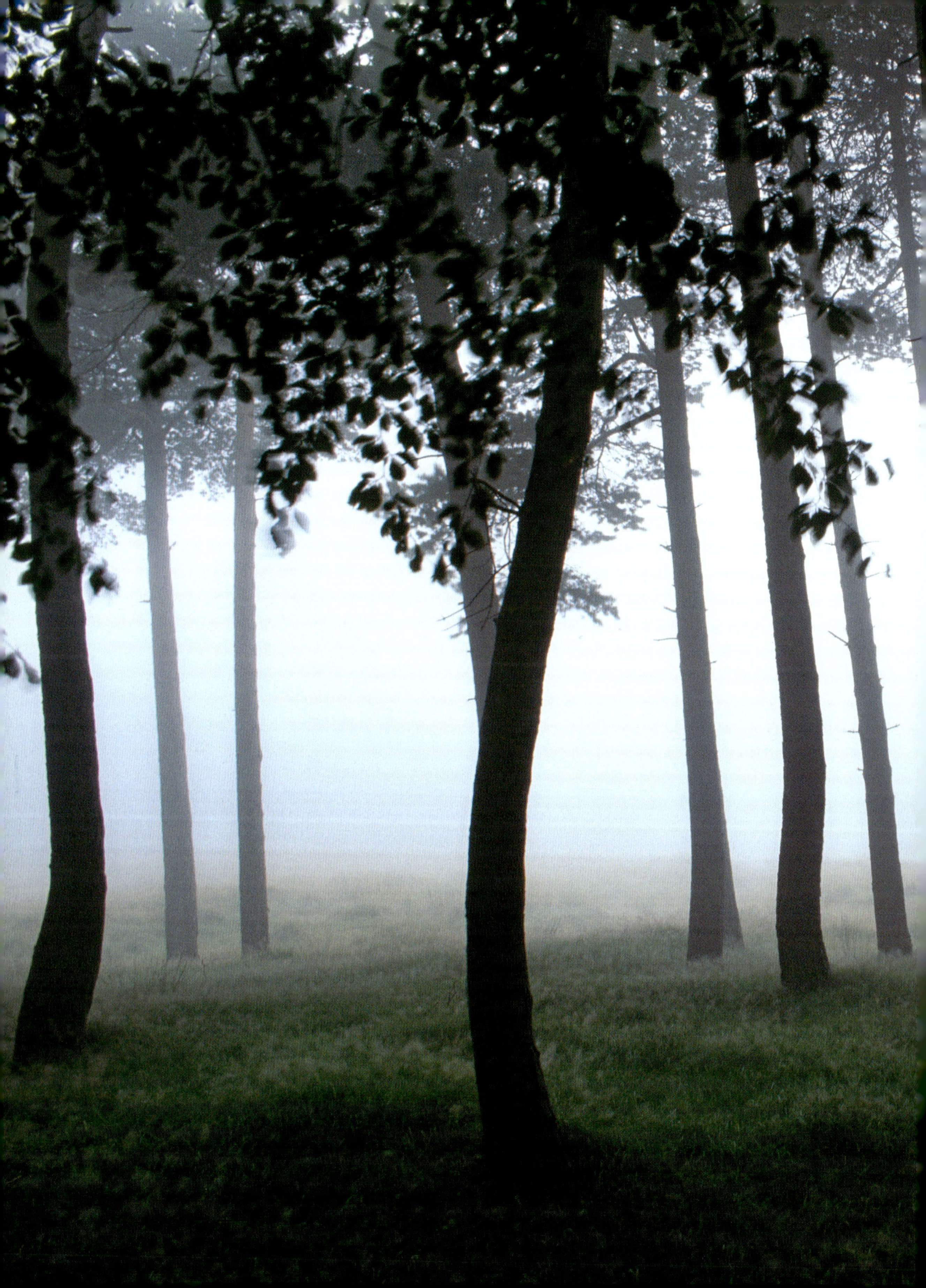

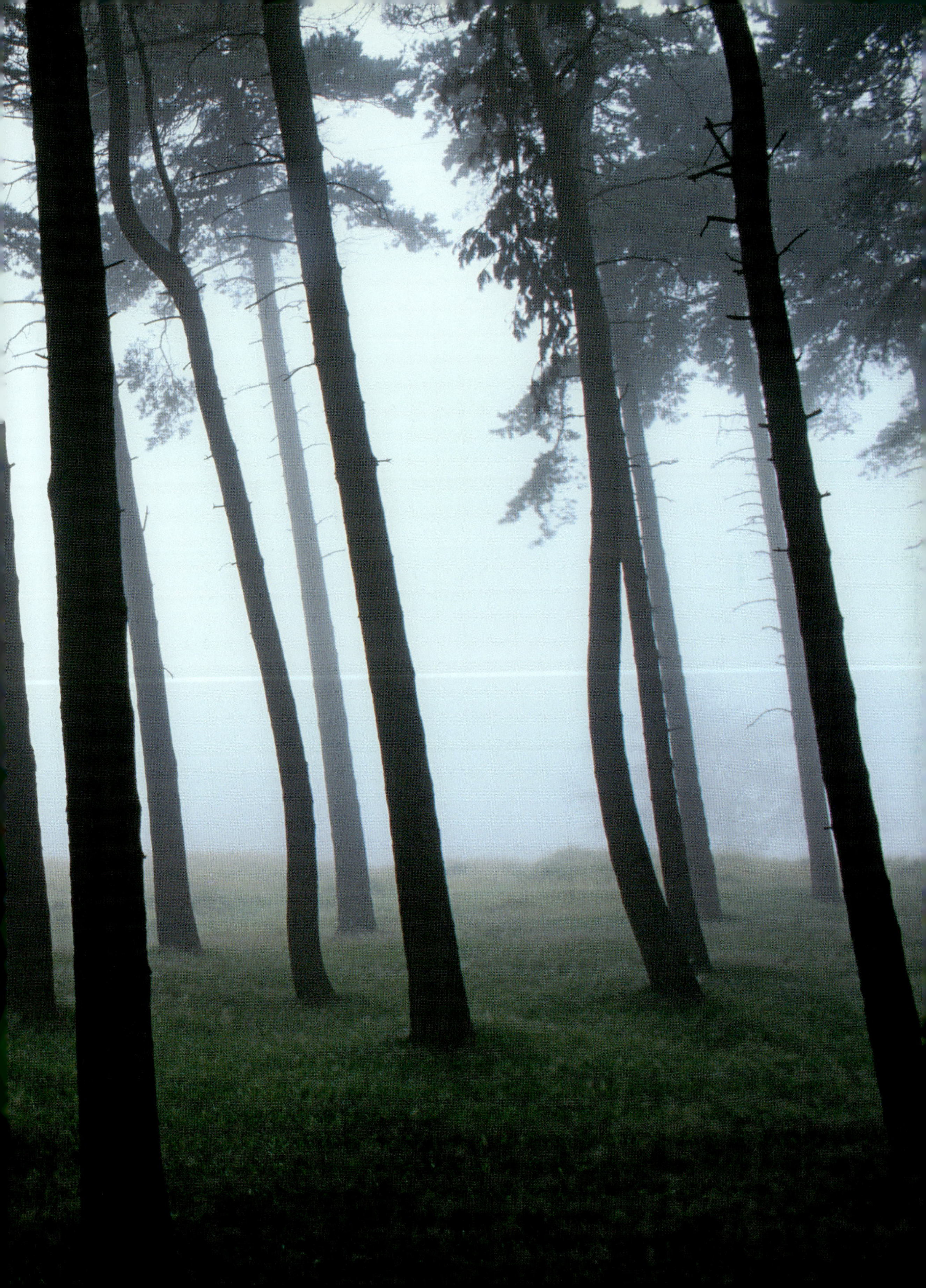

▼ The Woolpacks, Kinder

Amazing shaped boulders are scattered all over this area and were apparently the inspiration to the sculptor Henry Moore, and you can see why. The imagination runs wild as all sorts of forms and creatures can be created from their shapes. At around 1970 feet/600m on the southern edge of the Kinder Plateau, it is a wild, bleak place surrounded by blanket bog and peat groughs. I know only too well, as once on a failed mission to photograph them in moonlight, I found myself up here in the pitch black with no decent torch one evening. I got down safely, but will be better prepared next time!

▶ The Kissing Stones, Bleaklow

Also known as 'The Wain Stones', this amusing formation is found just off the Pennine Way near Bleaklow Head. I was incredibly lucky with the weather when I took this and am pleased there were some clouds looming in the background to give it atmosphere. Often, this is a foreboding place full of peat bogs, where many people get lost and disorientated if the mist descends, as it so often does. I've been back but have never had such good lighting conditions again. This could be taken in any month of the year as the surroundings never change – just black, squelchy peat. Summer or winter are probably the best seasons, when the ground is either frozen or dry.

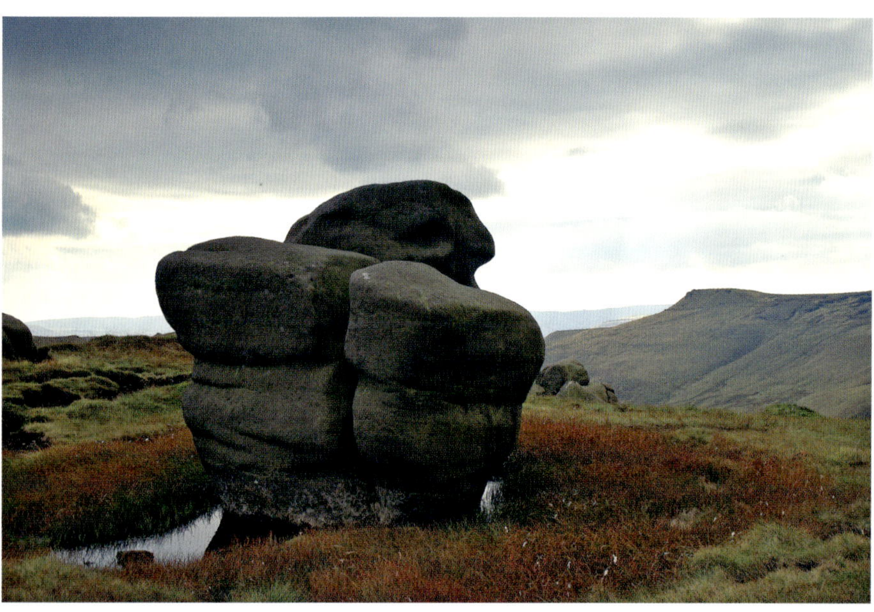

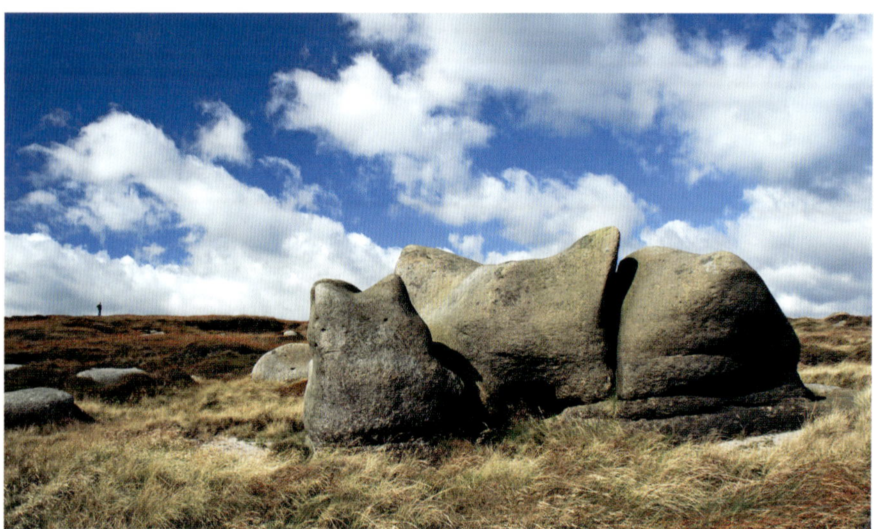

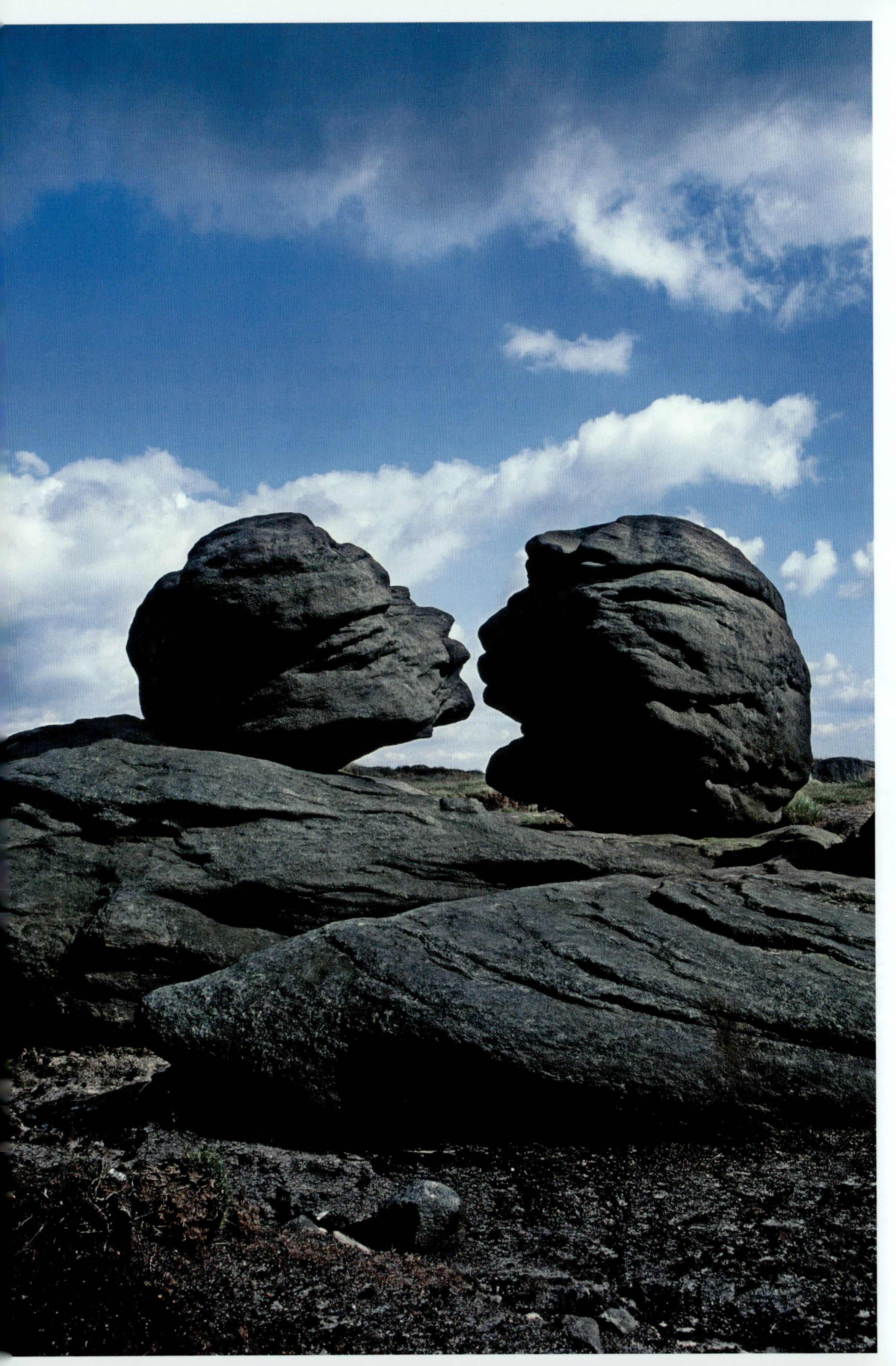

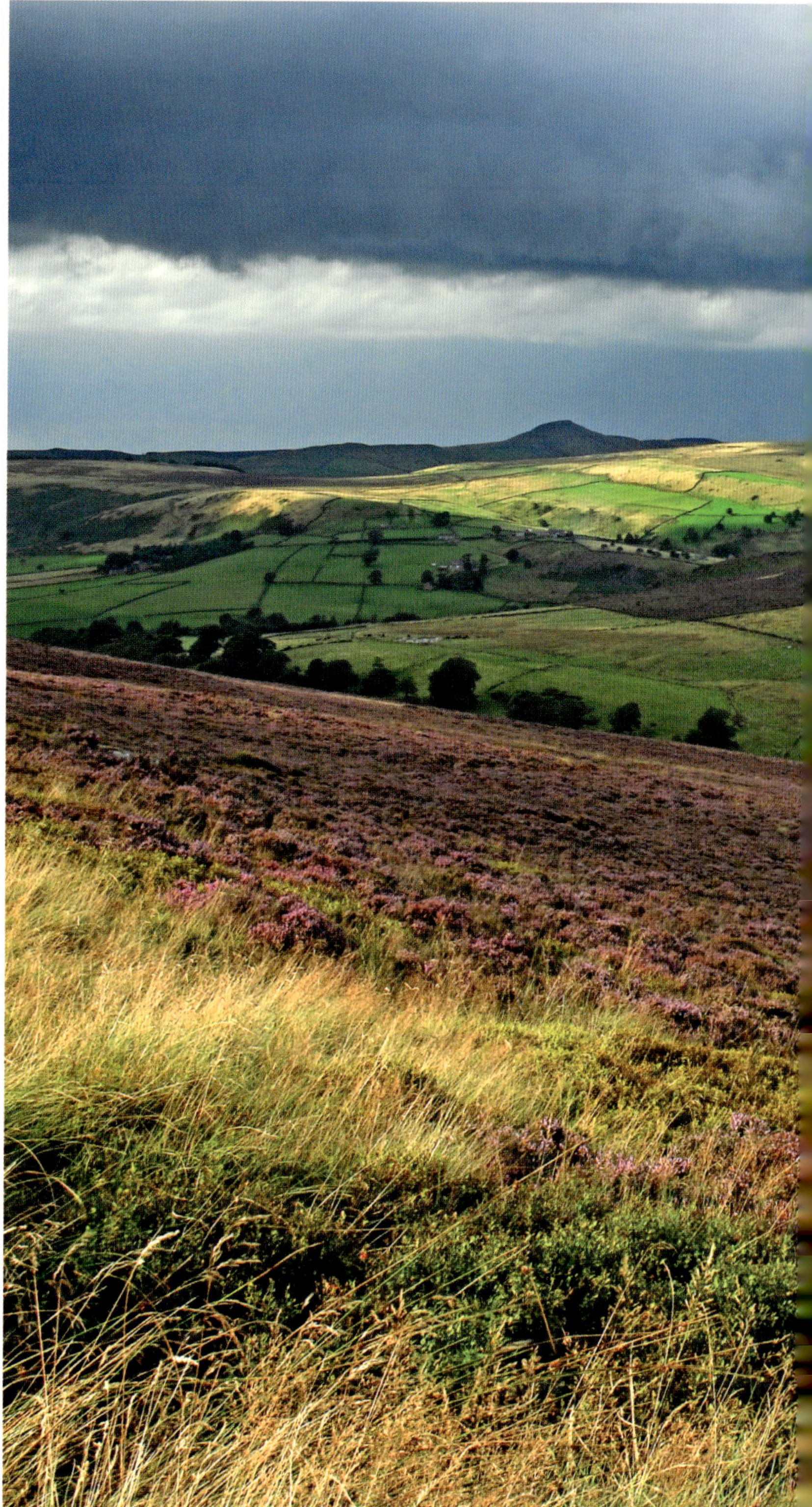

Rowan near Goldsitch Moss looking towards Shutlingsloe

Late in August rowan trees start to glow with red berries and I'd noticed that this year seemed particularly good. It was an extremely blustery afternoon, just the stormy weather I was looking for, so I headed off to a rowan tree I'd spotted the year before among the heather behind the Roaches. Here, we look over Gradbach towards Shutlingsloe, which is in dark shadow from the encroaching storm clouds.

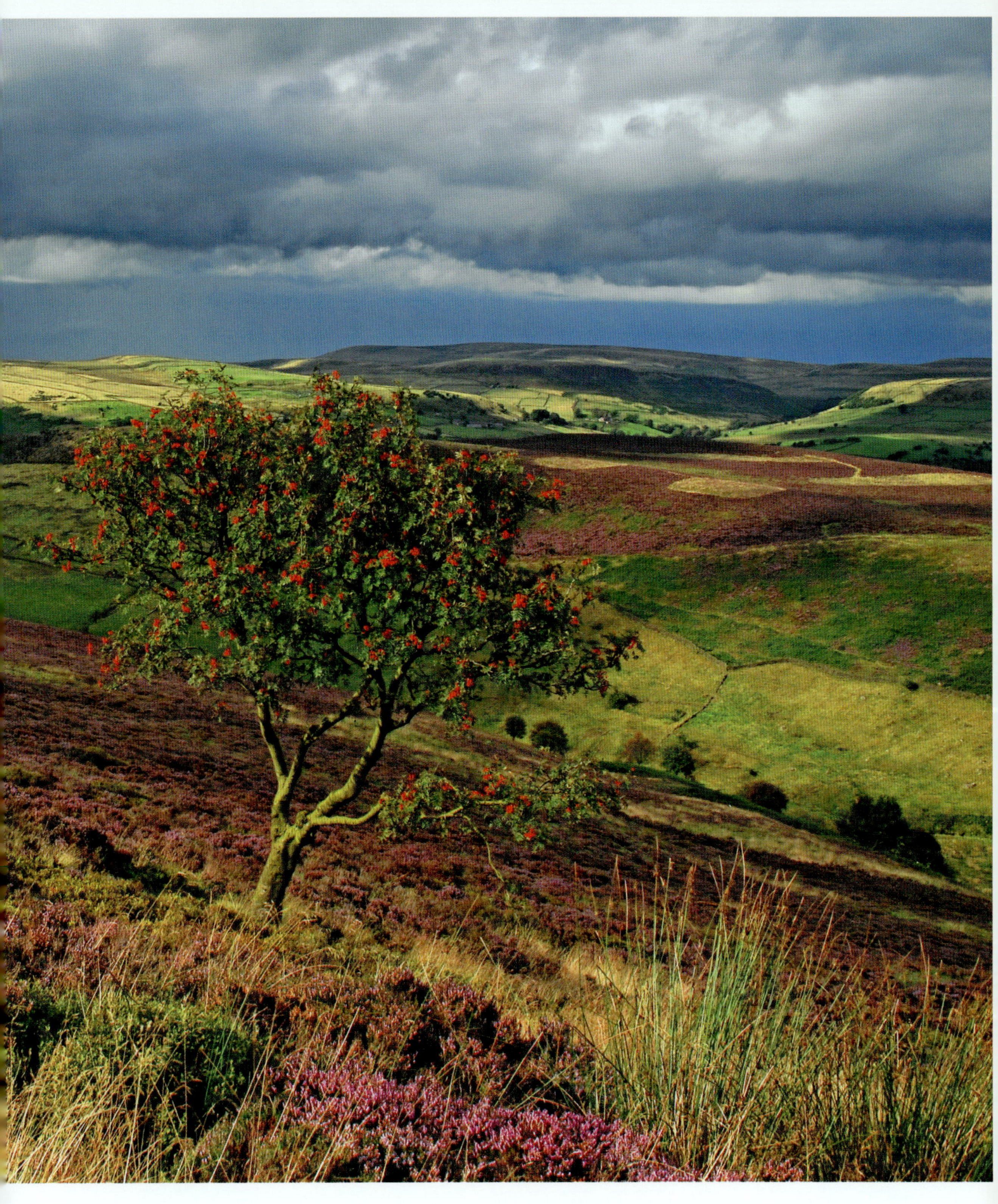

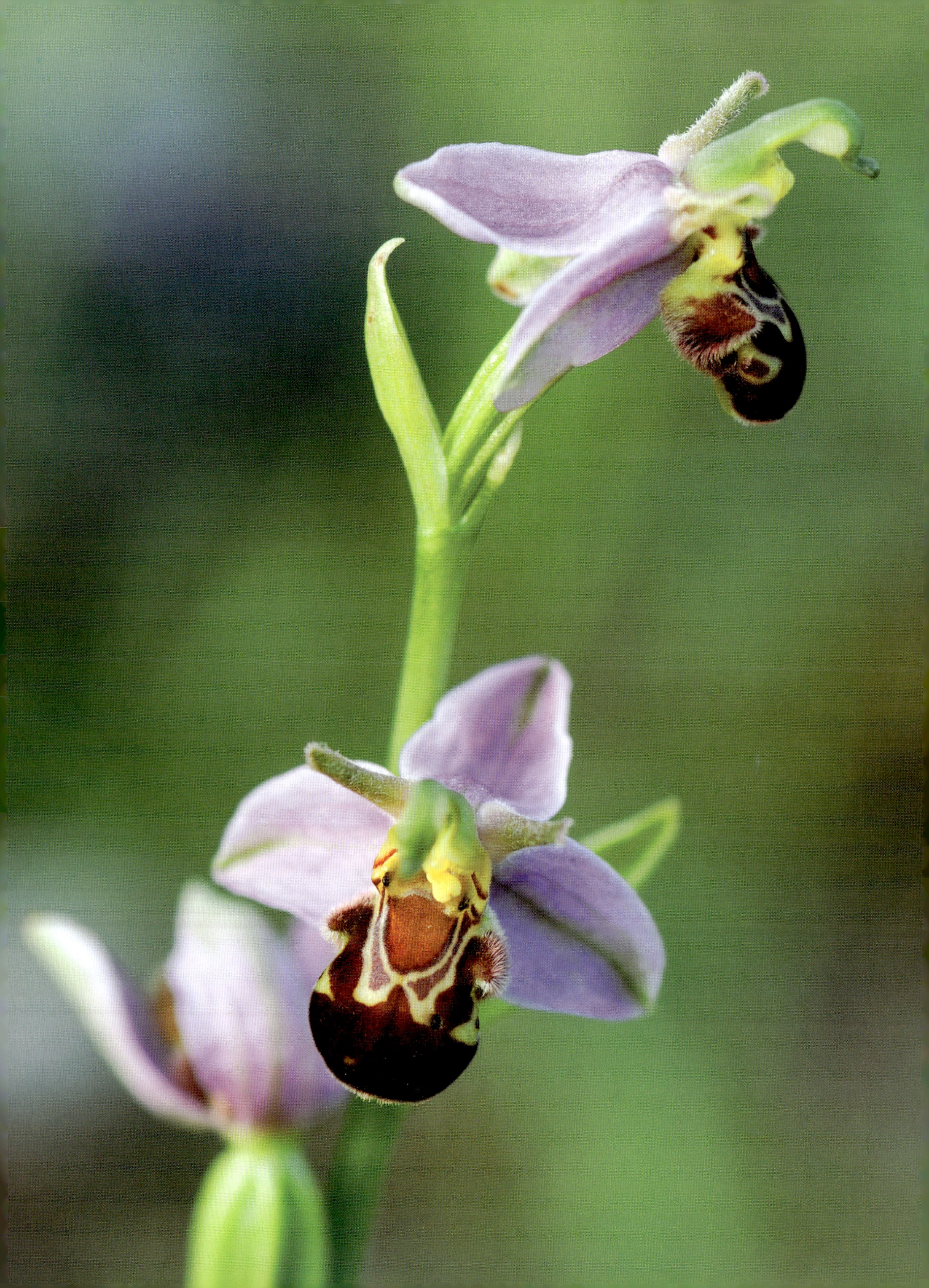

◀ Bee orchid, Miller's Dale

I'm no botanist, but when I first stumbled upon this orchid years ago in Miller's Dale, I knew it had to be a bee orchid from its amazing resemblance to a bumble bee. I was unprepared and took the best photo I could with my equipment back then. It was 14 years later before I returned in July 2009 to photograph it again. This time there seemed fewer around which was slightly worrying and emphasises how important it is to protect and respect our rarer species. Through my work I'm constantly being reminded of how clever nature can be, and fervently hope it can continue to stand up to our interference.

▼ Storm approaching Roach End

There was a huge thunderstorm developing over Bosley Cloud out west on the Cheshire Plain. I love black skies as a backdrop to acid green fields. Here we have what I call a 'stripey picture' – three layers of colour which I tried to create from the heather, fields and sky. The backlit black walls add that little extra dimension, together with the sheep of course. Seconds after I took this I got drenched and raced back to the car as the loud thunderclaps intensified.

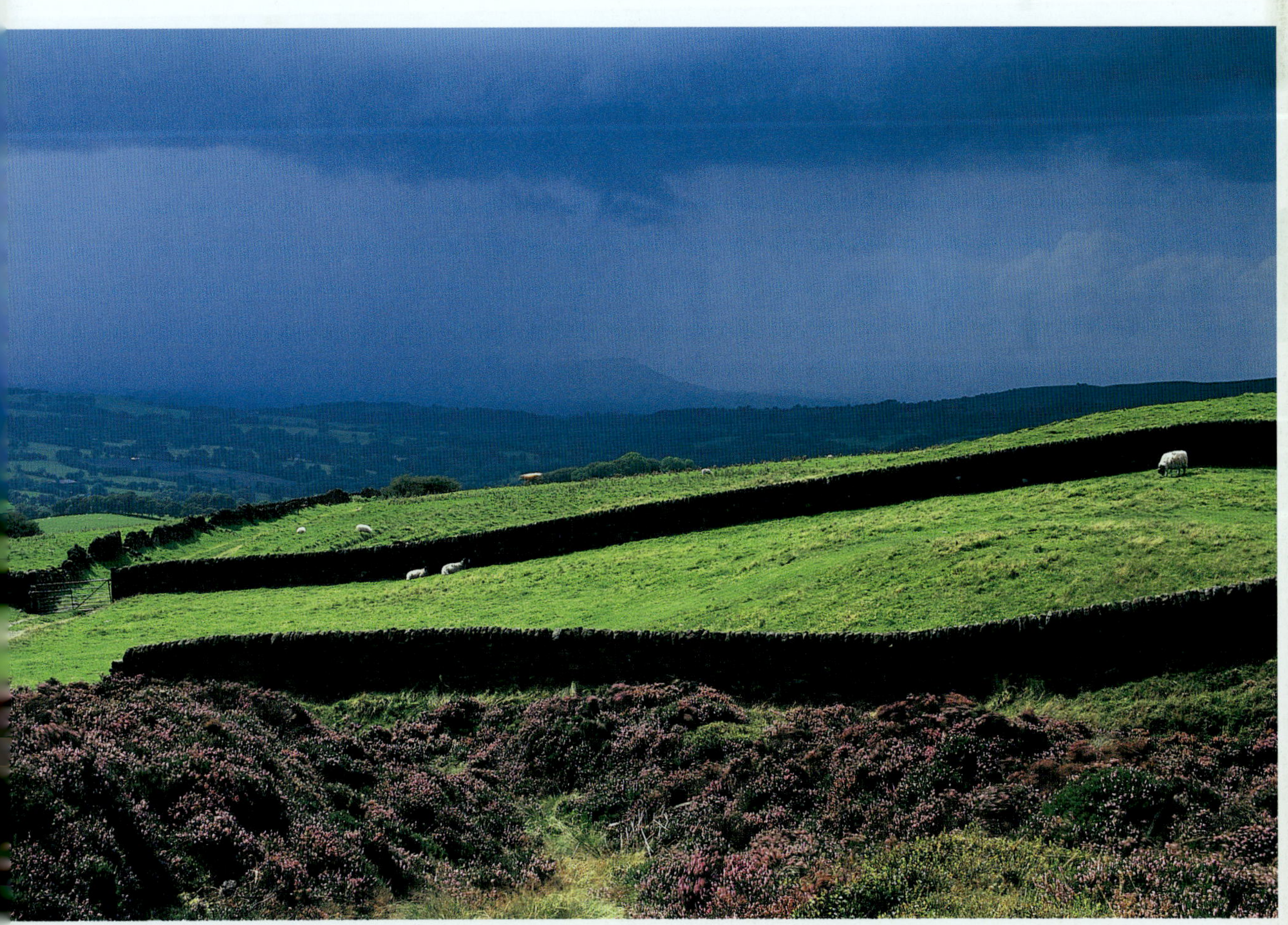

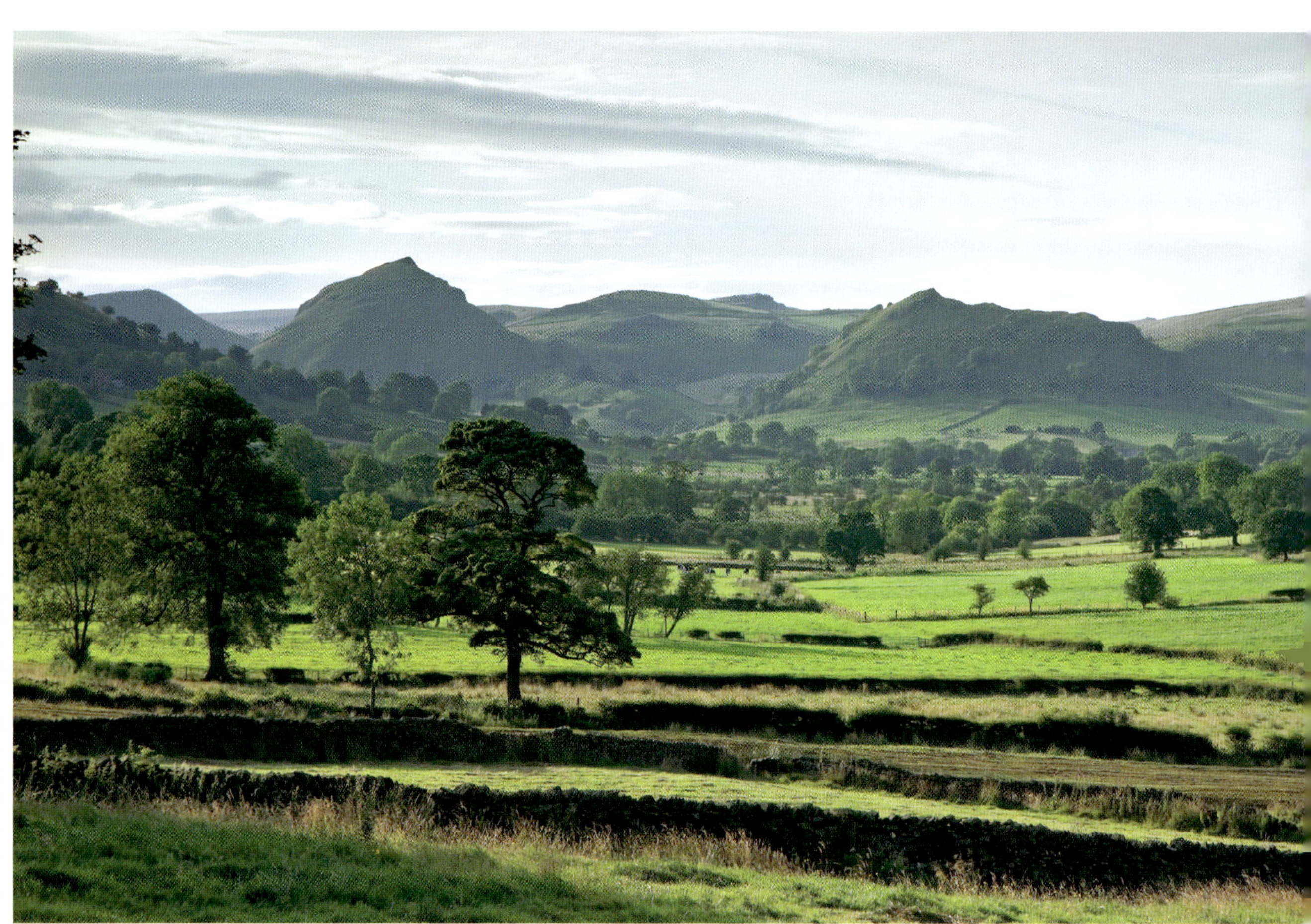

▲ Chrome and Parkhouse Hills near Longnor

Looking north west across the meadows between Longnor and Crowdicote in the Upper Dove valley we see the only true peaks of the Peak District - Chrome Hill to the left and Parkhouse Hill on the right. These were formed from the harder reef limestone as this area was submerged under a shallow tropical sea some 350 million years ago. I've had numerous visits to this spot over the years in order to capture them in the right light – preferably soft side lighting. Unfortunately, it means missing tea and waiting until late, ideally on an evening with a little cloud. Either there is too much cloud or I'm too late and the left hand side is in shadow, or too early and the light is flat. Another tricky one! I'm still not satisfied and will return again, I'm sure.

▶ Field patterns below Grindslow Knoll, Edale

Around the golden hour, sunlight sculpts out the velvety contours of the head of the Edale Valley which lies in the shadow of the Kinder massif. A field barn, one of many on these sheep- grazed pastures, is the main point of interest in this image. Only in late evening of the summer months can we get back-lighting showing up the undulations probably caused by landslips in the unstable shale rock below. The walls show the enclosure fields and the intake land from medieval times.

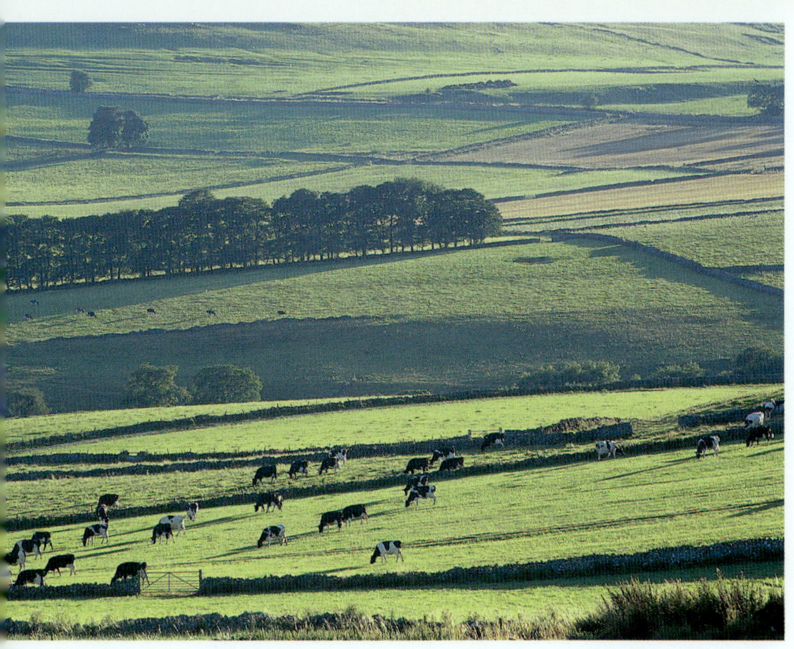

Another 'stripey' picture. Late, low evening light picks up the contours of the landscape, the bright and dark green tones separated by the occasional walls, trees and ploughed fields. Apart from the fantastic light, what particularly attracted me was the way the cows were all lined up in the same direction. I needed to use my long telephoto lens to compress the undulations and enlarge the cows in the composition. I can't quite remember, but I can only assume it was breezy and they all had their backs into wind.

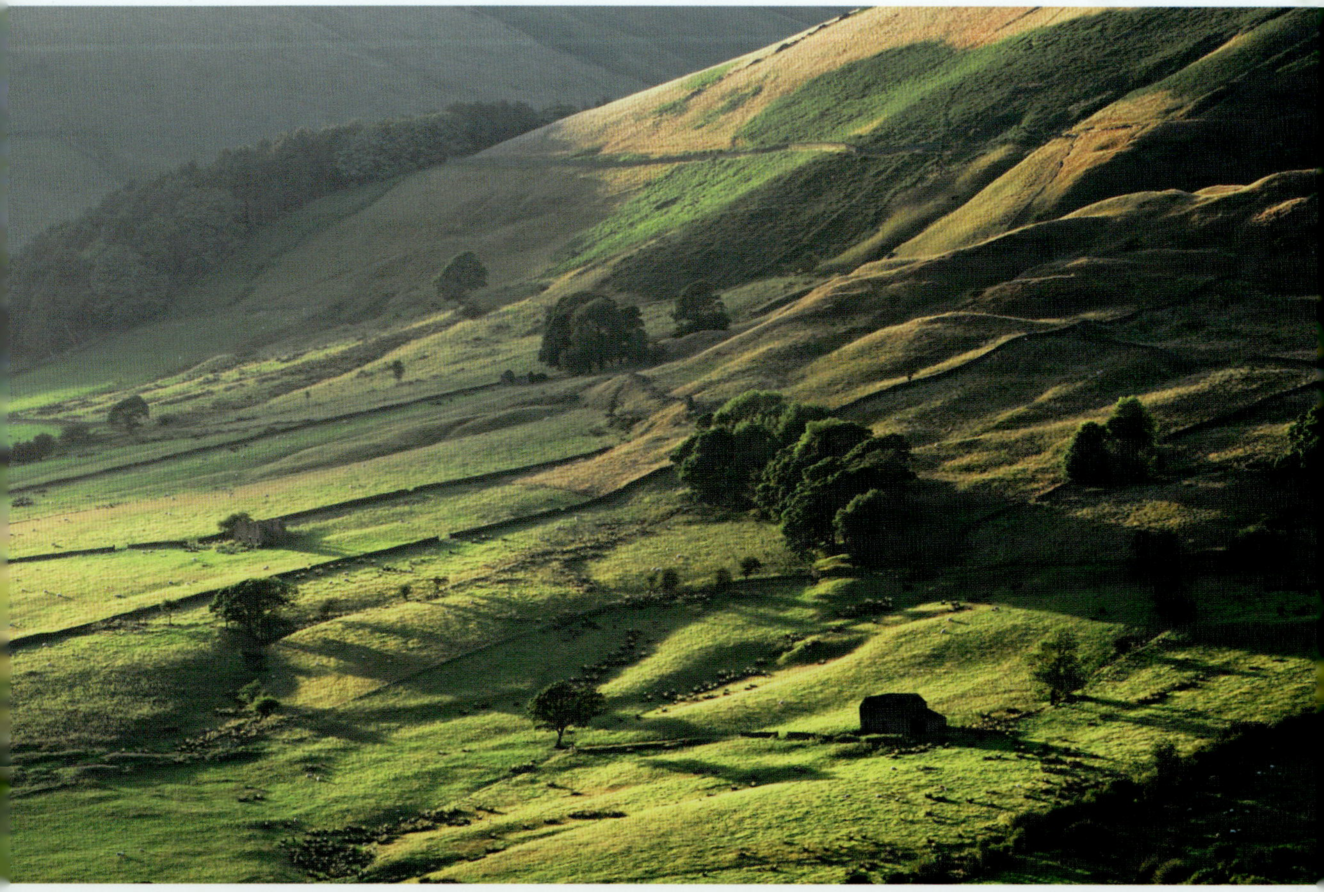

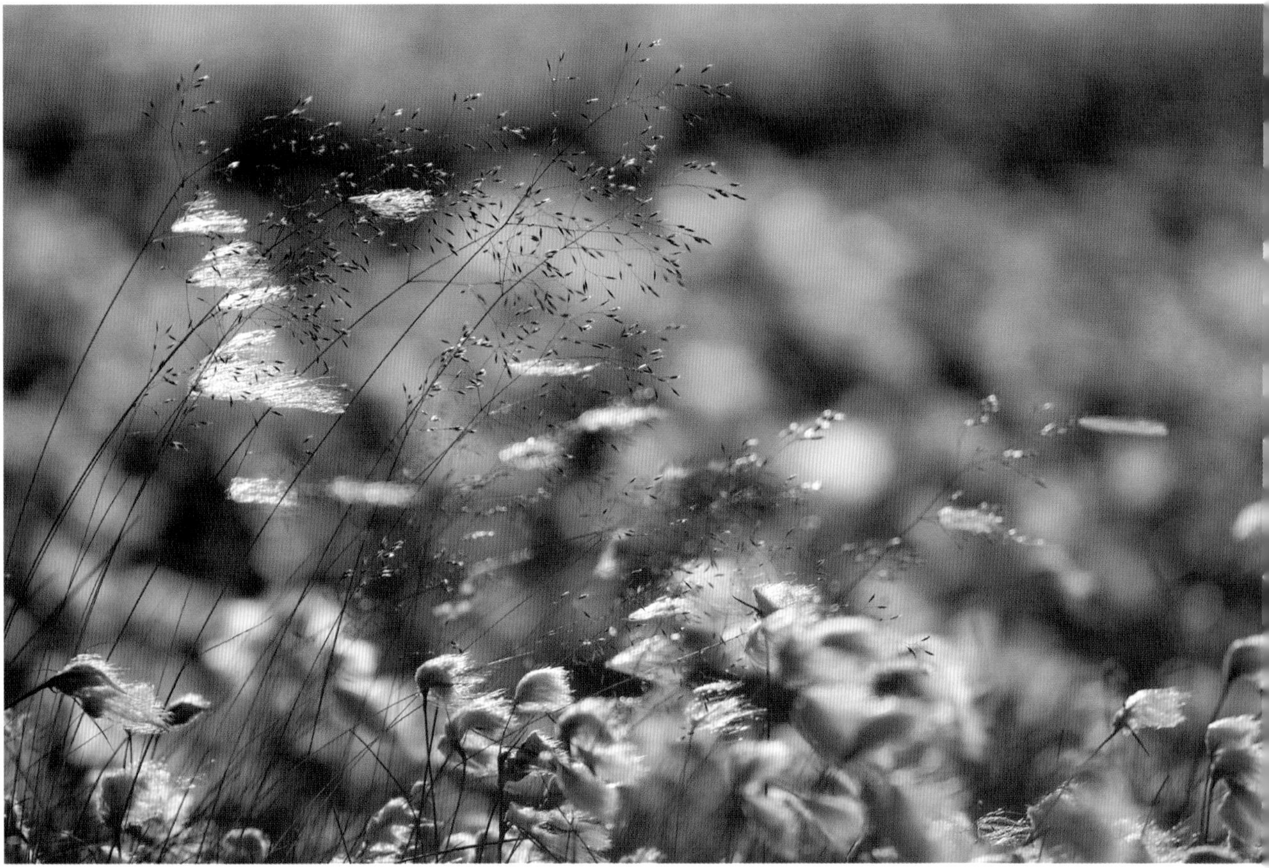

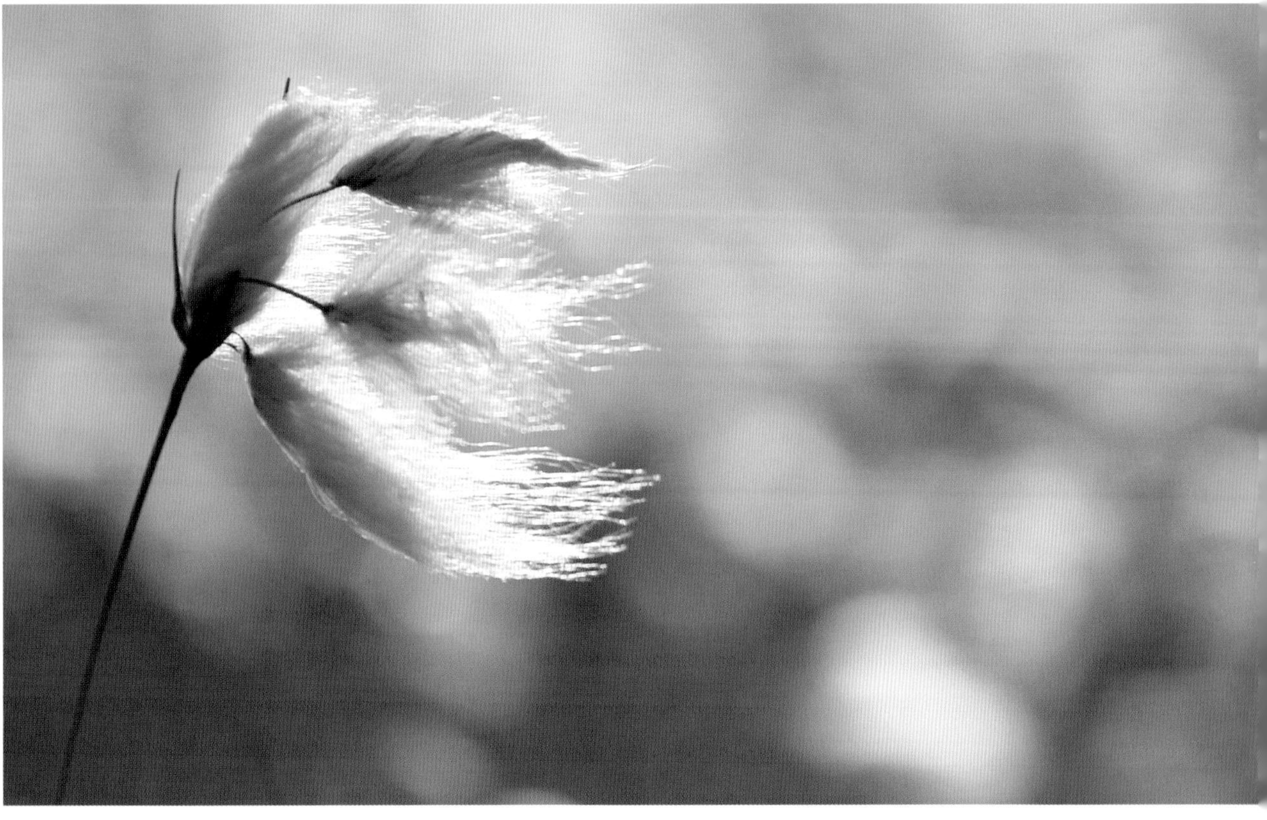

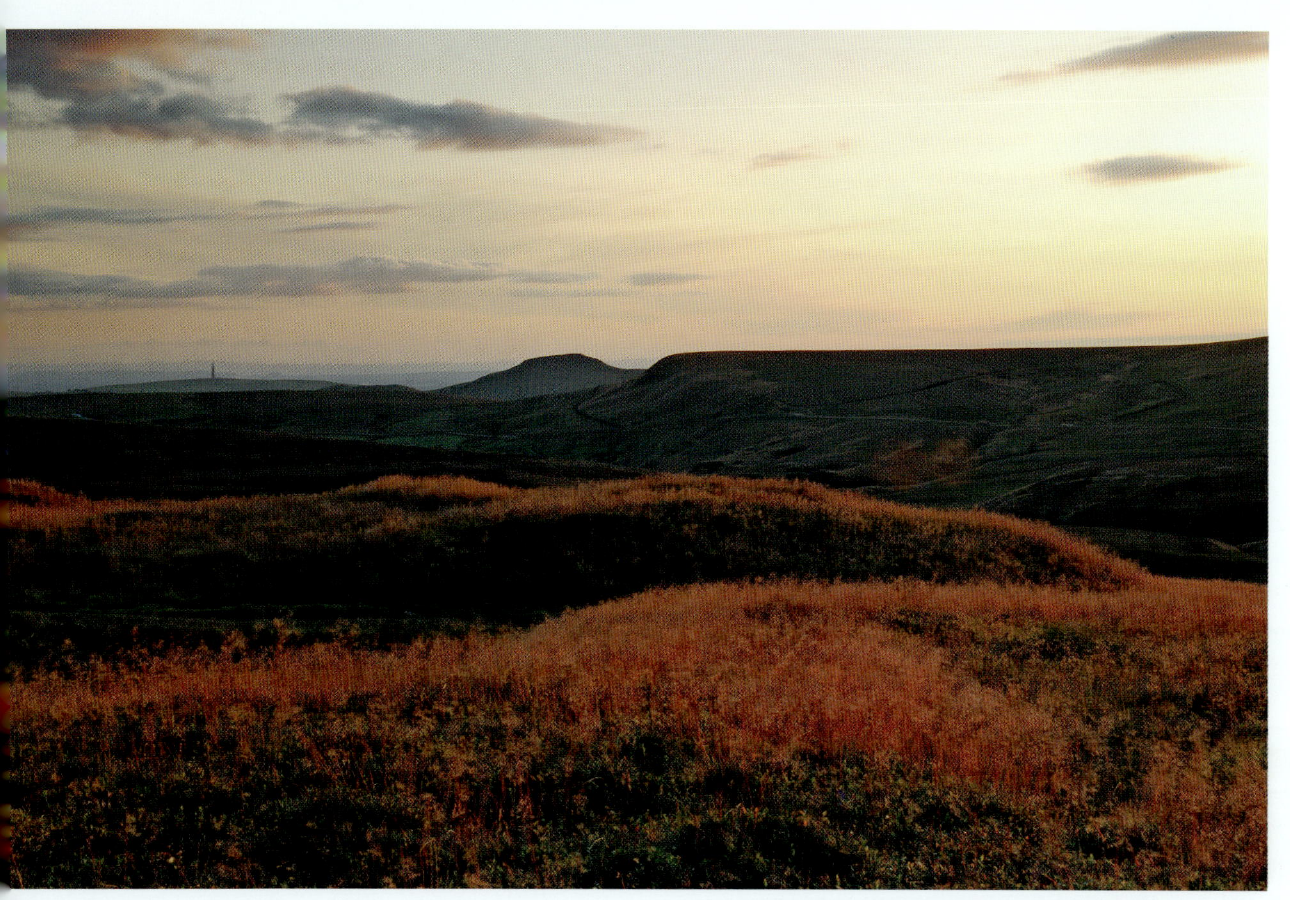

◀ Cotton grass on Axe Edge

Blowing in a stiff breeze, these cotton heads glowed golden in the late evening sunshine. Here on Axe Edge between Buxton and Macclesfield, they carpet the landscape creating a wonderful sight. By August, they are slightly longer and more ragged than when they first emerge on boggy, peaty ground back in June, when they appear just like cotton balls on sticks.

Searching for a sunset on Cheeks Hill, I was drawn towards this beautiful carpet of soft, feathery grass glowing red under the pink sky. The low sun skimmed the surface creating mini valleys and ridges, drawing my eye to the distant Shutlingsloe and the communications tower at Croker Hill. It wasn't easy to get here. What looked like a quick march across the moor ended in a precarious balancing act between tussocks above deep pools of squelchy peat. I zig-zagged my way across the moor, leaping from tuft to tuft trying not to break my ankles. It was getting dark by the time I got back to my car. Luckily, my ankles were intact and I was not sucked under the oozing black bog never to be seen again.

Bamford Edge

Late afternoon light illuminates this gritstone escarpment above the village of Bamford seen below in full autumn glory. Normally, the classic view from here is taken looking north west over the Ladybower Reservoir, but on this evening I turned my camera southwards to capture the way the golden light had picked out every crevice on this weathered gritstone tor. Once again, my trusty sheep wandered into the scene, but not quite in the right places for my liking.

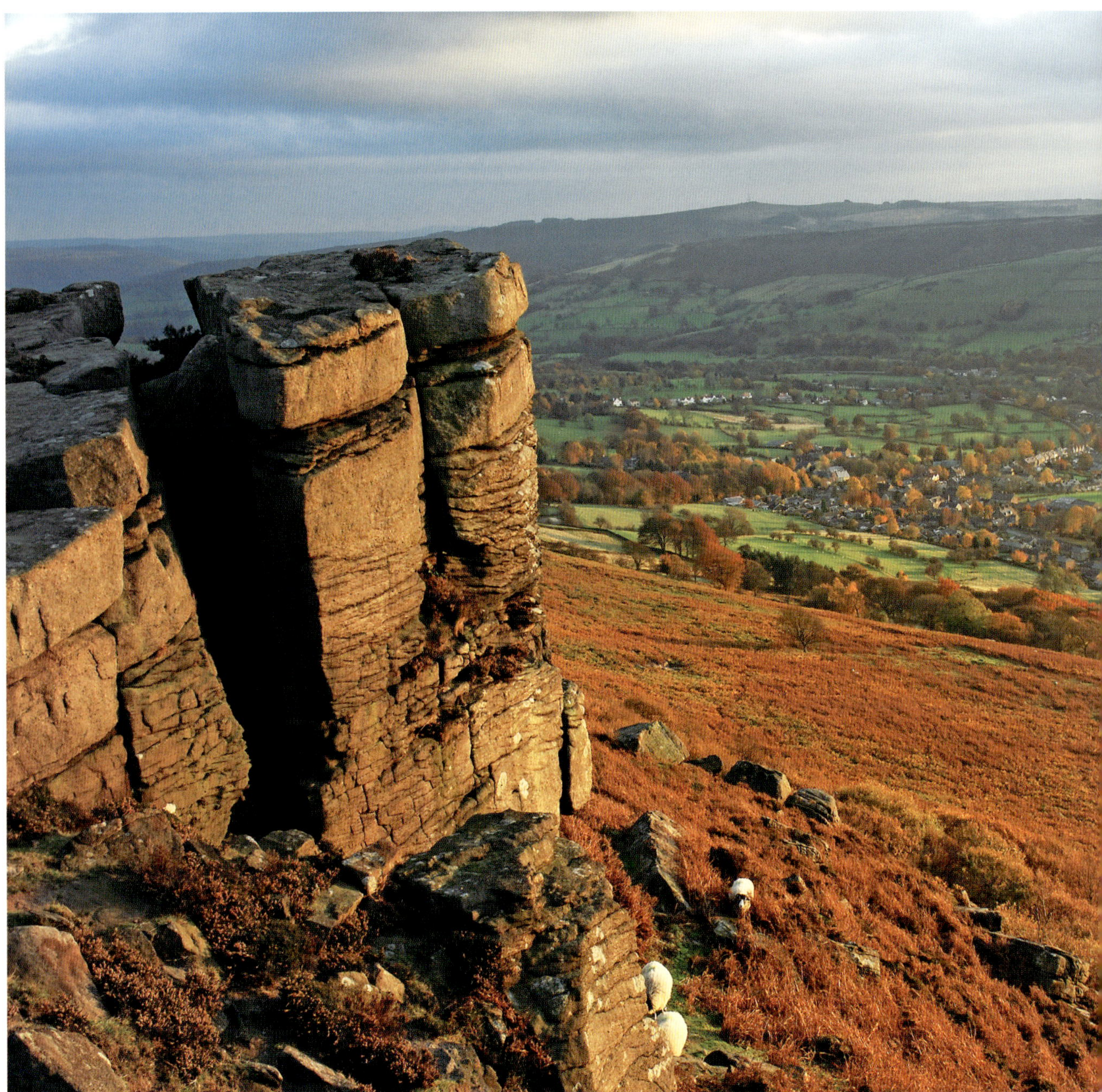

SEPTEMBER–OCTOBER

Sunrise time 06.18–07.09 **Sunset time** 19.59–16.39
Sunrise direction E–ESE **Sunset direction** W–WSW
Autumn Equinox Sep 22nd **Sunrise** 06.55 **Sunset** 19.07

Stormy skies, scarlet berries and fiery bracken

The autumnal equinox on September 22nd is another time of year when the landscape changes rapidly. Those warm, balmy summer days with high pressure and settled conditions still abound at the beginning of September often better than in August. The moorland is still purple with heather, but gradually as the days shorten and get colder, the nuances of autumn creep in. The purple fades to shades of brown, hawthorn berries begin to ripen turning the bushes red and the rowan trees already laden with berries start to be stripped by hungry birds.

By mid October, many deciduous trees begin to turn a yellow, gold, green mix and bracken-clad hillsides and moorlands are russet or fiery orange. Even the ash trees, always last to lose their leaves, look better as their dark branches begin to show through the paler green canopy giving structure and interest in the limestone dales. As the stormy Atlantic lows blow in, there is an explosion of colour and dramatic light of outstanding quality. This is one of my favourite and busiest times. Spoilt for choice, it's often a frantic affair dashing around everywhere trying to capture all this wonderful colour when weather permits. In addition, we begin to get those atmospheric morning mists forming more frequently.

It's all quite exhausting but at least it's over by the early evening and a normal social and family life can resume.

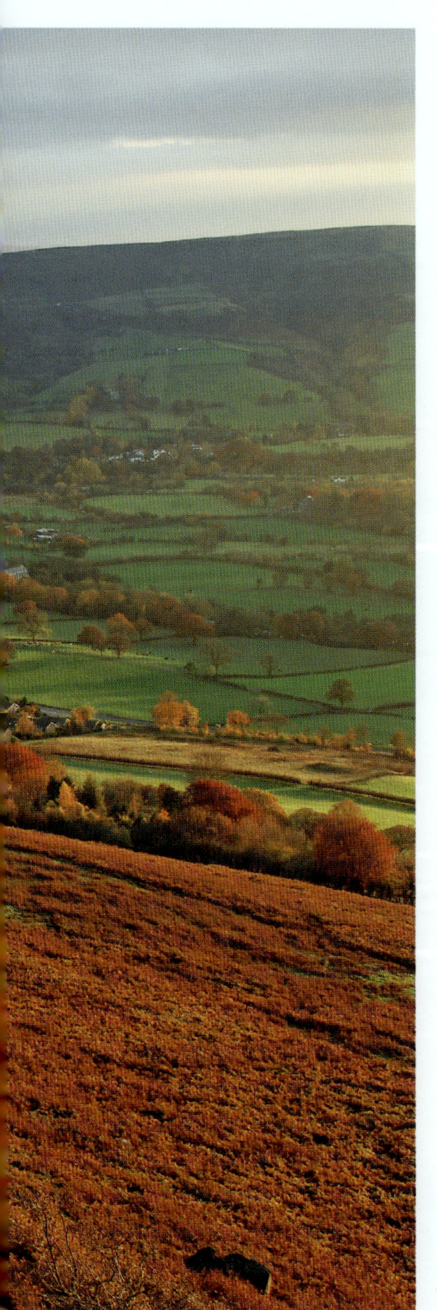

▼ Storm clouds approaching Stanton Moor

The Nine Ladies Stone Circle is surrounded by a lovely
silver birch wood. As storm clouds were fast approaching,
I hurried to photograph it backlit against the stormy sky,
the stark trees on the left adding drama. I also like the
shine on the bracken in the foreground.

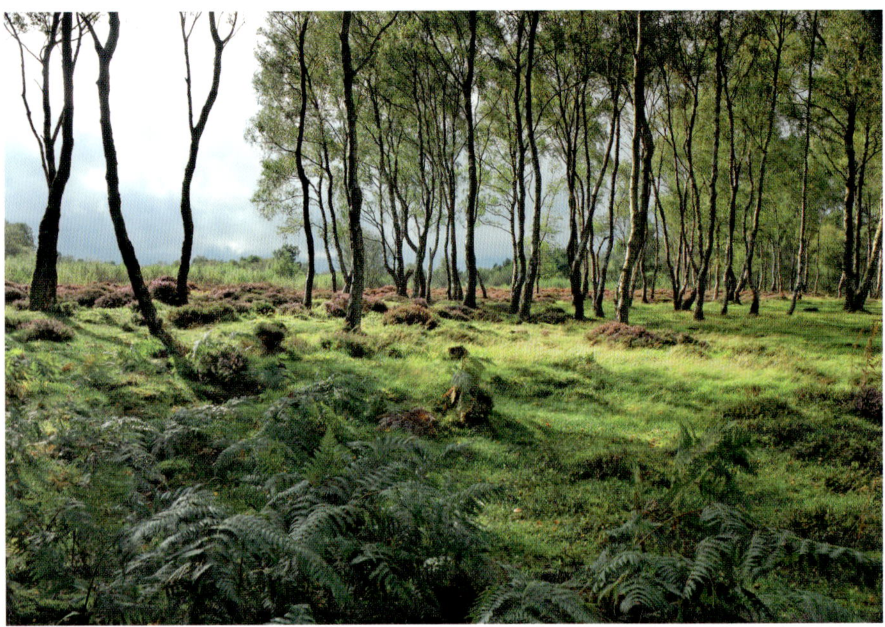

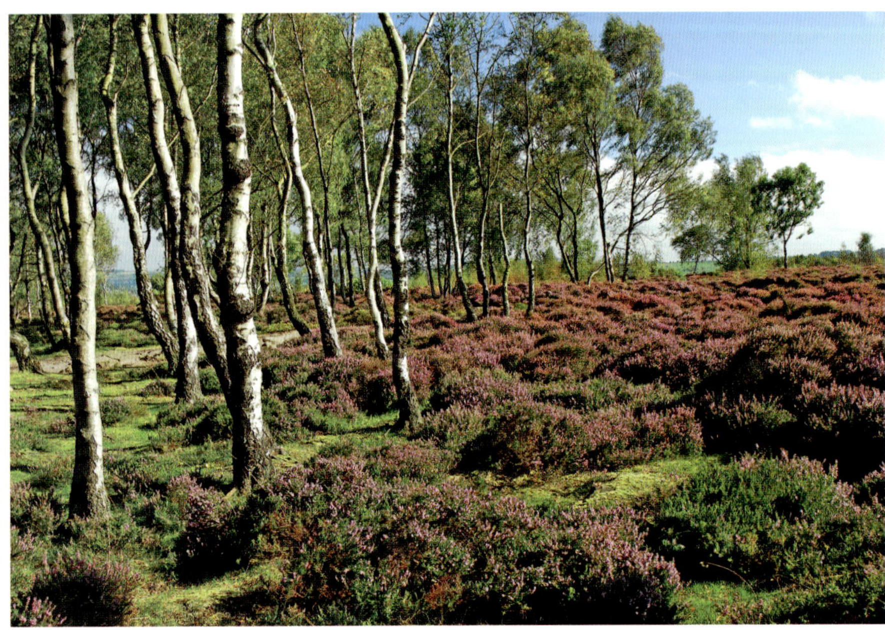

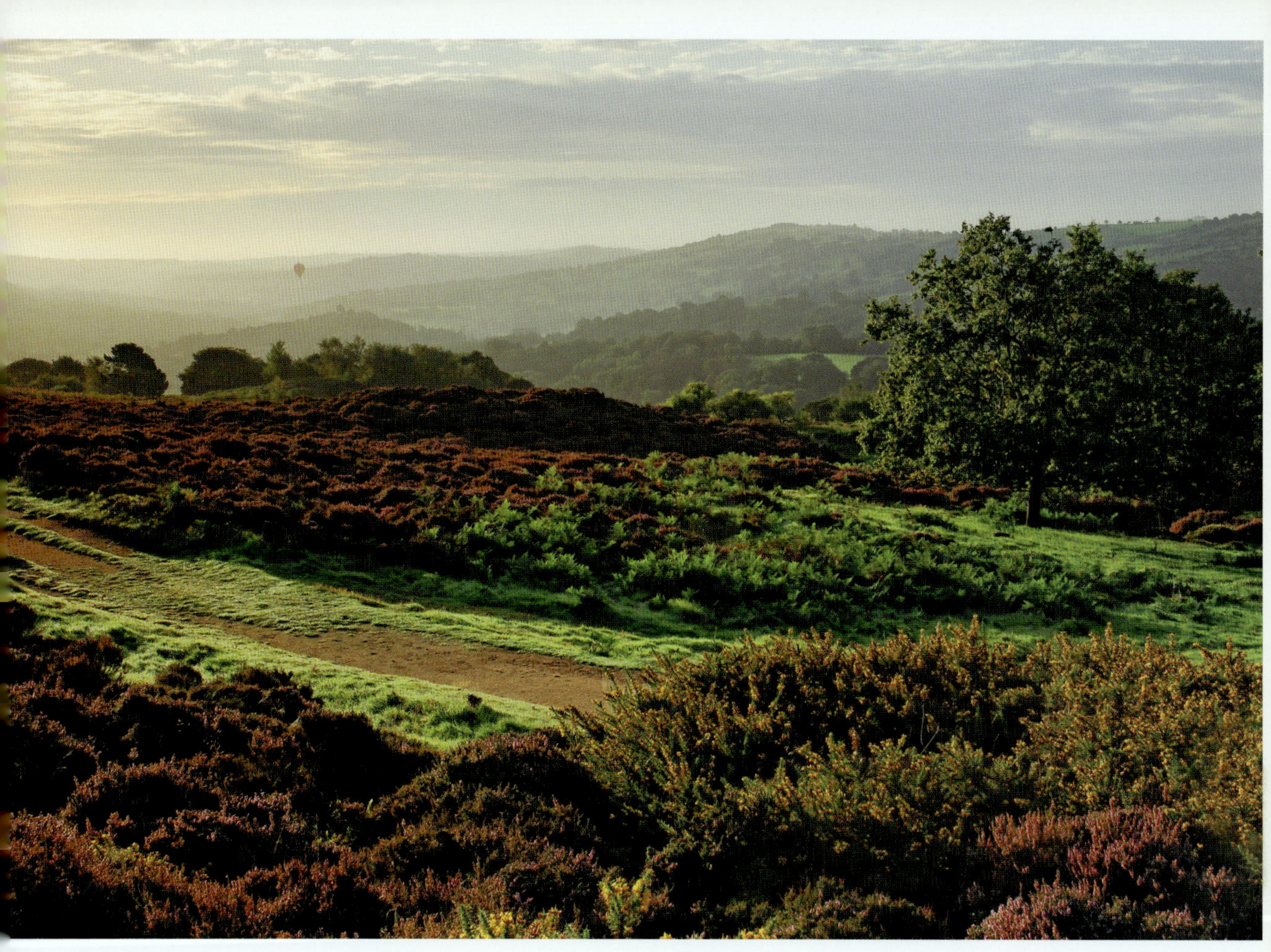

▲ After dawn on Stanton Moor

The gritstone plateau of Stanton Moor near Matlock is a scheduled ancient monument and an important ritual site in the Bronze Age, about 4000 years ago. Since then it has been used for farming, settlement and quarrying. Among the heather and silver birch is the Nine Ladies Stone Circle which is still regularly visited by people carrying out their own rituals and who believe it holds special powers. For 10 years, dedicated protestors camped out in the woods on the edge of the moor, fighting to prevent a nearby quarry expansion. They finally succeeded in 2007 and have now left. Having checked out the heather the afternoon before, I decided to drag myself out for the following dawn knowing that the light would be special at this hour. Here, we look across the heather and gorse towards an old track, probably one of the old packhorse routes. In the distance is a balloon drifting over the moor towards the distant hills around Matlock.

◀ Silver birch woodland near Nine Ladies

Taken in strong afternoon sunshine on the wood and moorland edge on a September afternoon, the heather is still looking good. The silvery trunks of the birch glow as they are lit from the side.

▼ Hawthorn near Parkhouse Hill, Dowel Dale

Dowel Dale is a charming little limestone dale just south of
Buxton and not far from the famous High Edge raceway.
This hawthorn tree blows vigorously in the wind as it points
us up to the steep reef limestone slopes to the summit of
Parkhouse Hill, one of the few real peaks in the Peak District.
I remember setting up my tripod on the lower slopes of
Chrome Hill to get this precise composition, which was rather
tricky on the steep, rocky terrain. After slipping down a few
times, I finished covered in mud, but pleased I'd found
a new angle on this dramatic little peak.

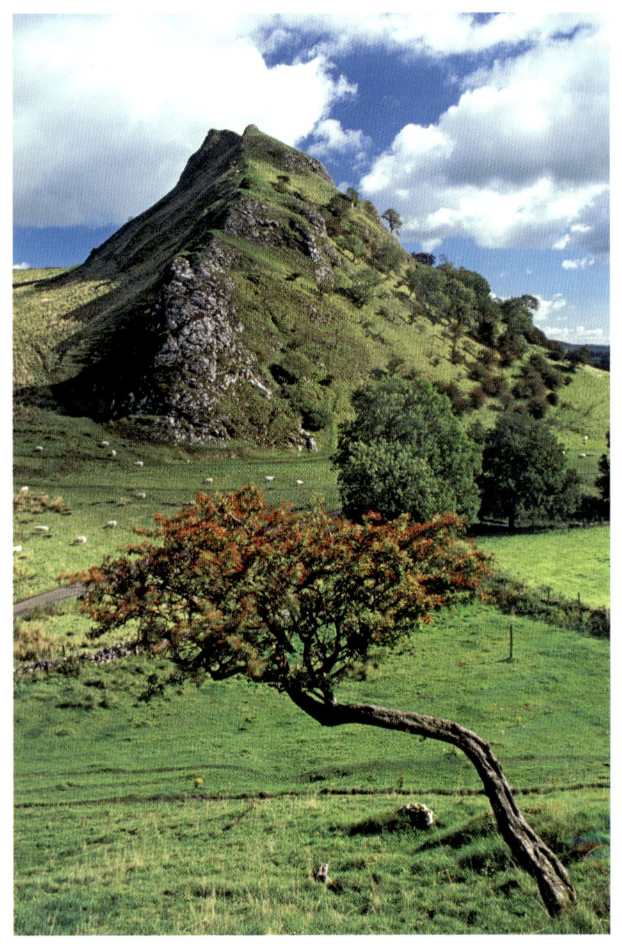

▶ Shadows over Winnats Pass

Winnats Pass near Castleton is one of the most spectacular
reef limestone features of the Peak. With its towering rocky
pinnacles above grassy slopes, this long canyon is now
thought to have been an under-sea channel through tropical
coral reefs formed around 350 million years ago. Here, I am
standing above the pass on precarious ground buffeted by
the strong wind and updraft from the steep slopes below.
Interesting shadows cast from the craggy pinnacles along
the ridge add drama. I would have liked to have stood on
the limestone crag we see in the middle to get a different
composition but, this time, my fear of heights beat my desire
for a better picture. The tiny sheep on the top right gives us
some sense of scale.

▶ Bunster Hill and Dovedale from Thorpe Cloud

From the perilously steep slopes of Thorpe Cloud I am looking almost vertically down into the popular but crowded Dovedale, taking care not to topple over or dislodge any loose stones onto anyone below (which someone did to me recently from here). The shadow formed from Bunster Hill follows the course of the River Dove along this beautiful ash-wooded valley with its limestone caves, crags and pinnacles. On the far horizon at the same height as myself is the village of Alstonefield. Taken earlier in the day with the sun directly behind me would have given a flat, featureless scene. It's the shadows that make this image. The tiny specks in the valley below are people giving the picture a sense of scale.

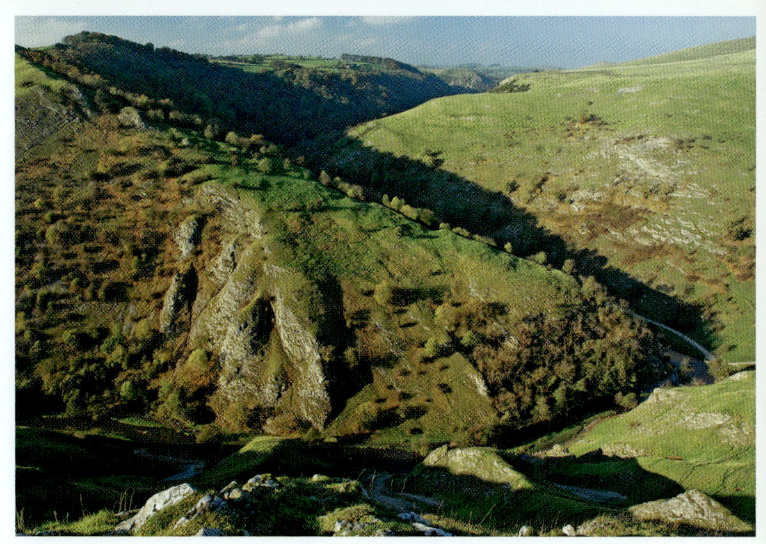

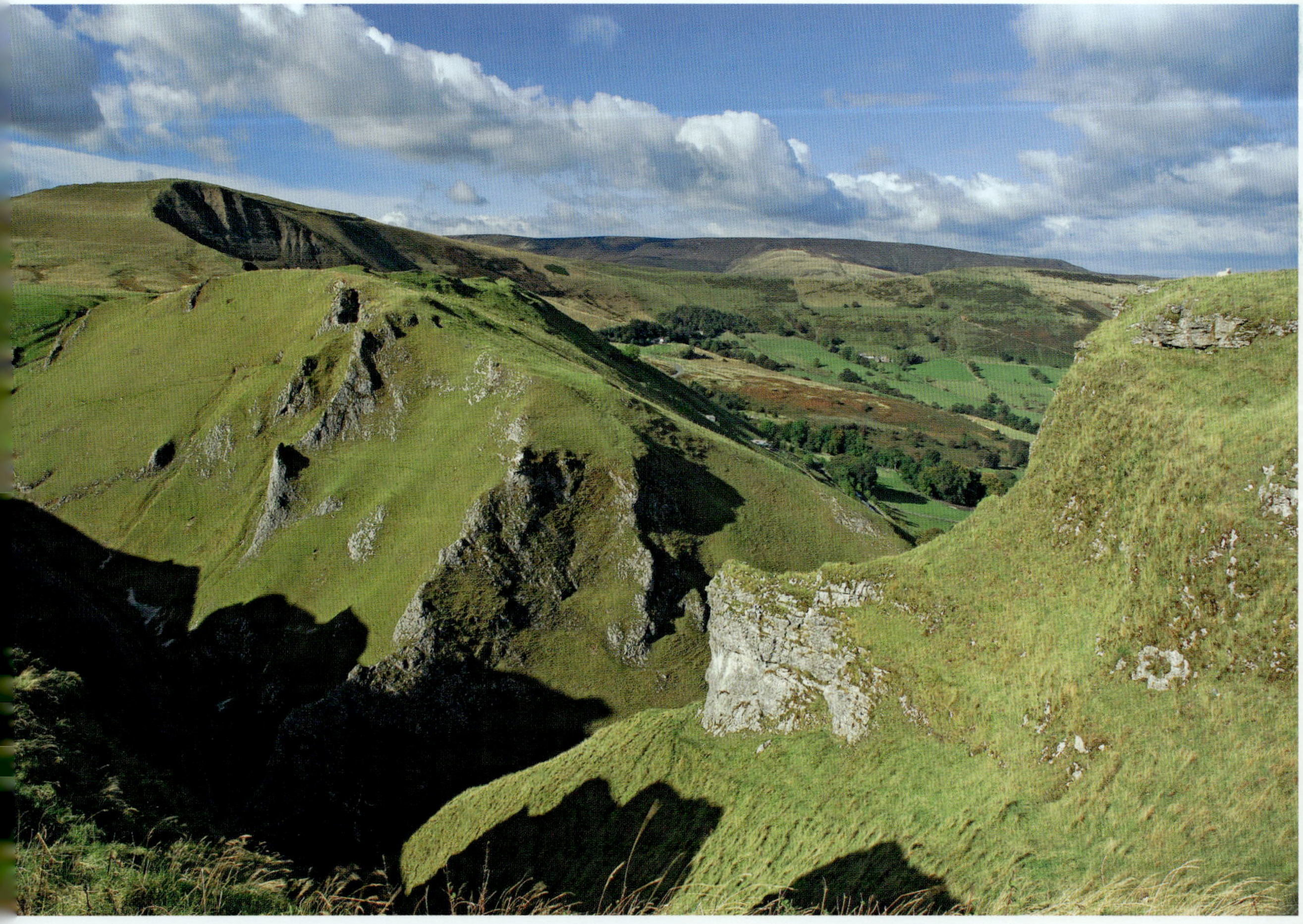

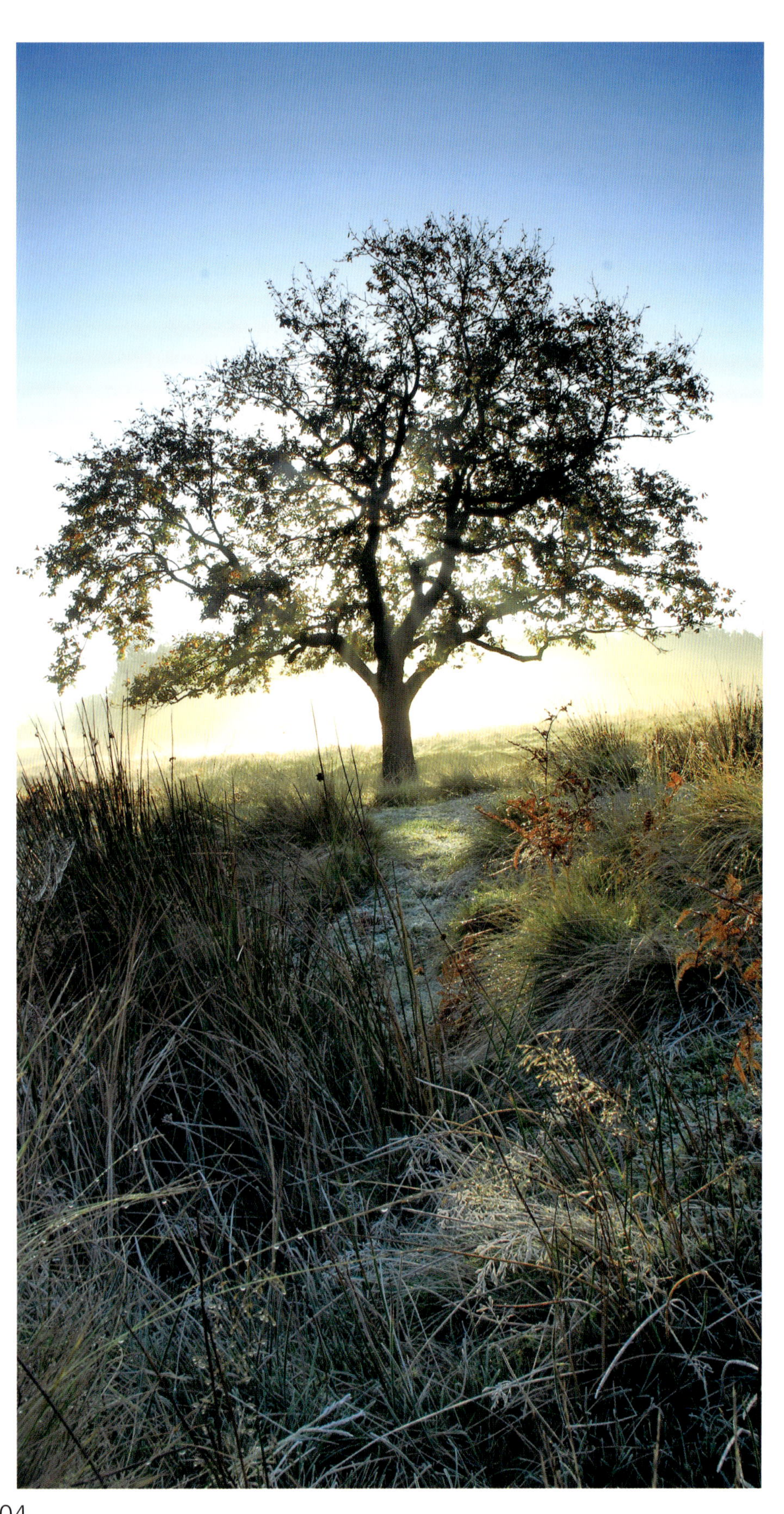

◀ Morning frost and dew on the Longshaw Estate

Taken on the same morning as the sunbeams opposite, there was an incredible dew on the grasses twinkling in the morning sunlight and pockets of frost still surviving in the shadows. The mist had almost cleared from this tree, so any chance of more sunbeams had gone but I perservered with the tricky lighting, shooting straight into the sun to get the atmosphere I wanted.

Chasing sunbeams and sheep on the Longshaw Estate ▼

Looking out one morning I noticed a low-lying mist in the distance, but it was clear and sunny above. I'd long imagined capturing sunbeams through a misty woodland, but had never quite managed to be in the right place at the right time. Maybe this morning I would be lucky, so I set off in search of the right level of mist to create this phenomenon. If I was too low and the mist too thick the sun would not penetrate; too high and there would not be enough mist to give the 'beamy' effect. I headed for the National Trust's Longshaw Estate above Grindleford where I could see the mist was the right sort of thickness. I chased sunbeams around the woodland and happened to bump into this sheep which popped out from behind a tree. Careful stalking and I managed to capture him standing in a beam of light, his condensed breath in the cool air adding to my composition. I couldn't have asked for a better model. It was a shame about the scruffy bits of thistle everywhere, but you can't have everything.

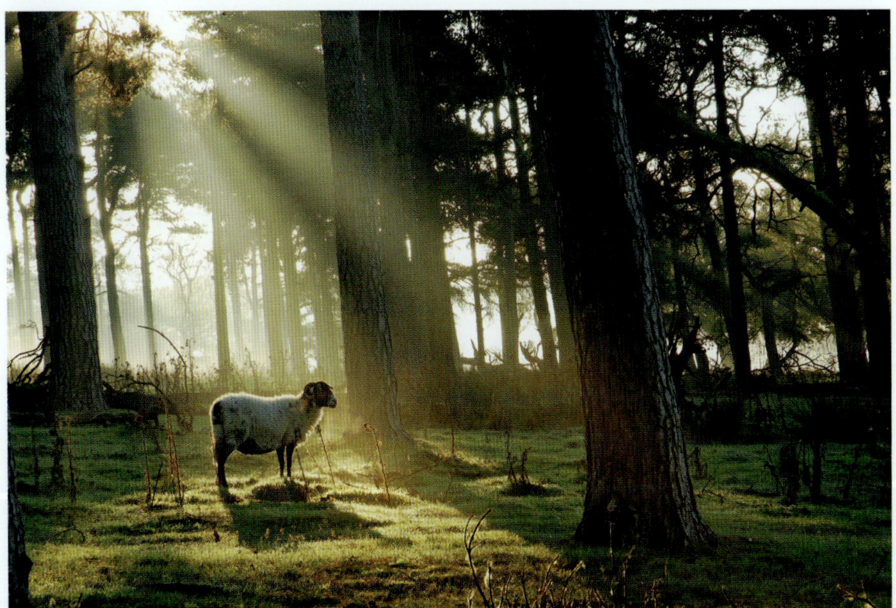

▶ Cranberry Bed

One of my favourite places away from the crowds is high in the Upper Derwent Valley just north of Slippery Stones bridge where I wander for peace and solitude. Looking down onto Cranberry Bed from Swine Side, I noticed the River Derwent like a ribbon of light snaking its way through the valley, the undulations sculpted out by the low afternoon October light. By the river we see a few surviving native oak, birch and rowan scattered around.

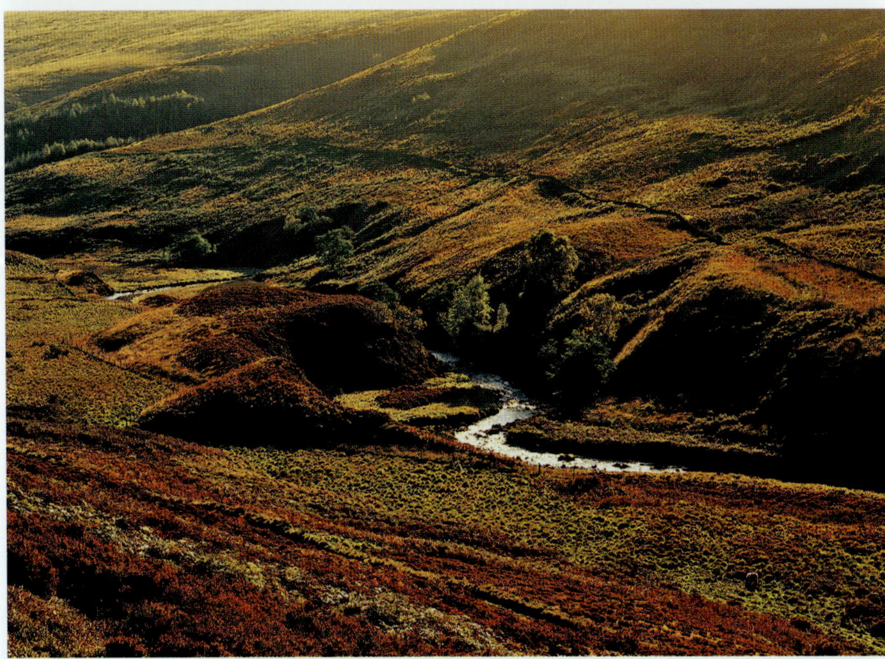

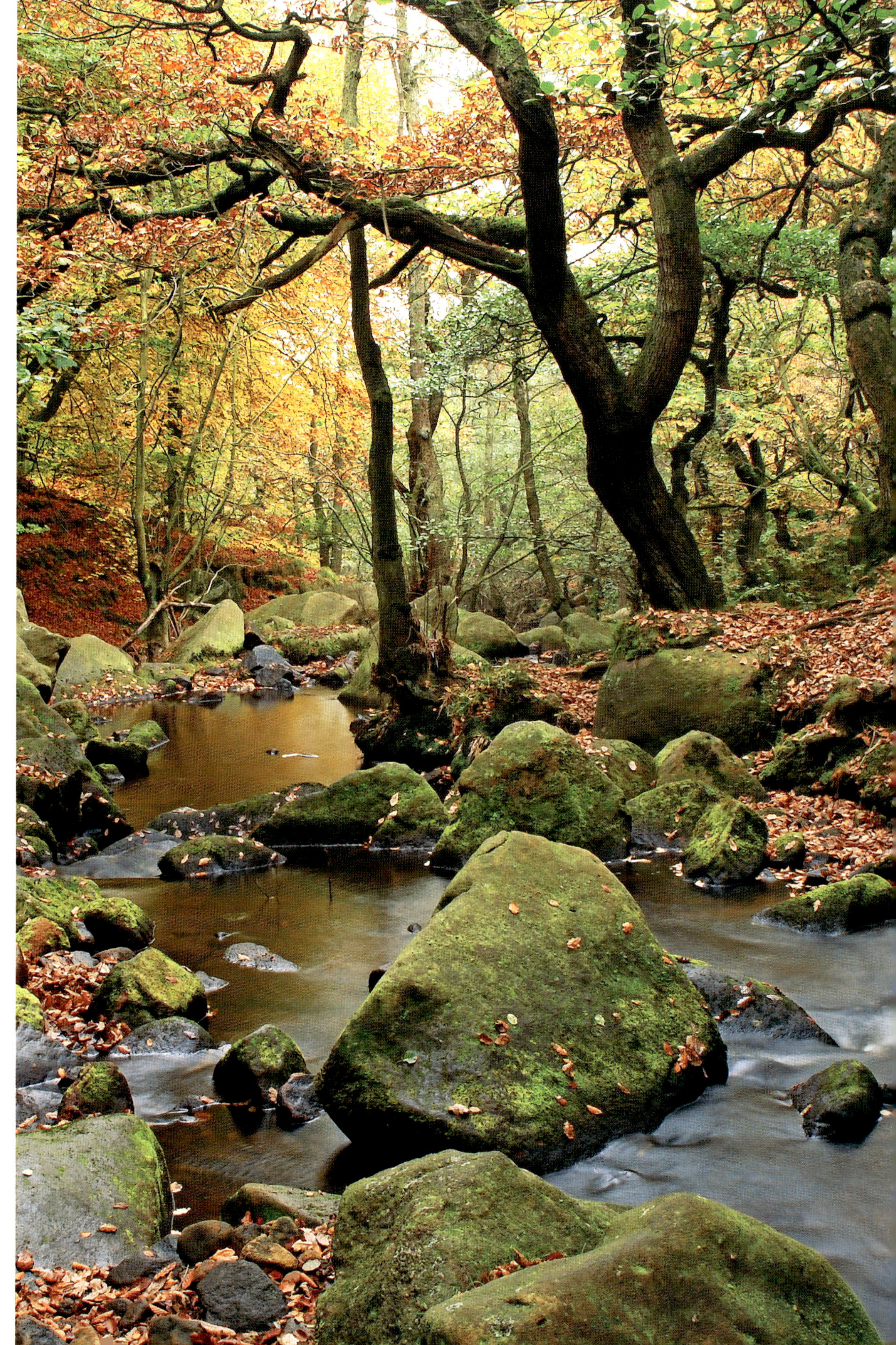

▼ Millstone and gnarled beech tree in Yarncliffe Wood

It was the spooky old tree roots crawling over the boulder that initially caught my eye back in the late 1990's (see page 48–49). This is another of those images which took me years of repeat visits before I managed to catch some half decent light falling on this abandoned millstone in 2004. When I arrived, the light was over in minutes so I had to work quickly. Since then, I've been back in all weathers and seasons and never experienced the right light again. Sometimes I think it would be much easier and less time consuming to be a painter. Some people might think I scattered those beech leaves over the millstone, but they had fallen naturally and the rain had enhanced their colour. If I had tried, I would have made it look slightly odd I'm sure. In my opinion, photographers, artists, and even Photoshop can't compete with the beauty of nature.

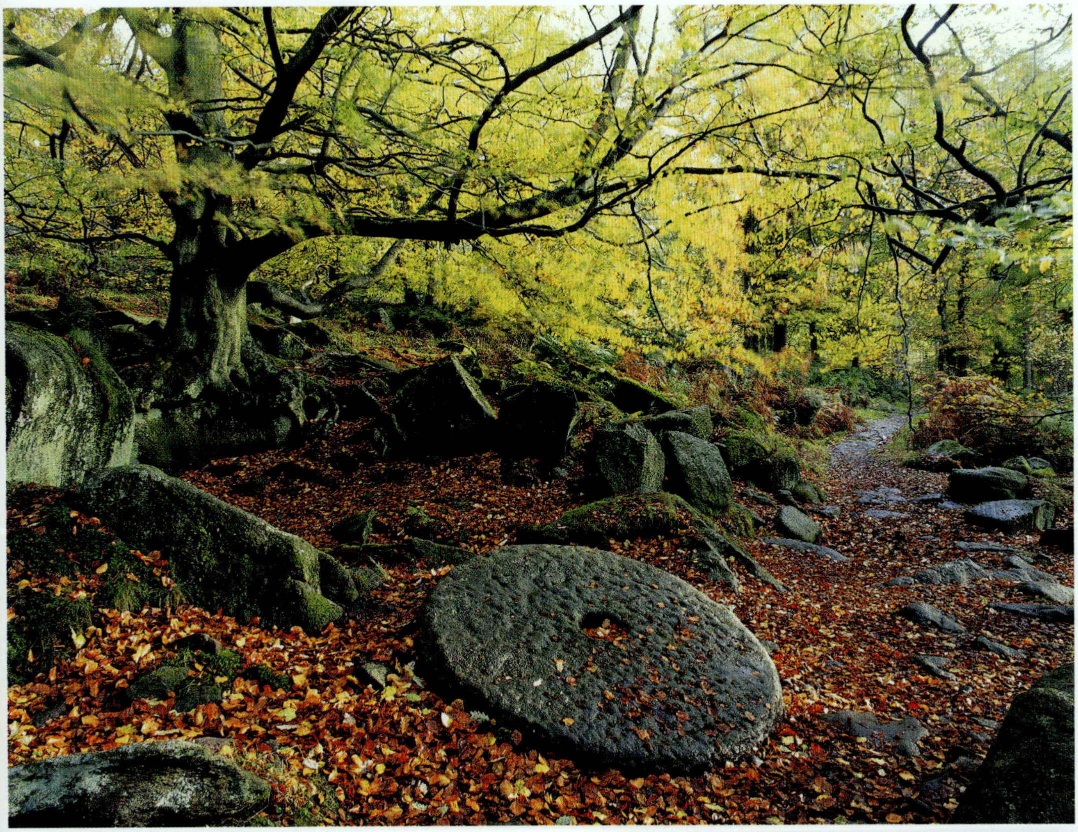

◀ Padley Gorge ▶

This must be one of the most popular photographic locations in the Peak at this time of year as it has endless opportunities for stunning images. It's a real gem with Padley Brook tumbling and cascading over gritstone boulders through semi-natural oak and beech woodland, the autumn leaves appearing to snow down forming a golden carpet. Peaty water coming down from high on the moors cascades over one of the many rocky falls in the gorge. Under the damp, dark canopy, velvety green moss grows over the boulders, contrasting well with the freshly fallen golden beech leaves.

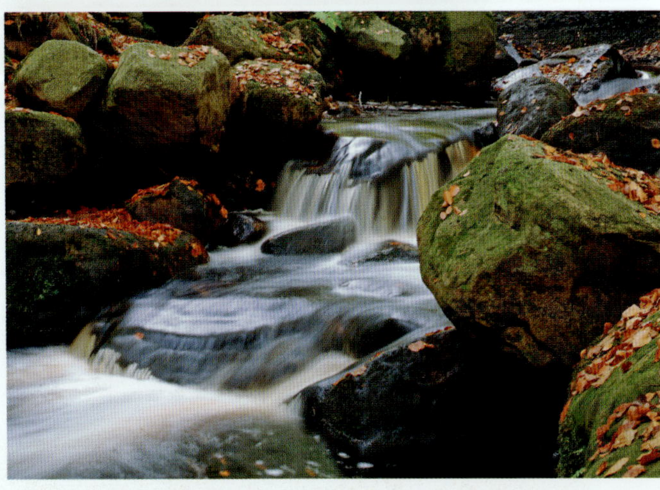

▼ View from High Wheeldon towards Chrome Hill

There are magnificent views all around from the conical summit of High Wheeldon (1,384 feet/422m), near Earl Sterndale. We are looking along a ridge of reef limestone across Aldery Cliff, Hitter Hill, Parkhouse Hill and Chrome Hill, (locally known as the 'Dragon's Back') in the distance. I got here with only seconds to spare as the light went patchy after this and I hung around for another hour on this blustery hill top waiting for better conditions. It was my last chance to catch the autumn leaves, now hanging on by a thread at the end of this wet and windy October.

▶ Monsal Dale

Standing at the honeypot of Monsal Head looking north west down the valley towards Cressbrook, the little village clings to the steep slopes above the River Wye in a manner not dissimilar to those on Alpine pastures. On this windy October afternoon, the clouds were scudding across the sky casting interesting shadows across the landscape, with no two images being the same. The colours and quality of light on this occasion gave the image the quality of a painting, something I always strive to achieve. Being useless myself in the art of painting, I try to do it through my photography.

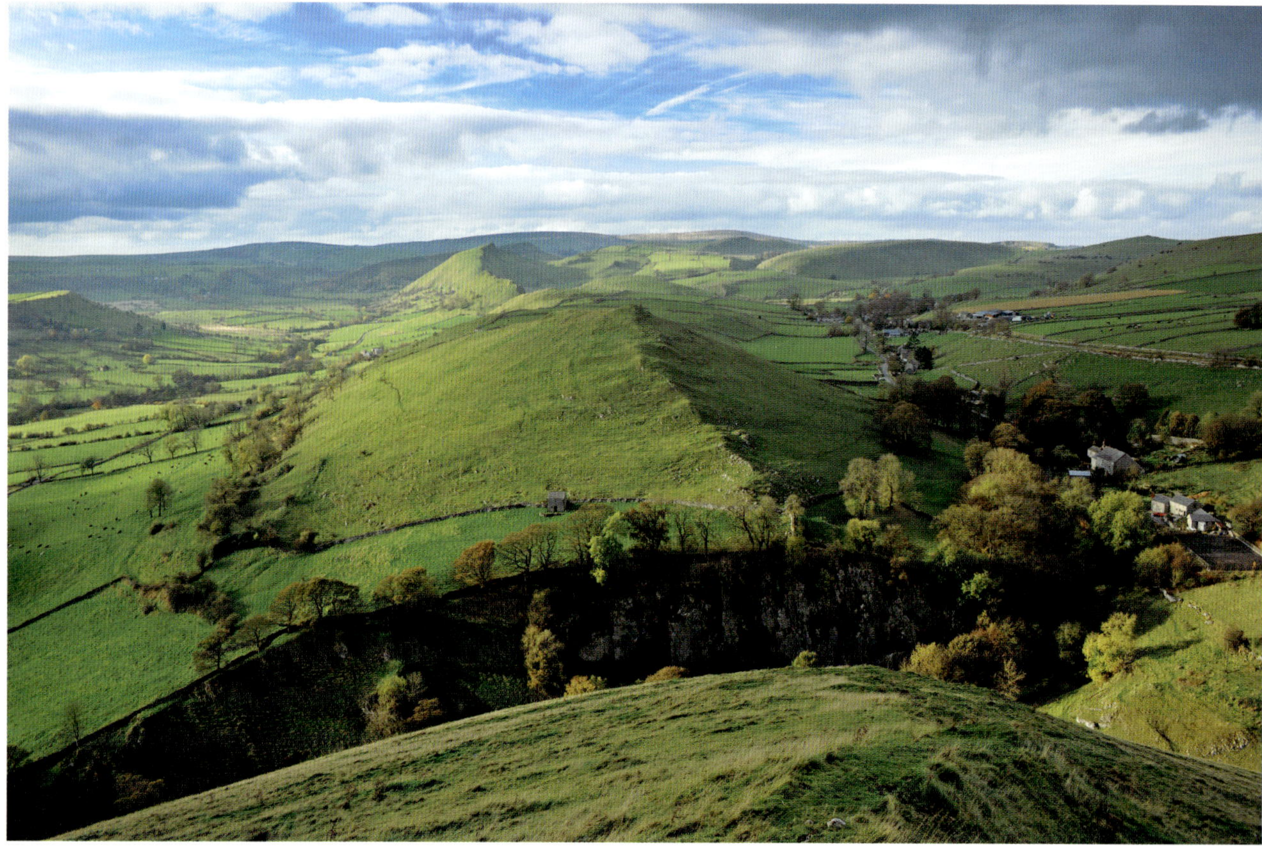

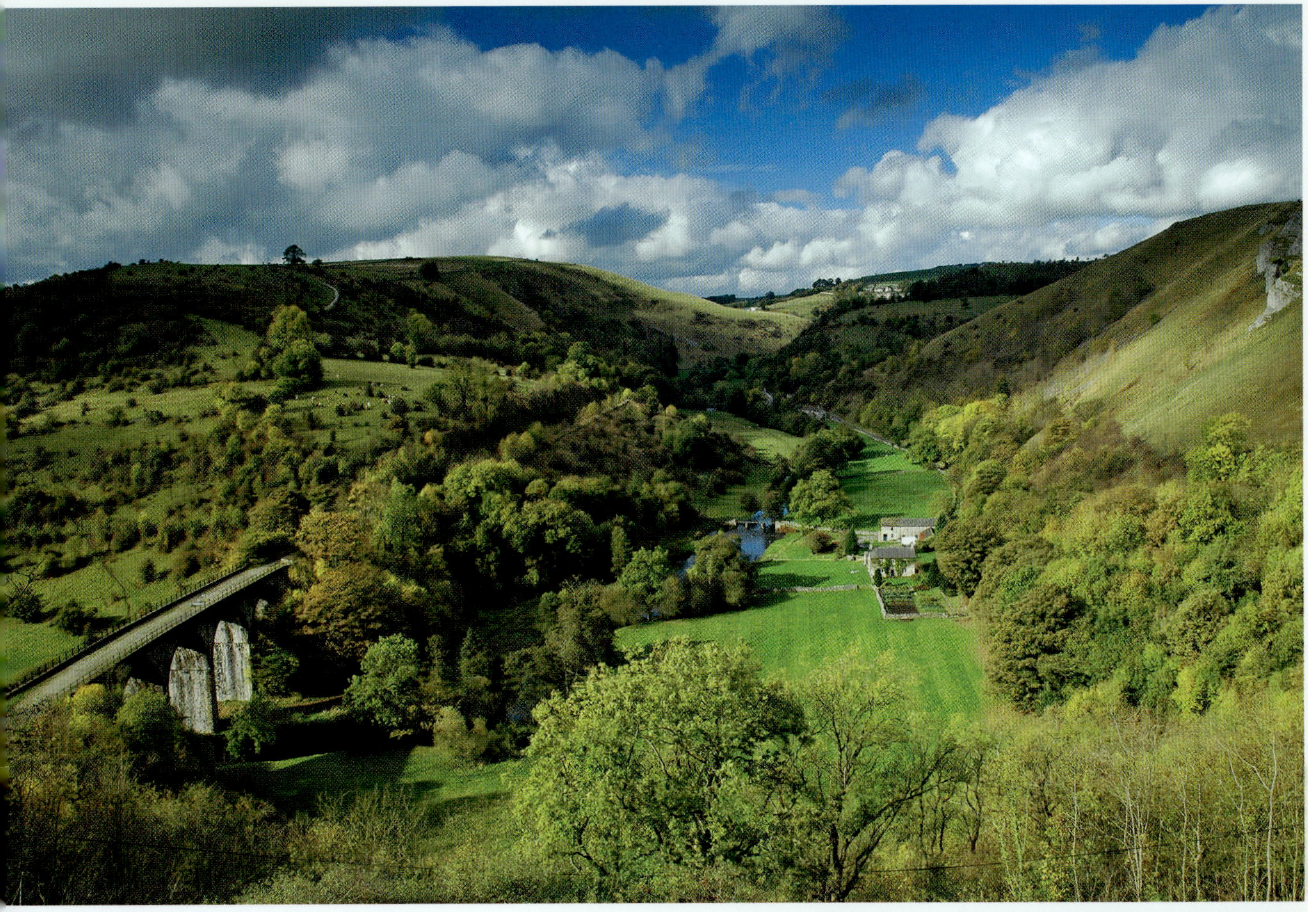

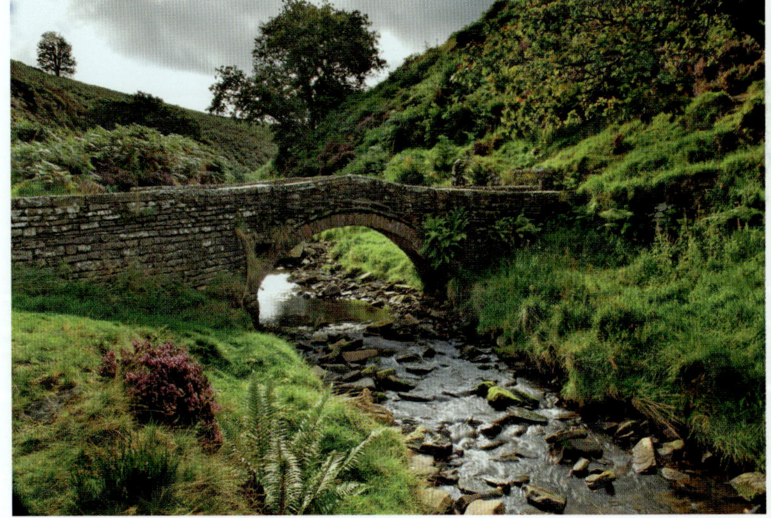

▶ Packhorse Bridge, Goyt Valley

This little packhorse bridge over the River Goyt was once used by salt traders, but not in its current location near Goytsclough quarry. Massive changes came to the valley in 1938 when Stockport's increasing demand for water forced the building of the Fernilee, and 30 years later, the Errwood Reservoirs. As well as rebuilding the little bridge further upstream, it also meant the demolition of Errwood Hall, the beautiful Victorian home of the wealthy Grimshawe family who chose this remote location to build the hall in 1830. It also saw the end to the thriving farming community dating back to the 1500's, a gunpowder factory, paintworks and a railway line. However, the Upper Goyt Valley is still beautiful and the little bridge backlit by the early morning sun sits well in its relatively new home.

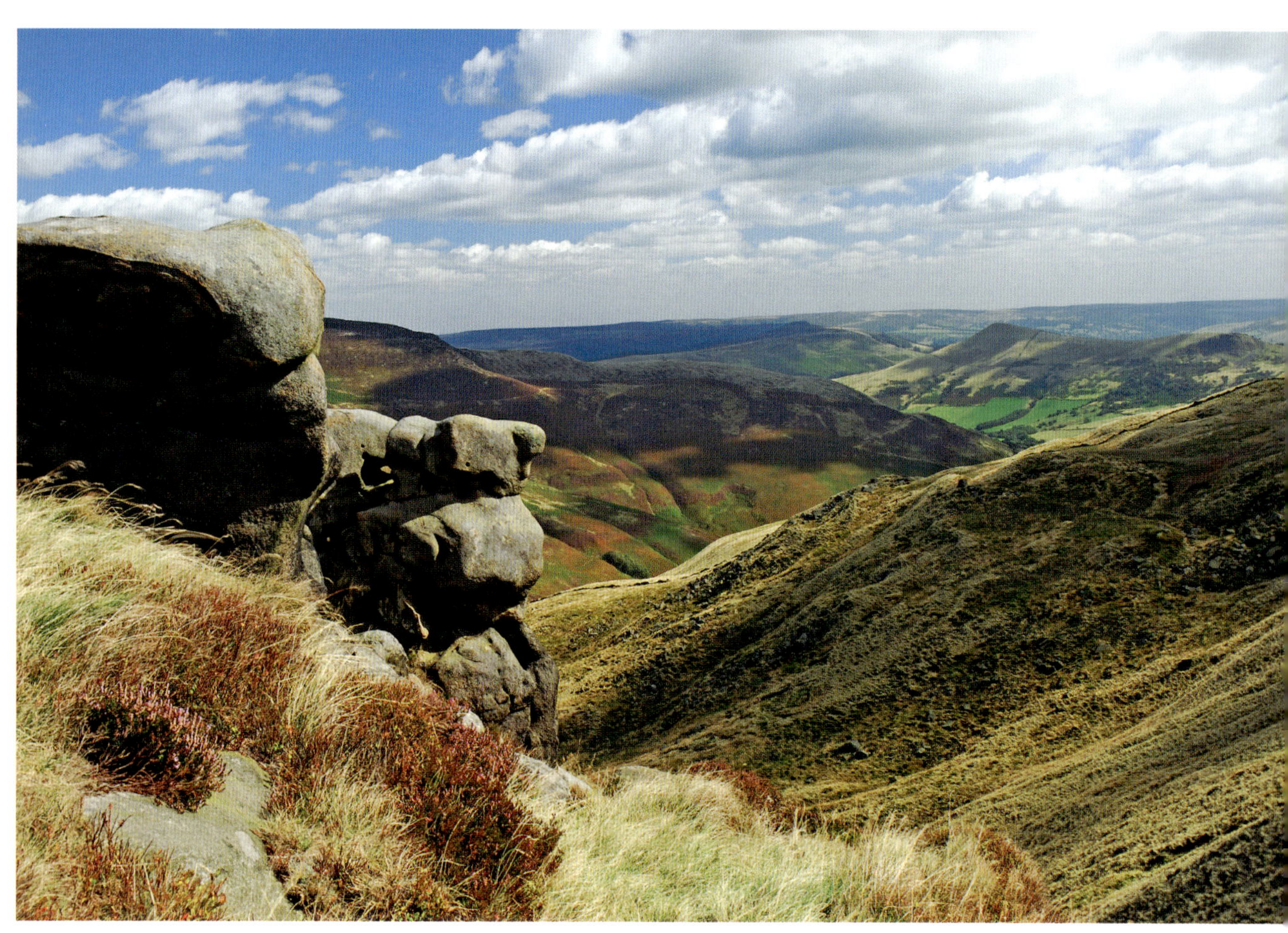

▲ Looking down into Grindsbrook from the Kinder plateau

After struggling up the rocky scramble at the head of Grindsbrook with heavy camera bags, I popped out the top on the Kinder Plateau at about 1,800 feet/550m near these amazing wrinkled gritstone formations. Here, I am looking back down the valley towards Back Tor, Lose Hill and Win Hill in the far distance. Initially attracted by the rocks, I then noticed the many triangles formed from the soft grasses, side-lit rocks and shadows from the scudding clouds across the valley which all help in the composition of a more interesting image.

▶ Last light on Robin Hood's Stride

Alternatively known as Mock Beggar's Hall, this gritstone outcrop stands on Harthill Moor near the Harthill Stone Circle. Charging there for a sunset, I could see heavy cloud encroaching from the west. Unfortunately, when I got there it was covered in people scrambling around enjoying the views. By the time they had left, the sun had dropped into the cloudbank. However, I could just see a chink of clear sky below the cloud, and from past experience I knew that these conditions can be fruitful, so I waited. No light explosion happened, but beneath the cloud the last rays of sunlight emerged and lit the top of the crag in a pinky hue for a few seconds. Now peaceful and silent, just myself and a couple of climbers were there to witness it including the one on the top. Quite magical.

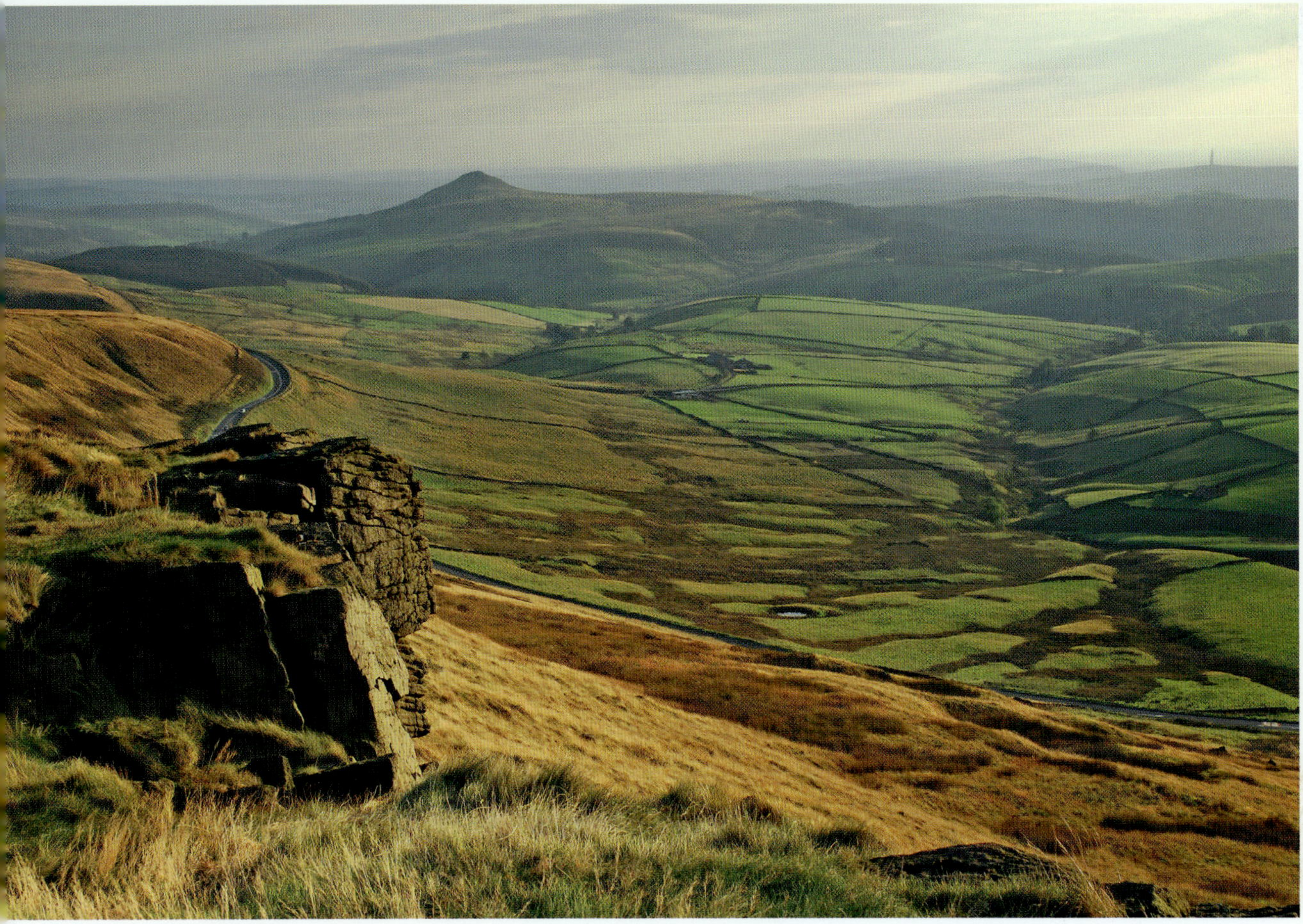

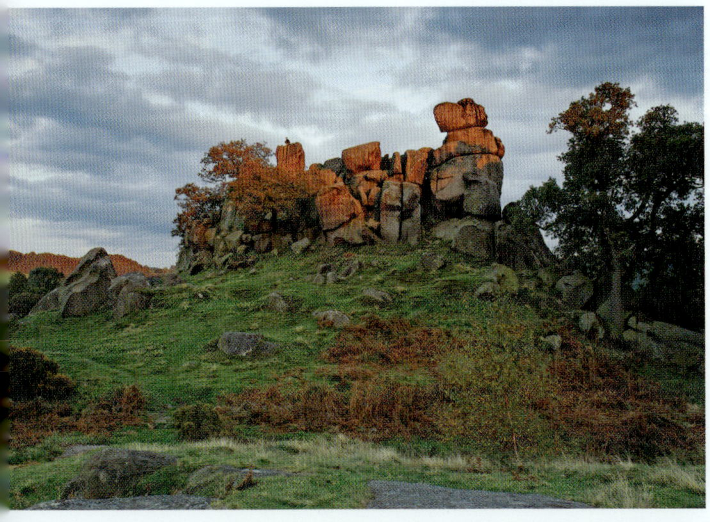

▲ View from Shining Tor

Standing on the sandstone summit of Shining Tor in Cheshire at 1,834 feet/559m, we are looking south west towards Shutlingsloe and Macclesfield Forest across the notorious A537 Cat and Fiddle Buxton to Macclesfield road, classed as one of the most dangerous in Britain. In winter at a height of 1,640 feet/500m near its summit, it's certainly prone to ice and drifting snow but I suspect it's the long sweeping bends that encourage people to use it as a race track that's the cause of most accidents. Shining Tor rises up from the Goyt Valley in the east to form a lovely ridge with Cat's Tor to the north. Boggy, wild moorland gives way to tamer, undulating green fields which are picked out well in the September evening light. I'm already too late in the year to get the sunlight on these foreground rocks. For this I must come back one evening next summer.

Stormy day on Stanage

Stanage Edge has to be one of the most spectacular places to be on a stormy afternoon. The west facing four-mile/6km long gritstone outcrop reputed to be one of the longest inland cliffs in Britain is famous for its many climbing routes, some pioneered back in the 1890's by climbers such as JW Puttrell. There are spectacular views down into the Hope Valley and towards Win Hill and Lose Hill. Here, we are looking north towards the Derwent Valley where Crook Hill and Whinstone Lee Tor are caught in a fleeting patch of sunlight. The clearest light is often on post cold front days when the weather can be stormy and extremely windy. Today was no exception. I wanted to capture the wonderful colour contrast of the fiery bracken against the mauve stormy sky. Balancing my tripod precariously near the edge, with a heightened feeling of vertigo and buffeted by the incredibly gusty wind, I was struggling to see through wind-whipped hair and watery eyes. Keira Knightley was tied on to stop her falling off while filming for *Pride and Prejudice* here. I just had to suffer for my art and hold on. With the vibration of my tripod in the wind, I had to use a faster shutter speed and wider aperture than I would have liked, consequently losing some depth of field in the foreground.

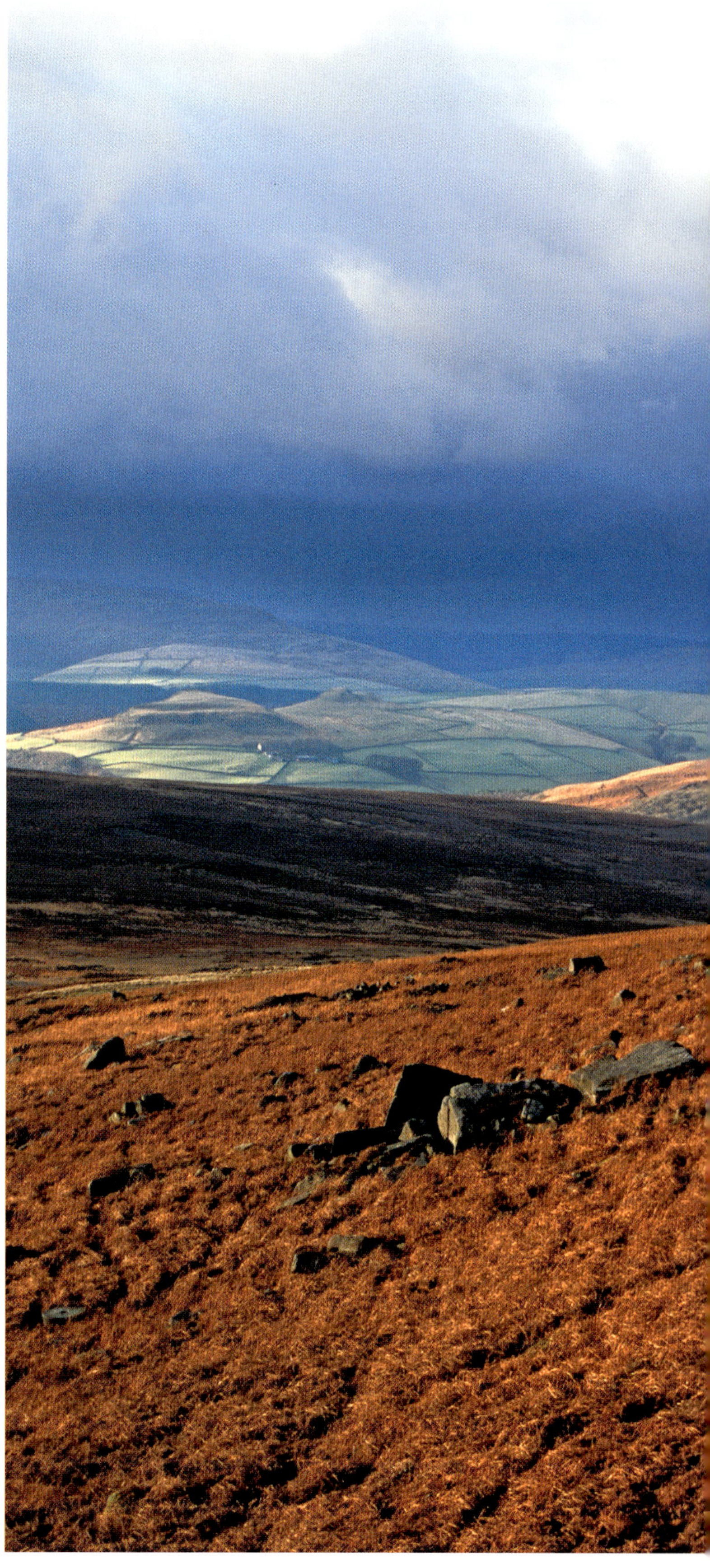

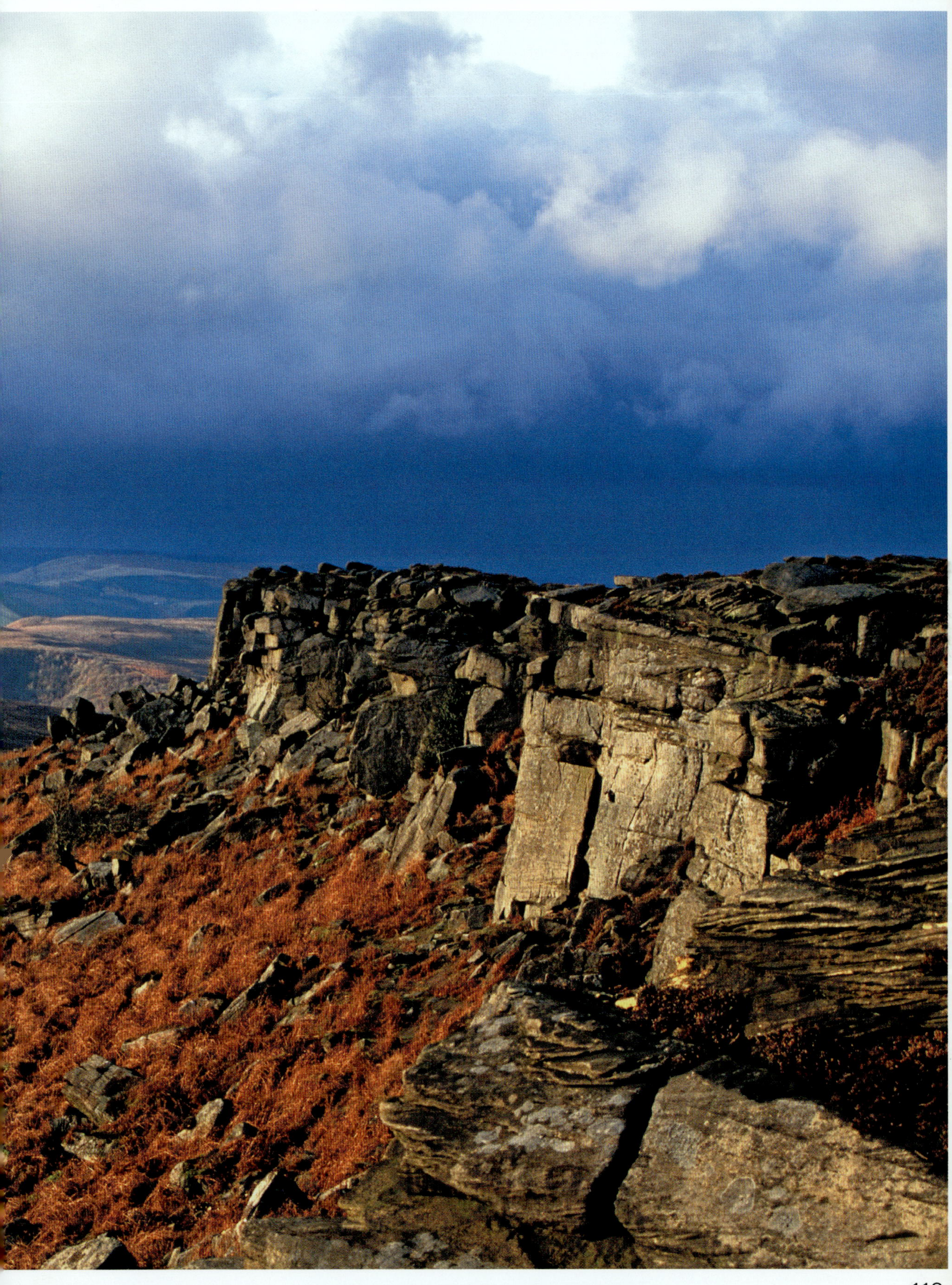

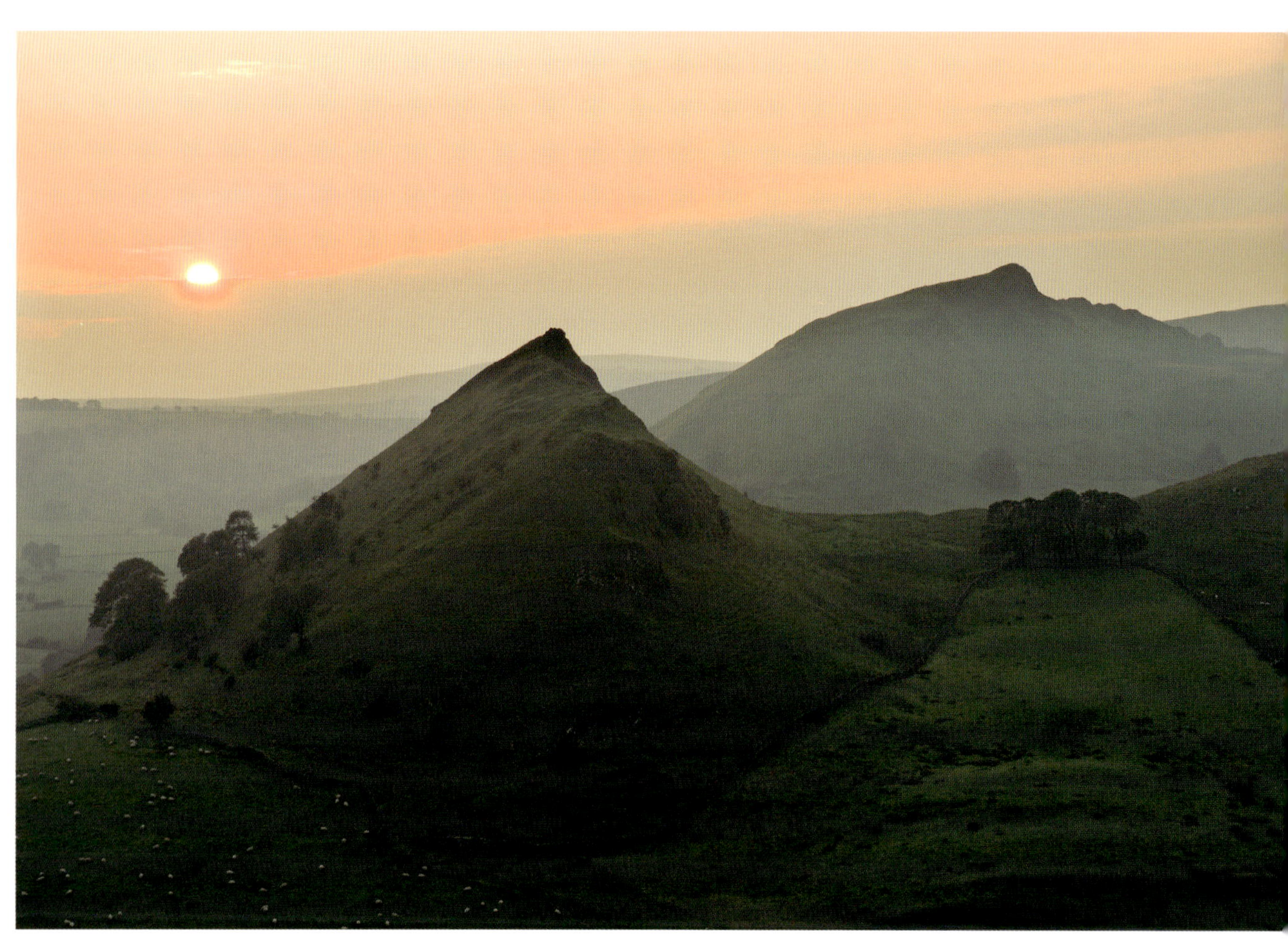

Sunset over Parkhouse
and Chrome Hills

This was another chance photograph. Driving back from
Buxton one September evening at around 6.45pm after an
exhausting day teaching a photography course, I noticed
the sun appear from behind a cloud bank and the sky
began to take on an orange glow. With the sun dropping
fast into more cloud, I had to think of a suitable location
quickly. Screeching to a stop in Earl Sterndale, I parked
my car and raced up the hill behind the Quiet Woman pub.
My chest pounding from the exertion, and I fumbled to get
my camera equipment set up. With only seconds to spare,
I captured this image. Earlier on, my hunger and exhaustion
almost forced me to drive straight home, but an inner urge
to photograph a sunset won. I'm glad it did.

Sunrise over Hope Valley Cement Works

This was one of the first pictures I took with my new camera. A surprise misty dawn caught me unprepared. I rushed out of the house in a fluster, only to get to this location without the base plate of my tripod fixed to the camera. The chimney was rising out of the mist like a rocket against the pink sky. Frustratingly, I had to balance the camera precariously on top of the tripod. With such low light levels it's a wonder it came out as anything but a blurry mess.

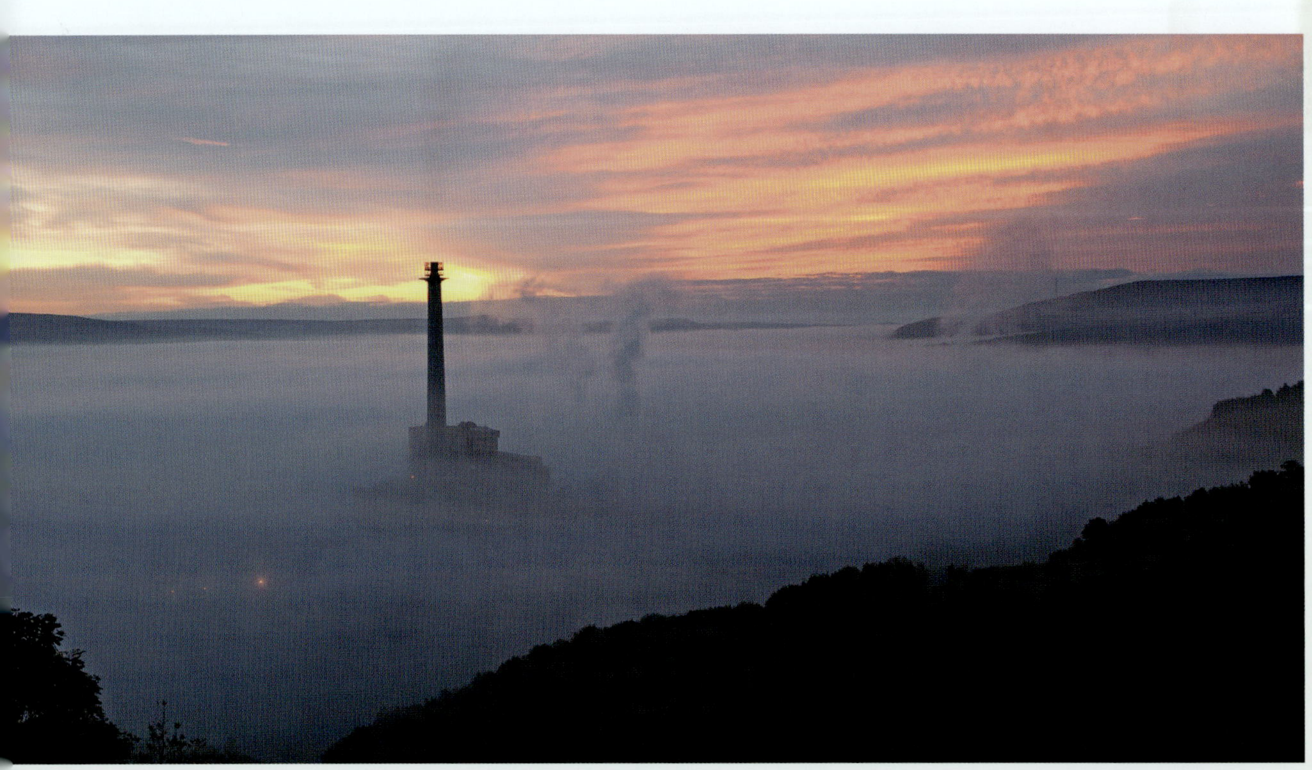

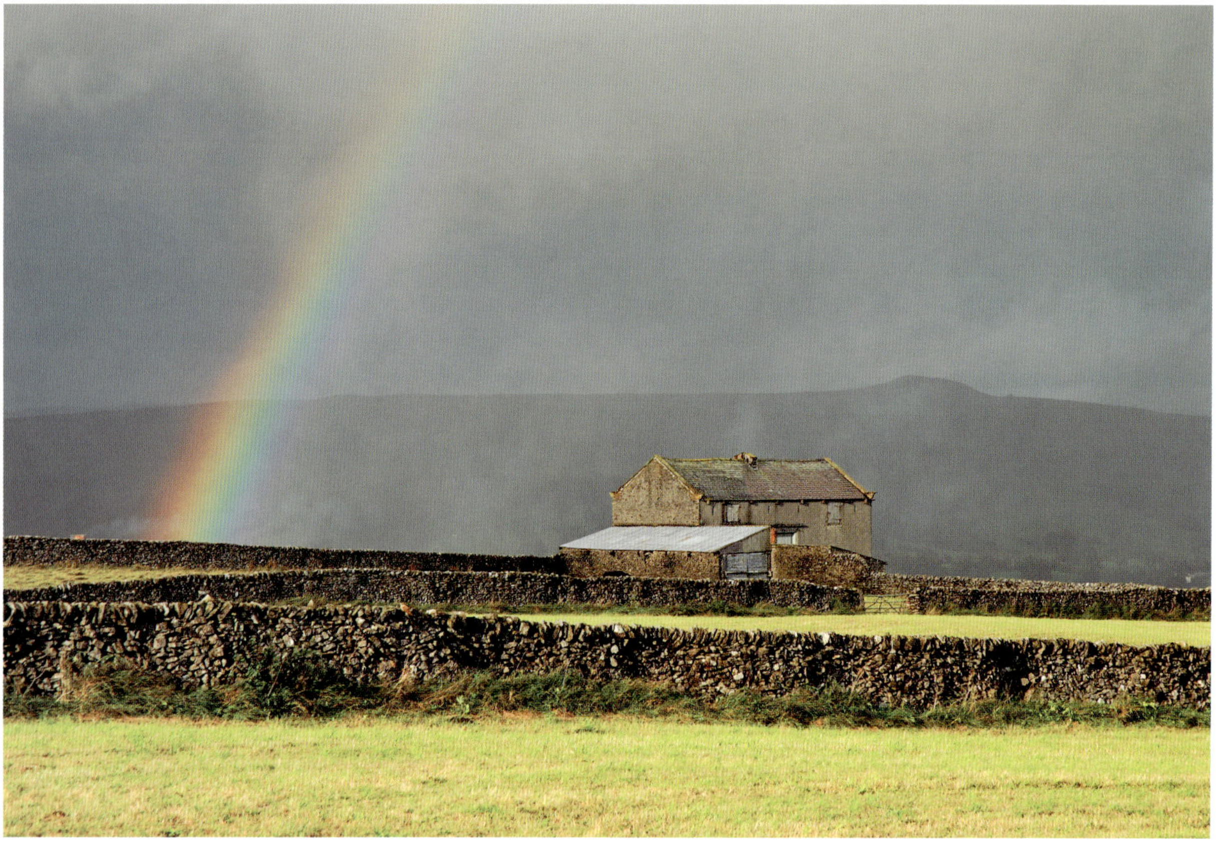

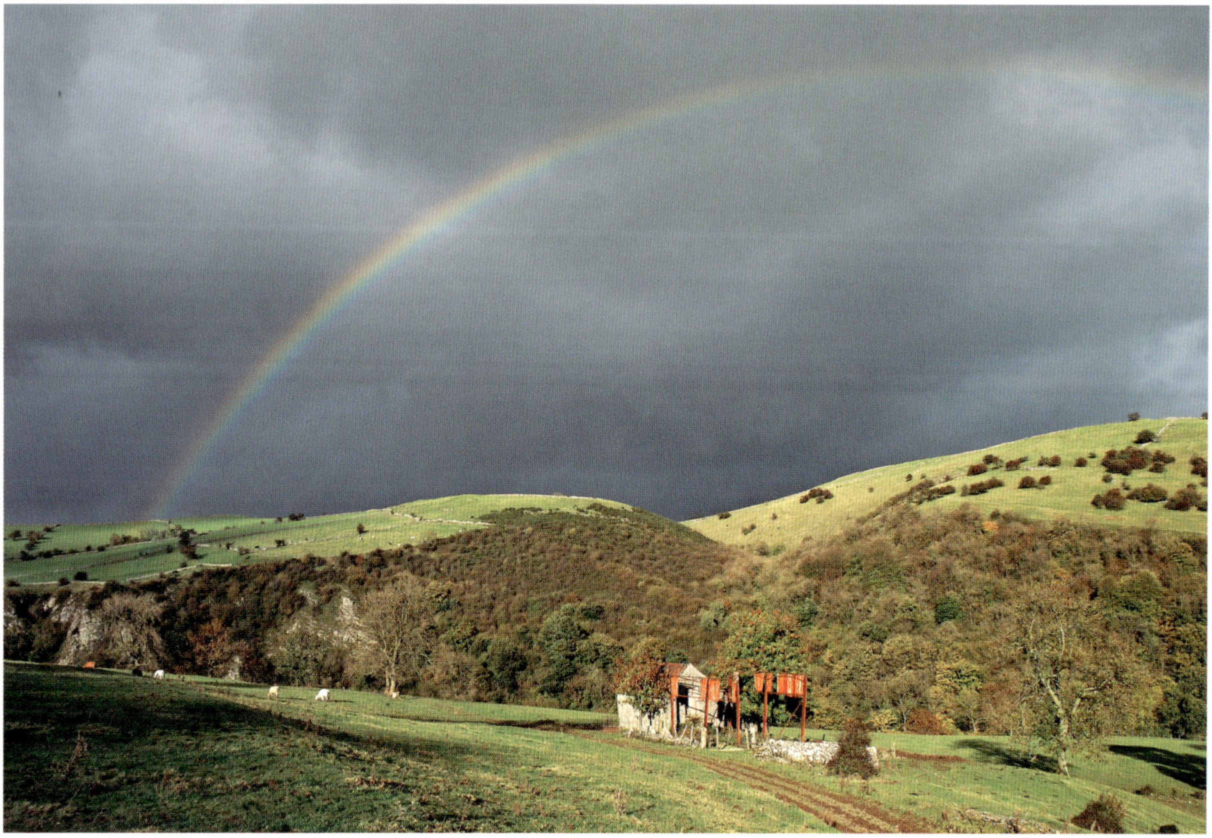

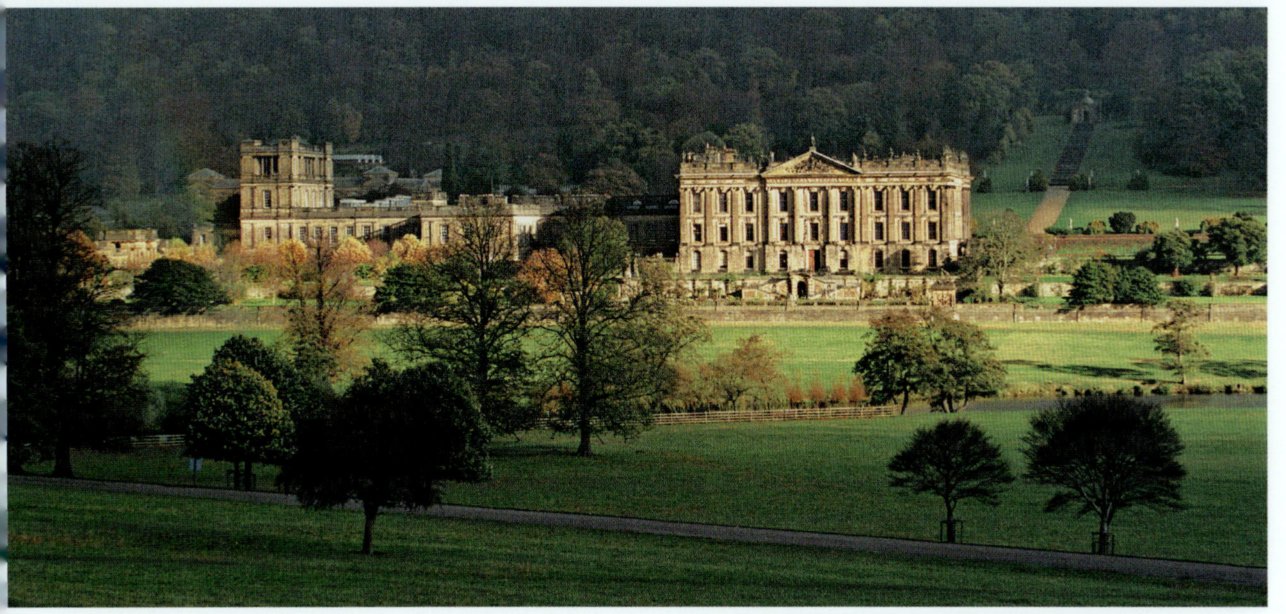

◀ Rainbow over barn above Bradwell

This stormy time of year is great for rainbows. I caught this vivid one on the way to Bradwell, just after an extremely heavy shower. In the background we can see the distinctive outline of Win Hill still being lashed with rain squalls. Patches of white cloud from the clearing shower can be seen above but it is also interspersed with smoke from the nearby Lafarge Cement Works in the Hope Valley below. It all adds to the atmosphere.

◀ Rainbow over Beeston Tor and the Manifold Valley

About a mile/2km downstream of Wetton Mill rising above the River Manifold lies Beeston Tor, a spectacular limestone crag popular with climbers. It is also where the River Hamps converges with the Manifold. Climbing up from Beeston Tor to walk south towards Throwley Hall, I looked back to see dark storm clouds and a spectacular rainbow over the valley. The sunlit white cows compliment the colour of the limestone and the ruined barn and rusty old shelter add a colourful focal point along the muddy track. As a big black cloud was about to obliterate the sun, there was no time to set up my tripod, so I had to hold the camera steady as best I could.

▲ Chatsworth light

Home of the Duke and Duchess of Devonshire, Chatsworth must be one of the most lavish and popular stately homes in England. It has a magnificent setting, sitting on the banks of the River Derwent and nestling below heather moorland and wooded hillsides among 1000 acres/400ha of parkland created by the famous landscape gardener Lancelot 'Capability' Brown in the late 1800's. With its many rare art treasures and ever changing exhibitions of contemporary sculptures by leading international artists scattered around its wonderful 105 acre/42ha garden, it's easy to see why it attracts thousands of visitors each year.

As expected, it's much photographed and I wanted to try to get something different. One very cold, stormy day in September many years ago, I did manage this atmospheric shot. Sunlight was fleeting from the passing showers, the play of light constantly moving across the landscape, but, after a two-hour wait I got what I wanted. For a few seconds a beam of sunlight spotlit the house leaving everything else in darkness. Perfect!

Evening sunset below Bretton Edge

However much you pre-visualise and plan, you never quite know quite when a great photograph will appear by chance in front of you. I was driving back home along Bretton Edge one evening, and the scene which presented itself could have been a Tuscan dawn rather than a Derbyshire sunset. Unusually for this time of day, the mist was forming on the landscape beneath a watery sun creating a soft pastel canvas across the White Peak plateau. Quite breathtaking. With the bare essential camera equipment always to hand, I used my grey graduate filter to keep detail in the sky and tried to keep the sun out of the shot to reduce the risk of flare.

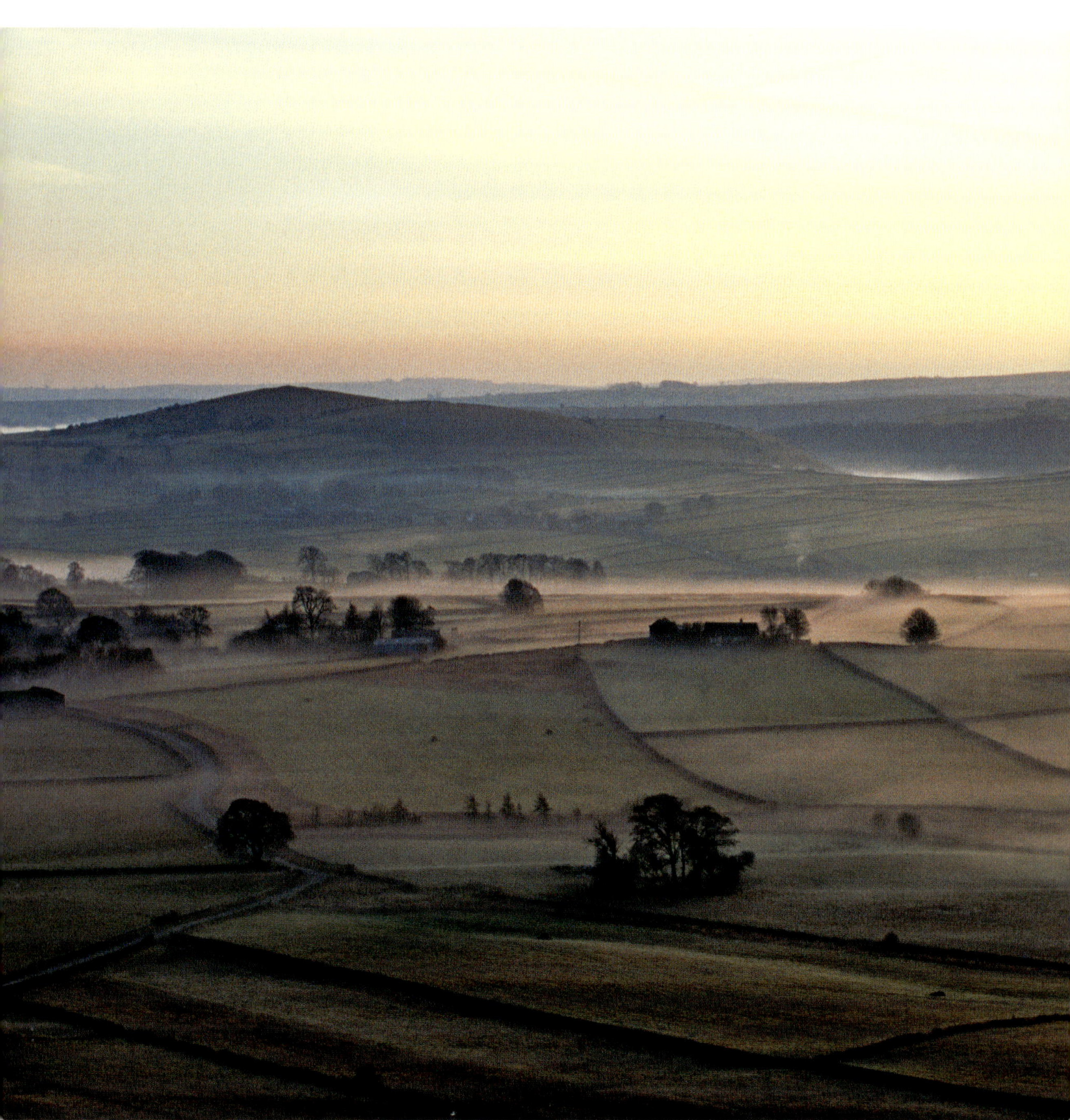

NOVEMBER–DECEMBER

Sunrise time 07.08-08.25 **Sunset time** 16.37- 15.59
Sunrise direction SE **Sunset direction** SW
Winter solstice Dec 21st **Sunrise** 08.23 **Sunset** 15.51

Nature's Tapestry and Light Sculpture

As new growth stops, chemical changes in the deciduous foliage bring a kaleidoscope of colour. Green chlorophyll production ceases, revealing an enormous range of red and golden pigments beneath. So be quick, with these delicate autumn leaves hanging on by a thread, the slightest frost and wind can put a speedy end to this colourful display. It's time to head for larch woodlands like the Upper Derwent Valley. The falling needles create a spectacular carpet and the colours so intense the landscape appears on fire. The gritstone moorland is equally magnificent with its golden sedges against dark brooding skies.

The down side with this time of year is the very low, short arc of the sun. For this reason higher ground is best. Many valleys only get sunlight for a brief period in the day and some not at all. On sunny days many of the limestone dales are in shadow and difficult to photograph unless overcast with low contrast conditions. Heavy frost or snow transforms the landscape. Hoar frost forms fantastic riverside ice sculptures in the still, damp air of sheltered dales. Moreover, low oblique sunlight has warmer tones and creates wonderful long shadows throughout the day, unlike summer.

I love winter photography, but the cold comes quickly and always takes me by surprise. I suddenly find myself tramping in icy winds through wet wild moorland woefully unprepared, without the hot flask of coffee and extra food I carry later on. But I soon toughen up and summer seems just a memory.

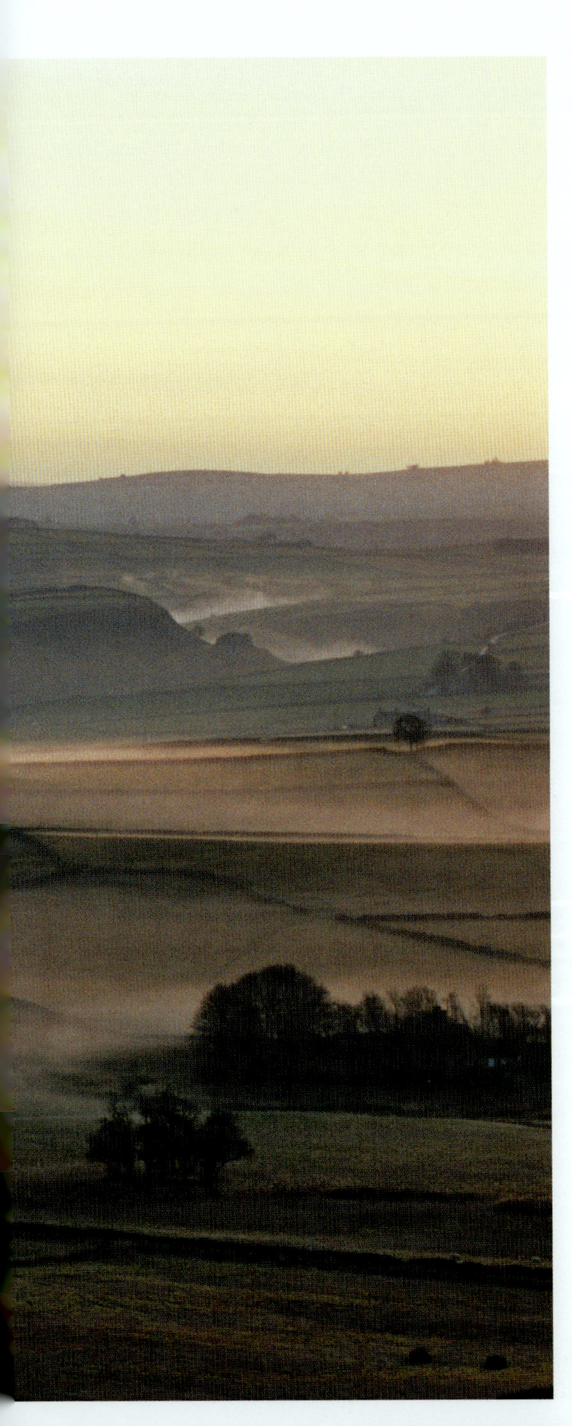

▶ Reflections in Derwent Reservoir

Back in 1996 using transparency film, I took this successful
single chance photograph one stormy day in November
while out walking with friends. I went back year after
year trying to re-capture that image again, only to be
disappointed by low water levels, less colour, or the wrong
light. Exactly 11 years later I managed to get something
similar on my digital camera with the wonderful colours on
the larch trees, a slightly stormy sky and quiet reflections in
the lake, but I still prefer the original one shown here.

▶ Looking down on Howden Dam

A crystal clear November day and the Upper Derwent
Valley is in all its autumnal splendour as I look down from
high on Abbey Bank towards the overflowing Howden
Dam and the surrounding moors. This area is a proper
wilderness; there is no habitation or roads north of Howden
until you hit the Woodhead Pass some 5½ miles/9km north.
In the far distance is the watershed of Howden Edge
(1,686ft/514m) which leads westwards on to Bleaklow
(2,068ft/630m). Although managed for grouse shooting,
this area covers some of the wildest and most remote
moors in the Peak District where you can experience a
real feeling of solitude. It's the nearest thing we've got
to Scotland in the Peak and brilliant for practising your
navigational skills.

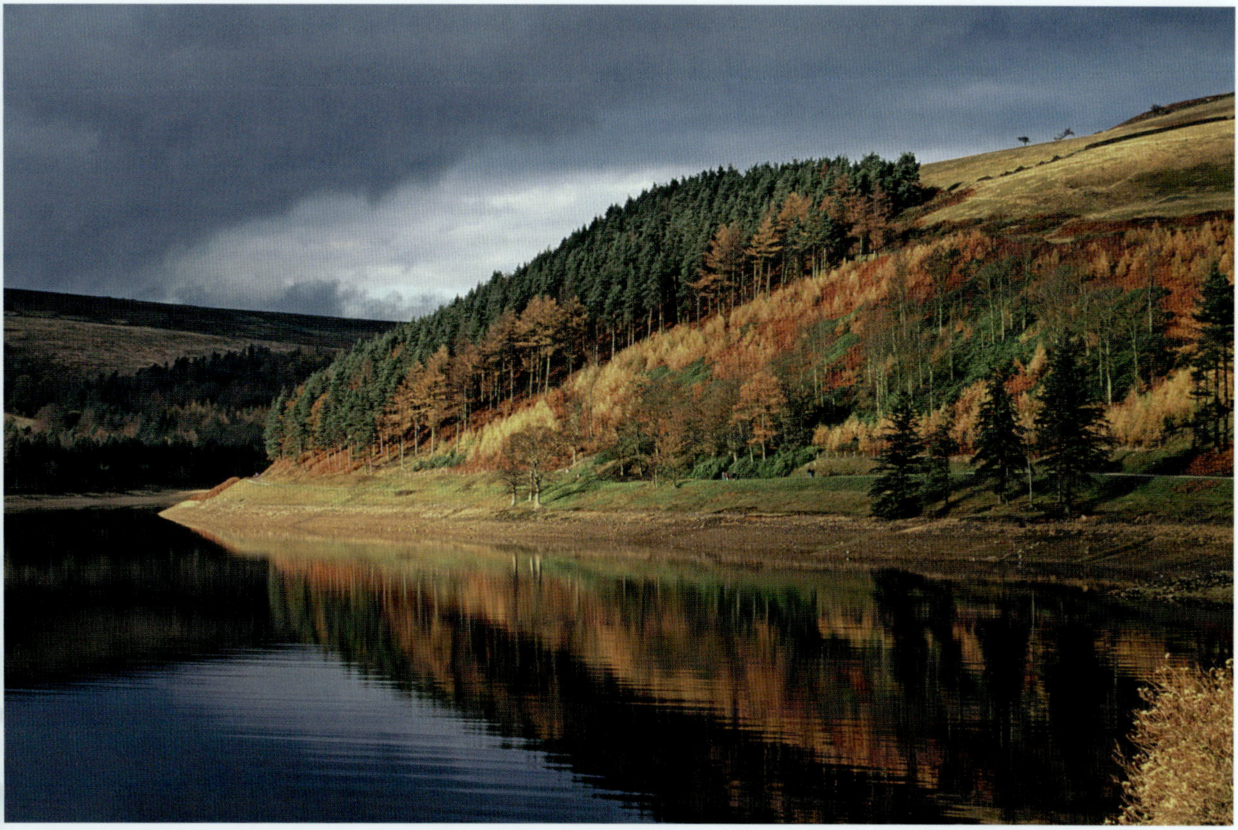

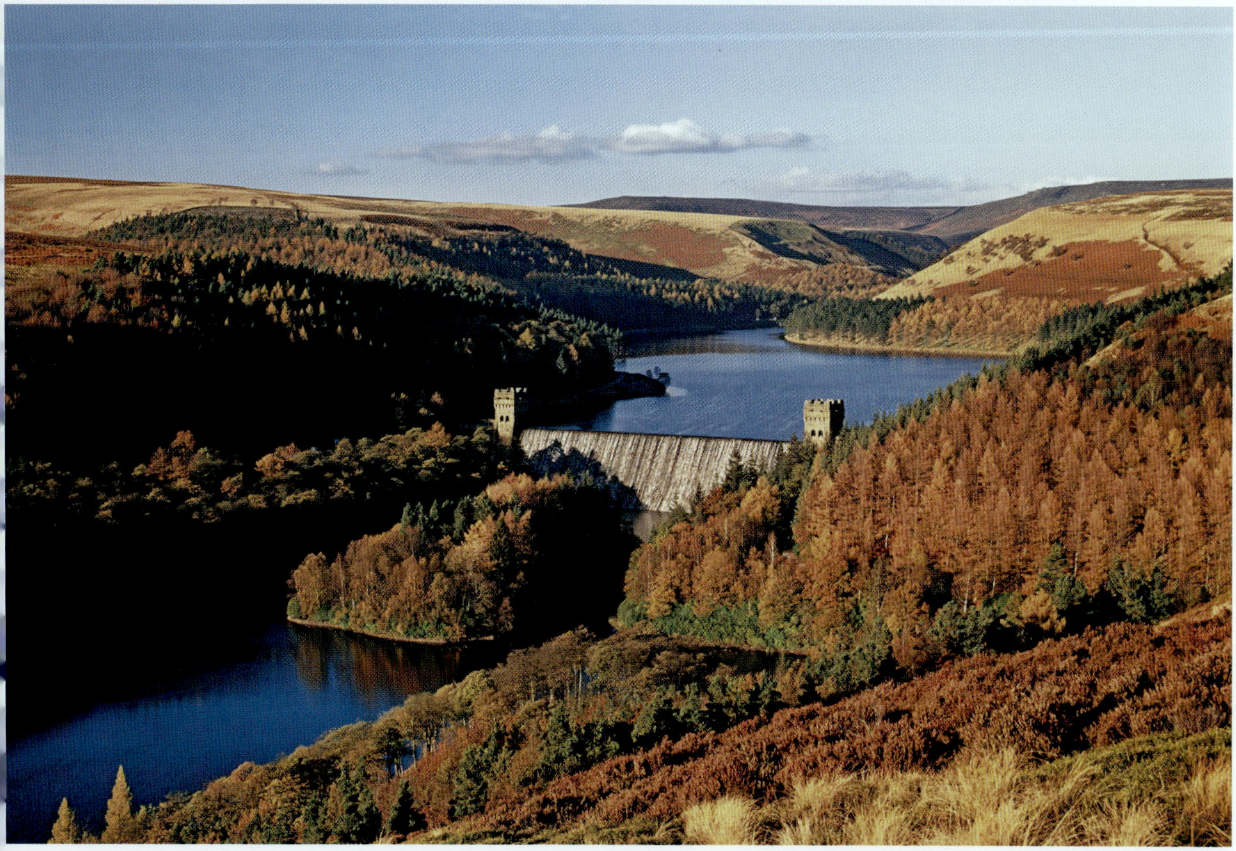

▼ Sheep gathering below Stanage

Often you can be on your way to a planned location and the unexpected appears, a photograph which can never be planned or recreated. The main thing is to spot it, have your 'image antenna' on at all times, and be able to react quickly enough before it disappears into a memory. This is what happened one sunny day in November on my way to Stanage. I was aiming to photograph a view I'd had in mind for years. On reaching my location I was disappointed, it was not lit how I'd planned and didn't have impact so I left taking no pictures. But on returning to my car, I walked past these sheep herded into an enclosure. I didn't see the potential at first, but then I came back and stalked around. Luckily I had my long lens with me and put it on. My reliable woolly models did the rest.

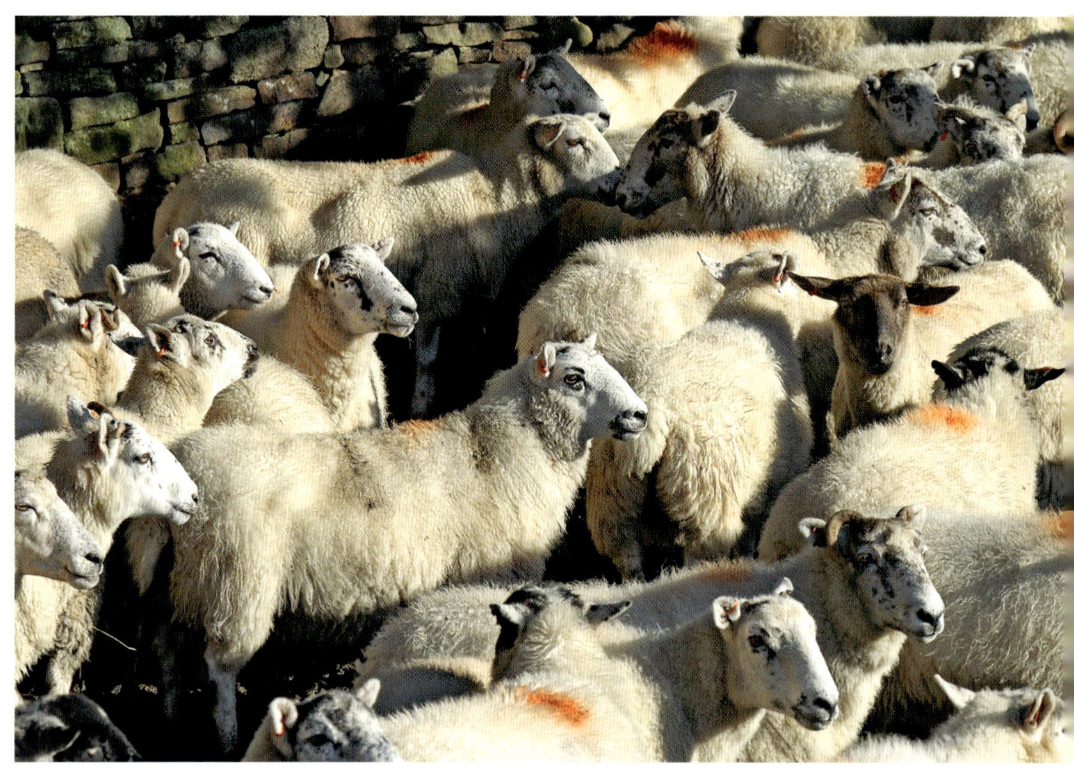

▶ Deserted house, The Roaches

This deserted house with its burnt out roof is in a fitting setting on the bleak moors behind the Roaches. Lit strongly by afternoon winter light, I waited for stormy clouds to pass overhead and add to the atmosphere. I hunted for some foreground and found this old fence post and the remains of a wall.

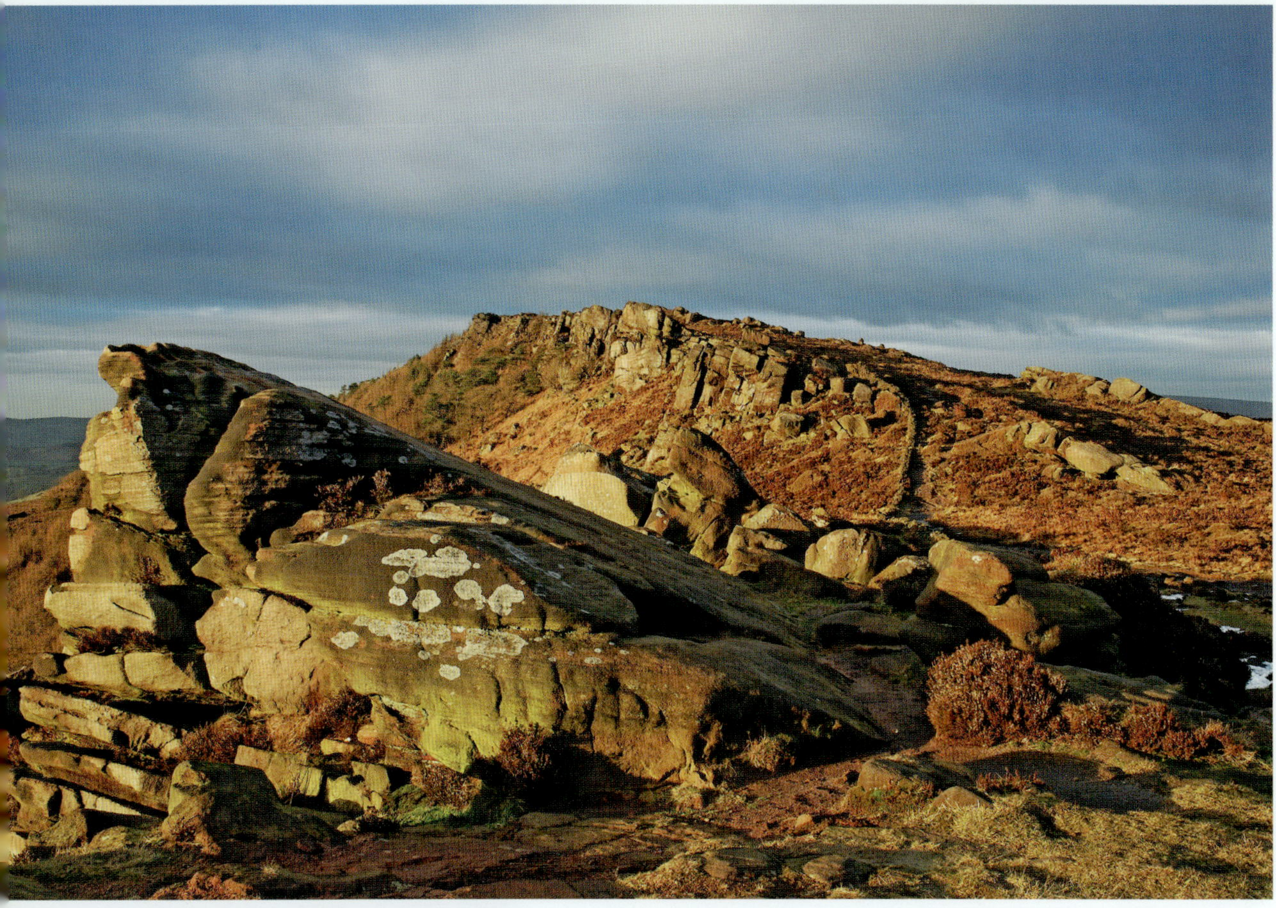

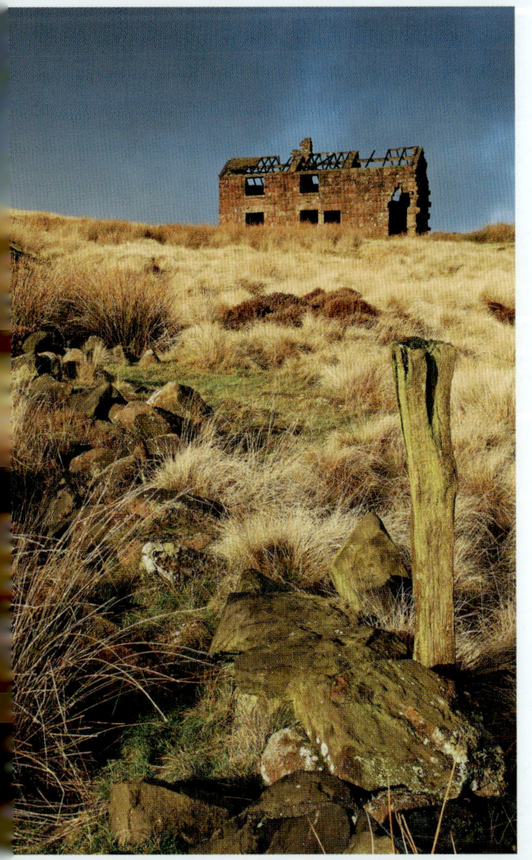

▲ Winter afternoon along the Roaches

Turning to look north, the sharp winter light gave a strong sculptured image as it fell sideways across the ridge. I particularly liked the triangle shape formed as it lights the rocks in the foreground.

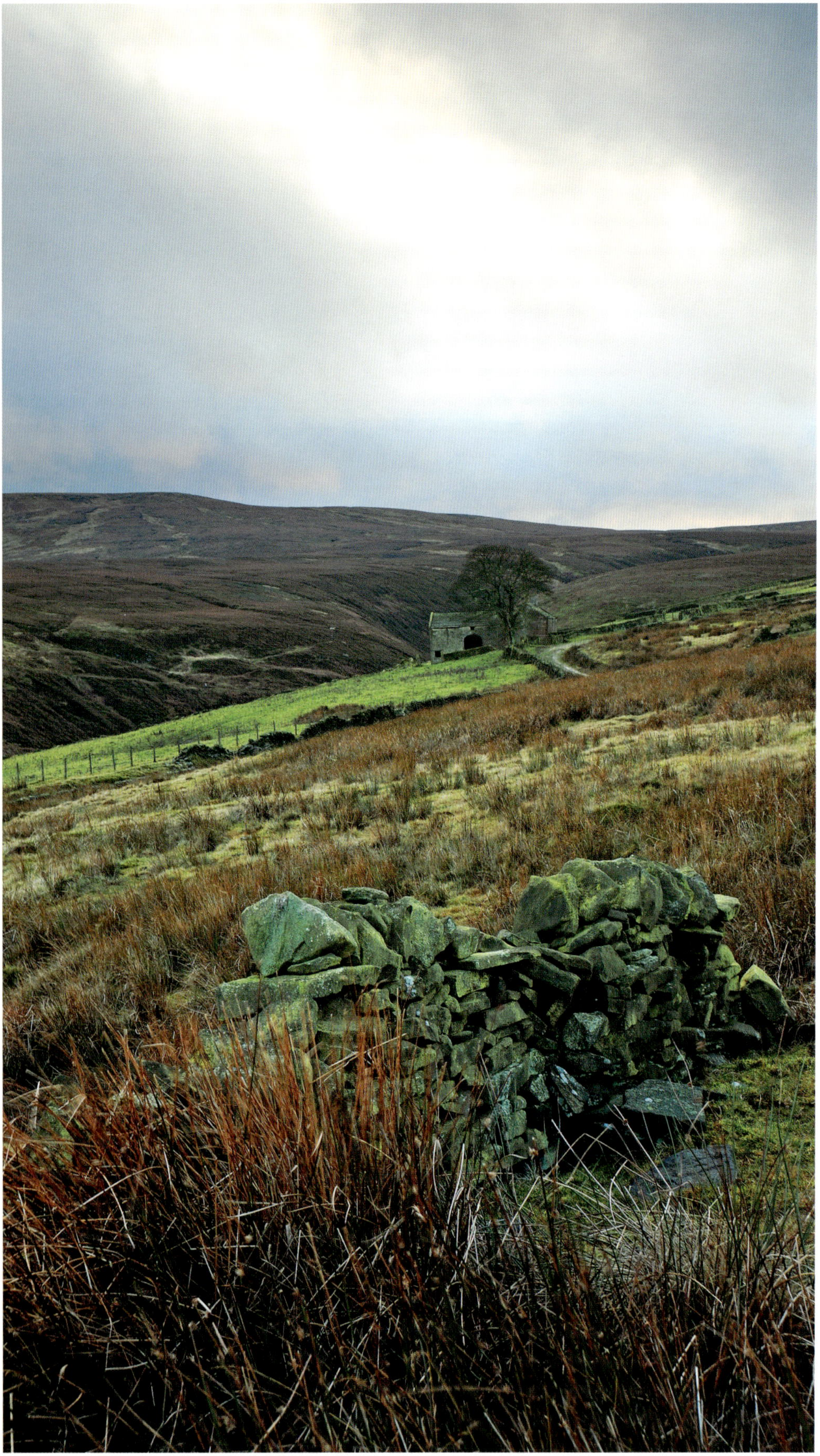

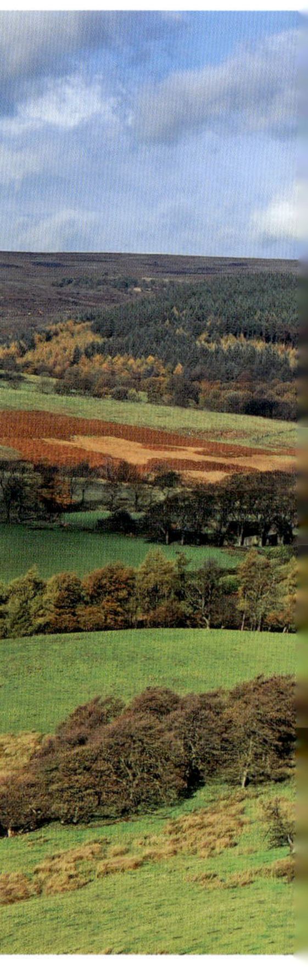

◀ Kirklees Way and Wessenden Head Moor

Looking up towards Black Hill and Wessenden Head Moor, I was drawn towards the tumbledown farm of Bartin, fitting in this wilder landscape of the northern Peak. Sadly, this was the first and only visit I have ever made here, so I had to make the most of the drab lighting conditions, using the lichen covered wall as foreground. A faint clearance in the sky towards sunset lifted the image slightly, but I'd love to come back when conditions are good and explore more, as it's a great area with loads of potential.

▼ Strines and the Boot Folly

Water drains down from the moors east of Derwent Edge to the reservoirs around Bradfield, built to satisfy the needs of Sheffield as demand for water soared during the Industrial Revolution. Strines reservoir was completed in 1871 after the terrible Dale Dyke Dam disaster in 1864, when 244 people were killed lower downstream. Standing proudly above Strines is Boot's Folly, built by Charles Boot (related to Henry Boot founder of the construction company) in 1927 to provide work during the recession. He lived in nearby Sugworth Hall which can be seen on the right hand side and later in Bents House to the left.

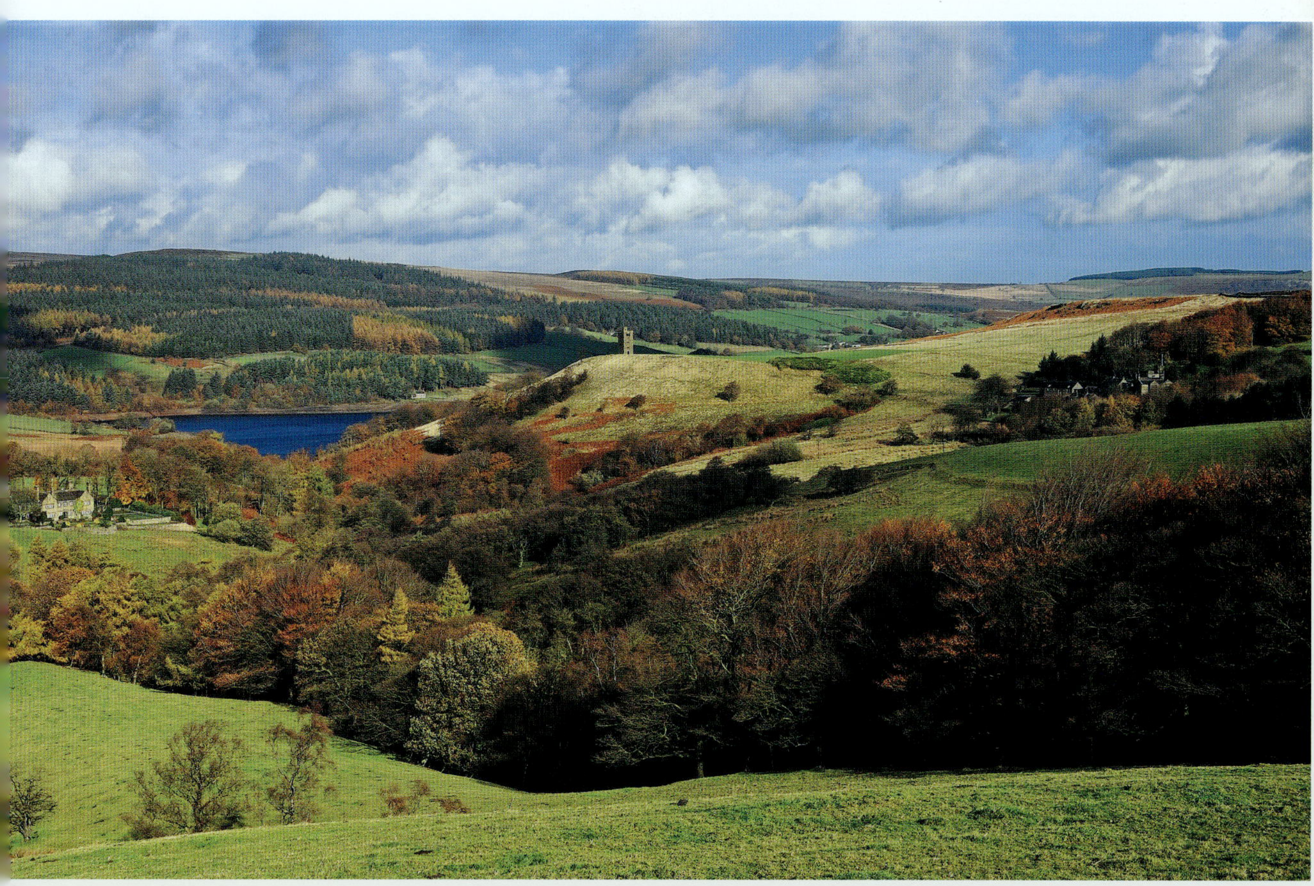

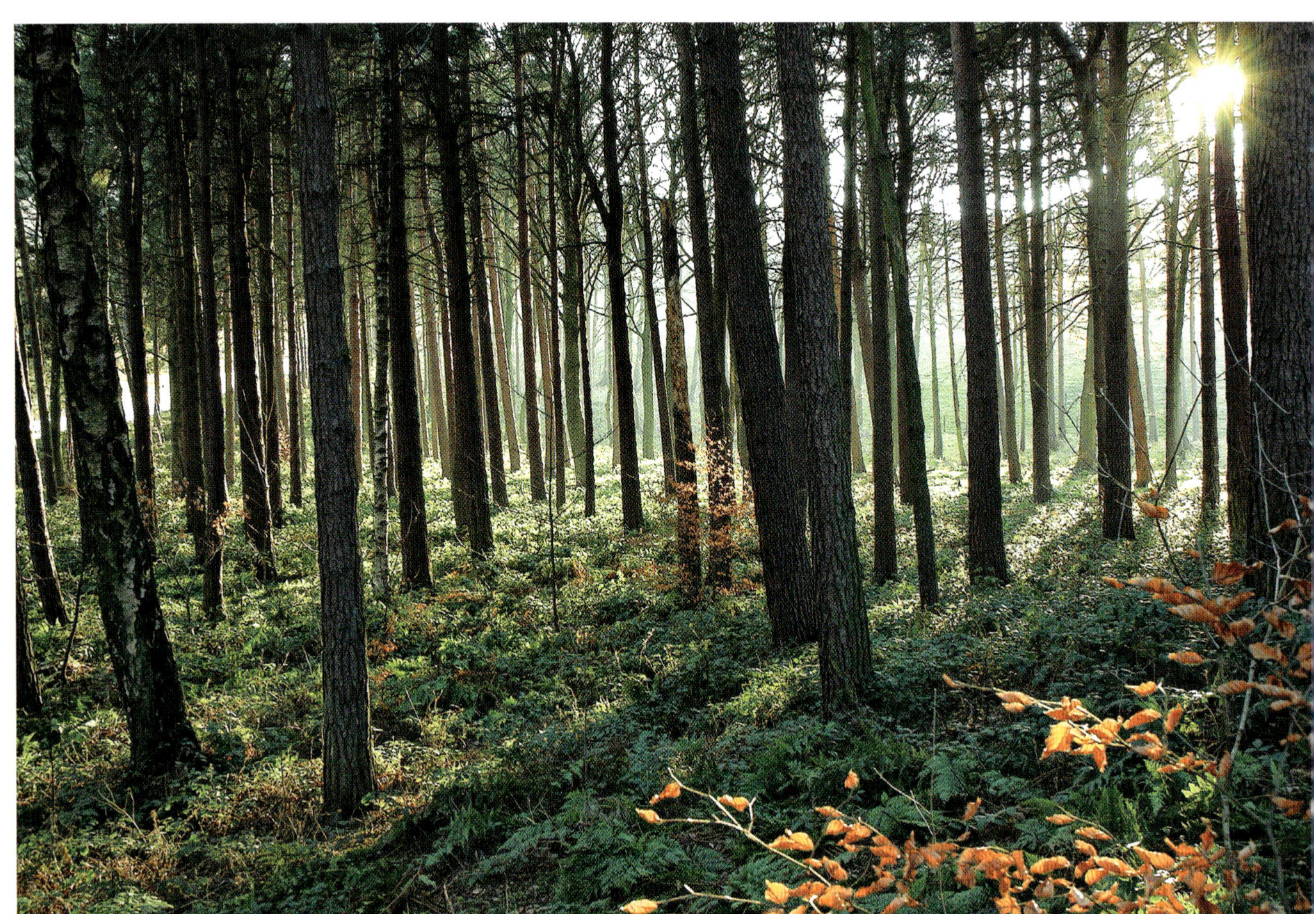

Strines woodland

Afternoon sunlight streams through this conifer wood near
Strines Reservoir picking out the few remaining orange
beech leaves. I was on an exploratory trip and had no idea
this wood was here. Feeling it had a lot of potential,
I vowed I would return on a misty day, but, so far, have
never managed to get back.

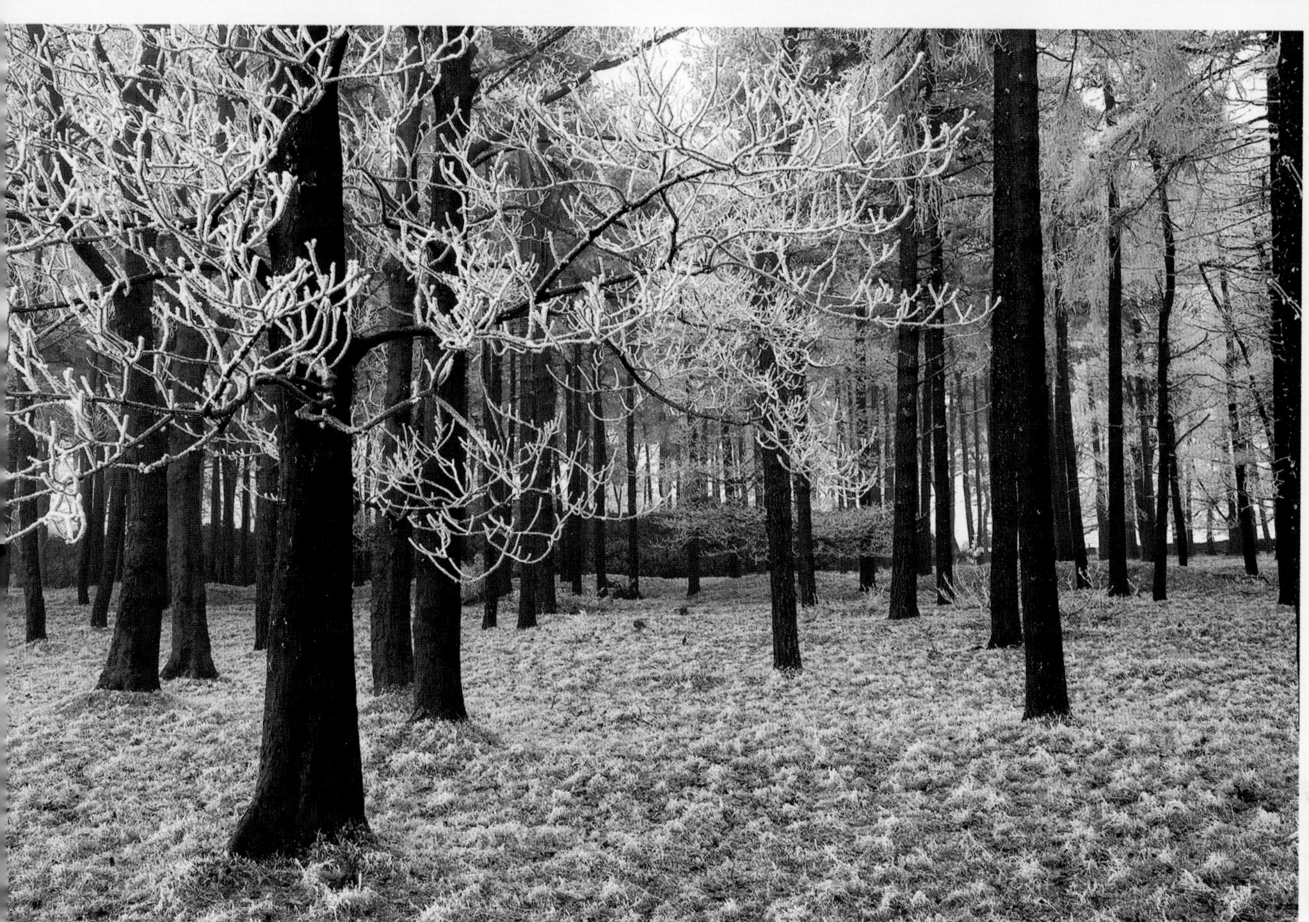

Rime on conifers near
Sir William Hill, Eyam Moor

This is a wonderful example of trees laden with rime.
On this gloomy morning, the branches of the nearest tree
loomed out of the mist like stag's antlers. What would have
made the picture perfect would be a lovely red deer stag
to emerge and stand next to the tree. However, no such
luck. I never have seen deer in this area so didn't wait
around for one. Sheep would have been a good substitute
but they weren't around either.

Snow-laden silver birch near Millstone Edge

This was an unusual treat - a brilliantly sunny, frosty, snowy day in November when the snow kept on the trees all day. It gave you a real 'good to be alive' feeling which injects you with energy. This time I didn't have to dash around madly, but could crunch gently through this winter wonderland. The only down side was that the battery on my medium format film camera went flat with the cold and my spare didn't work either. I would have been extremely frustrated, but luckily, I had my digital camera with me as a back up.

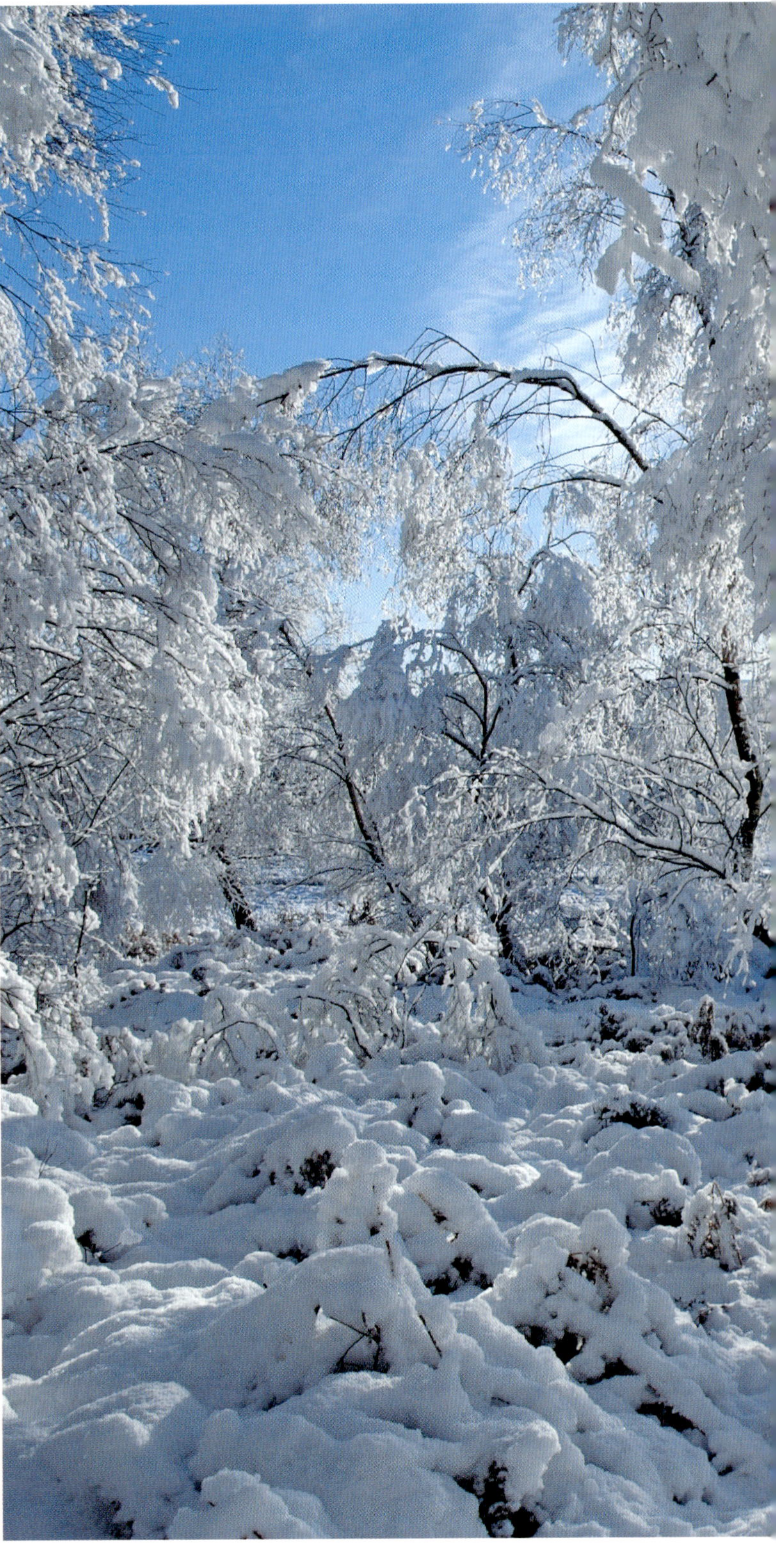

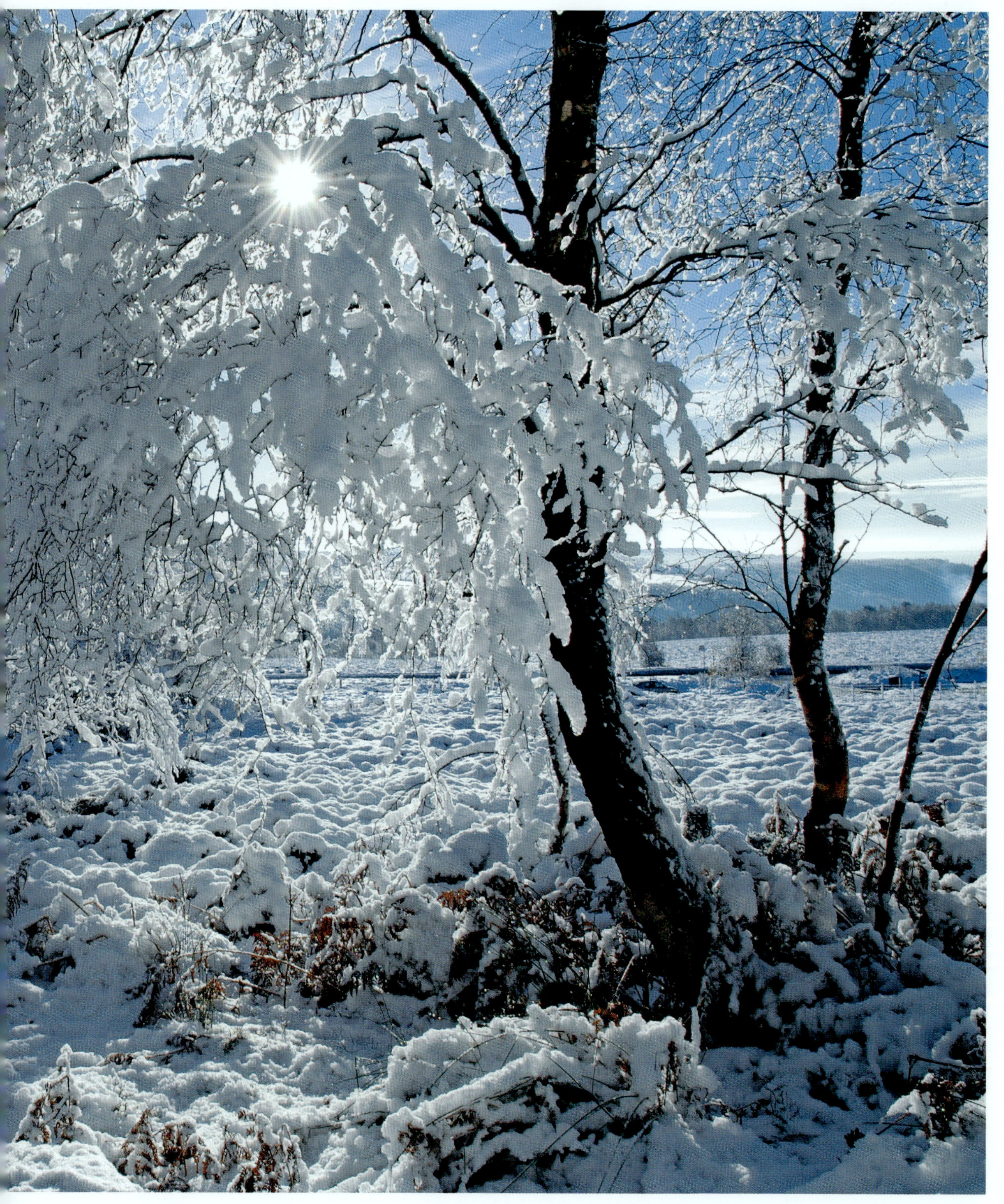

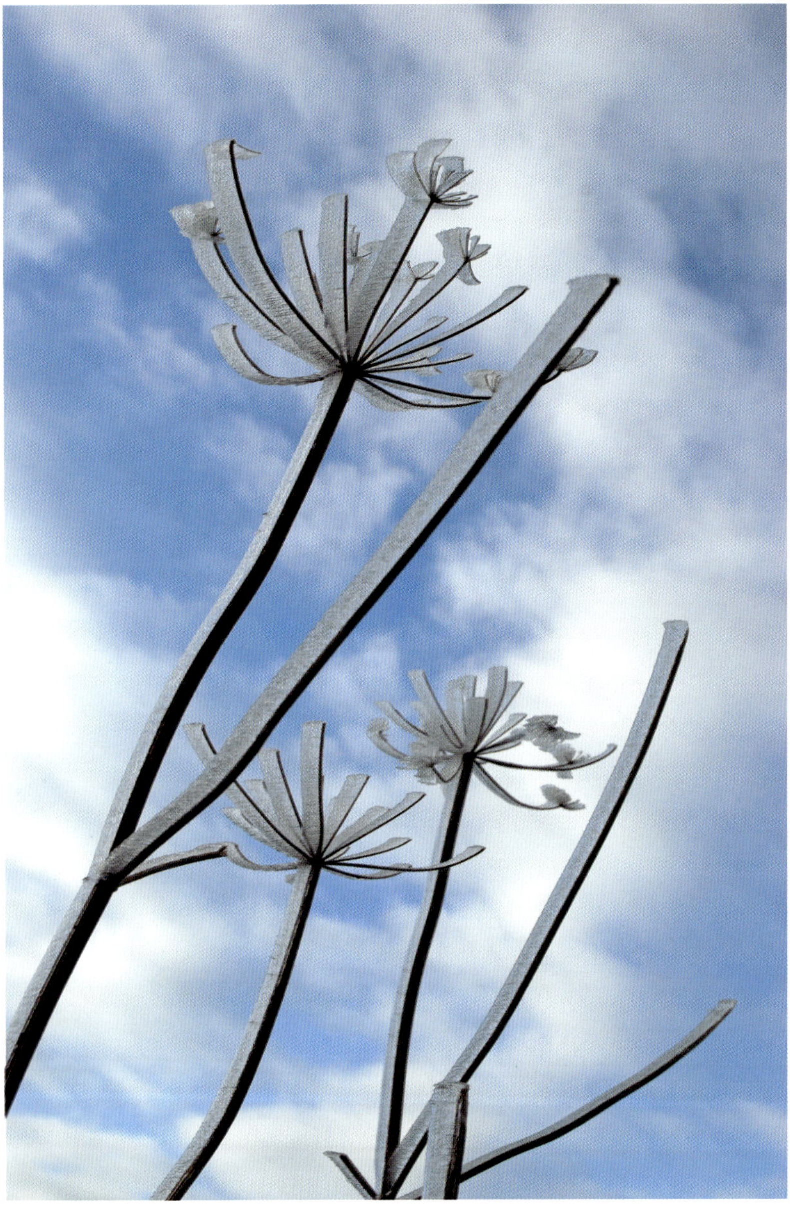

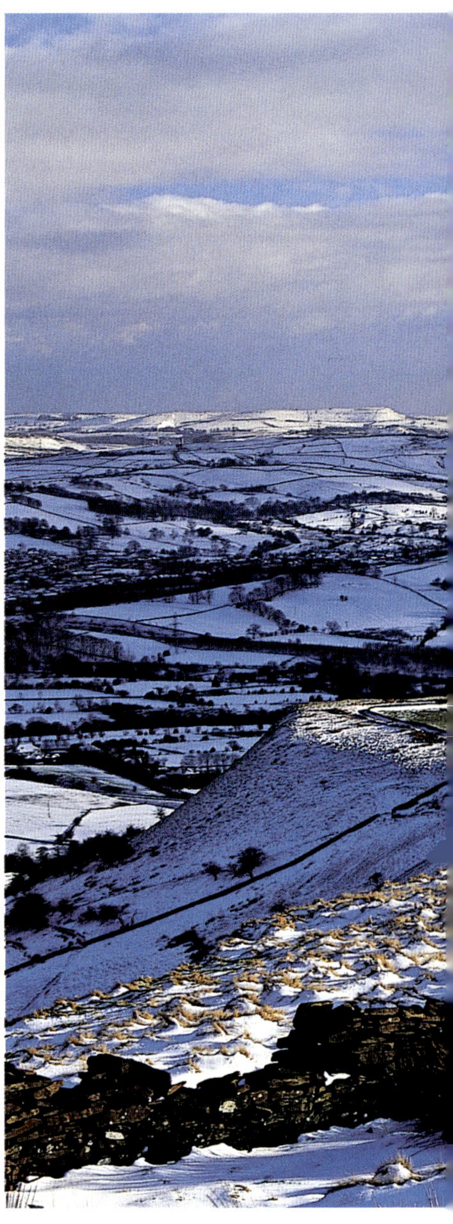

Rime frost on hogweed

Rime is a deposit of needle-like ice crystals formed by
the freezing of water droplets in fog onto solid objects.
It transforms the landscape into a crystal wonderland,
coating trees, grasses, seed heads, walls and rocks with
its spiky crystals. If there has been a slight breeze, the
crystals grow sideways, as in the case of this hogweed,
creating a wonderful natural sculpture. I lay on my stomach
in the icy grass in order to photograph it against the ideal
backdrop of a simple blue sky. Freezing cold and numb,
I returned home for breakfast and hot tea.

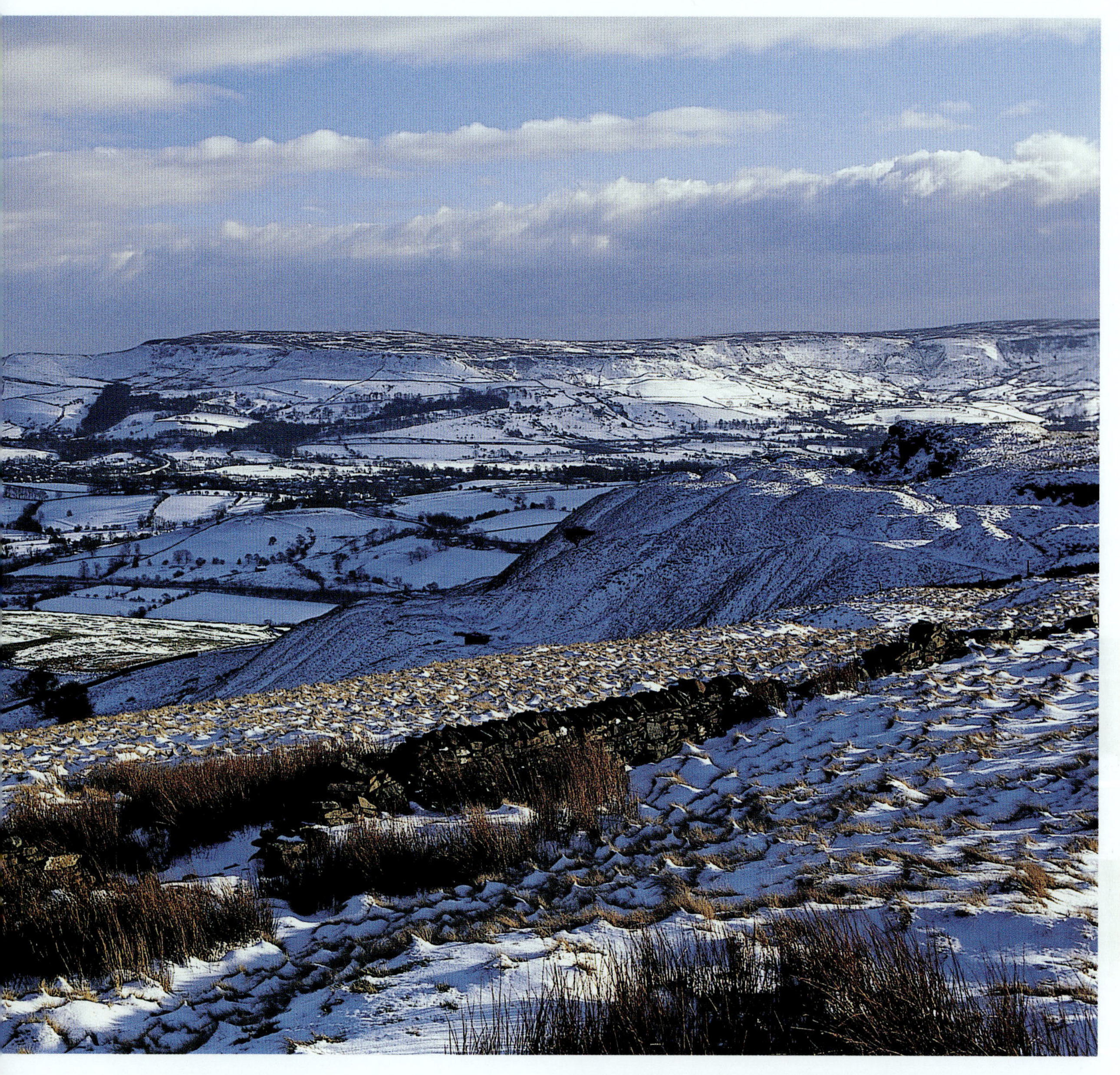

Chinley Churn in winter

Just north of Chinley rise Cracken Edge and Chinley Churn (1,480ft/451m). The crags are the remains of an old gritstone slate quarry where the spoil heaps are now grassy mounds and form a pleasant walk with wonderful views. Here we are looking south towards Chapel-en-le-Frith, Castle Naze and Combs Moss. There are also wonderful views north eastwards towards Mount Famine, South Head and Kinder behind. A dusting of snow transforms the landscape and tussocks of moorland grasses pop through, appearing golden in the winter afternoon light.

▼ Woodland below Gardom's Edge

I've noticed that often after a dry late summer/early autumn the colours are fantastic. Unfortunately, the summers of late have been wet and colours more muted. This, on the other hand, was a brilliant year taken some time ago. I used my long lens to zoom in on the mainly silver birch and larch woodland, attracted by the silvery skeletons shining through the shimmering golden foliage. As I write, we have just had the wettest and windiest November on record. Sun was scarce and the leaves soon blew off. This may be a sign of things to come, so this photograph will become increasingly special.

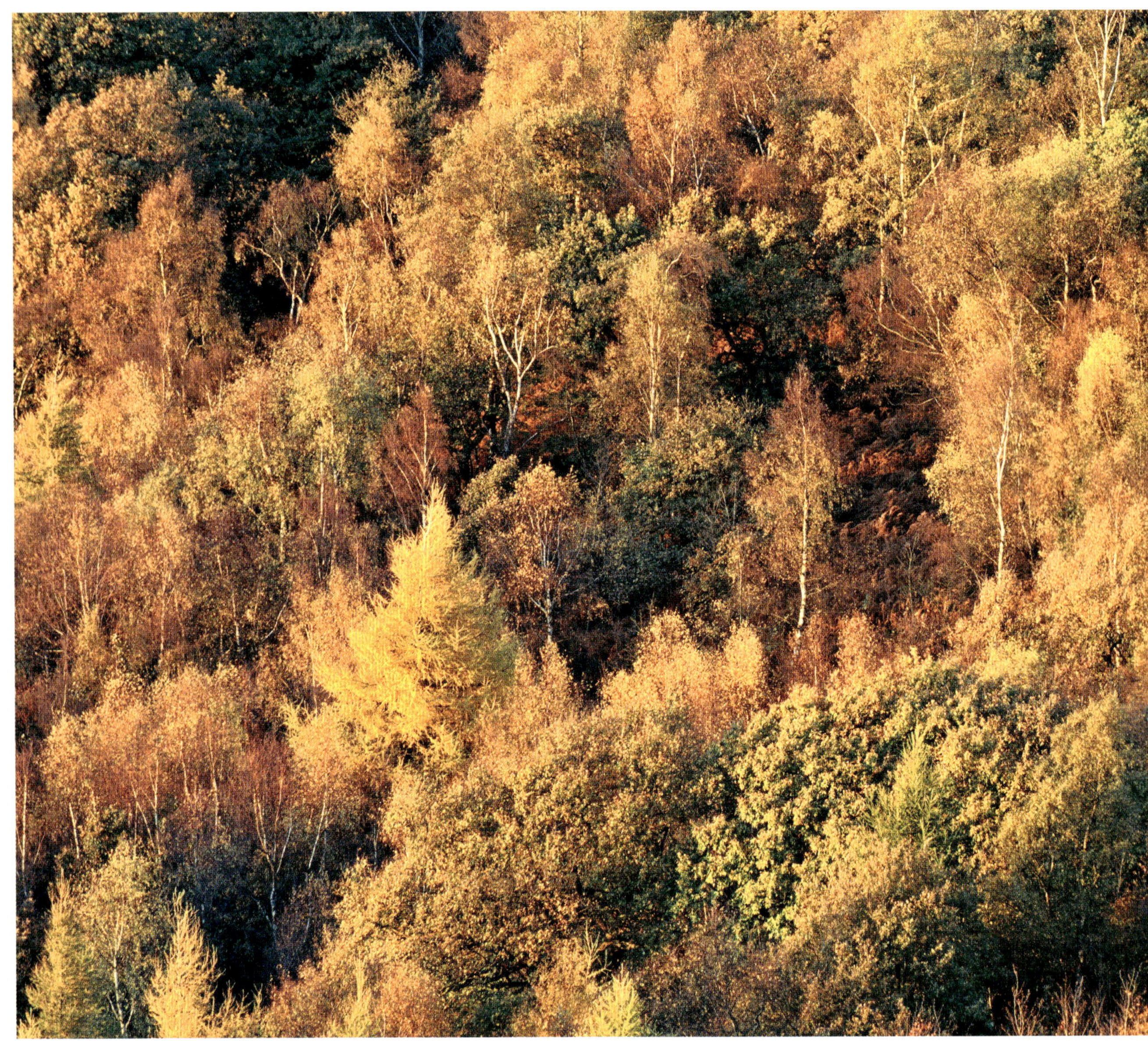

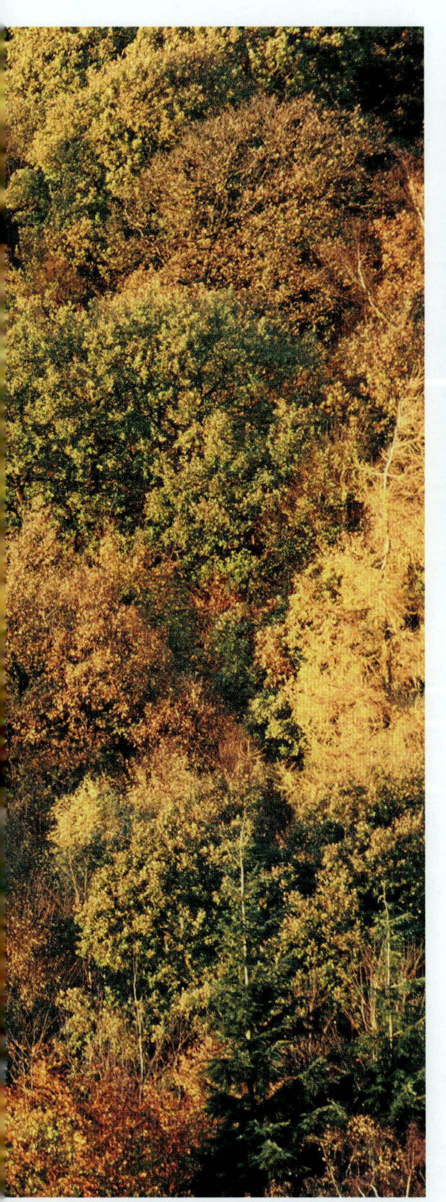

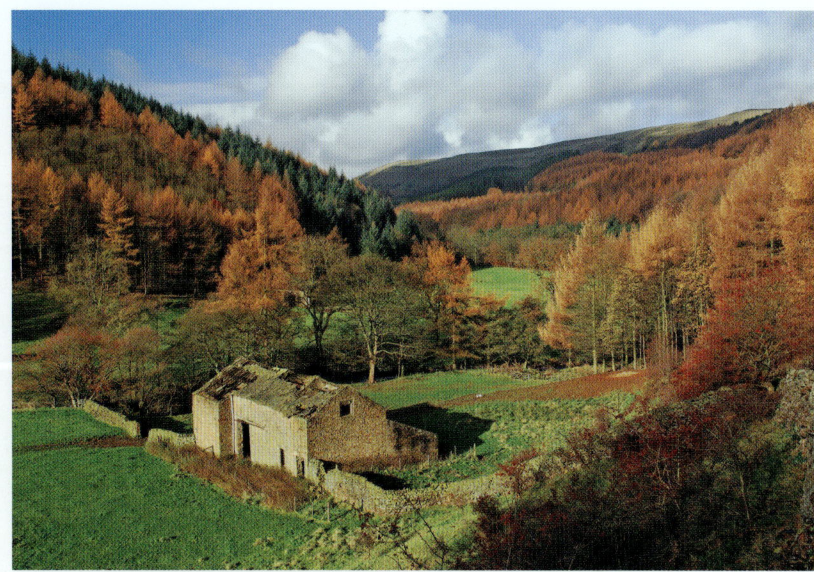

▲ The Woodlands Valley, Snake Pass

It's so easy for people to whizz past this lovely old barn in the Woodlands Valley by the side of the notorious Snake Pass, the A57 Glossop to Sheffield road. This beautiful valley is probably at its best in autumn, the burnt orange colour of larch needles contrasting with the green fields. I had just captured a glimpse of the sunlit hawthorn covered in crimson berries, but could have done with getting there a little earlier to avoid the shadow cast over it from a nearby tree. Yet another place I need to return to one day in October or November.

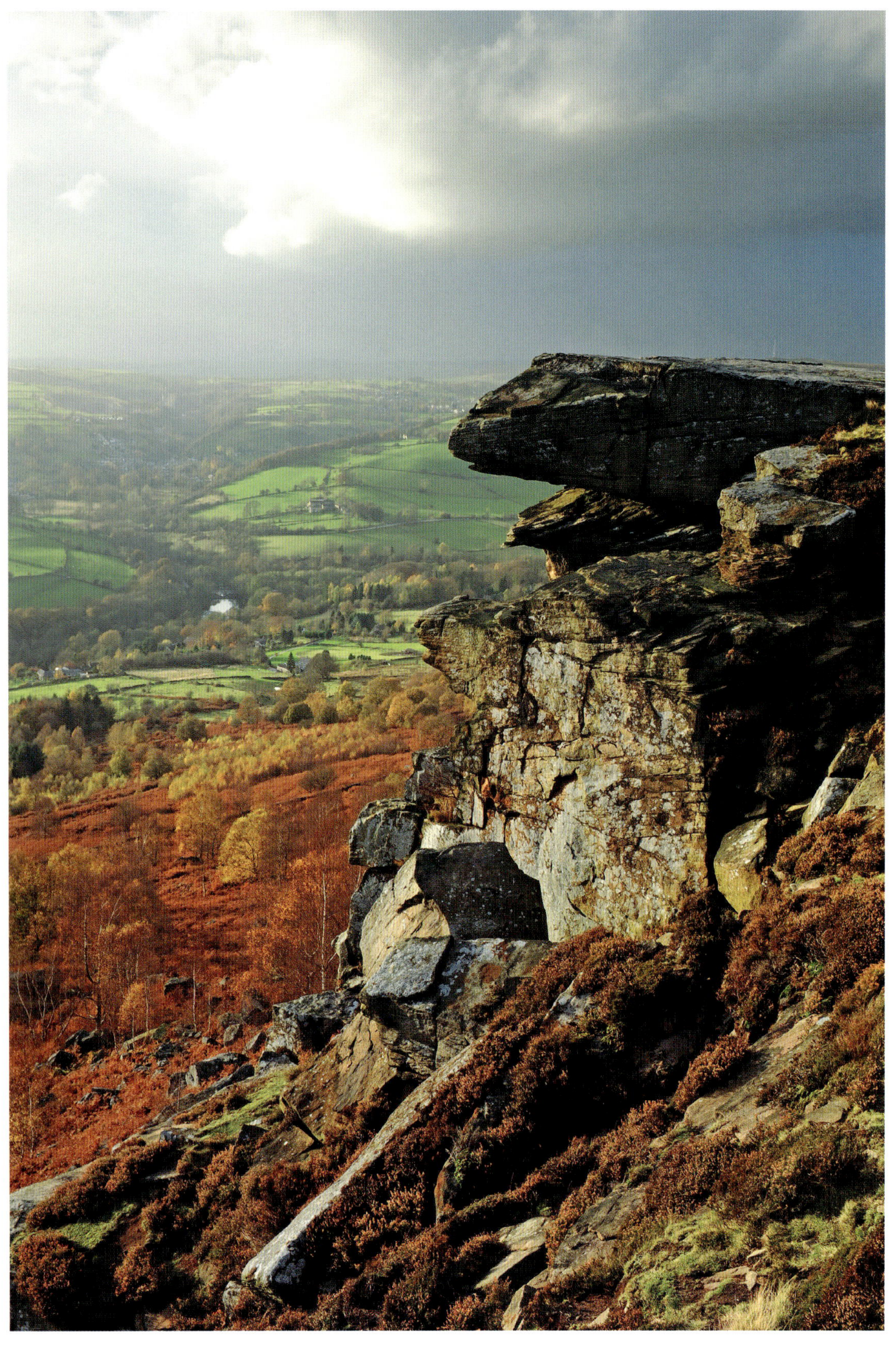

◀ Curbar Edge looking northwards.

One of the most popular of the Peak's Eastern Edges, Curbar Edge is a wonderful, south west facing gritstone outcrop which runs northwards into Froggatt Edge. These two edges combined are a great place for a gentle evening stroll on a sunny evening to watch the sun go down. This rocky outcrop on Curbar lit up by the late afternoon sunlight resembles a lizard's mouth,and is a popular challenge for climbers. Here, we look out over the lower slopes covered with golden silver birch and fiery bracken down towards the villages of Froggatt and Stoney Middleton. The pale patch mid distance is not a blemish but the reflection of sky in the River Derwent below.

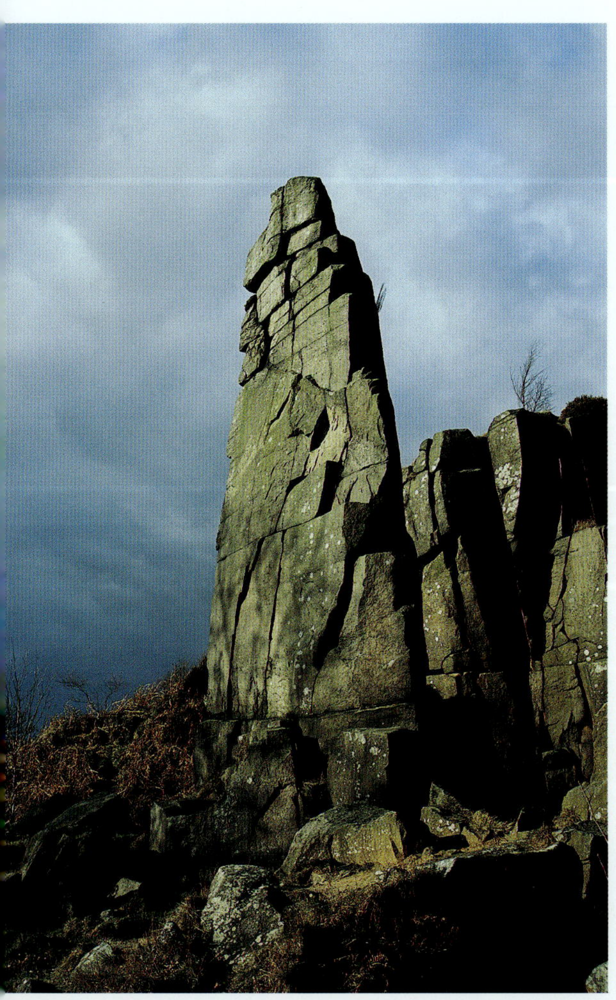

◀ Pinnacle near Tumbling Hill, Nether Padley

Reminding me of Napes Needle on Great Gable, I came across this gritstone pinnacle many years ago and thought it had photographic potential. The low winter lighting has done it justice, creating strong shadows as it rises into the stormy sky. I needed a climber to give it scale, but as it is considerably smaller than the Cumbrian classic, it would probably ruin the dramatic look.

▼ Mist in Winnats Pass

On a freezing December morning I climbed above the mist on the slopes of Mam Tor to see it swirling below in Winnats Pass. It was as if the earth was on fire. In the immediate foreground, under a thin veil of cloud, you can just see the undulations and debris from the landslips of the unstable shales which give Mam Tor its nickname of 'The Shivering Mountain.'

▶ Curbar blizzard

Standing on Curbar Edge one cold December afternoon, I was constantly hit by face-tingling blizzards. I find these conditions a challenge, trying to keep my tripod steady in the gusty conditions, but I also find the experience totally exhilarating and addictive, my face stinging and fresh. Tiny glimpses of afternoon sunlight were struggling through the storms, backlighting the distant fields and hills as sheets of hail, sleet and snow were driven through.

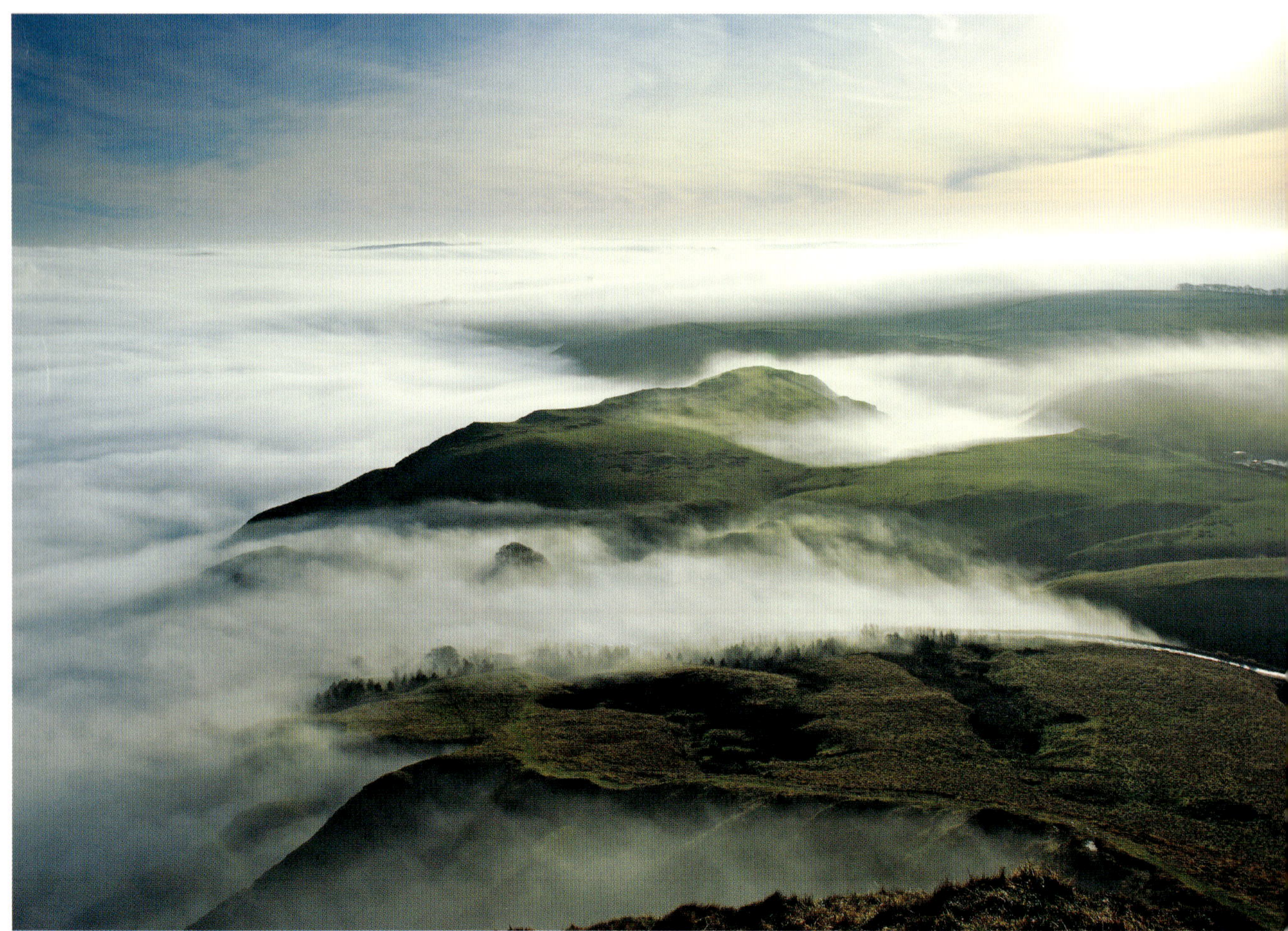

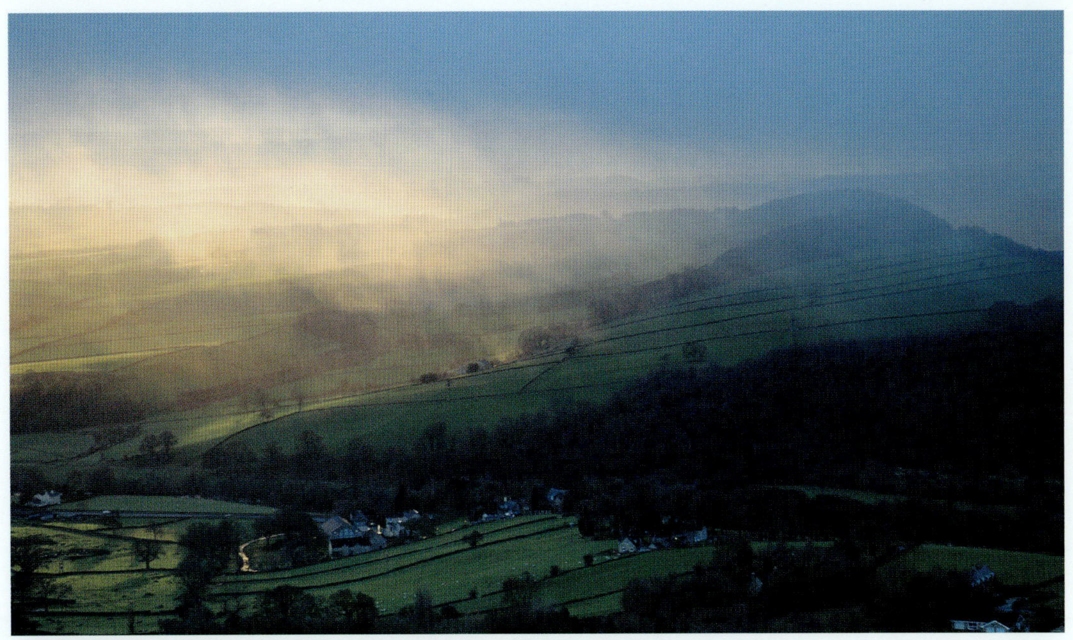

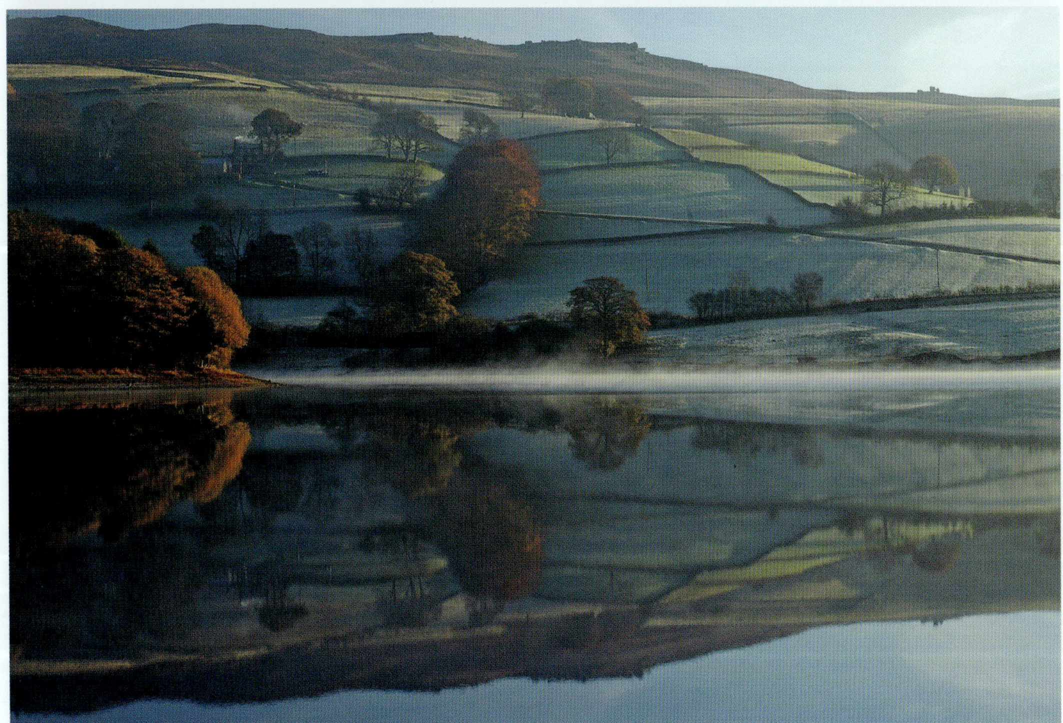

▲ Morning mist over Ladybower

Ladybower appears to be steaming on this quiet chilly
November morning. Smoke billows from the chimney of
Ashes Farm, one of the few remaining sheep farms in this
valley, and up above is Derwent Edge where we can see
the aptly named Coach and Horses (The Wheelstones)
rocks on the skyline. Beneath the water lie the ruined
remains of Derwent village.

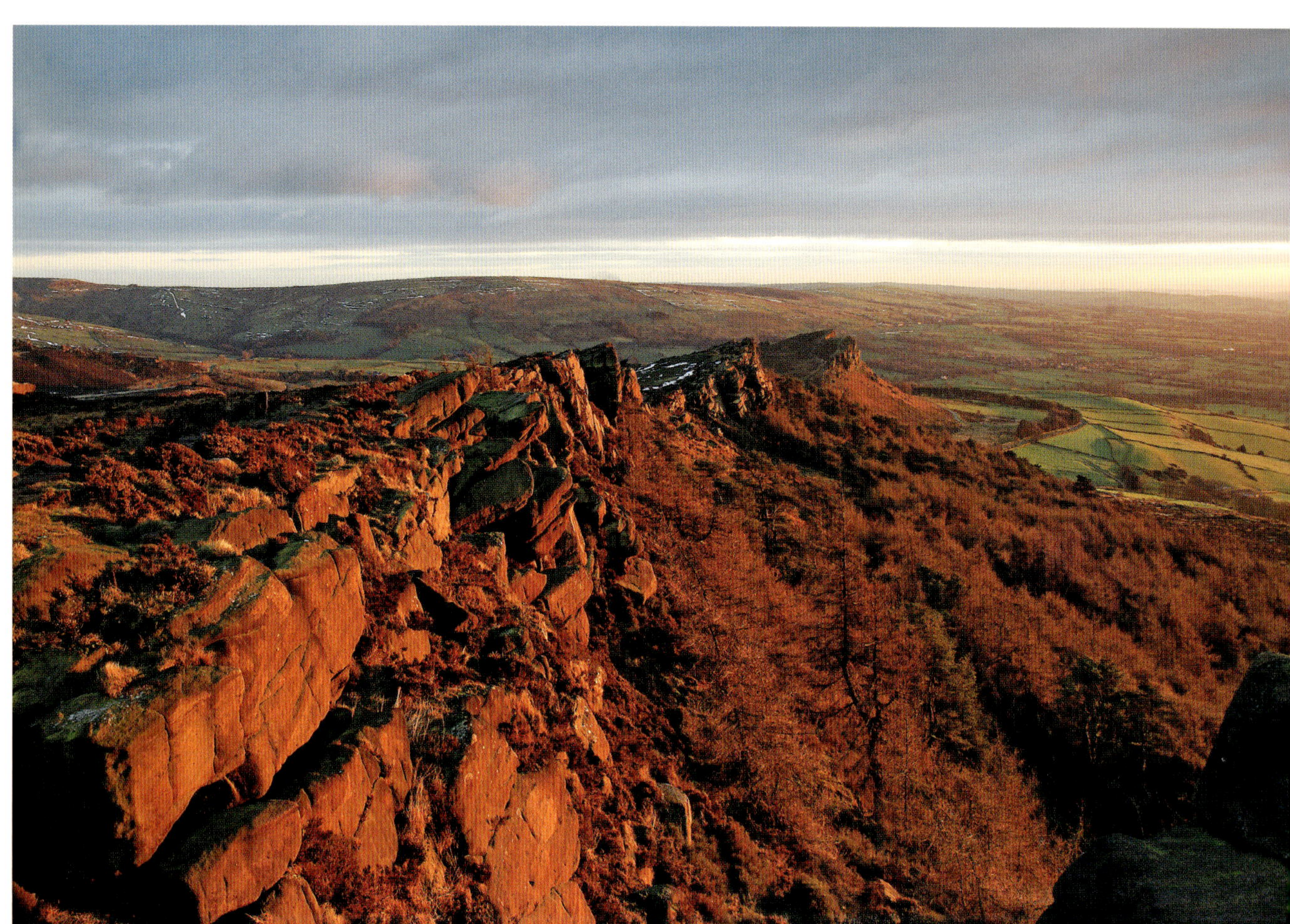

The Roaches at dusk

This image looks outrageously red and unreal, but it is not from any fancy filter or Photoshop magic, it is as I saw it. These pink-hued rocks, formed from successive layers of grit and sandstone high in iron content, look fiery red at dusk in the red/orange light of the setting sun. The Roaches emerge like fins out of the flatlands near Leek and are the start of the striking gritstone scenery of the Staffordshire Moorlands. They rise in two tiers up above a larch and pine woodland, creating a playground for rock climbers. At their southern end is Hen Cloud which stands proud at 1,345 feet/410m which you can just see as the final link in the Roaches chain.

Doxey Pool at sunset

Looking in the opposite direction to the previous picture, I managed to capture the last rays of sunlight as they illuminated the distant hills and higher rocks around Doxey Pool. The low ridge of rocks in front of the pool casts it in shadow and we can see the amazing reddening effect of the sun on the rocks, compared to those in shade which appear green from their covering of lichen. It was well below freezing as you can see from the chunks of ice scattered around the frozen pond. All I had to do now was to descend safely in fading light and icy conditions. Tricky, but worth it for such a successful afternoon's photography.

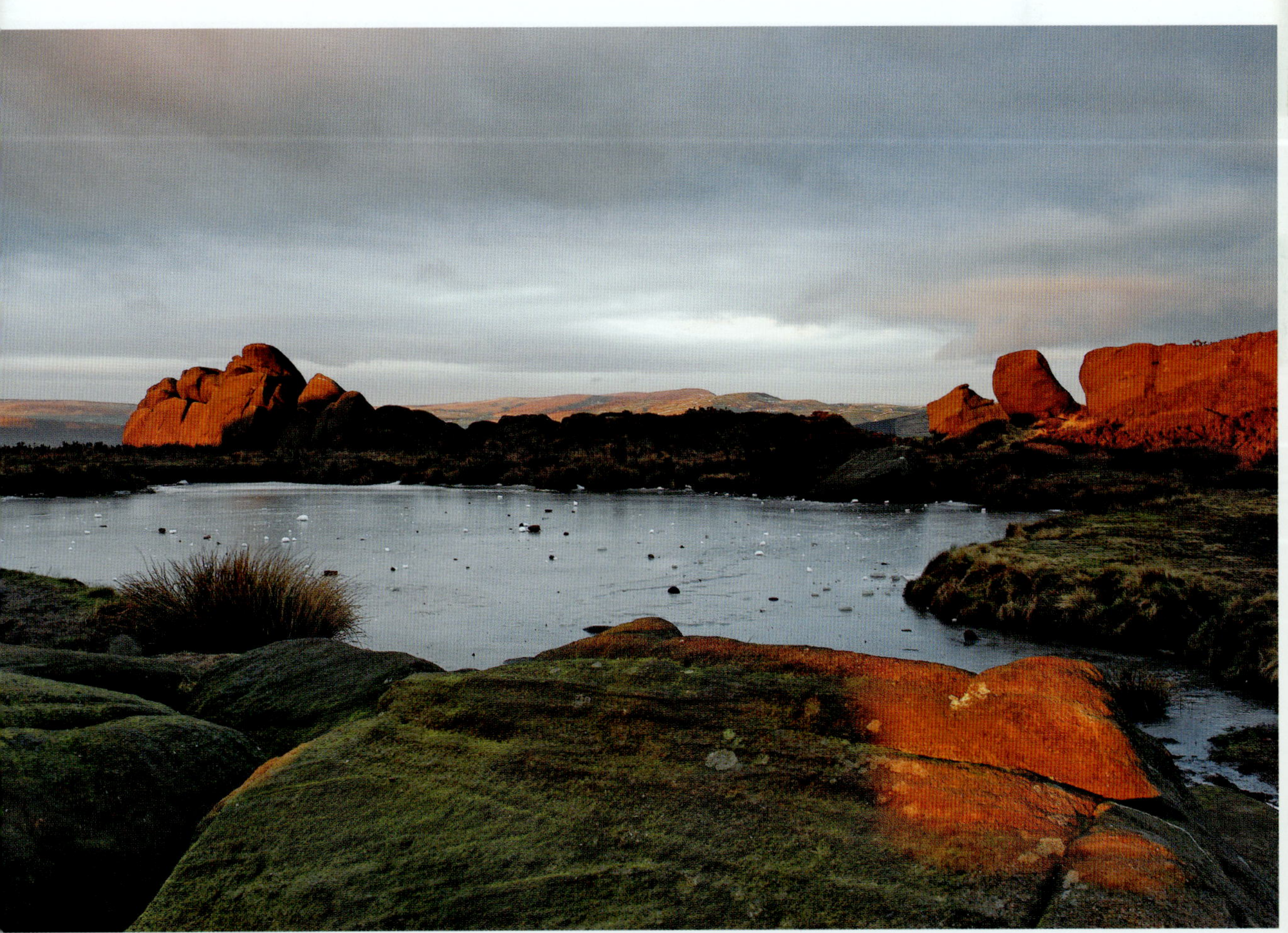

PHOTOGRAPHY NOTES

In this section I will discuss a few technical things which I feel were important in photographing the images for this book.

Philosophy

As a traditional landscape photographer, my aim is simple. It is to spot beautiful lighting, compositions and situations in nature and then try and record them to reproduce that scene as accurately as possible. Although incredibly time consuming, it's better to start with the best image we can in the right light rather than try and 'fiddle' a bad one in post processing later, or, heaven forbid, drop a false sky in, as I've sometimes heard people do.

In my opinion, when things are manipulated too much they look odd somehow and leave the realms of landscape photography to become something else. Admittedly, a camera's sensor or film will never see things quite the way our eyes do, the biggest problem being the narrower tonal range that they can cope with. Our eyes adjust constantly and can see more details in shadows and highlights giving us a much greater range. We can also 'fiddle' things in the camera, depending on the filters we use, choice of aperture and lenses, to create blurry backgrounds or shutter speeds to record movement. In the end I suppose we are artists, but I prefer to paint with the light that is there at the point of capture, not afterwards.

Post Processing

Personally, I hate spending time on computers, and would rather spend it out in the field, so I try and do as little post processing as possible. Using Adobe Photoshop I do slight alterations with levels to tweak contrast and brightness selectively in adjustment layers. Occasionally, I'll adjust the colour balance, hue and saturation but rarely need to if the photograph is taken with the correct white balance in the first place. Sometimes the tonal range is too great to be captured by one exposure, and if there is not a vaguely horizontal line between the brighter (usually sky) and darker areas where grey graduated neutral density filters can be used to even it out (see later), then two

images must be taken, one exposed for the darker and midtone areas, and one for the brighter part of the image. For this they must be taken on a tripod to ensure there has been no movement between them so that they can be superimposed later in Photoshop. The correctly exposed part from each image is then blended together to re-create what your eye saw.

I find this slightly tedious and a problem if there is something moving - usually trees or plants blowing in the breeze. If I can capture the whole tonal range in one shot I prefer to process a RAW file twice, once corrected for highlights and then again for the dark and mid-tone areas to produce two separate images. These can then be superimposed and blended together more easily as they are from the same original file.

Film versus digital

I found the discipline of using transparency film useful and, therefore made an easy transition to digital. There is a constant film versus digital debate. It's a personal thing and I like and still use both for different reasons. Nowadays with most cameras having greater than 6 mega pixels resolution, it's getting increasingly difficult to distinguish between the two for quality.

The advantage of digital is the instant feedback on both your composition and exposures using the review and histogram displays on the back. It's like having your own portable mini-lab. I will often walk round checking quick compositions to see if they work before setting up properly on the tripod and ensuring depth of field, focusing, exposure and timing for the light are correct. It's a great experimental tool. The down side of digital for me is the time spent afterwards, reviewing them on the computer and processing. Here, film wins for me. Once the picture is taken, I send the transparency roll off for someone else to process and await eagerly for them to return. When they do, I throw them all on a lightbox, study them quickly with a loupe and throw the bad ones in the bin. Job done in half an hour. I also like the way the transmitted light makes them glow rich and vibrant back at me, oozing quality. The computer screen just doesn't do that for me. Unfortunately nowadays, most people want things digitised, so the

transparencies do now need to go through the scanning process, and I'm back on my computer again.

Photographing details in the landscape

Ideally for macro, plant photography or details in the landscape, I choose soft, diffuse lighting conditions, bright but overcast as if the sun is behind a big white handkerchief, giving a large light source. Contrast is then low and highlights are not burnt out enabling details to be recorded in both the shadow and highlight areas.

Focusing and depth of field becomes critical with this kind of photography as the latter is not only affected by aperture, but is reduced significantly by using longer lenses and being close to your subject. Knowing where to focus and using the depth of field preview button on your camera is invaluable to check that backgrounds are enough out of focus not to be too fussy, but your subject is as sharp as possible where you want it to be.

As a rough rule of thumb, I'll focus about a third of the way into the picture as depth of field extends about a third in front and two-thirds behind your point of focus. I'll then quickly check using my DOF preview button and adjust focusing or apertures to get the effect I want. Subject blur is a problem if there is a breeze and shutter speeds are slow, due to the small apertures needed for a decent depth of field when you are so close. For this reason I favour early mornings for plant photography as the air is usually calmer before thermals have time to develop. With these small depths of field (or plane of sharpness), it's best to try and keep the subject area parallel to your camera. If this is a forest floor or low to the ground, it means fighting with your tripod's central column and contorting yourself into all sorts of uncomfortable positions. A bean bag is sometimes useful, or propping your camera on a rucksack and wedging it still if you have no suitable tripod.

LIGHTING AND USE OF FILTERS
Polarising filters

For most of the images in this book I have used either side-lighting or back-lighting by timing my visits if it's a planned shot. This gives more depth to the image as shadows and highlights are created giving a more three dimensional effect, showing up relief in the landscape, in contrast to when the sun is directly behind you, where the image can then appear flat and featureless. In addition, polarising filters work to full effect, giving a punchier image when the camera is pointing at 90 degrees to the sun. At 180 degrees, there is little or no effect. Put simply, a polariser cuts out surface reflections resulting in more saturated colours as most foliage has a slight sheen. It also has the effect of deepening blue skies, highlighting the contrast with white clouds and cutting out haze. This is probably the most important filter in landscape photography as it cannot be easily replicated in post processing.

Grey graduate filters

My next most used filters are grey (neutral density) graduated filters for evening out tonal differences in an image. They transmit all colours of the spectrum evenly, hence giving no colour casts to the image. They are a rectangular piece of glass or plastic with a clear part at the bottom becoming gradually darker grey towards the top. There are different strengths of filters which have different degrees of darkness measured in stops, their use depends on how large the tone difference is (in stops) between the light and dark areas we are trying to even out. The dark part is aligned in the filter holder across the brightest part of the image. As it is a horizontal line with a choice of hard or soft gradation, it works best if the line between dark and light areas is vaguely straight (not in a V shaped valley!). It can be tilted upside-down e.g .if the land is brighter than the sky, or even diagonally as in an unevenly lit street or valley for example.

Colour correction/warm up filters

When using daylight balanced film I occasionally need to use the yellow warm up filters to balance out the cool blue casts recorded on overcast days or in shadow where the light source is deficient in the warmer red/yellow tones. These filters come in different strengths depending on the degree of "warming up" you need. For digital capture these filters are not necessary, as adjustments of the white balance controls either in camera or in post processing has the same effect as adding a coloured filter. When the sun is low in the sky shining through the earth's lower atmosphere it is more effective at scattering the shorter wavelengths (the blue light). This results in the light illuminating the scene at around sunset or sunrise being enriched in the warmer red tones, hence why we get the lovely warm pastel pink shades at this time. As this is pleasing to the eye, I tend not to use colour correction filters and leave the white balance set to either sunny or cloudy to keep or even enhance the warm tones slightly. Fuji Velvia film also records a slightly warmer image than your eye may see.

Neutral density filters

Neutral density filters are probably the ones I use least. They are similar to the grey graduate but grey all over, giving the effect of simply cutting out the light entering the camera resulting in reduced exposure time. It's useful if you want to record movement in an image and conditions are too bright for a slow shutter speed or if you want to use a wider aperture to give a soft focus background. Again, it is measured in stops depending on how much light you wish to cut out. I'm often working with slow enough shutter speeds and don't need them.

EQUIPMENT

CAMERAS AND LENSES USED

Film cameras

35mm Nikon F90 and F90X with the following lenses:
Nikon 17-35mm F4/5.6
Tokina 28-70 F2.8
Sigma 100-300mm F4
Nikon 105mm macro F2.8

Mamiya 645 with 35mm, 80mm and
150mm lenses

Pentax 6 x7 with 45mm and 105mm
lenses

Digital cameras

Nikon D70 and D200 with use of the above 35mm film lenses and:
Nikon 18-70mm F 3.5-4.5 G ED DX
Nikon D700 FX full frame digital with use of the above Nikon film lenses and:
Nikon 24-85mm F2.8-4 D

Tripods

Manfrotto 190ProB and O55CXPRO3 with a lightweight magnesium head and quick release plate attached to the camera.

Film

Fuji Velvia 50 ISO transparency film for its superb fine grain and saturated colours, particularly on dull days. This is the film I've used almost exclusively for this book.
Fuji Provia 100 ISO transparency film

Filters

Circular polariser in either a Cokin or Lee filter system with adapter rings so that you only need to buy one filter if you have different lenses of varying thread size. They also have slots for positioning other filters to be used together with this filter.

Neutral density graduated Lee 1 stop (0.3), 2 stop (0.6) and 3 stop (0.9) soft gradation filters

Neutral Density   Cokin 2 stop (2x)

Warm up (film only)   Cokin 81A or 81B series

Accessories

Nikon Cable release, Jessops hot shoe spirit level, small Lastolite reflector.

INDEX OF PLACES, FLORA AND FAUNA

RECOMMENDED READING

Kinder Scout, Portrait of a Mountain edited by Roly Smith (Derbyshire County Council, 2002).

Wild Peak – Mark Hamblin (Halsgrove, 2003)

The Peak District – Fran Halsall (Frances Lincoln, 2008)

Peak District - John Barnatt and Ken Smith (English Heritage/ BTBatsford, 1997)

Rambler's Guide to The Peak District – Roly Smith and Karen Frenkel (Harper Collins, 2000)

First Light – Joe Cornish (Argentum, Aurum Press, 2002)

Websites

Peak National Park Authority
www. peakdistrict.gov.uk

Natural England
www. naturalengland.org.uk

Moors for the Future
www. moorsforthefuture.org.uk

National Trust
www. nationaltrust.org.uk

For sunrise, sunset and moon rise times
www. timeanddate.com

(all times are quoted for Manchester in this book)

Maps

Ordnance Survey Explorer OL24 White Peak (1:25,000)

Ordnance Survey Explorer OL1 Dark Peak (1: 25,000)

ACKNOWLEDGEMENTS

Many thanks go to the friends and family who have supported and encouraged me throughout this work and have put up with my absence and neglect during the latter few months whilst finishing this book. I would also like to thank the following people:

Tina Hook, Jane and John Entwistle, Julia Woodman, and Alex Hyde for their offers of help in the final editing stages, although I ran out of time and was not able to make use of their skills:

Fran Halsall for supplying me with initial map templates for me to build on.

Edwin, Helen and Laura Hirst, Catarina Gueben and Chris Foster who pushed and helped me to finish in the final few days around New Year 2010.

Many colleagues, both photographers and clients who have given me confidence in my work particularly those from the Peak Photo Centre, (now Simon Watkinson Training Ltd) where I worked as a landscape tutor for a number of years.

My editor Roly Smith for encouraging and enabling me to do this book in the first place.

And my husband David, for his endless patience, advice, support, and pushing me out in all weathers when I needed it!

Prints
Archival prints and prints on canvas are available of any of the images from this book. See www.karenfrenkel.info for contact details and prices.

TECHNICAL DETAILS

A tripod is used in all pictures unless marked with a * which means it is hand held.
T = top, B = bottom, L = left, R = right
GG = grey grad or neutral density graduated filter
Order = **Page**, Camera, Film/ISO, lens/mm, Exposure, Filters, Date/Time

1. Pentax 6x7, Velvia 50, 105, 1/2 sec @ f22, polariser, Aug 04 late aft **2.** Nikon F90, Velvia 50, 28-70, 1/4 sec @ f16, none, Oct 02 aft **4.** Nikon F90, Velvia 50, 28-70, not recorded, none, Nov 98 16.00 approx **6.** Nikon F90, Velvia 50, 28-70, 1/8 sec @ f22, polariser, Nov 01 15.00 approx. **8T.** Nikon F90, Velvia 50, 28-70, not recorded, polariser, Sep 02, 14.00 approx **8B.** Nikon D200, 100, 18-70, 8 sec @ f16, polariser, 28/10/07 17.17 **9.** Nikon F90, Velvia 50, 28-70, not recorded, 0.9GG, Aug 98 aft **10.** Nikon D70, 400, 18-70, 1/25 sec @ f20, polariser, 0.6GG, 20/10/05 13.14 **11.** Nikon D70, 200, 100-300, 1/160 sec @ f8, none, 6/5/05 13.36 **13.** Nikon F90, Velvia 50, 28-70, 1/2 sec @ f 16, polariser, Jan 98 aft **14.** Nikon D200, 100, 18-70, 1/6 sec @ f18, polariser, 0.3GG, 23/1/08 12.15 **15.** Nikon F90, Velvia 50, 100-300, 1/30 sec @ f8, none, Feb 02 morn **16.** Nikon D200, 100, 100-300, 1/10 sec @ f20, none, 25/1/07 14.45 **17L.** Nikon D200, 100, 100-300, 0.8 sec @ f22, none, 17/2/08 11.00 **17R.** Nikon D200, 100, 100-300, 0.6 sec @ f22, none, 17/2/08, 11.18 **18.** Nikon F90, Sensia 200, 100-300, 1/30 sec @ f22, polariser, Jan 01 morn **19.** Nikon F90, Sensia 200, 100-300, 1/15 sec @ f22, polariser, Jan 01 morn **20.** Nikon D70, 200, 100-300, 1/160 sec @ f22, none, 18/2/06 10.20 **22.** Nikon F90, Velvia 50, 28-70, 1/60 @ f22, polariser, Jan 03 morn **23.** Nikon D200, 100, 18-70, 1/20sec @ f 22, polariser, 22/1/09 12.30 **24.** Mamiya 645, Velvia 50, 80, 1/4 sec @ f22, none, Feb 04 morn **25.** Pentax 6x7, Velvia 50, 45, 30 sec @ f22, none, Feb 04 morn **26.** Nikon D200, 100, 18-70, 1/3sec @ f14, polariser, 0.6GG, 7/1/09 16.42 **28T.** Nikon F90, Velvia 50, 28-70, not recorded, polariser, Jan 02 16.00 approx **28B.** Nikon D200, 100, 17-55, 1/2 sec @ f 16, polariser, 0.6 GG, 8/2/09 08.35 **29.** Nikon F90, Velvia 50, 28-70, 1/4 sec @ f22, polariser, 0.6 GG, 3/1/00 08.30 approx **30.** Nikon F90, Velvia 50, 28-70, 1/60 sec @ f22, polariser, Jan 00 morn **31.** Mamiya 645, Velvia 50, 80, 1/5 sec @ f 22, polariser, 22/1/07 12.30 **32.** Nikon D200, 100, 18-70, 1/2 sec @ f 22 (panned down) none, 27/1/09 10.40 **33.** Nikon D200, 100, 18-70, 1/4 sec @ f22, none, 19/2/08 11.00 **34.** Nikon D200, 200, 100-300, 1/13 sec @ f14, polariser, 9/3/08

16.45 **36.** Nikon F90, Velvia 50, 28-70, 1/4 sec @ f22, polariser, 0.6GG, Mar 02, 14.00 approx **37.** Nikon F90, Velvia 50, 28-70, 1/30 sec @ f16, none, Mar 01 12.00 approx 38. Mamiya 645, Velvia 50, 80, 1/15 sec @ f22, polariser, 4/3/06 10.30 **39.** Nikon D70, 200, 18-70, 1/15 sec @ f18, 0.9 GG, 6/3/06 16.56 **40.** Nikon F90, Velvia 50, 28-70, 1/4 sec @ f16, polariser, Mar 98 late morn **41.** Mamiya 645, Velvia 50, 35, 1/5 sec @ f16, polariser, Apr 06, 10.00 **42.** Mamiya 645, Velvia 50, 80, 1/15 sec @ f22, polariser, Mar 02, early aft **43.** Nikon D200, 100, 28-70, 1/8 sec @ f11, none, 7/3/07, 16.00 **44.** Nikon D200, 100, 18-70, 1.1 sec @ f14, 0.6 GG, 27/4/08 20.30 **45.** Nikon F90, Velvia 50, 100-300, not recorded, none, Apr 07 aft **46T.** Nikon D200 200, 18-70, 1/15 sec @ f14, polariser, 8/4/09 17.50 **46B.** Nikon D200, 200, 18-70, 1/10 sec @ f14, polariser, 14/4/08 18.40 **47.** Nikon D200, 400, 28-70, 1/50 sec @ f16, polariser, 0.6 GG, 6/3/07 14.38 **48.** Nikon D200, 100, 18-70, 1/3 sec @ f13, polariser, 15/4/08 11.00 **50.** Nikon D200, 200, 100-300, 1/6 sec @ f8, none, 14/3/07 12.00 **51.** Nikon D70, 200, 18-70, 1/20 sec @ f22, none, 25/4/05 15.00 **52.** Nikon D200, 200, 105 macro, 1/30 sec @ f16, none, 18/4/09 17.12 **53T.** Nikon D70, 400, 100-300, 1/100 sec @ f6.3, none, 30/4/07 13.44 **53B.** Nikon D200, 200, 100-300, 1/320 sec @ f8, polariser, 2/4/09 16.38 **54.** Nikon D700, 400, 105 macro, 1/125 sec @ f8, none, 11/6/10 10.27 **56T.** Nikon D200, 125, 18-70, 1/6 sec @ f16, polariser, 3/6/07 20.11 **56B.** Nikon D200, 200, 18-70, 1/20 sec @ f16, polariser, 11/6/09 13.41 **57.** Nikon D200, 125, 18-70, 1/8 sec @ f16, polariser, 0.6GG, 18/5/07 18.00 **58.** Nikon D200, 200, 18-70, 1.1 sec @ f13, polariser, 6/5/09 18.41 **60TL.** Nikon D200, 200, 105 macro, 1/30 sec @ f5.6, polariser, 18/5/09 11.26 **60TR.** Nikon D200, 200, 100-300, 1/40 sec @ f8, none, 8/5/08 11.22 **60B.** Nikon D70, 200, 18-70, 1/13 sec @ f22, polariser, 12/5/05 16.43 **61.** Nikon D200, 100, 105 macro, 1/50 sec @ f7.1, none, 11/4/07 14.21 **62.** Pentax 6x7, Velvia 50, 105, 1/15 sec @ f22, none, Jun 04 20.30 approx **64.** Nikon D200, 100, 18-70, 1/4 sec @ f16, polariser, 11/5/09 17.45 **65.** Nikon D200, 100, 18-70, 0.8 sec @ F18, polariser, 10/6/09 11.01 **66.** Nikon D200, 200, 18-70, 1/25 sec @ f11, polariser, 0.6GG, 1/5/08 18.11 **67.** Nikon D70, 200, 18-70, 1/250 sec @ f11, none, 23/5/06 09.11 **68T.** Nikon D200, 200, 18-70, 1/20 sec @ f11, polariser, 2/5/09 12.37 **68B.** Mamiya 645, Velvia 50, 80, 1 sec @ f22, polariser, 5/5/06 17.00 **69.** Nikon F90, Velvia 50, 28-70, 1/4 sec @ f16, polariser, 2/5/99 10.00 approx **70.** Mamiya 645, Velvia 50, 80, 1/4 sec @ f22, none, May 04 14.00 approx **71T.** Nikon F90, Velvia 50, 28-70, 1/8 sec @ f22, polariser, Jun 99 late morn **71B.** Nikon F90, Velvia 50, 28-70, 1/8 sec @ f22,

polariser, Jun 99 late morn **72.** Mamiya 645, Velvia 50, 80, 1/8 sec @ f16, polariser, May 03 eve **73.** Mamiya 645, Velvia 50, 80, 1/15 sec @ f16, polariser, May 03 aft **74.** Nikon D200, 200, 18-70, 1/10 sec @ f13, polariser, 22/5/09 16.54 **75.** Nikon F90, Velvia 50, 28-70, 1/8 sec@ f11, polariser, 27/5/03 morn **76.** Nikon D200, 200, 18-70, 0.7 sec @ f11, polariser, 0.9GG, 31/8/07 19.42 **78T.** Nikon D200, 200, 18-70, 1/4 sec @ f14, polariser, 0.3GG, 31/8/09 06.43 **78B.** Nikon D200, 100, 18-70, 1/3 sec @ f22, polariser, 0.6GG, 21/8/06 17.16 **79.** Mamiya 645, Velvia 50, 80, 1/4 sec @ f22, polariser, Aug 04 11.00 approx **80.** Nikon D200, 200, 18-70, 1/5 sec @ f13, polariser, 0.6GG, 19/8/06 19.34 **82T.** Nikon F90, Velvia 50, 28-70, 1/4 sec @ f16, polariser, Aug 99 aft **82B.** Nikon D200, 200, 18-70, 1/30 sec @ f14, polariser, 0.6GG, 24/8/09 11.50 **83.** Pentax 6x7, Velvia 50, 105, 1/15 sec @ f16, polariser, Aug 04 aft **84T.** Pentax 6x7, Velvia 50, 105, 1/2 sec @ f22, polariser, 25/8/07 18.00 approx **84B.** Nikon D200, 200, 18-70, 1/13 sec @ f11, polariser, 0.9GG, 26/8/07 19.05 **85.** Nikon D200, 250, 18-70, 1/90 sec @ f11, polariser, 15/8/07 10.30 **86.** Nikon F90, Velvia 50, 28-70, 2 sec @ f22, none, Aug 04 06.00 **88T.** Nikon D70, 200, 18-70, 1/80 sec @ f10, 0.6GG, 28/8/05 15.15 * **88B.** Nikon D200, 100, 18-70, 1/45 sec @ f10, polariser, 29/8/07 13.35 * **89.** Nikon F90, Velvia 50, 28-70, not recorder, polariser, July 98 aft **90.** Nikon D200, 200, 18-70, 1/30 sec @ f14, polariser, 0.6GG, 25/8/09 16.30 **92.** Nikon D200, 200, 105 macro, 1/45 sec @ f8, none, 31/7/09 20.15 **93.** Nikon F90, Velvia 50, 28-70, not recorded, polariser, Aug 04 15.00 approx **94.** Nikon D200, 100, 18-70, 1/5 sec @ f16, polariser, 0.6GG, 30/7/08 19.18 **95T.** Nikon F90, Velvia 50, 100-300, not recorded, polariser, Aug 98 19.00 approx **95B.** Nikon D200, 200, 100-300, 1/80 sec @ f11, polariser, 29/7/08 20.00 **96T.** Nikon D200, 200, 100-300, 1/250 sec @ f5, none, 20/7/09 20.35 **96B.** Nikon D200, 200, 100-300, 1/250 sec @ f5, none, 20/7/09 20.32 **97.** Nikon D200, 200, 18-70, 1/2 sec @ f14, polariser, 0.9GG, 20/7/09 21.06 **98.** Nikon D200, 200, 18-70, 1/5 sec @ f11, polariser, 31/10/07 16.06 **100T.** Nikon D200, 200, 18-70, 1/25 sec @ f13, 0.9GG, 8/9/09 15.42 **100B.** Nikon D200, 200, 18-70, 1/20 sec @ f13, polariser, 8/9/09 13.36 **101.** Nikon D200, 200, 18-70, 1/13 sec @ f14, polariser, 0.6GG, 9/9/09 07.30 **102.** Nikon F50, Velvia 50, 28-70, 1/8 sec @ f22, polariser, Sep 04 late morn **103T.** Nikon D70, 200, 18-70, 1/13 sec @ f20, polariser, 27/10/05 13.27 **103B.** Nikon D200, 200, 18-70, 1/80 sec @ f10, polariser, 25/9/07 15.25 **104.** Nikon D200, 100, 18-70, 1/20 sec @ f16, none, 19/10/07 09.25 **105T.** Nikon D200, 100, 18-70, 1/10 sec @ f16, none, 19/10/07 09.12 **105B.** Pentax 6x7, Velvia 50,

105, 1/15 sec @ f22, none, 8/10/08 16.00 **106.** Nikon D200, 200, 18-70, 2.5 sec @ f18, polariser, 24/10/07 14.54 **107T.** Mamiya 645, Velvia 50, 35, 1/2 sec @ f22, polariser, 21/10/04 15.15 **107B.** Nikon D200, 200, 18-70, 1.1 sec @ f16, polariser, 14/10/08 15.38 **108.** Nikon D700, 200, 28-70, 1/6 sec @ f14, polariser, 0.6GG, 28/10/09 15.20 **109T.** Nikon D70, 400, 18-70, 1/25 sec @ f20, polariser, 0.6GG, 20/10/05 13.14 **109B.** Nikon D200, 100, 18-70, 1/5 sec @ f16, polariser, 0.9GG, 3/9/08 09.50 **110.** Nikon D200, 100, 18-70, 1/13 sec @ f14, polariser, 9/9/07 13.50 **111T.** Nikon D200, 200, 18-70, 1/15 sec @ f13, polariser, 0.6GG, 20/9/09 17.56 **111B.** Nikon D200, 200, 18-70, 0.7 sec @ f11, 0.3 GG, 23/9/09 19.48 **112.** Nikon F90, Velvia 50, 28-70, 1/30 sec @ f8, polariser, Oct 2000 aft **114.** Nikon D200, 100, 18-70, 1/15 sec @ f14, 0.6GG, 17/9/08 18.49 **115.** Nikon D700, 400, 28-70, 1/15 sec @ f10, 0.6 GG, 5/10/09 07.09 **116T.** Nikon D200, 200, 18-70, 1/200 sec @ f9, none, 1/10/08 16.44 **116B.** Nikon D200, 250, 18-70, 1/200 sec @ f11, none, 26/10/08 15.34 * **117.** Nikon F90, Sensia 100, 28-70 , not recorded, none, Sep 95 late morn **118.** Nikon F90, Velvia 50, 28-70, not recorded, 0.9GG, Nov 03 16.00 approx **121T.** Nikon F90, Velvia 50, 28-70, not recorded, polariser, Nov 96 aft **121B.** Nikon F90, Velvia 50, 28-70, not recorded, polariser, Nov 05 aft **122.** Nikon D70, 200, 100-300, 1/250 sec @ f11, none, 1/11/05 09.30 **123T.** Nikon D200, 200, 18-70, 1/3 sec @ f16, polariser, 10/12/08 14.43 **123B.** Nikon D200, 100, 18-70, 1/10 sec @ f20, polariser, 0.3GG, 10/12/08 13.34 **124.** Nikon D700, 200, 24-85, 1/20 sec @ f14, 0.6GG, 6/12/09 15.38 **125.** Nikon D700, 200, 28-70, 1/50 sec @ f11, polariser, 0.6 GG, 3/11/09 11.40 **126.** Nikon D70, 400, 18-70, 1/25 sec @ f8, polariser, 28/11/06 14.45 **127.** Pentax 6x7, Velvia 50, 105, 1/4 sec @ f22, none, 2/2/06 11.30 **128.** Nikon D70, 200, 18-70, 1/200 @ f16, none, 19/11/04 10.34 **130.** Nikon D200, 100, 18-70, 1/125 @ f10, none, 13/12/07 10.51 * **131.** Nikon F90, Velvia 50, 28-70, not recorded, polariser, Dec 02 aft **132.** Nikon F90, Velvia 50, 100-300, 1/4 sec @ f16, polariser, Nov 02 aft **133.** Nikon D200, 200, 18-70, 1/30 sec @ f11, polariser, 19/11/06 11.22 **134.** Nikon D700, 200, 28-70, 1/8 sec @ f16, polariser, 3/11/09 16.11 **135.** Nikon F90, Velvia 50, 28-70, not recorded, polariser, Nov 01 aft **136.** Nikon D200, 100, 18-70, 1/25 sec @ f14, 0.9 GG, 22/12/07 0.19 **137T.** Nikon D70, 200, 18-70, 1/30 sec @ f5.6, none, 17/12/04 15.18 **137B.** Nikon D70, 200, 18-70, 1/8 sec @ f20, polariser, 21/11/05, 09.15 **138.** Nikon D200, 200, 18-70, 0.7 sec @ f14, polariser, 0.6GG, 10/12/08 15.39 **139.** Nikon D200, 200, 18-70, 1 sec @ f18, 0.3 GG, 10/12/08 15.36

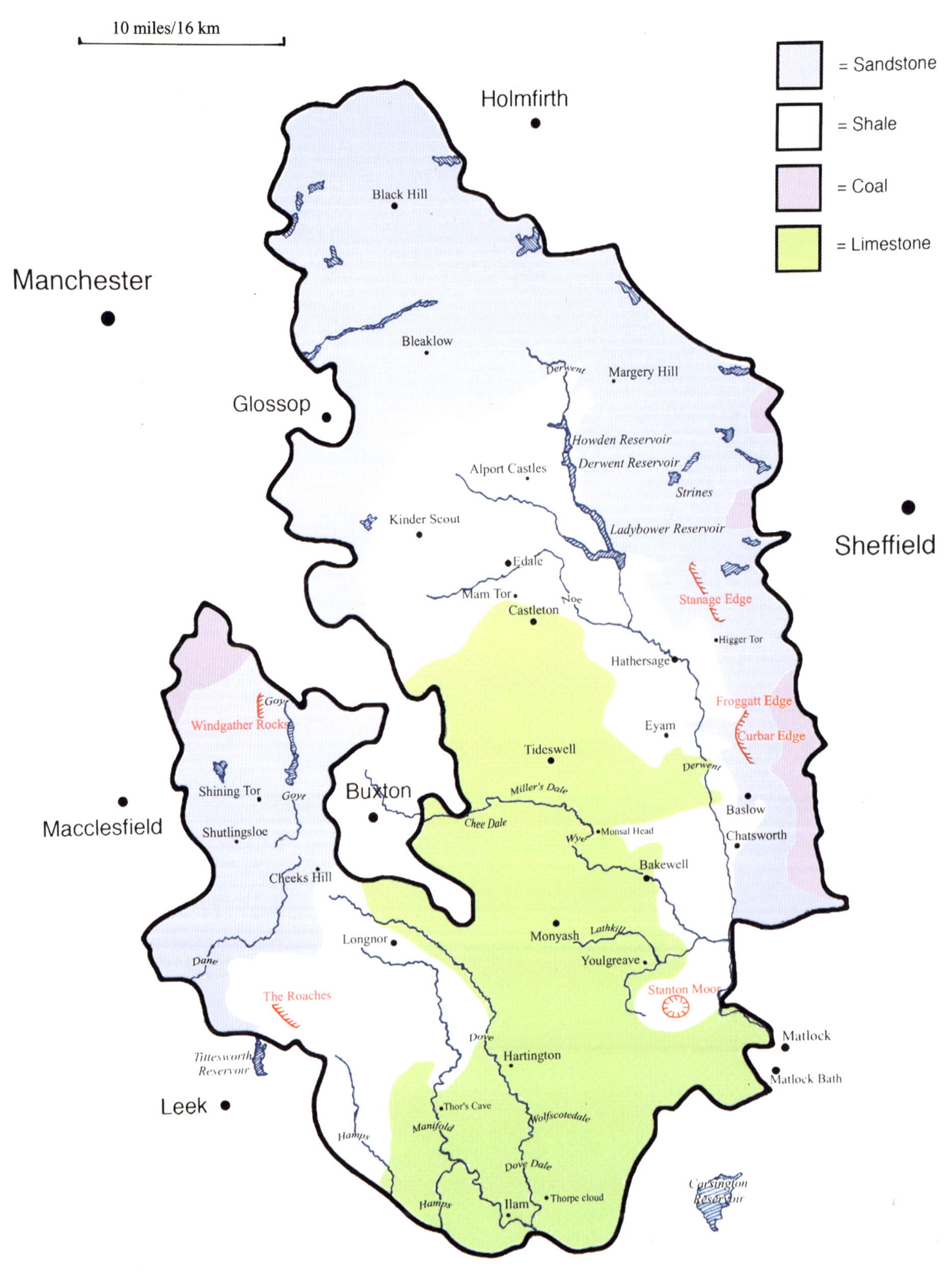
The Peak District
10 miles/16 km
= Sandstone
= Shale
= Coal
= Limestone
Holmfirth
Manchester
Black Hill
Bleaklow
Glossop
Derwent
Margery Hill
Howden Reservoir
Derwent Reservoir
Alport Castles
Strines
Kinder Scout
Ladybower Reservoir
Sheffield
Edale
Stanage Edge
Mam Tor
Noe
Castleton
Higger Tor
Hathersage
Froggatt Edge
Goyt
Windgather Rocks
Eyam
Curbar Edge
Tideswell
Derwent
Shining Tor
Goyt
Buxton
Miller's Dale
Chee Dale
Baslow
Macclesfield
Shutlingsloe
Wye
Monsal Head
Chatsworth
Bakewell
Cheeks Hill
Monyash
Lathkill
Longnor
Youlgreave
Dane
Stanton Moor
The Roaches
Matlock
Tittesworth
Reservoir
Hartington
Matlock Bath
Leek
Dove
Wolfscotedale
Hamps
Manifold
Thor's Cave
Dove Dale
Carsington
Reservoir
Hamps
Ilam
Thorpe cloud
Ashbourne